Leadership Without
Easy Answers

Leadership Without Easy Answers

Ronald A. Heifetz

The Belknap Press of
Harvard University Press
Cambridge, Massachusetts
London, England

Library of Congress Cataloging in Publication Data

Heifetz, Ronald A. (Ronald Abadian), 1951–
Leadership without easy answers / Ronald A. Heifetz.
p. cm.
Includes bibliographical references (p.   ) and index.
ISBN 0-674-51858-6 (acid-free paper)
1. Leadership. I. Title.
HM141.H385 1994
303.3′4—dc20

94-15184
CIP

To Sousan

Contents

Foreword

Richard E. Neustadt

This book is the product of teaching.

The Kennedy School of Government at Harvard University teaches students at four levels: undergraduates in voluntary, noncredit study groups; recent graduates in two-year Masters programs; midcareer students, on average ten years older, in one-year Masters programs; and senior officials, civil as well as military, in a range of short courses called "executive programs." Much of what we teach is adapted from traditional disciplines thought to be particularly relevant for public policy and its analysis, mainly from economics, political science, political philosophy, and sociology.

Some courses, however, are framed not by disciplinary concepts but rather by the questions our experienced students draw urgently from their own work in public life. "Exercising Leadership," a course offered in various versions at all graduate levels of our student body, attempts to give students insight on, and useful tools for working in, a range of roles, unofficial and official, where leading others can become essential to effective performance. Some of our students seek such roles in elective politics, some in the military, some in law or medicine, more in civilian bureaucracies, public, nonprofit and private—but all will have the lead role thrust at them, perforce, as task or opportunity, through the group memberships that mark their professional and personal lives. Knowing this from experience, our more mature students press us for something they can learn about leadership—and take with them back to work.

But what? A decade ago we asked Dr. Heifetz, a young psychiatrist, as well as a skilled musician, who had also studied with us and so knew his fellows well, to take that question and address it afresh in concert with our students. He has done so ever since. This book is the result.

I find it a striking achievement. It presents concrete prescriptions resting on hypotheses immediately relevant for anyone who needs to take the lead in almost any sort of social situation, under almost any organizational conditions. Heifetz illustrates what he prescribes both from the vantage point of highest public office and from that of intimate interpersonal relations. On the one hand, here are the likes of Lyndon Johnson, Martin Luther King Jr., and Mahatma Gandhi, both in triumph and in tragedy. On the other hand, here are military officers and men, doctors and patients, college students, and local civic groups. Some manage, some butcher, the leader-follower relationship. Some, like LBJ, do both in turn. The cast of characters is varied, wide-ranging, and unfailingly of interest, sketched with precision, touched by empathy, and always on point: illustrating something a practitioner can try to do (or avoid doing) in a concrete effort to take leadership on something in particular, sometimes from a position of authority, sometimes not.

This prescriptiveness is what distinguishes Heifetz's book from most works in a literature on leadership as broad as it is diverse. In the English language alone it cascades down from Shakespeare to contemporary sociologists, from Samuel Pepys to contemporary memoirs and biographers. Mostly it describes, prescribing, if at all, only by inference, the inference of analogy: "If the shoe fits, wear it." Heifetz, in contrast, uses description only to illustrate, and his illustrations serve only to reinforce his analysis, which is prescriptive. It rests upon hypotheses of social interaction, some of which have roots in Freudian psychology, some in anthropology, some in music, but all of which have been exposed to long years of refinement by the harsh light of reactions from practitioners in public life with work to do, as well as lives to live.

Heifetz's ten years with practitioner-students has done for him somewhat the same thing seven years of Washington experience once did for me, and it has brought him, among other places, to the same ground I traversed more than thirty years ago in *Presidential Power*. That is the ground occupied by the maker of choices in a political system's highest formal authority, from whom leadership is both expected and resisted by others as matters of course. I dealt with one such, the American President in the then contemporary setting. I sought rules of thumb to help him think strategically. All I could prescribe for such a one was that he think today about tomorrow's implications in each act of choice, with special reference to his prospects for prestige and reputation. This may have been good advice, as far as it went, but it was ambiguous: It jumbled up the long run with the short. So it was hard to apply predictively with confidence—as subsequent observers, even Presidents, have found.

Heifetz's advice is richer, more suggestive, hence I hope more usable, because his analysis goes deeper into what an authority figure of that sort could do, both to inform himself and to guide purported followers. Take note of social stresses; they are clues to needed work. Take note of attacks upon you: they are clues to work avoidance. Do not try to do the work yourself; instead, provide those followers a holding environment within which you challenge them. Then get up on the balcony—afford yourself perspective on the scene—to spot the pitfalls and to take corrective action, changing pace or path. These are terms of art; I leave it to Heifetz to define them. But I happily acknowledge that, taken together, his rules of thumb are likelier than mine were to help a person in the role of chief executive, or some such, build effective strategy.

A further strength in Heifetz, which I cannot claim, is that his rules of thumb address strategic thinking not only by leaders in positions of authority but also by those lacking such positions, endeavoring to stir their neighbors from the side, or from the rear. Some years ago, I talked with two state legislators both of whom felt they had gained much from the Heifetz course. The one, a committee chairman, went home confident he could steer his committee better than before. The other, younger, a "backbencher," went home feeling able to convince and move his seniors, chairs included, from behind!

So "leadership" for Heifetz is distinct from the positions of authority which usually are thought to be its starting point. His rules of thumb, his principles, apply to anyone who itches to get something done through and in company with others. That is a widespread sensation, especially in a democracy like ours, the universe Heifetz addresses. It follows that this book should be widely read, used, and taught. I hope it is.

Cambridge, 1994

Leadership Without
Easy Answers

Introduction

On Wednesday, April 29, 1992, Los Angeles exploded in the most violent and destructive American urban riots of the century.[1] The acquittal of four white policemen for criminal assault in the widely televised beating of black motorist Rodney King unleashed a fury of looting, arson, and killing painfully reminiscent of the 1960s. Thousands of federal troops helped to restore order, but not before fifty-two people were dead, hundreds were wounded, and more than one billion dollars worth of property was destroyed.[2] On Friday evening, two days later, President George Bush, in a nationally televised speech, focused on the immediate sources of distress, condemning the violence and promising a swift restoration of order while suggesting federal action to ensure justice for King. He did not use his authority to mobilize commitment to the larger questions that underlay the riots—racism and chronic economic disparity.[3]

Coincidentally during the riots, I was in Washington, D.C., consulting in the government. The following three questions came up repeatedly: Was Bush exercising leadership? What criteria could we use to judge his actions as events were unfolding, without the benefit of historical hindsight? Was his focus too narrow in responding to symptoms rather than causes, or was it a necessary short-term tactic in a strategy to address the larger issues? This book, the product of a decade's research and teaching at Harvard University's John F. Kennedy School of Government, addresses questions such as these about leadership, authority, and the challenge of tackling very hard problems.

1

Today we face a crisis in leadership in many areas of public and private life. Yet we misconceive the nature of these leadership crises. We attribute our problems too readily to our politicians and executives, as if they were the cause of them. We frequently use them as scapegoats. Although people in authority may not be a ready source of answers, rarely are they the source of our pains. Pinning the blame on authority provides us with a simple accounting for our predicaments. "Throw out the rascals! *They're* the reason we're in this mess!" Yet our current crises may have more to do with the scale, interdependence, and perceived uncontrollability of modern economic and political life. The paucity of leadership may perpetuate our quandaries, but seldom is it the basis for them.

Furthermore, in a crisis we tend to look for the wrong kind of leadership. We call for someone with answers, decision, strength, and a map of the future, someone who knows where we ought to be going—in short, someone who can make hard problems simple. But problems like the Los Angeles riots are not simple. Instead of looking for saviors, we should be calling for leadership that will challenge us to face problems for which there are no simple, painless solutions—problems that require us to learn new ways.

We have many such problems: uncompetitive industry, drug abuse, poverty, poor public education, environmental hazards, ethnic strife, budget deficits, economic dislocation, and obstacles to constructive foreign relations. Making progress on these problems demands not just someone who provides answers from on high but changes in our attitudes, behavior, and values. To meet challenges such as these, we need a different idea of leadership and a new social contract that promote our adaptive capacities, rather than inappropriate expectations of authority. We need to reconceive and revitalize our civic life and the meaning of citizenship.

These challenges are the subject of this book. To introduce them, it seems only fair that I introduce myself and the baggage and resources I carry into this study. I am a psychiatrist, musician, and lecturer in public policy at the Kennedy School of Government, where I direct the school's Leadership Education Project. As a physician, I carry several biases. The first is a belief that many problems are embedded in complicated and interactive systems. In medicine, for example, we want to know how the body will react to the opening in its defenses when illness sets in.

Most professionals have a systems bias. Car mechanics, business executives, and urban planners think systemically about problems, focusing on the interacting parts of a car, business, or city. They often intervene in a part of the system distant from the location of the symptom. When a car fails to start in the morning, a mechanic rarely locates the problem in the key switch itself, but several feet away in the battery, starter, an electrical connection, or the alternator. When citizens of Los Angeles rioted in response to the court's decision in the case concerning Rodney King, the problem was not just police brutality but injustice writ large—the festering issues of unemployment, poverty, inequity, and prejudice.

The second bias from biology is to assume that much of behavior reflects an adaptation to circumstances. An organism's responses to stress—whether the stress is induced by the climate, competition, food supply, sexual activity, or parenthood—represent adaptations developed over the course of evolution. Often, biological adaptations are transformative, enabling new species to thrive in changing environments. A most dramatic example is the evolution of our human hands, which seem to have been the trigger for a series of major adaptive leaps, including upright posture and the human brain.[4] Together, these responses to ecological challenge have given us the means to transform our world.

By adapting socially, I mean developing the organizational and cultural capacity to meet problems successfully according to our values and purposes. And when there are conflicts over values and purposes, which happen frequently, the clarification and integration of competing values itself becomes adaptive work.

As in biology, social adaptations run the gamut from minor to transformative change. By adapting, I do not mean accepting the status quo, or resigning ourselves to a new and bad situation. When President Bush first met with members of his Cabinet to respond to the Iraqi invasion of Kuwait, Nicholas Brady, the Treasury Secretary, presented a strategy for coping with high oil prices in the near, medium, and long term were Iraq to stay in Kuwait and keep prices up. But Bush emphatically refused to *"adapt"* to this invasion.[5] His use of the term makes sense and communicates clearly, but it is not the way I use the term here. By adaptation I do not mean merely *coping*, even though coping may at times be a critical part of adapting.

The orchestration of many countries along with the United Nations to meet the challenge of a belligerent Iraq was the beginning of adaptive work par excellence. To break old myths in the Middle East, form new international alliances, invigorate the United Nations, and bring together much of the world community required many people around the globe to clarify values and change attitudes, beliefs, and behavior. A new world order that requires people to learn better ways of living together would be an enormous social adaptation, were we to achieve it. Of course, adaptation requires accomplishment as well as aspiration.

As a third bias, I think of authority relationships in terms of service. My job as a physician consists of helping people solve the problems for which I have some expertise. That is why they authorize me: Authority is a trust. If in some problem situations my latitude for action—my authorization—must expand, then the bases of my trust may have to change.

Furthermore, having a service orientation means having at once a practical and prescriptive view. In being "practical," I look for ways to apply theory and research to everyday problems. In "prescribing," I give advice, not simply by taking the patient's complaint at face value but by interpreting it. Problems often present themselves ambiguously. I interpret complaints both as symptoms of biological stress and as indicators of psychological or social imbalance in the individual's work and support system. I include the patient's environment in my analysis of problems. Similarly, outside the context of medicine, I consider a CEO's complaint about his loss of power as a symptom of an underlying problem within his organization. Perhaps the CEO's influence has diminished because he recently broached disturbing issues in his organization, and the response was to wall him off. In the medical sense, it would be poor practice to give advice based simply on someone's initial complaint. Prescription requires analyzing the problem in the larger system.

This may sound obvious, but its implications are not. Many consultants and theorists of leadership think they have completed their task by advising the executive or politician on how to gain more power, if that is what he asks for. In some cases, they may be right. Yet it is not always enough simply to give someone what he thinks he wants. One may have to interpret the executive's wishes in the context of problems facing the organization in order to help him clarify the systemic problem so that he can then clarify what he wants. Perhaps he would rather move the organization to face an issue that is being avoided than to simply regain power. Perhaps he would willingly trade power to mobilize attention to the issue. Perhaps he has identified an issue not quite ripe for his organization's attention and should slow down. The loss of power may indicate that the issue requires a change in tactics.

As a psychiatrist, I believe that many adaptive and communicative processes are unconscious, and I learn about them by inference. People do not always say what they "really think" or understand why they do what they do. Moreover, many difficulties with making headway on problems arise from poorly orchestrated and unresolved conflicts—internal contradictions in values, beliefs, and habit. Furthermore, I also believe that people's defenses deserve respect. In identifying and raising issues, I assume that people and their social systems are doing the best they can given their adaptive capacity and the challenges they are up against. I assume they are working on real problems, even if the manner of work is distorted and riddled with avoidance. Their behavior is their effort to adapt. As a consequence, I intervene in people's lives and social systems with the aim of increasing their adaptive capacity—their ability to clarify values and make progress on the problems those values define.

Finally, psychiatry has a bias regarding how people accomplish adaptive work. In psychotherapy, people adapt more successfully to their environments, given their purposes and values, by facing painful circumstances and developing new attitudes and behaviors. They learn to distinguish reality from fantasy, resolve internal conflicts, and put harsh events into perspective. They learn to live with things that cannot be changed and take responsibility for those that can. By improving their ability to reflect, strengthening their tolerance for frustration, and understanding their own blind spots and patterns of resistance to facing problems, they improve their general adaptive capacity for future challenge.

Policy experts proceed with a similar bias. They help communities by interpreting and analyzing problems, distinguishing cause from effect, fact from fiction, and formulating and offering possible solutions. They too believe that facing problems is better than neglecting them. Indeed, they complain, quite understandably, about the resistance they meet to the troubling information they gather, analyze, and offer.

As a musician, I bring several metaphors from music to the study of leadership. Music teaches that dissonance is an integral part of harmony. Without conflict and tension, music lacks dynamism and movement. The composer and the improvisational musician alike must contain the dissonance within a frame that holds the audience's attention until resolution is found.

Music also teaches to distinguish the varieties of silence: restless, energized, bored, tranquil, and sublime.[6] With silence one creates moments so that something new can be heard; one holds the tension in an audience or working group, or punctuates important phrases, allowing time for the message to settle.

Creating music takes place in relation to structures and audiences. Structural limits provide scaffolding for creativity. Plato put it this way: "If there is no contradictory impression, there is nothing to awaken reflection."[7] People create in relation to something or someone. Although the audience may be safely tucked inside the composer's mind, still it is there. Because we do not think of creativity as a product of relationship, audiences often do not know their power. In a hall of five thousand, one person in the back of the second balcony talking to a neighbor or getting up to leave has all too real an impact. So too, in politics and organizations, people mistakenly look to an authority figure, presuming that he or she performs independently of them.

Music teaches what it means to think and learn with the heart. In part, it means having access to emotions and viewing them as a resource rather than a liability. It also means having the patience to find meanings left implicit. When I was a student in the Master Class of Gregor Piatigorsky, the great Russian cellist, we cellists would play a phrase of Brahms or Shostakovich, and Piatigorsky would launch into a story that seemed at first to come from nowhere with no apparent relevance to what we were doing. In time, he would often land hawklike on his subject. But sometimes the challenge of finding the connection was ours. If we looked hard, we could usually discern his intent, or find our own lesson beyond his intent. We had to take responsibility for our learning.

With this background, I have spent the last ten years developing and teaching courses in leadership and authority to young adult, midcareer, and executive students at Harvard. They have come from governments, nonprofit institutions, and profit-making enterprises throughout the United States and abroad. They have included top- and middle-level managers in public agencies and private businesses, members of Congress, congressional staff, mayors, state legislators, city officials, entry-level public servants, diplomats, all levels of military officers, foreign officials, journalists, community organizers, and heads of banks. A few have been graduate students in law, business, education, divinity, medicine, public health, and international development.

These practitioner students, many hundreds of them by now, have given me the means to develop, test, and refine a set of ideas about leadership. Beginning with the assumptions and metaphors of my past, I have plied them for their wisdom. This book is the product of our joint daily efforts to elucidate their successes and failures.

Teaching students who are practitioners has forced me to look for the fine line between generalization and practical guidance. Generalizations are needed to speak to students from every conceivable kind of organization and culture. I could not teach so varied a group without looking for generic ideas. Yet at no time could I get away with teaching theory disconnected from reality, as I might with a class of undergraduates. Practitioners have little patience for ideas that fail to speak to real experience. My students have forced me to develop a general theory that has practical application.[8]

My practitioner students have directed my attention to the difficulties they see in exercising leadership and have slanted my theory in the direction of the kinds of adaptive work that generate perceptions of loss, real or imagined, by people facing change. In contrast, I have spent much less time on other forms of adaptive work, for example, the entrepreneurial challenge of spotting and seizing untapped opportunities or the challenge of sustaining excellence in a well-functioning operation.

The theory presented here is empirical in the sense that it reflects engagement with real problems. But it is not empirical in the rigorous sense of methodically categorizing and selecting cases on which to examine and test the full range of possible hypotheses. In the emerging field of leadership analysis, this book represents theory-building—an effort to provide a powerful and practical conceptual framework from which to launch more focused empirical research. The book provides a source of ideas, interpretations, and conjectures, many of which are illustrated but none of which is proven.

My view of leadership is organized around two key distinctions: between technical and adaptive problems, and between leadership and authority. The first points to the different modes of action required to deal with routine problems in contrast with those that demand innovation and learning; the second provides a framework for assessing resources and developing a leadership strategy depending upon whether one has or does not have authority. Viewed in these ways, for example, our questions about Bush's leadership and the Los Angeles riots become: What adaptive challenges in Los Angeles and the country at large gave rise to the riots? And what resources and constraints associated with presidential authority in an election year did Bush have for leading the nation in meeting those challenges? Furthermore, how could people without authority, or with less authority, exercise leadership on the issues without waiting for the President?

Steeped as I am in the U.S. constitutional system, my conception of leadership is shaped fundamentally by it. If my argument has relevance for people from societies with other politics, that would be fortuitous. This is an argument about the strategies of leadership most suitable to a democratic society, as well as for economic institutions that aspire to compete in the modern world, and for other institutions that need to inspire intense commitment of members (particularly those ascribing to modern norms of democracy and self-expression) rather than mere compliance.

Part One presents an overview of the meaning of leadership, focusing particularly on the concepts of adaptation and authority. Parts Two and Three focus on strategies of leading with and without authority. Part Four concludes with practical recommendations for leading and staying alive.

Throughout these discussions I use cases not as evidence but to illustrate theory and enrich speculation about how individuals might think about leadership in a variety of settings. Some of these stories may touch on the reader's experience. They include interpersonal, small group, and organizational problems, as well as local, national, and international affairs. Some are part of our recent and shared history: "Star Wars," civil rights, and Vietnam. Although most of the cases are taken from the public realm, these ideas have been tested in other contexts as well: businesses, religious institutions, schools, and nonprofit organizations.

This book is meant for those who lead in this place and time. Although I count on my colleagues in the academy to analyze, test, refine, and deepen this argument, my aim here is to provide the practitioner with a practical philosophy of leadership—an orienting set of questions and options for confronting the hardest of problems without getting killed, badly wounded, or pushed aside.

Part I

Setting the Frame

1

Values in Leadership

Leadership arouses passion. The exercise and even the study of leadership stirs feeling because leadership engages our values. Indeed, the term itself is value-laden. When we call for leadership in our organizations and politics, we call for something we prize. If one asks: "Would you rather be known as a leader or a manager? A follower or a leader?" the response is usually "a leader." The term *leadership* involves our self-images and moral codes.

Yet the way we talk about leadership betrays confusion. On one hand, we use the word to denote people and actions of merit. During an election year, we want "a leader" for President, rather than "another politician." In our organizations, we evaluate managers for their "leadership," by which we mean a particular constellation of valued abilities. When we look abroad, we fasten the term to people like Gorbachev, Walesa, De Klerk, or Mandela, people we admire for their values, courage, commitment, and skill. On the other hand, we insist that the word leadership is value-free. We say that Pablo Escobar, head of the Medellín drug cartel, was a "leader," even if we detested his values, because he motivated followers to realize his vision.[1] Our media routinely use the term leader to denote people in authority or people who have a following. We talk about the leader of the gang, the mob, the organization—the person who is given informal or formal authority by others—regardless of the values they represent or the product they play a key part in producing.

We cannot continue to have it both ways. We may like to use the

13

word *leadership* as if it were value-free, particularly in an age of science and mathematics, so that we can describe far-ranging phenomena and people with consistency. Yet when we do so, we ignore the other half of ourselves that in the next breath speaks of leadership as something we desperately need more of. We cannot talk about a crisis in leadership and then say leadership is value-free. Do we merely mean that we have too few people in our midst who can gather a following? Surely, we are not asking for more messiahs of Waco and Jonestown who meet people's needs by offering tempting visions of rapture and sacrifice.[2] The contradiction in our common understanding clouds not only the clarity of our thinking and scholarship; it shapes the quality of leadership we praise, teach, and get.[3]

Understandably, scholars who have studied "leadership" have tended to side with the value-free connotation of the term because it lends itself more easily to analytic reasoning and empirical examination.[4] But this will not do for them any more than it will do for practitioners of leadership who intervene in organizations and communities everyday. Rigor in social science does not require that we ignore values; it simply requires being explicit about the values we study. There is no neutral ground from which to construct notions and theories of leadership because leadership terms, loaded with emotional content, carry with them implicit norms and values. For example, when we equate leadership with holding high office or exerting great influence, we reinforce a tendency to value station and power. We are not simply studying or using power; we unwittingly communicate that power has intrinsic worth.

We have to take sides. When we teach, write about, and model the exercise of leadership, we inevitably support or challenge people's conceptions of themselves, their roles, and most importantly their ideas about how social systems make progress on problems. Leadership is a normative concept because implicit in people's notions of leadership are images of a social contract. Imagine the differences in behavior when people operate with the idea that "leadership means influencing the community to follow the leader's vision" versus "leadership means influencing the community to face its problems." In the first instance, influence is the mark of leadership; a leader gets people to accept his vision, and communities address problems by looking to him. If something goes wrong, the fault lies with the leader.[5] In the second, progress on problems is the measure of leadership; leaders mobilize people to face problems, and communities make progress on problems because leaders challenge and help them do so. If something goes wrong, the fault lies with both leaders and the community.

This second image of leadership—mobilizing people to tackle tough problems—is the image at the heart of this book. This conception builds upon, yet differs from, the culturally dominant views. For example, in popular conceptions of politics, leadership generally refers to the exercise of influence: the leader stands out in front—usually in high office—influencing others. The person may also be the most influential member of a popular movement operating with little if any formal authority, such as Lech Walesa or the Ayotollah Khomeini (before they took political office).

In business, we see an evolution of the concept of leadership. For decades, the term leadership referred to the people who hold top management positions and the functions they serve. In our common usage, it still does. Recently, however, business people have drawn a distinction between leadership and management, and exercising leadership has also come to mean providing a vision and influencing others to realize it through noncoercive means.[6]

In the military, the term leadership commonly refers to people in positions of command, who show the way. Perhaps because warfare has played a central role historically in the development of our conceptions of leadership and authority, it is not surprising that the ancient linguistic root of the word "to lead" means "to go forth, die."[7] In our time, leadership in the military aims to draw forth a person's highest qualities, by influence more than coercion. "Be all that you can be" implies preparation based on the potential that resides in the enlistees when they enter. In the final test, however, the troops achieve the goals prescribed by the leaders in command.[8]

In biology, leadership is the activity of flying at the front of a flock of geese, or maintaining order in social relations and food gathering among primates. The leader has a particular set of physical attributes (big, colorful, fast, assertive). The leader functions as a focal point of attention by which the rest of the group instinctively organizes itself. Leadership is equated with prominence and dominance.

In horse racing, a field some would say bears a resemblance to politics, leading simply means being out in front. The jockey of the lead horse is leading nobody, except perhaps unintentionally to the extent that other jockeys set strategy and strive harder to overtake him.

There seem to be two common denominators of these various views: station and influence. Hence, many scholarly approaches to the study of leadership during the last two hundred years focus on the phenomena of prominent and influential people.[9] Theorists ask the following important questions: How and why do particular individuals gain power in an organization or society? What are their personal characteristics? What functions do they serve? How do they realize their vision? How do they move history, or does history move them? What motivates them and how do they motivate others?[10]

Hidden Values in Theories of Leadership

Perhaps the first theory of leadership—and the one that continues to be entrenched in American culture—emerged from the nineteenth-century notion that history is the story of great men and their impact on society. (Women were not even considered candidates for greatness.) Thomas Carlyle crystallized this view in his 1841 volume *On Heroes, Hero-Worship, and the Heroic in History*. Although various scientific studies discount the idea, this *trait approach* continues to set the terms of popular debate.[11] Indeed, it saw a revival during the 1980s.[12] Based on this view, trait theorists since Carlyle have examined the personality characteristics of "great men," positing that the rise to power is rooted in a "heroic" set of personal talents, skills, or physical characteristics. As Sidney Hook described in *The Hero in History* (1943), some men are eventful, while others are event-making.[13]

In reaction to the great-man theory of history, *situationalists* argued that history is much more than the effects of these men on their time. Indeed, social theorists like Herbert Spencer (1884) suggested that the times produce the person and not the other way around. In a sense, situationalists were not interested in leadership per se. "Historymakers" were interesting because they stood at the vortex of powerful political and social forces, which themselves were of interest. Thus, the more or less contemporaneous emergence of the United

States' first great leaders—Jefferson, Washington, Adams, Madison, Hamilton, Monroe, Benjamin Franklin—is attributed not to a demographic fluke but to the extraordinary times in which these men lived. Instead of asserting that all of them shared a common set of traits, situationalists suggest that the times called forth an assortment of men with various talents and leadership styles. Indeed, many of them performed marvelously in some jobs but quite poorly in others.[14] Thus, "What an individual actually *does* when acting as a leader is in large part dependent upon characteristics of the situation in which he functions."[15]

Beginning in the 1950s, theorists began (not surprisingly) to synthesize the trait approach with the situationalist view. Empirical studies had begun to show that no single constellation of traits was associated with leadership. Although this finding did not negate the idea that individuals "make" history, it did suggest that different situations demand different personalities and call for different behaviors. Primary among these synthetic approaches is *contingency theory*, which posits that the appropriate style of leadership is contingent on the requirements of the particular situation. For example, some situations require controlling or autocratic behavior and others participative or democratic behavior.[16]

The field of inquiry soon expanded into the specific interactions between leaders and followers—the *transactions* by which an individual gains influence and sustains it over time.[17] The process is based on reciprocity. Leaders not only influence followers but are under their influence as well.[18] A leader earns influence by adjusting to the expectations of followers. In one variant of the transactional approach, the leader reaps the benefits of status and influence in exchange for reducing uncertainty and providing followers with a basis for action.[19] In another variant, bargaining and persuasion are the essence of political power, requiring a keen understanding of the interests of various stakeholders, both professional and public.[20]

Each of these theories is generally considered to be value-free, but in fact their values are simply hidden. The great-man or trait approach places value on the historymaker, the person with extraordinary influence. Although the approach does not specify in what direction influence must be wielded to constitute leadership, the very suggestion that the mark of a great man is his historical impact on society gives us a particular perspective on greatness. Placing Hitler in the same general category as Gandhi or Lincoln does not render the theory value-free. On the contrary, it simply leaves its central value—influence—implicit.[21]

The situational approach, ironically, does something similar. It departs radically from the great-man view by suggesting that certain people emerge to prominence because the times and social forces call them forth. Yet leaders are still assumed to be those people who gain prominence in society. The people that a trait theorist would select to study from history, the situational theorist would select as well.

Contingency theory, synthesizing the great-man and situational approaches, also began with a value-free image of itself. It examines which decisionmaking style fits which situational contingency in order for the decisionmaker to maintain control of the process. Sometimes a directive, task-oriented style is the most effective, and at other times a participative, relationship-oriented style is required. Yet even in this more specific rendition of the traditional view, the mark of leadership is still influence, or control.[22]

Advocates of transactional approaches, focusing on how influence is gained and maintained, also see themselves as value-neutral. Although they describe elegantly the relational dynamics of influence, they do not evaluate the purpose to which influence is put or the way purposes are derived. By stating that the mark of leadership is influence over outcomes, these theorists unwittingly enter the value realm. Leadership-as-influence implicitly promotes influence as an orienting value, perpetuating a confusion between means and ends.[23]

These four general approaches attempt to define leadership objectively, without making value judgments. When defining leadership in terms of prominence, authority, and influence, however, these theories introduce value-biases implicitly without declaring their introduction and without arguing for the necessity of the values introduced.[24] From a research point of view, this presents no real problem. Indeed, it simplifies the analytic task. The problem emerges when we communicate and model these descriptions as "leadership" because "leadership" in many cultures is a normative idea—it represents a set of orienting values, as do words like "hero" and "champion."[25] If we leave the value implications of our teaching and practice unaddressed, we encourage people, perhaps unwittingly, to aspire to great influence or high office, regardless of what they do there.[26] We would be on safer ground were we to discard the loaded term leadership altogether and simply describe the dynamics of prominence, power, influence, and historical causation.[27]

Although these theories were designed primarily for value-free description and analysis, they still shed light on how to think about practice. For example, the trait theorists encourage us to believe that individuals can indeed make a difference. No activist can operate without that assumption. Furthermore, the decades of scholarship devoted to sifting and analyzing generic skills provide us with some basis to define the goals of leadership education. The situational approach directs us toward examining how the activity of leadership differs depending on the context. Coupled with the contingency approach, it tells us that the task of contextual diagnosis is central to leadership. In addition, it provides a host of variables to consider in analyzing different situations and the style of leadership that might apply. This will be critical to those who lead. For example, contingency theory frames the key question: Which situations call for authoritarian behavior and which demand "democratic" processes?[28] The transactional theorists contribute the basic idea that authority consists of reciprocal relationships: people in authority influence constituents, but constituents also influence them. We forget this at our peril.

Toward a Prescriptive Concept of Leadership

In this study I will use four criteria to develop a definition of leadership that takes values into account. First, the definition must sufficiently resemble current cultural assumptions so that, when feasible, one's normal understanding of what it means to lead will apply. Second, the definition should be practical, so that practitioners can make use of it. Third, it should point toward socially useful activities. Finally, the concept should offer a broad definition of social usefulness.

How might we go about defining the term leadership in a way that employs our current knowledge, and the values associated with it? Leadership, which has long been linked to the exercise of authority or influence, usually suggests playing a prominent and coordinating role in an organization or society. To capture these uses of the term in a definition, we can use the word "mobilize," which connotes motivating, organizing, orienting, and focusing attention.

Rather than define leadership either as a position of authority in a social structure or as a personal set of characteristics, we may find it a great deal more useful to define leadership as an *activity*.[29] This allows for leadership from multiple positions in a social structure. A President and a clerk can both lead. It also allows for the use of a variety of abilities depending on the demands of the culture and situation. Personal abilities are resources for leadership applied differently in different contexts. As we know, at times they are not applied at all. Many people never exercise leadership, even though they have the personal qualities we might commonly associate with it.[30] By unhinging leadership from personality traits, we permit observations of the many different ways in which people exercise plenty of leadership everyday without "being leaders."

The common personalistic orientation to the term leadership, with its assumption that "leaders are born and not made," is quite dangerous. It fosters both self-delusion and irresponsibility. For those who consider themselves "born leaders," free of an orienting philosophy and strategy of leadership, their grandiosity is a set-up for a rude awakening and for blindly doing damage. Minimally, they can waste the time and effort of a community on projects that go, if not over a cliff, then at least in circles.[31] Conversely, those who consider themselves "not leaders" escape responsibility for taking action, or for learning how to take action, when they see the need. In the face of critical problems, they say, "I'm not a leader, what can I do?"[32]

So, we ought to focus on leadership as an activity—the activity of a citizen from any walk of life mobilizing people to do something. But what is the socially useful something? What mode of leadership is likely to generate socially useful outcomes? Several approaches to these questions might work. We could imagine that a leader is more likely to produce socially useful outcomes by setting goals that meet the needs of both the leader and followers.[33] This has the benefit of distinguishing leadership from merely "getting people to do what you want them to do." Leadership is more than influence.

Even so, setting a goal to meet the needs of the community may give no definition of what those needs are. If a leader personally wants to turn away from the difficulty of problems, and so do his constituents, does he exercise leadership by coming up with a fake remedy?

To address this problem, the leadership theorist James MacGregor Burns suggested that socially useful goals not only have to meet the needs of followers, they also should elevate followers to a higher moral level. Calling this *transformational leadership,* he posits that people begin with the need for survival and security, and once those needs are met, concern themselves with "higher" needs like affection, belonging, the common good, or serving others.[34] This approach has the benefit of provoking discussion about how to construct a hierarchy of orienting values. However, a hierarchy that would apply across cultures and organizational settings risks either being so general as to be impractical or so specific as to be culturally imperialistic in its application.

We might also say that leadership has a higher probability of producing socially useful results when defined in terms of legitimate authority, with legitimacy based on a set of procedures by which power is conferred from the many to the few. This view is attractive because we might stop glorifying usurpations of power as leadership. But by restraining the exercise of leadership to legitimate authority, we also leave no room for leadership that challenges the legitimacy of authority or the system of authorization itself.[35] No doubt, there are risks to freeing leadership from its moorings of legitimate authority. To take one celebrated case, perhaps we risk encouraging committed zealots like Oliver North. Yet we also face an important possibility: social progress may require that someone push the system to its limit. Perhaps Andrei Sakharov served such a role in the democratization of the former Soviet Union. Hence, a person who leads may have to risk his moral state, and not just his health and job, to protect his moral state.[36] Defining leadership in terms of legitimate authority excludes those who faced moral doubt and deep regret by defying authority. Vaclav Havel, Lech Walesa, Aung San Suu Kyi, Martin Luther King Jr., Margaret Sanger, and Mohandas Gandhi, to name a few, risked social disaster by unleashing uncontrollable social forces.

Business schools and schools of management commonly define leadership and its usefulness with respect to organizational effectiveness. Effectiveness means reaching viable decisions that implement the goals of the organization. This definition has the benefit of being generally applicable, but it provides no real guide to determine the nature or formation of those goals.[37] Which goals should we pursue? What constitutes effectiveness in addition to the ability to generate profits? From the perspective of a town official viewing a local corporation, effectiveness at implementation seems an insufficient criterion. A chemical plant may be quite effective at earning a profit while it dangerously pollutes the local water supply. We are left with the question: Effective at what?

This study examines the usefulness of viewing leadership in terms of adaptive work. Adaptive work consists of the learning required to address conflicts in the values people hold, or to diminish the gap between the values people stand for and the reality they face. Adaptive work requires a change in values, beliefs, or behavior. The exposure and orchestration of conflict—internal contradictions—within individuals and constituencies provide the leverage for mobilizing people to learn new ways.[38]

In this view, getting people to clarify what matters most, in what balance, with what trade-offs, becomes a central task. In the case of a local industry that pollutes the river, people want clean water, but they also want jobs. Community and company interests frequently overlap and clash, with conflicts taking place not only among factions but also within the lives of individual citizens who themselves may have competing needs. Leadership requires orchestrating these conflicts among and within the interested parties, and not just between the members and formal shareholders of the organization. Who should play a part in the deliberations is not a given, but is itself a critical strategic question. Strategy begins with asking: Which stakeholders have to adjust their ways to make progress on this problem? How can one sequence the issues or strengthen the bonds that join the stakeholders together as a community of interests so that they withstand the stresses of problem-solving?

To clarify a complex situation such as this requires multiple vantage points, each of which adds a piece to the puzzle. Just as clarifying a vision demands reality testing, reality testing is not a value-free process. Values are shaped and refined by rubbing against real problems, and people interpret their problems according to the values they hold. Different values shed light on the different opportunities and facets of a situation. The implication is important: *the inclusion of competing value perspectives may be essential to adaptive success.* In the long run, an industrial polluter will fail if it neglects the interests of its community. Given the spread of environmental values, it may not always be able to move across borders. Conversely, the community may lose its economic base if it neglects the interests of its industry.

The point here is to provide a guide to goal formation and strategy. In selecting adaptive work as a guide, one considers not only the values that the goal represents, but also the goal's ability to mobilize people to face, rather than avoid, tough realities and conflicts. The hardest and most valuable task of leadership may be advancing goals and designing strategy that promote adaptive work.[39]

Does this forsake the image of leadership as a visionary activity? Not at all. It places emphasis on the act of giving clarity and articulation to a community's guiding values. Neither providing a map for the future that disregards value conflicts nor providing an easy way out that neglects the facts will suffice for leadership.[40] Guiding values are interpreted in the context of problems demanding definition and action.[41] People discover and respond to the future as much as they plan it. Those who lead have to learn from events and take advantage of the unplanned opportunities that events uncover.[42] They have to improvise. In the midst of the Great Depression, Franklin Roosevelt called for "bold, persistent experimentation." As he put it, "It is common sense to take a method and try it. If it fails, admit it frankly and try another. But above all, try something."[43]

As an example to compare these frames of reference, we can use the case of Roosevelt's adversary, Adolf Hitler. When influence alone defines leadership, Hitler qualifies as an authentic and successful leader: he mobilized a nation to follow his vision. Indeed, he inspired millions of people to organize their lives by his word. Even with the added criterion that goals have to meet the needs of both leader and follower, we would say that Hitler led. His many followers in Germany shared his goals. He was not simply forcing his sentiments and views on everyone. He reached office, in part, by articulating the pains and hopes of many people.

Furthermore, by the standard of organizational effectiveness,

Hitler exercised formidable leadership. Within hundreds of specific decisionmaking instances, Hitler succeeded in developing the effectiveness of German organizations. He set the goal of restoring the German economy, and for a period of time he succeeded.

If we assume that leadership must not only meet the needs of followers but also must elevate them, we render a different judgment. Hitler wielded power, but he did not lead.[44] He played to people's basest needs and fears. If he inspired people toward the common good of Germany, it was the good of a truncated and exclusive society feeding off others. By the standard of legitimate authority, Hitler also does not qualify as a leader. Elected once by a plurality of Germans in 1933, he destroyed the nascent democratic political apparatus and maintained his political dominance through terror.

By the criterion of adaptive work used here, we would also say that Hitler failed to exercise leadership. Although dramatically mobilizing his society, both socially and economically, he did so primarily in the direction of avoiding tough realities. By providing illusions of grandeur, internal scapegoats, and external enemies, Hitler misdiagnosed Germany's ills and brought his nation to disaster.[45] He exercised leadership no more than a charlatan practices medicine when providing fake remedies.[46]

There are several advantages to viewing leadership in terms of adaptive work. First, it points to the pivotal importance of reality testing in producing socially useful outcomes—the process of weighing one interpretation of a problem and its sources of evidence against others. Without this process, problem definitions fail to model the situation causing distress.[47] Conceptions of leadership that do not value reality testing encourage people to realize their vision, however faulty their sight. Thus, Hitler's error was diagnostic as well as moral.[48] To produce adaptive work, a vision must track the contours of reality; it has to have accuracy, and not simply imagination and appeal.[49]

In addition, focusing on adaptive work allows us to evaluate leadership in process rather than wait until the outcome is clear. We could have spotted Hitler's faulty reality testing early on. He gave plenty of clues. His election in 1933 based on a platform of exaltation and scapegoating would have made us question the health of the problem-solving apparatus in the German society, notwithstanding the appearance of legitimate authority flowing from a democratic election. We would not have had to wait for the results of his efforts.

Furthermore, in using the criterion of adaptive work, we need not impose our own hierarchy of human needs on the genuinely expressed needs of Germany at the time. In analyzing a community's response to hard realities, we would ask the following questions: Are its members testing their views of the problem against competing views within the community or are they defensively sticking to a particular perspective and suppressing others? Are people testing seriously the relationship between means and ends? Are conflicts over values and the morality of various means open to examination? Are policies analyzed and evaluated to distinguish fact from fiction?

In Nazi Germany, Hitler suppressed the competition among German perspectives. He established a norm of conformity that excluded the views that could test his vision of Germany's problems. Hence, Germany could not test the hypothetical relationship between current economic conditions and the citizenship of Jews.[50] How establishing a "land free of Jews" would restore Germany was not subject to open scrutiny, either as a technical or moral prescription. Even in military operations, German policymakers lost the flexibility to respond to changed conditions. The ideal of will produced decisions that disregarded complex circumstances.

Working within the society's own frame of reference becomes particularly important in cases less obvious than Nazi Germany. For example, an international development consultant might plan a series of interventions into a foreign culture. To assess that culture's objectives according to her own values may be dangerous. But she can help assess the quality of work without imposing her beliefs. She can evaluate the extent to which the culture fails to address the problems arising from the culture's own values and purposes. And perhaps more significantly if she has any leverage, she may be able to help or push the society to do the hard work of clarifying its competing values and purposes, and of facing the painful trade-offs and adjustments required to narrow the gap between current conditions and purposes. If the society bans certain parties, disenfranchises segments of the population, or uses torture and repression, what value perspective is obliterated among those being silenced? What aspects of reality that they see are being kept hidden? What might she do to encourage the factions of the culture to speed their own change of attitudes, habits, and beliefs?

Because leadership affects many lives, the concept we use must be spacious. It has to allow for the values of various cultures and organizations. It cannot be imperialistic. Yet we cannot beg the issue altogether by saying that leadership is value-free and define it simply in terms of its instruments (influence, formal powers, prominence) or personal resources (skills, bearing, temperament). Those who listen to us do more with what we say. They turn instruments and resources into values that orient their professional lives.

In this study, leadership is oriented by the task of doing adaptive work. As we shall see, influence and authority are primary factors in doing adaptive work, but they also bring constraints. They are instruments and not ends. Tackling tough problems—problems that often require an evolution of values—is the end of leadership; getting that work done is its essence.

Our societies and organizations clearly need leadership in the sense developed here. We are facing major adaptive challenges. We need a view of leadership that provides a practical orientation so that we can evaluate events and action in process, without waiting for outcomes. We also need a governor on our tendencies to become arrogant and grandiose in our visions, to flee from harsh realities and the dailyness of leadership. Terms like transformational leadership fuel such grandiosity. Furthermore, as we shall see, a strategy of leadership to accomplish adaptive work accounts for several conditions and values that are consonant with the demands of a democratic society. In addition to reality testing, these include respecting conflict, negotiation, and a diversity of views within a community; increasing community cohesion; developing norms of responsibility-taking, learning, and innovation; and keeping social distress within a bearable range.

Yet this concept of leadership has potential drawbacks that require investigation. The word adaptation too readily connotes coping, as if one must passively submit to an unbending reality. It may often be true that there are unbending realities that we should face rather than avoid, but since much of social reality is a product of social arrangements, and physical reality has become increasingly amenable to technological impact, there is obviously a great deal of plasticity to many of our realities, and we would do ourselves a disservice to adopt a coping relationship to them.[51] In addition, because adaptation is a metaphor from biology where the objective is survival, leadership as "activity to mobilize adaptation" may connote an overemphasis on survival. Clearly, we have a host of quite precious values—liberty, equality, human welfare, justice, and community—for which we take risks, and a concept of adaptation applied to human organizations and societies must account for these squarely. With these concerns in mind, we turn to a deeper examination of adaptive work.

2

To Lead or Mislead?

Living systems seek equilibrium. They respond to stress by working to regain balance.[1] If the human body becomes infected by bacteria, the system responds to fight off the infection and restore health. When people walk outdoors on a hot summer day, they sweat and move slowly to maintain a constant internal temperature of 98.6 degrees Fahrenheit. When a fire burns down a forest, the seeds that routinely blow in from a distance now take root in the ash. Knocked out of equilibrium, living systems summon a set of restorative responses.[2]

These responses to disequilibrium are the product of evolutionary adaptations that transformed into routine problems what were once nearly overwhelming threats. Looking backward in time, we marvel at the abundant success of these adaptations and the breadth of exploited opportunities. Yet we tend to notice the successes and innovations more than the failures. By definition, the successes survive while the failures disappear. The roads of evolution are strewn with the bones of creatures that could not thrive in the next environment. In natural selection, the failures abound alongside the successes. Evolution works by trial and error.[3]

Developing a robust adaptation to a new challenge is, in a sense, a learning process for a species. Through the hit-or-miss survival of some individuals over others, a species makes its way toward new adaptive capacities. As the survivors pass on to their offspring the traits that gave them a slight edge in the competition for resources, these better-adapted capacities become "hardwired" into the genetic programs of the species; the gene pool that determines the anatomical features and refinements of the next generation becomes changed. For example, human beings have developed the ability to speak in words and invent complex languages. These developments occurred because of new genetic recombinations and random mutations that happened to enhance the survival and reproductive capacity of our ancestors. These features have now become part of our inheritance.

Nature, however, is not farsighted. In fact, it has no foresight at all. Biological adaptation is not the result of planning or design on the part of a species, but is merely the outcome when some individual happens to be born with a trait that equips it to survive and reproduce in a changed environment. This variation is usually the result of a genetic "accident"—a mutation—and is often detrimental to the individual. But when the environment changes, the variation that might have been a disadvantage in the previous environment can suddenly present a distinct advantage.

For example, in England prior to the industrial revolution, most peppered moths were light-colored, resembling the heavy growths of pale-colored lichens that covered the tree trunks where they lived. Their light coloring protected the moths from their predators through camouflage. But during the industrial revolution, tree trunks in heavily industrialized parts of England became bare because polluting gases killed the lichens. The exposed dark trunks no longer provided camouflage for lighter moths, which were eaten by birds, but now protected the few darker variants. These better-adapted individuals survived and reproduced, thus pushing the local population toward gradual adaptive change. In nonindustrialized areas, the lighter-colored moths continued to thrive as before.[4]

Of course, if a species adapts to its current challenge, it still may not overcome the next one. Natural selection improvises, and improvises again, without any vision of what problems it might face ahead.

As amazing as it may seem that variation and natural selection have created red flowers, trees bearing pine cones, birds that sing, or camels, it seems just as extraordinary that adaptive processes have produced human beings with the capacity to learn. Because our genetic hardwiring gives us both social predispositions and intelligence, we humans can invent, reflect, and develop complex social systems that carry the lessons of our past.[5] We can thrive in cold climates because we have learned to clothe, shelter, and organize our communities, and pass on the know-how to our progeny.

Not only can we learn, but we can also manage our learning. We create rich cultures that pass on both what we know and how to discover more. We can give to others all sorts of lessons not in our genes. Nature has endowed us with the capacity to reflect on our problems and change our responses to them. Thus, Moses spent only two generations transforming an abject people into a self-governing society capable of fashioning laws that transcended the rule of kings.[6] Humanity has taken only 10,000 years to go from living as hunters and gatherers in well-circumscribed areas to developing a global economy and inventing the institutions and technologies that make it possible. We have new aspirations that generate new sets of opportunities and problems. Not only do we have vision, but we have the ability to analyze what we see. We can even temper our visions.

Yet many societies in human history have died rather than adapt. Clarifying aspirations, facing problems, and developing a set of socially adaptive responses is not easy. Just as individuals resist the pain and dislocation that comes with changing their attitudes and habits of behavior, societies resist learning as well. For a social system to learn, old patterns of relationship—balances of power, customary operating procedures, distributions of wealth—may be threatened. Old skills may be rendered useless. Beliefs, identity, and orienting values—images of justice, community, and responsibility—may be called into question. Humans can learn and cultures can change, but how much and how fast?

Adaptive Work

The concept of adaptation arises from efforts to understand biological evolution. Applied to the change of cultures and societies, the concept becomes a useful, if inexact, metaphor. Species change as the genetic program changes; cultures change by learning.[7] Evolution is a matter of chance—a fortuitous fit between random variation and new environmental pressures; societies, by contrast, can respond to new pressures with deliberation and planning. Evolution has no "purpose"—survival is our only measure of its success; societies generate purposes beyond survival.

The first and second differences between biological and cultural adaptation seem to pose little conceptual difficulty. We know intuitively that communities change through a variety of learning processes and sometimes with foresight and planning. This last difference, however, requires a refashioning of the metaphor if we are to use it to describe social change. The concept of adaptation applied to culture raises the question: Adapt to what, for what purpose?

In biology, survival of individual members of a species and their gene-carrying kin basically define the direction in which the species adapts. A situation becomes a "problem" for the species, or more accurately an adaptive challenge, because it threatens the capacity of individuals to pass on their genetic heritage.

Adapting to human challenges requires that we go beyond the requirements of simply surviving. In human societies, adaptive work consists of efforts to close the gap between reality and a host of values not restricted to survival. We perceive problems whenever circumstances do not conform to the way we think things ought to be. Thus, adaptive work involves not only the assessment of reality but also the clarification of values.

These tasks are inextricably connected. Assessing circumstances is made complex because we cannot always define problems objectively. The methods of science make a major contribution to reality testing; yet they cannot reliably define our problems both because the scientific method has limited capacity to make predictions and because our problems can only be diagnosed in light of our values. With different values, we screen reality for different information and put the facts together into a different picture.[8] If a society values individual freedom, it will tend to highlight those aspects of reality that challenge freedom. And as a corollary, it will also be inclined to neglect those elements of reality upon which another society with another central value, like shared responsibility, will focus. The aspect of truth each sees depends significantly on who cares about what.[9]

Typically, a social system will honor some mix of values, and the competition within this mix largely explains why adaptive work so often involves conflict. People with competing values engage one another as they confront a shared situation from their own points of view. At its extreme, and in the absence of better methods of social change, the conflict over values can be violent. The Civil War changed the meaning of union and individual freedom.

Some realities will threaten the very existence of a society if not discovered and met early on by the value-clarifying and reality-testing functions of the society. In the view of many environmentalists, our focus on the production of wealth rather than coexistence with nature has led us to neglect fragile factors in our ecosystem. These factors may become relevant to us when finally they begin to challenge our central values of health and survival, but by then we may have paid a high price in damage already done, and the costs of adaptive adjustment may have increased enormously.

Consider the following story. Fifteen hundred years ago, a group of Polynesians migrated over one thousand miles across the ocean to discover and settle on Easter Island.[10] They found a land rich with palm forests but far less fertile for cultivation than the islands back home. Not only the land but the sea as well had limited resources. Without a reef barrier, offshore waters provided a marginal fishing environment.[11] Yet the settlers apparently developed the island in familiar ways, applying and varying the strategies already in their repertoire. The abundance of palm trees provided everything from clothing to shelter and boats, and so the islanders thrived. To safeguard their venture, they built extraordinary stone figures to honor the gods.

For one thousand years the settlers grew and prospered according to their ancient ways. Adaptation meant variations on known methods. Although maintaining their slash and burn modes of agriculture, they adapted their farming to the new environment by building walled structures, "manavai," and using craters to protect trees and plants from the winds. But as their population grew and the number of trees began to dwindle, they created a situation that their repertoire of responses could not master.

The beliefs that once played a central role in a robust society became impediments to further adaptation. The islanders built more elaborate places of worship and even grander stone figures. When honoring the gods did not succeed in renewing scarce resources, some religious observances became extreme. The "Birdman" cult, oriented perhaps by the idea that the powerful Pacific frigate bird might intercede with the spirits, became a dominant political force. The hereditary chief and the priests lost a measure of their authority. Huge statues, weighing up to fifty metric tons, were built and then toppled and decapitated to release their divine powers, their *mana*.

When nothing else seemed to work, people resorted to human sacrifice and cannibalism. Finally, clannish factionalism and the rise of strongmen in the two major communities on the island led to war and destruction. The people began to starve. When Dutch sailors arrived at the island on Easter day, 1722, the trees were gone. The few remaining islanders found no blessing in their "discovery" by Europeans. Men were sold into slavery, women were taken as mistresses, and small pox raged. Only a handful of people endured to pass on their language and legends.

With a perfect science of forecasting and with a perfectly adaptive social system, people would be able to foresee crucial new realities and make the necessary adjustments. Even divergent cultural values could be subsumed by the shared value of survival. But we have neither perfect science nor perfect adaptability. The presumed demise of Easter Island culture suggests, among other things, that the ability to adapt requires the productive interaction of different values through which each member or faction in a society sees reality and its challenges. Without conflicting frames of reference, the social system scrutinizes only limited features of its problematic environment. It operates at the mercy of its blind spots because it cannot prepare for what it does not see. The Easter Islanders valued their relationship with the divine spirits and assumed that the gods would adjust nature to their needs. In particular, the fertility of the land was thought to depend upon interactions between divine power and the hereditary chief. However, had the islanders also placed value on their direct relationship with nature, for example, they might have sensed the slow but growing changes in their relationship with natural resources, and adjusted accordingly.

Let's imagine that early in the decline of Easter Island a small group saw that the trees were the island's true source of sustenance. Suppose in their zeal, they began to admonish people to stop cutting them down. Vociferously, they brought the problem of diminishing trees to general attention and came into conflict with the values and habits of their neighbors, as well as the authority structure.

The traditionalists, however, interpreting the situation according to their old values, saw the diminishing resources as a problem in their relationship with the gods. So they built bigger and bigger statues to the divine spirits, occasionally feminizing them with breasts to promote the land's fertility and adding bird figures to some of them.[12] They saw no way to reconcile their view with the view of the tree zealots. Dominant in political and military power, they silenced the heretics.

From our perspective outside the system and with our knowledge, it is easy for us to see that both factions had a grasp of some critical dimensions of reality. The traditional view encompassed all those institutions, habits, common currencies, and values which had built the society. This view had adapted wonderfully in many ways to its environment, and it enriched people's spiritual and social lives; surely a sensible tree policy would not require turning all of those norms upside down.[13] The new view, however, encompassed an emerging reality that, if left unaccounted for, would lead to the destruction of everything else that was good on the island.

In this case, adaptive work would mean utilizing both traditional values and the values represented by those who recognized the society's direct dependency on natural resources. Each would have to learn from the other. Learning would require each party to interpret the problem somewhat differently. The traditionalists would have to amend their interpretive framework—their religious under-standing—to encompass the emerging evidence that the fertility of trees depended on the relationship not only between people and the gods but between people and trees. On the other hand, the zealots would have to accommodate their views to incorporate the long-standing evidence that the society depended on tree cutting to sustain its ways. It could not just stop cutting trees down.

Archaeologists do not yet know if the islanders were beginning to conserve and plant trees by the time of their demise. To be effective, trees would have to be grown at the same rate that they were being cut down or the crisis would merely be postponed. Indeed, to adapt, the islanders would have had to solve a variety of problems in addition to the farming of trees, such as population control and migration to distant shores. Progress on these, too, may have required the creativity generated by differences, but the story has been made simple to illustrate a point: the mix of values in a society provides multiple vantage points from which to view reality. Conflict and heterogeneity are resources for social learning. Although people may not come to share one another's values, they may learn vital information that would ordinarily be lost to view without engaging the perspectives of those who challenge them.

If we define problems by the disparity between values and circumstances, then an adaptive challenge is a particular kind of problem where the gap cannot be closed by the application of current technical know-how or routine behavior. To make progress, not only must invention and action change circumstances to align reality with values, but the values themselves may also have to change. Leadership will consist not of answers or assured visions but of taking action to clarify values. It asks questions like: What are we missing here? Are there values of competing groups that we suppress rather than apply to our understanding of the problem at hand? Are there shared values that might enable us to engage competing views? Ongoing adaptive capacity requires a rich and evolving mix of values to inform a society's process of reality testing. It requires leadership to fire and contain the forces of invention and change, and to extract the next step.

Disequilibrium Dynamics

Like living systems, social systems under threat try to restore equilibrium. Generally, equilibrium means stability in which the levels of stress within the political, social, and economic areas of the society are not increasing.[14] Yet there is nothing ideal or good about a state of equilibrium per se. Indeed, achieving adaptive change probably requires sustained periods of disequilibrium.[15] A society may operate without increasing levels of stress, quite oblivious to the bankruptcy that lies ahead. Without a general climate of urgency—the feeling that something must change—the society may do nothing until it is too late.[16] How to manage sustained periods of stress consequently poses a central question for the exercise of leadership.

The patterns of disequilibrium in a social system take three forms. First, the current problem presents no new challenge and a response from the current repertoire may restore equilibrium successfully. For example, when snow blocks an interstate highway passing through the mountains and generates momentary distress to drivers, highway snow clearing services remove the snow and restore traffic to a slow but steady level. The social system, experienced in the problem, has learned a set of responses to meet the challenge. The problem and its solution lie within the society's repertoire.

Second, when the society has no ready solution for the situation, the social system may still try to apply responses from its repertoire, but may only restore equilibrium in the short term and at the cost of long-term consequences. This may have been the case with the demise of the Easter Island civilization.

Third, the society may learn to meet the new challenge. First Meiji Japan and recently postwar Japan made numerous adjustments to political balances of power, mechanisms to distribute wealth, attitudes to foreign industrial know-how, skills for its labor force, and cultural values and norms. Although the 1990s reveal significant problems, Japanese society has adapted remarkably. Indeed, in the process of adapting, Japanese society seems self-consciously to have learned lessons about how to continue managing the adaptive process. Perhaps Japan's competitive edge consists of consciously insisting that it must learn.[17]

Thus, there are three basic possibilities. The current response may both restore equilibrium quickly and solve the problem. The current response may restore equilibrium in the short term through a variety of expedient measures but may not solve the underlying problem. Overwhelmed eventually by the challenge, the society may retreat to a constricted level of functioning or die. Finally, the current response cannot solve the problem, but the social system may mobilize to produce a new adaptation sufficient to meet the challenge.

Clearly, we are interested in knowing how to turn the second possibility into the third outcome. Our organizations and societies face many kinds of adaptive work that we cannot afford to avoid. Some problems, such as reviving competitiveness in international markets, require that the United States respond to changed circumstances, urgent issues, and creative opportunities. The renewal of ethnic strife in the destabilized post-cold war international system requires the invention of new methods for dealing with festering problems of racial enmity. The simultaneous increases in crime, prison population, and prevalence of drugs in the streets of the

United States require serious differentiation of fact from fiction and close reasoning about causes and effects. Clashes between the pro-choice and pro-life forces in the abortion debate demonstrate an inability to resolve conflicts in human values peacefully even when the parties have little economic interest. The United States continues to consume natural resources at a rate that does not recognize limits or live within them. Too often we fail to meet these kinds of challenge. Why is this so?

People fail to adapt for several reasons. In some cases they may misperceive the nature of the threat. Based on their experience and science, the people of Pompeii made a reasonable but tragic estimate of the risk that Vesuvius might erupt. In our age, we are fortunate to have discovered already our dependence on the ozone layer. In addition to threats within common knowledge, however, some threats remain to be discovered. People can respond only to those threats that they see.

In some other cases the society may perceive the threat, but the challenge may exceed the culture's adaptive capability. Innumerable human tribes and organizations have disappeared with the onslaught of disease, environmental challenge, invasion, or competition because they could not develop the ability or find the means to adjust appropriately.

Finally, people fail to adapt because of the distress provoked by the problem and the changes it demands. They resist the pain, anxiety, or conflict that accompanies a sustained interaction with the situation. Holding onto past assumptions, blaming authority, scapegoating, externalizing the enemy, denying the problem, jumping to conclusions, or finding a distracting issue may restore stability and feel less stressful than facing and taking responsibility for a complex challenge. These patterns of response to disequilibrium are called *work avoidance mechanisms* in this study, and they are similar to the defensive routines that operate in individuals, small groups, and organizations.[18]

Diagnostically, an organization or community may experience any one of these difficulties in adapting. But when one takes action, the final cause of adaptive failure—the tendency to avoid distress—holds the key to setting strategy. It frequently provides the ultimate impediment to adaptive change because the learning associated with identifying blind spots and options that others cannot see, or strengthening a community's problem-solving capacity, will generate conflict and distress. Thus, a key question for leadership becomes: How can one counteract the expected work avoidances and help people learn despite resistance?

Though differing in form depending on the culture and complexity of the social system, work avoidance mechanisms seem to operate in any social context. In a small group, less powerful members will sit back and "watch the gladiators fight" as the chairperson and a colleague who represents a challenging perspective engage in an angry exchange that diverts attention from the issues on the table and diminishes a sense of shared responsibility. In an organization, people will follow standard operating procedures even when they know the procedures do not fit the situation. In a community or nation, voters will choose "good news" candidates even when they suspect that progress on pressing problems will require hard adjustments on their part.

Yet though we frequently avoid adaptive work, we seldom do so deliberately. Work avoidance mechanisms are often unconscious, or at least disguised from the self. Sometimes they reflect comforting misdiagnoses of the situation—a social system may scapegoat one of its factions because of a dominant perception that the faction is indeed responsible for the problem. A mob that burns a man in effigy may believe that its problem would be solved if it could burn the man himself. Yet even killing an accused heretic like Salman Rushdie would do little to integrate the traditional and modern strains within Islamic societies. Nevertheless, people in motion striving to ease their struggle may wish to believe that getting the scapegoat provides the needed resolution.

Reality testing—the effort to grasp the problem fully—is often an early victim of disequilibrium. Initially, people will apply routine practices for realistically assessing and addressing problems. But if these do not pay early dividends, restoring equilibrium may take precedence over the prolonged uncertainty associated with weighing divergent views and facing the need for changing attitudes and beliefs. With sustained distress, people may lose sight of their purposes. They "take their eyes off the ball."

On a personal level, for example, consider a father's response to the continued irritability and crying of his child. At first the father reacts with care and curiosity, questioning the child to assess the source of frustration. Not succeeding, the father may jump to a solution (like offering the child food), even though he doesn't understand the problem. If that does not work, the father might try to impose the solution authoritatively (strongly urging the child to eat). By the time that fails, the father begins to feel quite frustrated himself. The child's sense of urgency has now rubbed off on the father. If the father has a large capacity to tolerate frustration, he may start over again; he may continue to test reality. He may calm himself and then ask more questions to determine the difficulty. On the other hand, if the father has reached his own limit of tolerance, he may instead begin to grasp whatever mechanism he has in his repertoire for alleviating tension, at the cost of continuing to explore various causes of the child's problem. For example, he may put the child in his room and close the door to avoid the crying, or he may hit the child. As the father begins to view distress as the problem rather than as a symptom, his aim and focus of attention change as well. He shifts unconsciously to reducing the distress per se, and in that effort avoids the work of figuring out what's wrong with the child, and what would be an adaptive response.[19]

Distinguishing work from work avoidance is no science. Each culture will have its own typical patterns of response to stress—work-producing as well as work-avoiding. While more research should clarify the distinction between productive and avoidance behaviors in different social systems, some rules of thumb are useful. One might detect work avoidance when the subject of discussion is suddenly taken off the table (as with diversions); when the level of stress associated with an issue suddenly drops (often following an apparent technical fix); when the focus shifts from attending to the problem itself to alleviating the symptoms of stress (as in the father's case above); or when responsibility for the problem is displaced to an easy target (as with scapegoating). One ought to take a skeptical stance, at least momentarily, when some action suddenly makes everybody feel good.

Of course, what looks like momentary periods of work avoidance from one vantage point may be part of someone else's strategy. Leadership often requires pacing the work in an effort to prepare people to undertake a hard task at a rate they can stand. At the moment of his speech during the Los Angeles riots, one could not know whether George Bush was leading the nation or fostering work avoidance. Even his previous patterns of behavior could not tell us with certainty because a President's political calculations change with circumstances as public opinion shifts. To judge, we would have to look at his next moves after restoring equilibrium. Did he use the event soon afterwards to mobilize people to tackle the complex issues that gave rise to the riots, or did he move on to issues less challenging to the nation and his candidacy for reelection? We cannot know what Bush would have done in a second term as President, but in his remaining nine months in office, he seemed by and large to beg the issue and let the nation off the hook.

The following case illustrates the dynamics of disequilibrium and work avoidance with a little more historical distance.

The Strategic Defense Initiative

On March 23, 1983, President Ronald Reagan announced a bold new plan to develop a technological shield that would protect the United States from nuclear attack. The Strategic Defense Initiative (SDI—commonly called "Star Wars") intended to make nuclear weapons "impotent and obsolete."[20]

Ronald Reagan's interest in an effective nuclear defense dated back at least to his days as Governor of California, when he toured the Livermore Labs guided by scientist Edward Teller. Later, in his presidential challenge to Gerald Ford in 1976, he criticized deterrence, "comparing it to two people with guns cocked at each other's head."[21] During his 1980 presidential campaign, he made this wishful reference to a nuclear defense:

> They actually are tracking several thousand objects in space . . . I think the thing that struck me was the irony that here, with this great technology of ours, we can do all of this, yet we cannot stop any of the weapons that are coming at us. I don't think there's been a time in history when there wasn't a defense against some kind of thrust, even back in the old-fashioned days when we had coast artillery that would stop invading ships.[22]

Like many Presidents, Reagan wanted to do a great deal more than had been done to defend his country, and some scientists, especially Teller, told him that a great deal more could be done. Troubled by what he saw as America's vulnerability to people in Moscow, yet with little if any input from his advisers in the Defense and State Departments, he embarked on SDI.[23] He presented it as a way of ensuring that the nation's security would no longer hinge on the threat of retaliation to nuclear attack. The United States would render itself invulnerable to attack in the first place, Reagan claimed: we would go from Mutually Assured Destruction to Mutually Assured Survival.

The solution offered by President Reagan—SDI—reflected the way he defined the problem of defense in the nuclear age. The President, Teller, and a few others saw the problem in terms of our vulnerability to attack. Should we be held hostage to any foreign power, let alone an uncontrollable and "evil empire"? Was the threat of retaliation sufficient to combat the workings of a fundamentally aggressive and deceitful Soviet Union? Reagan said no.[24]

Within the foreign policy establishment, however, there were strong competing views. Most arms control experts defined the problem not in terms of vulnerability per se but as the imbalance of vulnerability between the superpowers.[25] Security lay in *mutual* vulnerability. As long as neither side gained a significant advantage over the other, neither power would risk a nuclear war. Within this school of thought, one camp strongly favored further arms control agreements that would slow the nuclear arms race and create greater deterrent stability. Another camp felt the United States had given too much away to the Soviets already in previous arms control treaties, perceived a "window of vulnerability" through which the Soviets could conceivably launch a first-strike knock-out blow, and saw SDI as a way to defend American forces and deter any "optimistic" Soviet calculation that a first strike could succeed.

Significantly, there was common ground between these views. Nearly everyone agreed that even at the very best SDI would render the country invulnerable only to ballistic missiles and not to submarine-launched cruise missiles with nuclear warheads or planes carrying nuclear bombs and missiles.[26] In addition, SDI would not protect the United States from chemical or biological weapons carried by nonballistic means. There would be all sorts of ways our enemies could get us, despite SDI.

In other words, most policymakers and experts agreed that SDI was being vastly oversold as a space shield. Given even the most optimistic forecasts, SDI would fail to address the problem defined by President Reagan. The United States would remain vulnerable.

How then can we explain the President's initiative and his campaign to sell SDI to the public? Most of his advisers knew better. They saw SDI not as a panacea for vulnerability but either as a bargaining chip in arms control negotiations or as a means of protecting our own missile silos and thus strengthening our deterrent capability. They realized, however, that Reagan's view of SDI as a solution to deterrence was much more marketable.[27]

The President's advisers knew that the public would not buy SDI as a bargaining ploy or another weapons system; the costs were astronomical. Indeed, in early 1983 the nuclear freeze movement was gaining considerable popular momentum, and even the Catholic bishops—always stalwart anticommunists—were publicly questioning in a Pastoral Letter the morality of nuclear deterrence.[28] The nuclear issue had taken on a feeling of urgency. To disarm these opponents and restore equilibrium required exaggerating the potential benefits of SDI, suggesting that it might some day eliminate nuclear weapons altogether. Since Reagan felt passionately about the possibility of building an impenetrable shield, presenting it to the public this way was relatively easy.[29] Indeed, if the President's vision was fraught with internal contradictions, he seemed not to notice.[30]

The wishful thinking that apparently underlay the President's belief in SDI shaped a highly effective political campaign that looked like leadership, as it is most commonly conceived. With one bold stroke, Reagan dominated doves and moralists by staking a position that co-opted both. Who could argue with the goal of abolishing nuclear weapons altogether? Who could argue with the morality of a defensive strategy over Mutually Assured Destruction? In one short speech, Reagan took control of the public debate and recast it in his own terms. If leadership means getting people to rally behind one's own vision, then SDI is a case par excellence. Reagan came up with a vision that spoke to the hearts of millions of people who were willing to invest billions of dollars in its achievement. He had the vision, and he had the political skill to market it.

But was this leadership? If leadership turns on getting people to do adaptive work, then leadership begins with facing tough realities. Three questions ensue: For what tough reality was SDI a response? What beliefs, investments, and values would be threatened by facing that reality? And was SDI an adaptive response?

The tough reality was staggering, mutual vulnerability to nuclear attack. Reagan would not accept it. Although the United States had lived for more than thirty years in a state of mutual vulnerability, he apparently had never given up the "old-fashioned" view that U.S. national security should never depend on the wisdom, predictability, or sanity of adversaries. Mutual vulnerability as a defense relied much too much on the other side.

The reality of mutual vulnerability is not easy news to take. For thousands of years human beings have sought to protect themselves by constructing invulnerable defenses. Oceans, walls, moats, and mountains have protected communities from hostile neighbors. Sometimes these were breached, but often they remained inviolate. Only the advent of nuclear weapons in 1945 made our security absolutely contingent upon our capacity to manage relationships of vulnerability with other nuclear powers. No longer could anyone even hope to be "king of the mountain." No longer could our governments or tribal councils guarantee our safety from attack. The idea of nuclear deterrence—that vulnerability is desirable, as opposed to being simply unavoidable—shifted radically our conception of security. Security became a function of relating, more than isolation.[31]

Incorporating the tough reality of mutual vulnerability meant at least three major adjustments for Americans. First, our ethos of self-reliance had to be tempered by the reality of interdependence. With oceans separating us from our adversaries, Americans had virtually no experience with vulnerability prior to the Soviet Union's development of the atomic bomb. In contrast, most of the countries in Europe had been overrun by one neighbor or another many times in the last several hundred years.[32]

Furthermore, in a world of mutual vulnerability, we would have to relate differently to our enemies. If nuclear deterrence violates our moral sensibilities, then our only recourse is to pursue less dangerous relationships, even to transform them. For lessons in how this can work we have current history to draw upon. Although the British and French have enough nuclear weapons to decimate the United States, and each other, we do not fear them; neither do they fear each other. These relationships, although mutually vulnerable, consist of a sufficient set of mutual identifications, joint purposes, and rules of conduct to ensure mutual safety.

Hence, mutual trust often must be fashioned by shared enterprise and effort. Yet as President Nixon found in 1973 when he attempted to develop détente, creating a set of conditions for improved relations with the Soviets ran against the grain of Americans, who not only had been raised to view the Soviet Union as a godless, sinister place but also, for two generations, had sacrificed their lives and families to fight Soviet influence in Korea, in Vietnam, and in various skirmishes for client states and factions.[33]

Finally, facing mutual vulnerability would demand taking responsibility for America's role in producing bad outcomes. Managing an interdependent relationship requires accounting for one's own behavior in assessing the behavior of the other party.[34] Did we provoke or perpetuate Soviet hostility? For example, in a 1989 round of dialogues between the Soviet and American officials who had been centrally involved with the 1962 Cuban missile crisis, the American side learned that a key factor in the Soviet decision to ship nuclear missiles to Cuba was the perception that the United States planned eventually to invade Cuba and overthrow Castro. The officials in the Kennedy Administration, however, were far more aware of the *restraint* they had shown in both the Bay of Pigs invasion of Cuba eighteen months before and subsequent more subtle acts to destabilize the Castro regime. The connection between the Bay of Pigs attack and Soviet missiles in Cuba was by and large unseen by the Kennedy Administration.[35] Their assessment of Soviet motives in placing missiles in Cuba failed to appreciate the significance of their own role in provoking Soviet action.

SDI, then, can be viewed as a response to the distress generated by the stark reality of being vulnerable to nuclear annihilation.[36] Facing that reality involved major adjustments in public perspectives. Politically, the conflict over which of these adjustments the country should make surfaced in the Nuclear Freeze Movement, the Catholic Bishops Letter, and a strong conservative sentiment to refortify the military. After thirty years of festering, the strains within the nation as it struggled with the meaning of mutual vulnerability took on the feel of urgency. Given the responsibilities of his office, the President would have felt the urgency acutely, as well as the need to fashion a strong response.

Was Reagan's response adaptive? The answer may vary depending on the time-frame for analysis. Although some responses may sacrifice long-term progress for short-term equanimity, still short-term equanimity may provide a necessary footing for future progress. In retrospect, we can judge the robustness of President Reagan's response by examining how well our society has continued to function, that is, to refine and meet our aspirations. We can also analyze the effects of SDI on the system of international relations. But in the early 1990s, it is too early to know. On one hand, the current transformation of the former Soviet Union and Central and Eastern Europe can be seen partly as a product of the Reagan Administration's hard line on arms control, including SDI. The Soviets were forced to face their economic incapacity to keep up. On the other hand, one could argue that these transformations were largely the product of a host of internal processes of collapse. Rather than respond to the adaptive efforts in the Soviet Union, Reagan's policies made it ever more difficult for the United States to assist the Soviet transformation. Public backing for a flexible relationship with the Soviet Union had never been fostered, and the legacy of debt resulting from the huge costs of an expanded defense in the face of tax cuts created severe limitations on our economic capacity for assistance in the 1990s.

What counts to those who lead, however, is not retrospect but judgments made in process. In real time, we might predict the adaptive success of a policy by the following commonsense principle: an initiative that *addresses* the challenge facing the society is more likely to result in a robust adaptation than a response that *avoids* addressing the challenge. Was Reagan facing the hard, new reality?

Some people might say that SDI provided a bold new means to tackle the challenge of national security by eliminating the need to live in a mutually vulnerable world. Indeed, most of the public at one time thought so.[37] But virtually no public official, policy expert, or scientist believed it, with the exception perhaps of Reagan, Teller, and a few others. Even granted a perfectly working Star Wars defense, which few of them thought remotely possible, the United States would remain vulnerable. Furthermore, to maintain the viability of any strategic defense would likely require arms control agreements. To most people who had thought hard about these problems, the shield was a "nonstarter."[38] Surely, good public arguments could have been marshalled for SDI as a means to keep up with the Soviet research program, strengthen deterrence, or push the Soviets into bankruptcy. But that was not how Reagan made the argument. SDI, as presented by the President, deceived people.

How should misleading the public be understood? Sometimes deception is done quite deliberately as a tactic in a longer term strategy to bring people slowly to face up to tough realities. Such was Roosevelt's strategy in the 1940 presidential election in regard to bringing the United States into the war.[39] Roosevelt engaged in a strategy to pace the work of arming the public. More often, however, misleading is a way to disarm the public. President Johnson deceived Americans as he escalated the war in Vietnam, hoping to turn the corner on the war before people paid too much attention to it. As well, misleading can be a product of self-deception by authority in collusion with people's desire for good news.[40] This, perhaps, is the most dangerous case. A well-meaning President may avoid facing scientific evidence and distressing realities. SDI is both a case of deliberate deception by some officials to disarm the public and a case, it seems, of self-deception by Reagan in collusion with the public.[41]

Unprepared for living in a world of mutual vulnerability, many people took quick comfort in Reagan's policy. Indeed, no previous President had taken on the challenge of educating people, not even President Nixon, who canonized the policy of mutual vulnerability in the 1972 Anti-Ballistic Missile (ABM) Treaty. President Reagan's vision might not be very accurate, but it had great appeal as a technical fix.

It is quite likely that Reagan misled the country unwittingly. He believed in SDI not as another deterrent but as an end to deterrence. When people are challenged, the first line of defense is to apply the responses already in their repertoire. Given the high number of major problems human beings have sorted out through history, applying solutions from the repertoire makes obvious sense. The solution for new problems, however, may lie outside the repertoire, which is exactly when adaptive work is needed. That Reagan and much of the public harkened back to a previous adaptation to the security dilemma—constructing a barricade—is understandable given that neither he nor they had adjusted, even after thirty years, to the fundamental transformation in the nature of security brought on by nuclear arms.[42] In fact, Reagan's formidable political power derived, in large measure, from his combined abilities to sense intuitively what most people wanted to hear and to give it to them.

President Reagan shielded himself and the nation from adapting to the harsh but challenging new reality of interdependence in the modern world. Deterrence has been part of that reality.[43] Without facing the fact of interdependence, the public has been ill-prepared to understand, select, initiate, or support foreign and economic policies suited to the pursuit of better and safer relationships. Trade agreements, foreign assistance, environmental pacts, and foreign investment at home are a part of weaving this new fabric. Ironically, public officials often pay the price of deception. When reality catches up with illusions and constituents discover themselves poorly prepared for the current challenge, they get angry. It may be too soon in retrospect to know, but one wonders whether this dynamic of false hopes—played out in the case of domestic economic issues—brought into office not only a new President but also 110 new members of Congress amid shouts of "Clean the House" in 1992.

Reagan's illusory plan to protect people was not simply a product of his own person. It was also a product of the kinds of public expectations that fall on the shoulders of the nation's senior authority. Imagine how difficult it would have been for Reagan to have given a different kind of speech on March 23, 1983, one in which he spoke of the reality of the nation's vulnerability and dependence—the basic logic of deterrence—without any hope of escape except through an unforeseeable improvement in U.S.-Soviet relations. Perhaps he could have found a way to frame it in a positive light. "Now in human history," he might have said, "people are forced to invent better ways to contain aggression, less destructive ways to compete, and more powerful means to foster cooperation. On a path with fortress isolation at one end and good relations at the other, managed deterrence is measured progress. To move farther along that path toward cooperation is the challenge and opportunity of our age." He might then have made one of several cases for the multibillion dollar SDI. "SDI might not make the United States invulnerable, but it would both strengthen deterrence and sharply increase Soviet military costs, putting great strain on its economy should it choose to continue the arms race."

Unfortunately, people's expectations in times of distress often pull authority figures away from making such speeches. Reagan's actions ought not to surprise us. The question is, Why?

3

The Roots of Authority

Social living depends on authority. Indeed, our capacity to form authority relationships lies at the base of our organizations, from the family to the nation. From a human perspective, evolution reached a major milestone when animals began to live in groups, and authority and its precursors, dominance and deference, made this possible.[1] Our systems of authority serve vital social functions. Without comprehending these functions, one can no more exercise leadership than Boeing Aircraft can design airplanes and ignore gravity. Some of us may hate or distrust authority, but I doubt that we can do without some form of it.[2]

In our everyday language, we often equate leadership with authority. We routinely call leaders those who achieve high positions of authority even though, on reflection, we readily acknowledge the frequent lack of leadership they provide. Intuitively, we sense there is a difference. Usually, we attribute this difference to personal skill, temperament, and motives. Some people "have it" and some people don't. But rarely is the personal dimension the whole story. Context also plays a key part. Frequently, there are impediments to leadership intrinsic to the setting that would make it hard for anybody to lead.

One of these key impediments is authority. Because we so commonly equate leadership with authority, we fail to see the obstacles to leadership that come with authority itself. Having authority brings not only resources to bear but also serious constraints on the exercise of leadership. We need to understand these resources and constraints.

To do so, we first need to identify the indispensable functions that authority serves in our lives.

Authority relationships resemble the dominance and deference relationships of our primate ancestors.[3] Both among humans and among primates, social frameworks provide a host of competitive advantages compared to solitary living. To name a few, societies protect individuals against threat, secure a food supply, care for the young, and adapt to new environments.[4] Yet social living requires the coordination of individual behavior—a need served, in various ways and to varying degrees, by relationships of dominance and authority.[5] Of course, animal societies are very different from human societies, and many people are rightly skeptical about drawing tight inferences from primates to humans; they are leery of potential abuse. At a minimum, however, an exploration of animal societies provides a useful analogy when examining how human organizations and communities coordinate and cooperate to meet vital problems.[6]

The Functions of Dominance in Primate Societies

Dominance structures serve similar functions across species, although social arrangements vary in primate societies from fluid to rigidly hierarchical. Dominant animals take a prominent stance. They dominate the *attention* of the band, sometimes residing in the spatial center of the group. By providing a central focus of attention, the dominant animals often serve as reference points by which the rest of the band orient themselves. By keeping an occasional eye on the location and actions of central figures during the day's activities, each member knows roughly which direction to travel for food, what position to take in camp, with whom to mate, where to run for protection, and to whom to look for the restoration of order when a fight erupts within the band.[7]

This structuring of attention is found, for example, among mountain gorillas living in the lush forests and mountains of central Africa. Living in small groups averaging from seven to eighteen members, the gorilla society centers around one adult male, called the silverback because of the silver hair on his back and neck. When in rare circumstances three or four silverback males live in the same group, a clear hierarchy orders their association.[8] The adult females in the band have more fluid relationships. The hierarchy among them appears to be based on the order in which they join the group, though a mother with very young offspring has more privileges than other adult females. For example, she and her young are afforded greater protection by staying in close proximity to the silverback.[9]

According to observers such as George Schaller and Dian Fossey, the silverback provides the group with an obvious focal point of attention, situated often at its center.[10] All eyes look to him to maintain the daily routine. The group travels when he moves and maintains the general direction he sets. When a predator threatens the group, the silverback often charges in defense, with his fellow males close behind. Although gorillas have few natural predators other than man, leopards have been known to attack. The earth-shaking chest-thump and call of a silverback has terrifying effect. Not only does it alert the rest of the group to watch his moves for direction toward safety, it also initiates the process of defensive attack against intruders, including other gorilla groups that venture into his range. According to Schaller, when he "suddenly roars, the other animals know that something potentially dangerous is in the vicinity, and they congregate around, or behind, their leader."

The silverback provides the focal point that orients others to their place in the line while traveling for food. When the band moves in single file through the forest, he walks in front, followed by the mother with the youngest children, then a mixture of mothers with older children adjacent to other adult males, followed by other females and males, and at the tail end, an adult male. When they feed, members of the group spread out, but during rest periods they often cluster near the silverback. In particular, the young are drawn to him and stay close by. His role is pivotal; the group disintegrates without his unifying influence.

The silverback also serves a control function, mediating aggression within the group and maintaining stability.[11] Fights are infrequent, but when they do break out the dominant male is the one most likely to quell them. When he takes sides, which is unusual, he often stands with the younger individual.[12] But the silverback is not the only member of the group to maintain stability. The hierarchy operates at all levels of the group: adult females dominate juveniles, and juveniles dominate infants who have strayed from their mothers. According to Schaller, "Contrary to popular belief, [the] dominance hierarchy does not cause strife and dissension but promotes peace within the group, for it relegates each member to a certain status and position: every animal knows exactly where it stands in relation to every other animal."[13]

In addition, the silverback establishes and maintains norms of mating. He does not always dominate by intimidation and sheer brute force, however. It is not unusual for a female to switch groups to find another silverback more to her liking, often an older male. A silverback maintains his dominance, in large part, by attracting females and young. How he does this is not clear, but field studies strongly suggest that the members of his band want to be near him, and they follow him accordingly.

In contrast with the rigid hierarchy of the small gorilla band, chimpanzees have a far more fluid social system. Rich and sophisticated patterns of coalition politics, intercommunal fighting, and mechanisms of conflict resolution permeate daily life.[14] In the wild, a chimpanzee community will divide into small groups that mingle and interact. Daily decisions regarding travel are decentralized.

Nevertheless, the chimpanzee dominance hierarchy serves a set of social functions similar to those among mountain gorillas. Though chimpanzees live in communities of up to 105 members, the most constant social unit is the female and her offspring. She decides which direction to take, she protects her young from predators and, when conflicts break out in her group, she restores order.[15]

Adult males usually travel and feed alone or in all-male bands that vary in composition over a week's time, and their groups have their own dominance hierarchy. The dominant male—the alpha—may hold his position for as long as ten years.[16] Chimpanzees appear to be territorial, and the alpha male functions to loosely coordinate the males in maintaining the boundary of the larger community. Within that boundary, according to Jane Goodall, "Overall levels of aggression are likely to be low; each individual, in a manner of speaking, 'knows his place' relative to each other." But at the boundary, males display noisily to ward off potential intruders. The dominance structure, "while it cannot be said to develop in order to control aggression within a society, often functions in exactly this way." Render the status of the alpha doubtful, and the number of aggressive encounters may double.[17]

Rank among chimpanzees establishes norms of male and female pairing. For example, higher ranking females often mate with higher ranking males. During mating periods, the occasional absence of clear-cut dominance among aroused and aggressive males unleashes bedlam.

In the naturalistic setting of the Arnhem Zoo in the Netherlands, Frans De Waal has studied the political behavior of the world's largest community of captive chimpanzees. To human observers, the alpha male appears larger than life. He struts erect with his long hair standing on end, which makes him look twice as big as the others; and he displays himself with great drama and gusto, occasionally adding ferocity, it seems, for effect. He dominates central stage, and few other chimpanzees can keep from gazing at his actions. In human terms, he has charisma. When his dominance is challenged, however, human observers are amazed at the transformation. When, after months of contest and coalition-building, the small and seemingly insignificant challenger succeeds in winning the dominant position, he suddenly begins to strut erect with *his* hair standing on end, inflated to nearly twice his normal size, while the fallen alpha shrinks to half.[18] The role transforms his demeanor. Evidently, through his apparent transformation, the new alpha male becomes a source of arousal, by which he then provides a focal point of attention, a reference point, for social coordination.

The societies of chimpanzees and gorillas suggest that dominant members perform at least five social functions: (1) choosing the direction of group movement, (2) protecting the group from predators, (3) orienting members to their status and place, (4) controlling conflict, and (5) maintaining norms, including norms of mating and resource allocation. The style of a dominant chimpanzee may differ fundamentally from that of a silverback gorilla; each society inhabits different ecological niches and exhibits distinctive social patterns.[19] But each society apparently needs to have these five functions fulfilled, and each uses dominance and hierarchy to do so.

Human Societies

Before drawing analogies between these animals and human societies, at least three caveats are necessary. First, the hierarchies in primate societies involve small groups, at least by modern human standards. They contain as many as one hundred members, but not five hundred, one thousand, ten thousand, or millions. Extrapolating from nonhuman societies to humans jumps a hurdle not only between species but in levels of complexity. The pervasive phenomena of dominance among our closest primate relations does not imply that dominance is a *natural* organizing principle among humans. Even if dominance and deference did constitute natural human tendencies, these tendencies might represent vestigial behaviors that do not provide for the needs of complex human societies. They might be maladaptive.

Second, human societies may not coordinate themselves by the same mechanisms that other animal societies use. Indeed, there are pronounced differences among many species. As we have seen, gorilla societies appear far more rigid than chimpanzee societies, and gorilla boundaries of membership are less permeable and their lines of dominance are far more linear.

Third, we have seen the misuse of Darwin's theory in the form of social Darwinism: the ideas that (1) someone should dominate, and (2) those who do must deserve to. Racists and charlatans of all sorts have tried to rationalize their prejudices by fashioning biological arguments to support them. They invoke natural law. They confuse biological potentiality with biological determinism.[20] For example, men for ages have justified sexism with arguments that males dominate females in many animal societies, and therefore male domination must be natural. But reasoning by analogies must allow for the differences to lead to discoveries. Thus, among all primates, perhaps only humans can realize equality between the sexes.[21] The power of human learning enables human culture to ameliorate the expression of natural behaviors which present impediments to developing a civilized society.[22] Equality, and many other precious achievements, are products of heroic effort and hard-won cultural adaptation.

At best, animal behavior can help us identify the biological potential of human beings toward social activity. Understood in these terms, human inclinations, like the potential for aggression and tenderness, will take a variety of forms depending on the context and culture.[23] What we do with our inclinations is a product of learning. In regard to authority, our capacity to construct a wide array of societies with different authority structures suggests that we can shape the elemental inclinations for dominance and deference.

Dominance in Children. Even at the age of four, youngsters generate systems of stratification. A study of preschool children in Virginia showed that those who dominated the attention of others also won the most struggles over access to toys. Observers attached the label "high-ranking" to these dominant children. Middle- and low-ranking children focused their attention on those with higher rank than themselves rather than on those whom they could displace at the toy shelf. They also spent much more time glancing at high-ranking classmates than vice versa. Attention focused upward. In addition, the children tended to orient themselves spatially (to find their place) by locating those in their own rank and by staying in close proximity to them.[24] In other words, orientation by perceptions of dominance provided part of the glue that held the group together. In a Japanese nursery school, the early departure of the dominant child in the process of group formation resulted in the disintegration of the group structure.[25]

Dominant children serve other functions in addition to orientation. In a Munich study of four-year-old children, the child that commanded the most attention was also the one who most often initiated and organized games, interceded as a third party to break up disputes, and represented the group when interacting with another group. Children of lower rank tended to obey, imitate, smile, and offer presents to the high-ranking child.[26]

In a study of first-graders playing dodgeball, the child who appeared most skillful emerged in time as the dominant individual to whom the rest of the players looked for organization. By first and second grade, most children agreed on the individuals with two dominant characteristics: Who is the smartest? Who is the toughest? Yet few agreed on the identity of the least smart and least tough among them. Attention, again, focused upward in the hierarchy.[27]

Do inherited genes account for these patterns? Or do children absorb these patterns by imitating their elders and other children? Probably, both mechanisms play a role. At particular phases of development, children are receptive to picking up different kinds of lessons and cues, like language, climbing, or social grace. Our genetic heritage has given us a biological foundation upon which many behaviors are readily, almost inevitably learned.[28] Yet though children may be predisposed to learn about dominance and deference, *what* they learn about these relationships is largely a matter of culture and upbringing, as the great diversity of human societies attests.

The dominant children in these studies performed functions that resemble those of the dominant gorillas and chimpanzees in their troops: direction of activity, orientation to role and place, protection at the boundary of the group, and conflict reduction within the group. The children taking the dominant positions provided a focal point of attention that helped to coordinate their classmates.

Small Adult Groups. A similar picture emerges in laboratory studies of small adult groups in the United States.[29] Three generalizations emerge. First, when men and women who do not know one another form a new group and undertake a task, they routinely establish a hierarchy of roles. Second, the group often informally selects and authorizes one of its own members to chair the group in place of the person designated by the scientist in charge. Hence, formal and informal authority roles do not necessarily overlap.[30]

Third, the group looks to its chairperson for certain services.[31] The group orients itself in relation to her. Once settled on the hierarchy, the rest of the members seem to find their places and roles, and the level of tension within the group diminishes dramatically. At the same time, cohesion increases.[32] Authority provides orientation, which in turn diminishes stress and provides a hub of cohesive bonding as each member develops some tie with the chairperson.[33] Commonly, group members then look to her to direct attention to the task and its themes. Authority provides direction. If a crisis ensues, the group turns more of its attention to the chairperson, expecting her to solve the problem. If she does not fulfill that expectation, she loses status and sometimes the dominant role. The group expects the person in authority to provide solutions to crises and, as a corollary, the promise or hope that a solution will be found.[34]

These studies begin to suggest a psychological mechanism for the dynamics of authority. A group recognizes the presence of a problem when the level of stress in the group goes up. Stress arises from disorientation in the face of a complex task, and effective groups normally generate an authority structure in response, sometimes quite informally. The authority structure establishes places and roles for group members, including the role of chairperson, and by so doing creates a coordinating and problem-solving mechanism. When members know to whom to turn, they feel calmed.

As long as the person in authority can provide the services that keep the group composed, her authority will increase; if not, she may get deposed, or the group may fragment. Her latitude for frustrating the expectations of the group may grow if she has succeeded in the past in meeting the group's expectations; she can earn "idiosyncrasy credits."[35] But in a stressful situation in which she does not have the answers, she can also run out of credit.

From Dominance to Authority

I define authority as conferred power to perform a service. This definition will be useful to the practitioner of leadership as a reminder of two facts: First, authority is given and can be taken away. Second, authority is conferred as part of an exchange. Failure to meet the terms of exchange means the risk of losing one's authority: it can be taken back or given to another who promises to fulfill the bargain.[36]

The exchange of power for a service between principal and agent takes a characteristic form. The authorizing principal says to the authorized agent: "Given your know-how, I give you the power to make decisions to accomplish a service, and I'll follow those decisions as long as it appears to me that they serve my purposes."[37]

For example: (1) The U.S. Congress confers power to an agency in the form of authorizing legislation. Congress charges the agency to perform a service, and Congress will defer to the agency's decisions as long as it believes that the agency is doing its job. (2) A traffic light changes color on a street corner, and drivers defer to the red light. By deferring, drivers benefit from a service performed by the local highway department. They confer power to the civil authorities in exchange for the coordination provided by traffic lights. (3) When local constituents elect their state legislator, they confer power to the legislator over decisions that will affect their lives. In exchange, they expect the legislator to serve their needs as they perceive them. (4) Someone who accepts a position in a firm has authority within the scope of employment to act for the firm. The transaction is set forth in a job description. The individual, then, gains the powers and rewards that come with the position in exchange for performing a set of specified services.

In discussing adult groups, I have referred to authority and not dominance. As theoretical types of power relations, dominance and authority can be viewed as distinct. Dominance relationships are based on coercion or habitual deference; authority relationships are voluntary and conscious. In reality, however, these types of power relations often overlap.

Clearly, not all conscious exchanges involving power are acts of authorization. A prudent mugging victim defers to the thief with a gun and hands over his wallet, hoping that his deference will be met with freedom from physical harm. The deference is quite deliberate and the exchange clear-cut: freedom for money. But this is not an authority relationship. The victim does not *authorize* the gunman. The victim does not confer power for a service.[38]

All too often, power is just taken, and deference to it indicates no authorization whatsoever. Yet over time, if people become accustomed to deferring to dominant individuals or institutions and develop a set of familiar habits and payoffs in exchange for their continued deference, then the act of deference begins to look like conference. Deference over time may become authorization, even without deliberate decision.

Thus, not all authority relationships are the product of a conscious and deliberate conferring of power. Often, like dominance, they are produced by *habitual deference*.[39] Many of us have been so conditioned to defer to authority that we do not realize the extent to which we are the source of an authority's power.[40] We forget that we are the principals.[41] When we realize our collective power, the person in authority becomes vulnerable because we can retract the power we have given. Such was the American Revolution.

The overlap between conference and habitual deference is obvious in childhood. A young child does not confer power to parents, but defers. A child learns, and perhaps is predisposed, to look up to them. His life depends on it. Yet when the child grows older, he begins to consider how much power to continue giving his parents. For what help should he look to them? For what help should he look to others? What was previously habitual deference may become conference.

The extent to which different people are able to confer power rather than defer by habit differs markedly. Some people grow up aware that the choice to confer power lies within them. They learn to question conventional structures and participate in the exchange of power for services. They come to think of authority figures with mutuality. But many do not. Many people take their powerlessness for granted. If they have grown up disenfranchised, they may have good reason.

If conscious choosing versus habit does not neatly distinguish authority from dominance, perhaps the presence of coercion in the bargaining separates them. Although the example of mugging shows that a coercive power relationship is sometimes purely dominance, does that mean that all power relationships involving coercion are purely dominance, and not authorization? Clearly, every government has the means to coerce its citizens in order to maintain norms, control conflict, provide direction, and protect boundaries.[42] The courts and the police are inherently coercive. We manage a host of personal and socially defeating tendencies that we seek to inhibit in ourselves (unethical, impulsive, destructive behaviors) by authorizing coercive reinforcements to bolster our will. The threat of coercion is part of the authorization we give to the traffic police, for example, to prevent accidents at dangerous intersections. Not only do we want that threat to inhibit the impulses of other drivers, we also look to it at times to bridle our own. The speeding ticket that we contest one week may save our lives the next.

The events surrounding Gorbachev's disruption of the Soviet Union illustrate more fully the overlap between dominance and authority. The Soviet revolution of 1917 inherited a people conditioned during centuries of Czarist Russia to defer to the government. Stalin's domination reinforced this deference. In contrast, Gorbachev intended *perestroika,* the restructuring, to invert people's orientation to power. He intended to give local businesses and city governments the power and responsibility for solving their own problems, possibly in divergence with commands from the central government.[43]

But Gorbachev found that giving people power does not readily produce empowered and responsible citizens. Not only do people have to change their concepts of power and responsibility, they also have to give up the payoffs of deference: political and economic security. In the old system, people knew where the government stood; its services in the form of jobs and welfare were secure and predictable. Most people did not have to worry about getting fired or laid off, or going homeless or hungry. If civil unrest surfaced in the countryside, all knew that order would be restored. If a foreign nation threatened war, the government's protective response would be decisive. No one need worry about drug abuse either (except with alcohol) because the borders were sealed tight and the punishments for the crime predictable and severe.

In authority relationships, both principals and agents make choices.[44] In the Soviet Union, once Gorbachev made the choices explicit between the old way and the new, we saw significant resistance throughout the land to the insecurities that would come with a nontotalitarian government. Gorbachev cut against the grain, not just of party apparatchiks and government bureaucrats but of numerous Soviet citizens as well. Once they had a choice, many were not sure at all that they wanted to change the terms of agreement.[45]

The Soviet resistance to political and economic liberalization surprised many Americans because we thought of the Soviet people as "enchained citizens of a totalitarian government," and we assumed that the average citizen would immediately rejoice at having the same freedoms that we have. We believed that a small elite generated the authority of the Soviet government through coercive powers—that for the vast majority of people these were purely dominance relationships. The Soviet reactions to reform in the early 1990s, however, suggest that government by the people has many forms, and some of them resemble dictatorship. In fact, we failed to appreciate that the relationship between the public and its government entailed an implicit exchange for services, though not a bargain we would undertake, given our values and priorities. Many Soviet citizens struck a deal long ago with those who were vying for political power, trading various freedoms for security and equity.[46] Once the chance to gain those freedoms was at hand, it was not universally accepted that their costs were worth the gains. The free expression of nationalism, as well as economic hardships, broke the Soviet empire, but the pressures on national authorities from many citizens to return to a variation of the old order were so great that no one in the early 1990s could readily predict the outcome.

Often, the deal to confer power in exchange for a service is made so automatically that the phrase "social habit" may fit better than "social contract."[47] A contract is a deliberate arrangement between consenting parties. Yet many of us who grow up within one society know of no other set of possible arrangements. We have not "agreed" in the sense of deliberately choosing among a set of alternative options. We live in our worlds and carry on its bargains as we know them.[48]

The transformation of either a dominance or a habitual authority relationship into a social contract is no small event. These are revolutions. Even the idea itself that such transformations can be achieved signaled a major intellectual development. For many political activists during the American and French revolutions, Rousseau's contribution to the idea of "social contract" represented not a historical account of authority and its genesis but an *aspiration* for humanity.[49] Can we elevate our unconscious bargains to a conscious level of deliberate choosing?

The concept of social contract may be one cornerstone of democracy, yet democracy is not so easily achieved in light of our inclination to look to authority with overly expectant eyes. In part, democracy requires that average citizens become aware that they are indeed the principals and that those upon whom they confer power are their agents. They have also to bear the risks, the costs, and the fruits of shared responsibility and civic participation.

Authority and Culture

Beyond the capacity for authority and dominance, human evolution reached another major milestone with the development of the mental ability to internalize representations of authority as conscience.[50] Unlike many animals, we do not have to keep authority figures in our actual line of sight. We assimilate the lessons and habits of our seniors: parents, teachers, and others. Their voices and the values, beliefs, norms, and rules they embody can be both internalized and abstracted, that is, detached from the person.

Of course, the internalized voices within us do not sing in unison. Often, they do not even sing in harmony. We internalize a host of competing authorities, each with a different voice and perspective, as we grow up around a variety of people. Furthermore, we develop the psychological capacity to observe the internal counterpoint among these voices in any given problem situation (the voice of our mother, father, teacher, boss, spouse, friend) and to choose which voices to heed and which to ignore.[51]

The debates within us give us the room to choose. We can evaluate, weigh options, and try out competing points of view. Internal conflicts are both a burden and a blessing. It is hard to imagine what children would be like if they were to grow up surrounded by unanimity everywhere, with only one internalized voice of authority. Indeed, we can trace the richness, creativity, and complexity of our cultures and organizations to our ability as individuals to carry on an internal debate among a variety of voices, including the one we call our own.

Our capacity to internalize the teachings of authorities enables the formation of culture and, consequently, large and flexible societies and organization.[52] In a large social system, the norms that guide people's behavior have to be portable. We have to be able to act our parts as members of a society without constant reference to an authority figure. Thus, our cultural norms fulfill in many ways the social functions of authority.[53]

The existence of a robust culture, however, cannot replace entirely the need for an authority system. The office of authority provides a position about which people's expectations cluster.[54] Indeed, the perpetuation of the culture requires a trustworthy network of authorities so that children internalize a fairly coherent set of norms. In the absence of such a network, we see various patterns of behavior, some of them dysfunctional. For example, a society may perpetuate a subculture of crime, street gangs, teen-age pregnancy, and drug abuse when relentless poverty and prejudice compromise the network of local and parental authority, disconnecting it from the larger community, its authority structure, and its promise. Thus, children in many of our American cities grow up internalizing a deep distrust of societal authority and the norms it represents. The distrust then reinforces the subculture of disconnection, fueling a vicious cycle.[55]

In societies with well-established and coherent institutions, authority may primarily play a symbolic role as the embodiment of cultural norms. Indeed, during long periods of stability, the role of authority may even seem to vanish. But it never disappears entirely.[56] Apparently, people always need to glance, at least on occasion, toward some central figure, even if only a figurehead.

For example, in the !Kung civilization of southwestern Africa, cultural constructs seem to have replaced the need for strong authority.[57] Yet the authority figure still plays a role. In each band, the headman coordinates the use of water and gathered foods. The water and plants within a given area are "owned" collectively by the band, and the headman, as the visible symbol of the land to outsiders, controls the consumption of its resources. Thus, when !Kung visitors from other bands enter the area, they ask the headman for permission to use these resources.

By and large, however, well-established norms of resource allocation reduce the need for the headman to exert his authority. The headman's duties dwindle because the families of the band resolve conflicts and ration provisions as a routine. Even his job of deciding to which part of the territory the band should move to gather food is made simple because generally the band already knows where to go. The social functions of authority have largely been incorporated into a stable system of norms and rules carried within each family and member.

Hunting provides a vivid illustration. The practice of hunting supplies about 20 percent of a band's food, yet wild animals obviously do not confine themselves to anybody's land in open countryside. Consequently, the !Kung are faced frequently with potential conflicts over the rights to an animal shot by one band on the land of another. One obvious mechanism to resolve such a dispute would entail establishing a superior authority to both bands, for example, a tribal council to establish and enforce laws. The !Kung mechanism, however, is to establish a tribal norm. An animal is the property of whoever appears to have killed it (the person whose arrow first pierces and stays in the animal). This norm is agreed upon by the various bands, and few disputes arise. The norm is reinforced by other norms. Food is shared among members of a band so that nobody gains that much from an individual kill, and nobody loses that much, dampening the stakes in any individual dispute.

Ultimately, the headman is accountable for the maintenance of these norms, but under stable conditions the norms lessen greatly the effort required of him.[58] The function of the headman is to *symbolize* the norms and their continuity. For example, when members of the !Kung were asked what would happen if an outsider were found stealing food, they responded that the headman would be responsible for "chasing him away." And if anyone attempted to join the band and partake in its food without proper kinship affiliation, the headman would be expected to tell them, "You are not a relative. You must not come to live in my band." However, no one could recall such events ever taking place.[59]

Stress and Charismatic Authority

We have seen that dominance relationships serve key social functions in animal societies, and that in human societies, cultural norms partially take the place of authority relationships in coordinating social activity. By and large, however, we have looked at already established communities unchallenged by sharp divisive conflict or extraordinary external pressure. Indeed, these stable situations are the daily workings of our lives. Authorities usually have the know-how to fulfill our expectations. And what they do not provide in terms of guidance, prevailing cultural norms provide. In Max Weber's terms, both the traditional and bureaucratic forms of authority suffice in helping to hold the community together and solve routine problems.[60]

However, what happens at the start-up of an organization when corporate norms have yet to be formed, or when an established society faces an adaptive challenge and must renew itself? At the beginning of an organization's life, the authority's job of directing, protecting, orienting, resolving conflicts, and establishing norms becomes paramount. He may appear larger than life because he is indeed doing so much. As the source of the organization's energy, he infuses people's work with meaning. As the founding father, he is likely to be invested with charisma by those around him.[61] Many founding fathers are remembered just so. Yet over time, as "a way of doing business" develops, the *office* of senior authority takes on a life of its own.[62] The charisma is transferred from the person to the office, where it then rubs off on whoever holds it; and depending on the stresses of the time and the person's ability to act as the repository of people's hopes, the magic may rub off a little or a lot.[63] Anyone who enters the Oval Office for the first time, no matter his rank, knows this feeling.

What happens after the start-up period and after routinization, when we face a new challenge and our norms and rules do not seem to work? The office itself and the routines it embodies can no longer carry the load, and we expect the officeholder to provide, as in the days of the founder, decisive direction, protection, orientation, control of conflict, and the restoration of norms.[64] We expect authorities to step into the breach. We lean on them to restore equilibrium.[65] We seek reassurance. Indeed, in March 1933, when Franklin Roosevelt became President at the depth of the Great Depression and in the midst of the national banking crisis, he was expected to do no less than save the people. Some even likened him to the Messiah. But not, quite fortunately, his wife. Eleanor Roosevelt called the inauguration "very, very solemn and a little terrifying because when Franklin got to that part of his speech when he said it might become necessary for him to assume powers ordinarily granted to a President in war time, he received his biggest demonstration."[66]

When the stress is severe, we seem especially willing to grant extraordinary power and give away our freedom.[67] In a historical study of thirty-five dictatorships, all of them emerged during times of social distress.[68] Unhinged from their habits, people look with greater intensity to authority figures for remedies.[69] We invest in them not only various formal powers with which to meet our needs but our personal trust that *they* can deliver. We rally to a person, a point, or a symbol; in so reacting we expect to discover, or to be told, how to respond. Hitler, who came to power only weeks before Roosevelt, described the phenomenon with great insight: "That is the mightiest mission of our Movement, namely, to give the searching and bewildered masses a new, firm belief, a belief which will not abandon them in these days of chaos, which they will swear and abide by, so that at least somewhere they will again find a place where their hearts can be at rest."[70]

We attribute charisma to people who voice our pains and provide us with promise. Sometimes in our desperation we do so without critical thought. Perhaps similar to chimpanzees who require an arousing alpha to serve as a reference point, we too in times of disorientation seem inclined to endow our authorities with idealized gifts. As long as they serve this need, we imagine them larger than life. We do not realize that the source of their charisma is our own yearning. What would have become of Adolf Hitler had he been born in normal times?[71]

When shared norms can no longer provide sufficient orientation, the capacity of authority relationships to contain the stresses of society provides a key backup system.[72] We will explore that resource in our discussion of *holding environments*. Mismanaged, however, dependency on authority discourages people from engaging with problems when they must. Instead of generating creativity and responsibility, charismatic authority can generate a mindless following or devolve into bureaucratic institutions that rely on central planning and control.[73] Creativity is stimulated by engaging with one's environment, but the skill of sensing local environments becomes dulled as people fasten their gaze on the charismatic figure or the chain of command for direction. Focusing upward, people lose touch with their communities, markets, and personal resources.

The social functions we call upon authority to serve need to be met. But how should they be met in the context of adaptive work, when distress rises in the society? How can one fashion and use authority relationships to mobilize rather than hinder a community's adaptive efforts?

Part II

Leading With Authority

4

Mobilizing Adaptive Work

In times of distress, we turn to authority. To the breaking point, we place our hopes and frustrations upon those whose presumed knowledge, wisdom, and skill show the promise of fulfillment. Authorities serve as repositories for our worries and aspirations, holding them, if they can, in exchange for the powers we give them.

In our organizations and in our politics, we look generally to our authorities for direction, protection, and order. Direction may take the form of vision, goals, strategy, and technique, but on some preconscious level, it may simply mean "finding the next feeding site." Protection may take the form of negotiating a favorable and mutually beneficial agreement with a competitor, but basically it connotes scanning the environment for threats and mobilizing the response. Order, as we began to view it in the previous chapter, consists of three things: orienting people to their places and roles, controlling internal conflict, and establishing and maintaining norms.[1]

It should be obvious from reflecting on our daily lives that authority relationships are enormously productive. The human capacity for generating complex systems of authority is essential to our extraordinary adaptability and creativity as social creatures. Without our innate abilities to organize ourselves to solve problems, much of what we call civilization likely would not exist.[2]

Yet many of us have mixed feelings about authority. Perhaps because we know from experience that authority relationships consist essentially of dependencies, some of us are ambivalent about giving power, and others are ambivalent about taking it. Having been disappointed or abused in these relationships, some of which may strongly resemble dominance, many of us do not like to be dependent, or depended upon. Dependency makes us feel vulnerable, controlled, or overwhelmed by the expectations other people place upon us.

Appropriate dependencies, however, arise every day. Whenever we develop an organization or a political community, we establish a system of authorizations by which various persons or groups coordinate their efforts and take on specialized roles and functions.[3] We construct a network of appropriate dependencies based on a realistic appraisal of what we and others can provide. In the programming division of a major Boston computer company, for example, Carol Lewis supervises John Edwards, who writes programs.[4] Carol depends on John for imaginative and timely production. In turn, John depends on Carol to provide him with clear specifications of the operations his computer programs should perform. In addition, Carol must provide John with a steady pay-check, computer time, workspace, and supplies. Furthermore, Carol has to maintain order in the workplace by orienting John to his role vis-à-vis other staff, resolving conflicts on joint projects and resources, and maintaining norms of warmth and civility around the office.

Manager and subordinate depend on each other. On one hand, if John disappoints Carol by failing to meet her expectations for quality and timeliness, she may reduce his authorization, either by subtly avoiding his advice on new projects, or by firing him. Similarly, if Carol disappoints John by failing to meet his expectations for direction, protection, and order, he may withdraw his support for her authority. He may undermine her position by making her look incompetent with her own supervisor; or he might diminish her reputation among her colleagues and subordinates. Or he may leave. On the other hand, when satisfying each other's expectations, Carol and John are inclined to reinforce each other's authority. Each increases the reputation and influence of the other.

Supervisor and supervisee are at once dependent and vulnerable. Their dependence derives from the importance of their relationship to the task at hand. Thus, to the extent that the dependence between

Carol and John functions realistically to meet a set of agreed upon goals, dependency seems quite appropriate. Carol and John depend on each other, not because either of them is a weak person but because, within the context of their organization, they have mutual interests and suitable skills to meet those interests.

In order to distinguish later between adaptive and maladaptive authority relationships, we need first to draw a line between appropriate and inappropriate dependencies. Consider the hospital personnel that staff the emergency room. Without an explicit hierarchy of authority by which to orchestrate the actions of a medical staff needing to provide a swift and coordinated response, chaos would ensue. Someone takes charge, usually a physician, and all eyes turn to her for cues and instructions. Information flows from all the members of the staff toward her: from the person monitoring the blood pressure, the person inserting the intravenous line and infusing medication, and the person monitoring the EKG. She provides a focus of attention that orients members of the team to their place and role; she provides direction; she stops any disruptive conflict that arises on the team.

In theory, however, if the members of the staff had worked together over a long period of time and had seen most of the kinds of situations that would come their way, each would know what role to take without much need for on-the-spot coordination or central decisionmaking. The functions generally served by authority would have been incorporated into the norms of the group. The likelihood of dysfunction in the absence of authority would diminish.[5] Yet most emergency rooms have rotations and turnovers in their teams, making a comprehensive set of norms unrealistic. Looking to the person in authority to serve critical functions therefore seems entirely appropriate.

The staff of an emergency room face a kind of problem similar to many everyday situations. These problems are *technical* in the sense that we know already how to respond to them. Often, they can only be accomplished with mastery and ingenuity. They are not easy, nor are they unimportant. Their solutions frequently save lives and require great organizational effort. These problems are technical because the necessary knowledge about them already has been digested and put in the form of a legitimized set of known organizational procedures guiding what to do and role authorizations guiding who should do it.

For these situations, we turn to authority with reasonable expectations. In our various social systems, our authority structures and the norms they maintain govern thousands of problem-solving processes. Meeting a host of vital and everyday problems, they are the product of previously accomplished adaptive work. Indeed, these systems took a long time for our cultures to develop. Over the course of history, we have successfully faced an array of adaptive challenges by developing new knowledge and organizations with new norms. Now that we have them, many of our problems have become routine. Our authority systems already "know" how to respond. And because we know how to respond, the stresses generated by these problems are temporary. For example, a car breaks down and a mechanic, an authority on fixing cars, is called in. A child breaks her arm and an orthopedic surgeon, an authority on fixing arms, is asked to set the bone. A social security check fails to arrive, and a local politician is called to "work the bureaucracy" for her constituent. The marketing department in a company is behind schedule in wrapping up a proposal for an important customer and the vice-president for marketing steps in to authorize a redeployment of staff to meet the deadline.

For many problems, however, no adequate response has yet been developed. Examples abound: poverty at home and abroad, industrial competitiveness, failing schools, drug abuse, the national debt, racial prejudice, ethnic strife, AIDS, environmental pollution. No organizational response can be called into play that will clearly resolve these kinds of problems. No clear expertise can be found, no single sage has general credibility, no established procedure will suffice. Stresses build up and produce a sense of urgency among certain groups within society and sometimes throughout society. In these situations, our inclination to look to authority may generate inappropriate dependencies.[6]

These are the times for leadership. Problems that cause persistent distress do so because the system of accepted dependencies being applied to them cannot do the job. We look to our authorities for answers they cannot provide. What happens, then? Authorities, under pressure to be decisive, sometimes fake the remedy or take action that avoids the issue by skirting it. We instigate drug wars across our border instead of facing the ills of our cities.[7] In the short term, of course, this may quell some of the distress at home. If the administration succeeds in shifting the public's attention to a substitute problem in a foreign nation, then the problem at home may cause less discontent. Attention is deflected from the issue, which *appears* to be taken care of. That more American citizens know the names Pablo Escobar, Medellín, and Manuel Noriega than know anything about their local drug treatment facility indicates how readily we invite distraction.[8] But in the long term, some problems get worse, and then frustration arises both with the problem situation and with those people in authority who were supposed to resolve it. In response to our frustration, we are likely to perpetuate the vicious cycle by looking *even more earnestly* to authority, but this time we look for someone new offering more certainty and better promises. We may rid ourselves of our current authorities in the hope that "if only we had the right leader our problems would be solved."[9]

Habitually seeking solutions from people in authority is maladaptive. Indeed, it is perhaps the essence of maladaptive behavior: the use of a response appropriate to one situation in another where it does not apply. Authority relationships are critical to doing work in many routine situations and, applied properly, can be used invaluably in more challenging times; yet misapplied, they serve to avoid work. The flight to authority is particularly dangerous for at least two reasons: first, because the work avoidance often occurs in response to our biggest problems and, second, because it disables some of our most important personal and collective resources for accomplishing adaptive work.

Distinguishing Adaptive from Technical Work

The practice of medicine illustrates the distinction between technical and adaptive problems, and the dynamics these problems generate. Patients come to physicians with symptoms and signs of illness. They hope that their doctor will be able to "fix" the problem, but they do not know if their hopes are well-founded. Often, the physician can indeed cure the illness. If a person has an infection, there are many times when the physician can say, "I have an antibiotic medication that will almost definitely cure you without any effort or life adjustment needed on your part. The medication is virtually harmless. I can give you one shot, or a week of pills, whichever you prefer." For the purposes of our discussion, we can call these technical situations Type I—situations in which the patient's expectations are realistic: the doctor can provide a solution and the problem can be defined, treated, and cured on the basis of (1) using the doctor's expertise, and (2) shifting the patient's burden primarily onto the doctor's shoulders. The patient appropriately *depends* on the doctor's know-how, and the doctor *depends* on the patient's trust, satisfaction, and willingness to arrange payment.

These Type I situations are somewhat mechanical: one can actually go to somebody and "get it fixed." Many medical and surgical problems are of this sort, and many of them are life-saving. From the doctor's point of view, these provide gratifying moments when she can say, "Finally somebody has brought me a problem that I can solve!" Although the patient's cooperation is crucial in these situations, the weight of problem-defining and problem-solving rests with the physician. The patient looks to her to provide a prescription that at once will offer direction (take this medicine), protection (the medicine will overcome the infection), and order (you should be able to resume normal activity within the week).

Of course, many situations that bring people to doctors are not so technical. We can separate these adaptive situations into Types II and III. In Type II situations, the problem is definable but no clear-cut solution is available. The doctor may have a solution in mind, but she cannot implement it. And a solution that cannot be implemented is not really a solution; it is simply an idea, a proposal. The patient must create the solution in Type II situations, though the doctor may play a central role. Heart disease sometimes presents a Type II problem. The patient can be restored to more or less full operating capacity, but only if he takes responsibility for his health by making appropriate life adjustments. In particular, he will have to consider the doctor's prescriptions for long-term medication, exercise, diet program, and stress reduction. He will have to choose among these. Type II situations can be managed in a mechanical way only partially by the physician. She diagnoses and prescribes, but her recommendations will have side effects requiring the patient's evaluation of the tradeoffs. What new balance should he reach between cutting down the intensity of his job, getting exercise, or eating better? The patient has to recognize his own problem enough to provoke adaptive change. The responsibility for meeting the problem has to be shared.

In these situations, the doctor's technical expertise allows her to define the problem and suggest solutions that may work. But merely giving the patient a technical answer does not help the patient. Her prescribing must actively involve the patient if she is to be effective. The patient needs to confront the choices and changes that face him. The doctor's technical answers mean nothing if the patient does not implement them. Only he can reset the priorities of his life. He has to learn new ways. And the doctor has to manage the learning process in order to help the patient help himself. The dependency on authority appropriate to technical situations becomes inappropriate in adaptive ones. The doctor's authority still provides a resource to help the patient respond, but beyond her substantive knowledge, she needs a different kind of expertise—the ability to help the patient do the work that only he can do.

Type III situations are even more difficult. The problem definition is not clear-cut, and technical fixes are not available. The situation calls for leadership that induces learning when even the doctor does not have a solution in mind. Learning is required both to define problems and implement solutions. Chronic illness and impending death from any cause often fit this category. In these situations, the doctor can continue to operate in a mechanical mode by diagnosing and prescribing remedies (and a "remedy" of some sort can usually be found). Yet doing so avoids the problem-defining and problem-solving work of both doctor and patient.

In Type II and III situations, *treating the illness* is too narrow a way for the patient and the physician to define the task. It applies a technical formulation to a nontechnical problem. When critical aspects of the situation are probably unchangeable, the problem becomes more than the medical condition. For example, if the patient's diagnosis is an advanced stage of cancer in which the likelihood of cure is remote, it may be useless—indeed, a denial of reality—to define the primary problem as cancer. Cancer, in this case, is a *condition.* To the limited extent it can be treated at all, it is only part of the problem. To define cancer as the primary problem leads everyone involved to concentrate on finding solutions to the cancer, thus diverting their attention from the real work at hand. The patient's real work consists of facing and making adjustments to harsh realities that go beyond his health condition and that include several possible problems: making the most out of his life; considering what his children may need after he is gone; preparing his wife, parents, loved ones, and friends; and completing valued professional tasks.

Table 1 summarizes the characteristics of the three types of situations.

Table 1. Situational Types

Situation	Problem definition	Solution and implementation	Primary locus of responsibility for the work	Kind of work
Type I	Clear	Clear	Physician	Technical
Type II	Clear	Requires learning	Physician and patient	Technical and adaptive
Type III	Requires learning	Requires learning	Patient > physician	Adaptive

Unfortunately, neither doctors nor patients are inclined to differentiate between technical and adaptive work. Indeed, the harsher the reality, the harder we look to authority for a remedy that saves us from adjustment. By and large, we want answers, not questions. Even the toughest individual tends to avoid realities that require adaptive work, searching instead for an authority, a physician, to provide the way out. And doctors, wanting deeply to fulfill the yearning for remedy, too often respond willingly to the pressures we place on them to focus narrowly on technical answers.

The doctor in the following case faced exactly these pressures.

Buchanan's Illness

Steve Buchanan was 42 years old when he noticed a pain in his back below the ribs on the right side.[10] It was the fall of 1985, and Steve, a strong-minded carpenter, had done all right in the spiraling Boston housing market of those years. He and his wife, Connie, had married young, and their three children were already teenagers. Connie, who had been working in the home, had recently begun to contemplate what she might do now that the children were getting old enough to leave.

Steve called the doctor whom he had known for ten years since he had suffered and passed a kidney stone. To Dr. Barbara Parsons, Steve's current complaint sounded like a repeat of the same problem, except milder. Yet a routine study suggested something else, possibly even cancer of the stomach. Without further tests—a CT scan, endoscopy—and possibly surgery, she couldn't be sure.

Up until that moment, Steve Buchanan and his family had no cause for alarm. They assumed the pain was nothing serious. Yet the need for a CT scan might signal something different. When Dr. Parsons told Steve about the test, however, she buffered the news by saying that there was no reason to be alarmed, that they were just playing it safe and making sure. Parsons saw no need to generate distress before knowing all the facts. Steve's response was informative: he agreed to the test saying, "No sweat, Doc, I'm sure it will be O.K."

Dr. Parsons had only bad news. In fact, the tests did indicate cancer of the stomach. Major surgery would be needed to take out the stomach and to find out the extent to which the cancer had spread. That was the technical side. Yet what was Dr. Parsons to say, particularly after Steve's subtle "instruction" to have O.K. news to tell?

The situation was nothing new to Parsons. Only a few patients in her thirty years of practice had ever said, "Doc, I'm hoping for the best, but just tell me what I've got." Most people needed time to take in information that demanded a major reorientation of their lives. And Parsons's job, as she saw it, was to help people like Steve accomplish that reorientation, but at a pace appropriate to them. So she told Steve the bad news, but again in buffered form.

Parsons buffered the news in two ways. First, she simply withheld information about the kind of cancer, the odds of curing it, and the likelihood of its spread. Instead, she told Steve that he had a "form of stomach cancer that she hoped was localized to the stomach" and that surgery would be necessary to take it out. Steve didn't ask for details about the disease.

Parsons's second form of buffering was more subtle. By emphasizing all the *actions* that the medical team would be taking, Parsons conveyed a tone of activism and decision that relieved Steve from having to do more than agree at this point. She told him, "Sometimes we find tumor cells in lymph nodes and if that is the case, we will probably need to give you chemotherapy after surgery." Action communicated more than words; it conveyed authoritative know-how upon which to rely.

Steve's surgery revealed what his CT scan anticipated. Cancer had spread beyond his stomach, and not all of the cancer could be removed. Statistically comparing his condition with the outcome of other people having the same form and spread of cancer, Dr. Parsons thought that Steve had a thirty percent chance of living more than a year and a five percent chance of living five years.

After surgery, Parsons entered Steve's room looking for clues to Steve's readiness to listen. Connie was there, too. Dr. Parsons appeared serious but not somber. She started with a question, "Hello Connie, Hi Steve, how do you feel after the surgery?" Steve responded, "This can't be real. I'm not ready for this." Connie asked, "Tell us the good news, Dr. Parsons, Steve's going to be O.K. isn't he?"

At this point, let's step back to contemplate what Dr. Parsons should do. If she were to do just what she felt like doing, she might weep and cry out, "I am heartbroken—the news from surgery is bad, very bad." Yet people in authority are not generally expected to let their emotions go, and that isn't what the Buchanans seemed to be asking for, either. Were Parsons to do what she felt like doing, Steve and Connie might be so disturbed by the suddenness of her outburst and the helplessness implied by her words that they might have fired her and found another doctor, someone who would fit their expectations—someone who would *contain their anxiety* by promising a return to normalcy. Indeed, Parsons had known patients who had spent their last months and their last savings searching all over the country and abroad for a doctor promising a cure. She had also known patients who had gone into deep immobilizing depression and people who had committed suicide upon getting bad news even though they would have had at least many months ahead of feeling healthy.

Parsons felt that she had to contain the Buchanans' anxiety to the extent that they indicated they needed it. Containing their anxiety meant, in operational terms, buffering the information and fulfilling their expectations of authority—for direction, protection, and restoring order. The same two techniques as before would apply: telling only some of the truth in the words, and conveying doctorly activism, know-how, and hopefulness in the tone of her actions.

Some people would view this strategic approach to doctoring as a parentalistic sham. Parsons did not. She saw no point in overwhelming people and families by demolishing the underpinnings of their dreams and plans in the name of "telling the truth." She felt that people's defenses deserved respect, and when facing adaptive challenges, people often need time. They need time to see their lives in a different light—to change their images of the future and the plans nurtured over a lifetime. They need time to tap their own strengths, to go against their natural inclination to depend inappropriately on authority when in distress. They need time to develop their own response ability. To Parsons, abdicating the duty to guide people through this process seemed cruel.

Yet buffering truth so persistently that patients live in a false state of security until the last weeks of life also seemed cruel, although it was not uncommon among her medical colleagues. The strategy of denial is popular because patients and their families are spared the work of adapting their lives to the conditions facing them. Being relieved of that work, they often delight in the doctor who seems always to have a hopeful word and a decisive next step. For the doctor, emotional gratification comes from serving that role. It satisfies one's aspiration to provide hope against hope, "to slay the dragon" and heal the sick. The harm is subtle, yet quite real. With major tasks left unfaced, major scars are left with the living. Unresolved conflicts between parent and child, husband and wife, and with friends and colleagues are left to fester. A time of healing is squandered. Financial questions and key professional priorities are neglected. Good-byes are said badly, if at all. And though the doctor may never hear about it, the surviving loved ones pay the price.

In light of surgery, Dr. Parsons switched gears in her mind. The situation was clearly a Type III and not a Type I problem. The Buchanans faced an adaptive challenge that could not be met solely by Parsons's technical expertise. Beyond her technical know-how, the situation demanded her leadership. Being a religious person, she thought of Scripture: leading people through the "valley of the shadow of death." She also knew the pitfalls of comparing herself with God; she did not fancy that she could see the future: all *she* had were statistics, and statistics only tell us the averages in a large group of people. Parsons's uncertainty made it easier to convey hope because statistics usually demonstrate the few who succeed against the odds. In any individual case, there is always reason for hope. No one can foresee the future of a particular patient with certainty. Of course, Parsons would also offer all the medical techniques that might give Steve the best odds. All that was the simple part.

More complex was the process of getting Steve and his family to adapt to the uncertain yet significant possibility that his life would end within the next few years. Parsons would have to *pace* this process depending on the rate at which the Buchanans could do this kind of work. Bringing to bear her ten years of experience with the family would help, but it would not be sufficient. Parsons knew that she would have to improvise, testing the waters with each step that she moved forward. She would now be in the business of diagnosing not a medical condition but the adaptive capacity of the patient, his family, and their social network.

Questions like these would guide her: How does this family handle stress? Do they bolster each other's resourcefulness, or do they take out their stresses on one another? Who in the family seems resilient and could serve as a bulwark in this process? Given what I know about this family, what are some of the definable problems they are likely to face regarding children, jobs, and finances?

The process would not be so delicate that Parsons had to worry about each and every mistake. Testing the waters meant that she had to take some risks in asking questions. Some of those questions might backfire, but she had some leeway. Her professional experience told her that she would have several chances to back off if she went too far—before destroying her relationship with the family.

In their first encounter after surgery, Steve and Connie's remarks indicated to Dr. Parsons that she should go slow. "I'm not ready for this." "Tell us the good news, Dr. Parsons." She thought that she should wait a few sessions before suggesting that they begin thinking about a contingency plan for the possibility of dying. So she responded in a hopeful way, withholding information without lying overtly. "Surgery went well. We think we got it all out. But we found some tumor cells in some of your lymph nodes. They can be a problem, so we will need to give you some drugs to try to control the little that's left, and hopefully prevent any further spread." Steve responded not by pressing Parsons to elaborate but by saying, "Well that's pretty close to what I expected. When will I be able to get out of the hospital and go home?" Connie smiled and remained silent, and the conversation focused on Steve's convalescence from surgery. Before leaving the room, Dr. Parsons asked if they had any questions, and they said they did not.

The rest of the week in the hospital was useful to Parsons as she acquainted herself more fully with Steve and Connie's world: their children, relatives, friends, and associates from work. These were the people who would play crucial roles in the adaptive process. Parsons didn't have much time, but with each daily encounter in Steve's hospital room, she widened her view of the world she would challenge with the questions she eventually would ask.

A month later in her office, after the oncologist gave Steve his first course of chemotherapy, Parsons raised the first tough question: "You know, there is always a possibility that the cancer can worsen in spite of the treatment. If that happens, people frequently don't survive. Have you two talked about that?" The response was a heavy silence, during which Parsons held steady, not offering a gesture of either encouragement or discouragement. After a minute or so, Connie spoke up anxiously, "I've tried to put the worst out of my mind, but I haven't been able to do that completely." There was a pressured quality to her speech, "I had a dream the other night in which I was alone with our kids in a strange town; I was frightened. I haven't wanted to think about it." Parsons then looked to Steve. "How about you?" Steve responded quickly, "Yeah, I felt differently when I went back to work this week. I can't explain it."

Parsons thought they had made it to first base. The subject could be discussed; the Buchanans had begun to face it on their own, at least unconsciously. Furthermore, they seemed to trust Parsons in their responses. They did not change the subject, or get angry with her for being pessimistic—indicators of unreadiness. Her relationship with them was evidently intact and sufficiently resilient, at least, to absorb this initial challenge. As a next step, she thought she had to structure and pace the discussion. If she were to leave it open-ended, Steve and Connie either might close up tight, not knowing how to proceed, or break open into a free-flowing expression of their feelings and fears. The first would be a step backwards, and the second might leave them feeling overwhelmed by their emotions, and consequently *less* strong and resourceful—qualities they would need in order to think through the adjustments ahead.

Parsons took what she thought would be a bearable next step. She wanted Steve to know that he had a new job to do. At the same time, she wanted to take some of the burden on her own shoulders. "Steve, I really want you to get yourself covered at work. You see, I don't want to be concerned about scheduling treatments and having to worry about your job. It would be much better for me if you could hand off your major responsibilities to one of your associates so we can fight this thing."

Steve squeezed Connie's hand tightly and smiled half-way, and it seemed to Parsons that they had achieved a good beginning. The last thing she had wanted to do was to destroy their hope. Conveying hope was truthful. Moreover, hope itself served as a powerful spur to the body's efforts to fight back. It seemed to Parsons that she had preserved hope at the same time that she had helped the Buchanans to begin organizing contingency plans for the worst outcome. With those plans in hand, the worst would never be as bad as those situations Parsons had seen previously when both patients and doctors joined in persistent denial.

The next steps were difficult. They required that Parsons continue to use her authority not to give answers but to hold the Buchanans in the process of adjustment and learning. Using her authority relationship, she could contain the stresses that the family would generate in facing this critical adaptive challenge. As long as the Buchanans entrusted her with their care, she could shoulder their pains. Serving as the repository of their pains, she had the power to manage the pace of giving those pains back—not so fast that the family would be overwhelmed, and not so slow that they would be unprepared to meet dying if it were to happen. Because they let her contain their anxiety, she had the power to manage how they would eventually work the issues.

Her capacity to hold was a product of her authority. But her authority came not simply from the medical community and from the state licensing board for physicians. All of that *formal* authority served as background for the *informal* authority the Buchanans gave her. If they lost faith in her efforts, they would find somebody else. Her formal authority meant nothing without the Buchanans' informal authorization that came with their trust. And maintaining that authorization, that trust, depended on meeting their expectations.

What did they expect? Steve and Connie initially expected Parsons to provide a cure, to shoulder the problem and solve it. When Parsons discovered that she probably could not solve the problem, she changed her mindset from exercising technical expertise to exercising leadership. But changing her own mindset was not enough. She also had to shift the expectations of her patient and his family. Otherwise, she would be constrained to operate in the technical mode, since that is what they initially had expected—remove the kidney stone. But shifting their expectations is a polite way of saying that she had to *fail their expectations at a rate they could stand.* Fundamentally, she had to fail their expectation that she could provide a cure. Later on, she would also frustrate their wishes that, for example, she would know just "what they should tell their children."

In failing expectations, as we have seen, Parsons took her time and acted gingerly. In maintaining her authority, she traded off expectations, failing some while meeting others. She met the expectation for decision, action, and hope. She also conveyed a sense of order. She structured and paced the process of adjustment by setting the agenda in their meetings; and by containing her own feelings, she communicated calm and control. By all of these means, she kept the level of distress down within a tolerable range.

In effect, the dependency changed. The family continued to make use of Parsons, depending on her for the services just described. But the dependency differed from what it initially had been when the family focused solely on getting a technical cure for the illness. Now, the doctor's *inability* to provide a cure meant that Steve and his family would have to develop *their own ability* to respond to the problem. What the doctor could not do, the patient would have to do, or the response would remain inadequate. Thus, in shifting from the dependence befitting technical situations to the dependence befitting adaptive situations, the patient—the authorizing principal—had to develop his own resourcefulness. The dependence on the doctor changed from looking to her for answers to looking for help in doing adaptive work.

In working toward an adaptive solution, doctor and patient broke the problem situation into definable and more technical components. The potentially unchanging conditions of the situation were identified so that those conditions, themselves, were not defined as problems. This required technical expertise. Cancer and the particular probability of dying was a *condition*. Given that condition, some of the family's problems were technical, Type I. For example, an accountant was hired to solve a set of financial problems. Still, other parts of the situation could be clearly defined, but no expert could solve them alone; these were Type II. The family had to learn. For example, Connie Buchanan had to prepare to return to wage-earning work. Experts helped, but the choices and adjustments were hers to make.

Fourteen months later, Steve died at home surrounded by his family. From Parsons point of view, there was achievement as well as failure. She had lost her patient. At the same time, the last year had been meaningful. The three children spent precious time with their father; they were given the chance to talk about all sorts of things that would help them continue to grow up. Connie, having begun a training program, was gradually getting ready for a job outside the home. Perhaps more importantly, Steve and Connie had discussed many intimate questions that strengthened Connie's courage and desire to continue living as fully as she could.

Leadership Expertise

The story of Steve and Connie suggests what an authority can do when the authority does not know the answer. In those situations, the authority can induce learning by asking hard questions and by recasting people's expectations to develop their response ability. In contrast, Plato argues in *The Republic* that people need a philosopher-king to counteract their ignorance. Using a medical analogy, he asserts that just as one sensibly turns to a physician to solve a medical problem, so also should a polity turn to a properly trained philosopher-king to solve problems of public policy.[11]

The notion of leadership developed here departs from Plato's perspective in a fundamental way. Plato argues that the expertise required of leadership is a substantive vision of the good. Yet Dr. Parsons has no such vision. When she switches from operating as a technician to operating as an agent of adaptive work, she does not know what adaptation the Buchanans ought to make. The expertise that derives from her professional experience tells her that major life adjustments of some sort are called for; it also provides practical guidance for stimulating those adjustments. In addition, her technical expertise gives her information about the medical conditions that are forcing the adaptive change. But she does not presume to know what the results should look like. True, she needs expertise, both technical expertise and leadership expertise. Her actions are nothing if not expert, but they are expert in the management of processes by which the people with the problem achieve the resolution.

Plato misunderstood the kind of expertise required of authorities because he failed to appreciate the medical difference between technical and adaptive work. As a consequence, he argued *as if* a restoration of health were the clear objective in all medical situations, a vision of the absolute good to which any reader might easily relate. Indeed, he may have used this analogy precisely because it conveyed in a concrete way his notion of the absolute good: restoring health. Who could argue? He then defined leadership essentially as answergiving—offering knowledge of the good and how to achieve it.

However, Steve Buchanan's case suggests that regaining health is often not the right orienting value. To focus on Steve's health rather than on Steve and his family's adaptive challenge would have misled them. Parsons's mode of operating shifted *away* from answer-giving authority toward the use of her authority to construct a relationship in which to raise and process tough questions.

Parsons used leadership and not just technical expertise.[12] She used her authority relationship like a containing vessel for the family's learning process. As one would use a pressure cooker, turning the heat up but keeping it within the carrying capacity of the vessel (its walls and relief valve), Parsons's authority gave her opportunities to regulate the levels of stress in the family to keep it within a tolerable yet productive range. She let pressure out by buffering the news, focusing on technical remedies, and organizing action. When she raised hard questions and left the adaptive work to the family, the pressure would rise. By deciding what to bring to their attention, she not only set the agenda, she also regulated stress.

Parsons helped the Buchanans take responsibility. She neither shielded them from their problems, nor did she abandon them. Developing responsibility—the ability to respond—took time and strategy. A large measure of the Buchanans' work involved emotional learning. The family had to grapple with the probability of great loss in order to think clearly and creatively about the specific changes they needed to make. It would have been wrong for her to assume that the Buchanans had that ability fully developed to begin with. They told her quite clearly that they were not ready for the news. Thus, Parsons began with the assumption that the family had the potential—the basic capacity—to take responsibility in this new situation, but likely would need help to employ it.

Implications

Although Plato set the precedent, analyzing leadership with a medical metaphor presents some difficulties. Doctor-patient relationships differ fundamentally from the relations of business executives, politicians, and public managers to their respective constituencies. Large social systems like organizations or polities present the manager with substantially more complex patterns than does the doctor-patient dyad. In a medical setting, a problem will lack clarity because the patient has not yet reasoned and separated the problem into Type I and II components. In a complex social system, a problem will lack clarity because a multitude of factions will have divergent opinions about both the nature of the problem and its possible solutions. One faction's fix is another faction's adaptive challenge. Competing values are often at stake. Furthermore, in a large social system the scientific experts often disagree even on the fundamental outlines of a problem, particularly at the early stages of problem definition.[13] Each faction will have its own expert. For example, witness the public debate about so scientific a question as global warming. Does global warming present a problem needing attention? Which scientist should we trust?[14]

Moreover, in medical illness, the patient has the problem. But in organizational and public life, there will be many relevant parties to a problem, diffusing responsibility for it. The critical strategic question becomes: Whose problem is it? And the answer is not so obvious. For example, who should take responsibility for drug abuse: police, parents, schools, clergy, taxpayers, the army, or some combination of these?

Still, medicine and politics present similar dilemmas. As we turn to large social systems, three general implications of the Buchanan story are worth considering. First, an authority figure exercising leadership has to tell the difference between technical and adaptive situations because they require different responses. She must ask the key differentiating question: *Does making progress on this problem require changes in people's values, attitudes, or habits of behavior?* If people recognize the problem and can repeat a well-worked solution, then she can engage an authoritative response with practical efficiency and effect. When Steve Buchanan had a kidney stone, Parsons took command and called in the right specialist to administer the cure. In situations that call for adaptive work, however, social systems must learn their way forward. Even when an authority has some clear ideas about what needs to be done, implementing change often requires adjustments in people's lives.

Hence, with adaptive problems, authority must look beyond authoritative solutions. Authoritative action may usefully provoke debate, rethinking, and other processes of social learning, but then it becomes a tool in a strategy to mobilize adaptive work *toward* a solution, rather than a direct means to institute one. When Parsons told Steve to hand off his major job responsibilities, she took authoritative action to provoke his thinking about difficult issues, and not really to ease the scheduling of treatments.

As suggested, this requires a shift in mindset. When using authoritative provocation as part of a strategy, one must be prepared for an eruption of distress in response to the provocation and to consider early on the next step. One has to take the heat in stride, seeing it as part of the process of engaging people in the issue. In contrast, the mindset which views authoritative action *as a solution* to an adaptive problem would logically view an aggravated community as an extraneous complication to making headway, rather than an inherent part of making progress. Operating with that mindset, an authority figure would likely respond defensively and inappropriately when the community retaliates.

Second, the Buchanan story suggests that having an authority relationship with people is both a resource for leadership and a constraint. Authority is a resource because it can provide the instruments and power to hold together and harness the distressing process of doing adaptive work. Authority is a constraint because it is contingent on meeting the expectations of constituents. Deviating from those expectations is perilous. Had Parsons not carefully monitored the trust of the family, she might have lost them.

Third, as learning takes place, Type III situations may be broken down partially if not completely into Type II and Type I components. This involves both process and technical expertise. When an authority distinguishes conditions from problems, she can bring tractable issues to people's attention. By managing attention to issues instead of dictating authoritative solutions, she allows invention. People create and sort through alternative problem definitions, clarify value trade-offs, and test potential avenues of action. Creativity and courage can sometimes transform adaptive challenges into technical problems by expanding people's technical capabilities.

For example, Parsons and the Buchanan family transformed the Type III problem of impending death into Type II and Type I parts. Steve and Connie started seeing a counselor to help them find a way to prepare the children. They called an accountant to help clarify their financial needs. And Connie used a local agency to begin a job search and professional training.

The following case illustrates these implications in a large and public system.

Tacoma

On July 12, 1983, the head of the U.S. Environmental Protection Agency (EPA), William Ruckelshaus, took unprecedented action in a case involving a copper plant owned by the American Smelting and Refining Company (Asarco) near Tacoma, Washington.[15] The Asarco plant was the only one in the nation to use copper ore with a high content of arsenic, and arsenic had been found to cause cancer. As authorized by Amendments to the Clean Air Act of 1970, Ruckelshaus was expected to decide what to do about the plant; in particular, he had to determine what constituted an "ample margin of safety" in the plant's operation to protect public health.

This was both a technically and politically difficult question. In the years since the 1970 Clean Air Act Amendments had been written, scientists were discovering that many hazardous wastes lacked a clear threshold of safety. Even a minuscule amount of "nonthreshold chemicals" could produce adverse effects. As Ruckelshaus put it in his June 1983 address to the National Academy of Sciences, "We must assume that life now takes place in a minefield of risks from hundreds, perhaps thousands, of substances. No more can we tell the public: You are home free with an adequate margin of safety."

The Asarco plant had long been regarded as one of the major polluters in the Northwestern United States, but it had also provided employment to generations of people since its opening in 1890. By 1983, nearly one hundred years later, the plant employed about 575 workers in the town of Ruston with a payroll of $23 million. It contributed significantly to the local economy through its purchases of $12 million worth of supplies, and it provided $13 million of revenue to auxiliary businesses in addition to paying $3 million in state and local taxes. If Asarco were to close the plant, the state of Washington would have to pay as much as $5.5 million in unemployment benefits. Closing the plant would be a devastating blow to a region where several major industries had not yet recovered from recession.[16]

Yet the numbers do not fully convey the significance of Asarco to Tacoma. A texture and a way of life had been woven around the plant. Seventy-year-old Owen Gallagher, a former mayor of Ruston and an employee of Asarco for forty-three years, spoke for many town residents when he told reporters from the *Chicago Tribune*: "I've worked in the plant all my life. So have my brothers, and so have my neighbors. We're not sick. This town was built around that plant. People came here looking for fire and smoke in the 1900's to find work. Now the government's complaining about that same smoke and trying to take our children's livelihood away."

The Asarco company itself was well aware of the pollution problem. Under pressure from the regional air pollution authority, Asarco had spent about $40 million since 1970 in equipment and practices to reduce emissions. In the late 1970s they had agreed to install, by 1984, secondary converter hoods at a cost of roughly $4 million to bring emissions down further. Indeed, the hoods were considered the best available technology to reduce pollution at a smelter like Asarco's. Going further would require one of three options: develop a new technology to reduce emissions; ship in low arsenic ore at high cost; or convert the entire plant to electric smelting, a different process altogether, at a projected cost of $150 million.

According to the company, any of these three options would force the closing of the plant. World copper prices had crashed between 1980 and 1982 from $1.45 per pound to 60 cents per pound. To break even, the Asarco plant required 82 cents per pound, which meant that at current prices it was losing money already.

The battle, like many environmental battles, was pitched between jobs and health. According to the EPA, installing the converter hoods as planned would reduce the risk of arsenic related cancer from four persons a year to one. Would this be acceptable? Did an "ample margin of safety" to protect public health require more? Should regulations demand zero emissions? Or was the livelihood generated by the plant worth the added risk of one case of cancer per year?

Complicating these questions was the fact that the emissions, and thus the risks of cancer, were spread out over a twelve mile area that involved people even at a distance from the plant and its jobs. For example, Vashon Island lay two miles offshore, but because of prevailing winds it became, as one resident put it, "the dumping grounds for these pollutants without any benefits such as jobs or Asarco tax payments." Many islanders were afraid of the high levels of arsenic found in the urine samples of their children and in the soil from their local gardens. Should they bear the side-effects of Asarco? People in the city of Tacoma were in the same predicament. Receiving tons of air pollution a year from the plant, and few tax benefits, one member of the Tacoma city council said it was as if "somebody [were] standing on the other side of the city line with a thirty-ought-six [rifle] and firing it into Tacoma."

Who should decide? By habit and statute, Ruckelshaus and the EPA were supposed to decide. The company and many of its workers looked to the EPA to confirm the acceptability of the actions they were about to take by spending $4 million on converter hoods. They were using the best available technology to reduce emissions from their plant. They looked to the EPA to resist taking action that would push them economically over the brink. Yet many area residents, along with environmental activists, looked to the EPA to provide "an ample margin of safety," and were quite willing to push the plant to the edge, if not over it, to reduce emissions significantly further.

Remarkably, Ruckelshaus, on July 12, 1983, refused publicly and dramatically to decide on his own. Going way beyond the perfunctory public hearings mandated by statute to accompany national rulemaking, Ruckelshaus proposed to engage the community at large in facing the problem. He announced the EPA's intention to solicit actively the views and wishes of the people that would be most affected by the EPA ruling. "For me to sit here in Washington and tell the people of Tacoma what is an acceptable risk would be at best arrogant and at worst inexcusable." As he later told the *Los Angeles Times:* "My view is that these are the kinds of tough, balancing questions that we're involved in here in this country in trying to regulate all kinds of hazardous substances. I don't like these questions either, but the societal issue is what risks are we willing to take and for what benefits?" Ruckelshaus even quoted Thomas Jefferson to back up his unprecedented stand: "If we think (the people) not enlightened enough to exercise their control with a wholesome discretion, the remedy is not to take it from them, but to inform their discretion."

Ernesta Barnes, the EPA's regional administrator in the Northwest, spoke to the local press as well on July 12. "We ask the public's help to consider the very difficult issues raised by arsenic air emissions. Together we must determine what is an 'acceptable' or 'reasonable' risk to public health from arsenic emissions." She announced that the usual public hearings would be preceded by "public workshops and other activities to inform you of the many technical issues involved."

Few people reacted positively. The press framed the issue starkly: "What cost a Life? EPA Asks Tacoma" *(Los Angeles Times),* "Smelter Workers Have Choice: Keep their Jobs or their Health" *(Chicago Tribune). The New York Times* ran an editorial that branded "Mr. Ruckelshaus as Caesar . . . who would ask the amphitheater crowd to signal with thumbs up or down whether a defeated gladiator should live or die." For Ruckelshaus to "impose such an impossible choice on Tacomans was . . . inexcusable." The head of the local chapter of the Sierra Club said, "It is up to the EPA to protect public health, not to ask the public what it is willing to sacrifice not to die from cancer." In the community's opinion as well, Ruckelshaus was neglecting his duties. Local citizens called it "copping out." "We elected people to run our government; we don't expect them to turn around and ask us to run it for them."

Ruckelshaus fought back in various encounters with the press. In a letter to *The New York Times,* he wrote, "Your Caesar analogy is seriously flawed. The Roman Caesars asked the crowd for thumbs up or down before sparing or condemning the gladiator. In Tacoma, the ones being asked for their reaction are at risk themselves. No one ever asked the gladiator his opinion, which may be the principal difference between Rome and the EPA."[17] "Listen," he told the *Los Angeles Times,* "I know people don't like these kinds of decisions. Welcome to the world of regulation. People have demanded to be involved and now I have involved them and they say: 'Don't ask that question.' What's the alternative? Don't involve them?"

Resistance to Ruckelshaus also ran high within the EPA itself. Never before had the agency pushed problems back into the laps of a community. Like most government officials, managers within the EPA took seriously their charge to solve problems on behalf of the public. Indeed, public involvement seemed so messy a process compared with rational and expert decisionmaking that even the public hearings demanded by law were seen more as a formality to be suffered than an essential component of the problem-solving process. As a regional staff member described, "At headquarters [in Washington, D.C.] they thought we were a bunch of bozos out here in the region. They could not understand why we were scrambling and bending over backwards to organize the workshops and put out easily digestible information for the public."

As one might expect, the three public workshops held that August were controversial and packed with people, including a large number of smelter workers, union representatives, local citizen organizations, and environmental groups. The first workshop was held on Vashon Island, and the last two in Tacoma itself. The format was the same for all three, and all were covered by local and national television.

After a formal presentation by the EPA staff, with graphs and charts to illustrate the technical facts regarding arsenic emission, dispersion, and the risk of illness, the audience was divided into smaller groups to facilitate individual responses. The EPA staff distributed several handouts with fact sheets, illustrations of how hooding helped control emissions, and excerpts from Ruckelshaus's National Academy of Sciences speech which outlined his philosophy (and Jefferson's) of public education. They then circulated among the groups to answer questions and record the comments of participants.

Many of the comments had little to do with verifiable facts. Hired by the EPA to observe, the dean of the School of Public Health at the University of Washington remarked on how "the personal nature of the complaints and questions made a striking counterpoint to the presentations of meteorological models and health effect extrapolations." People asked whether or not they could eat food from their Vashon Island gardens, how much soil should they remove to make it safe, how would their pets be affected. One woman asked, "Will my child die of cancer?"

The workshops had both immediate and subtle effects. Immediately, the EPA and the public learned some lessons. As one analyst for the EPA described, "We . . . got educated. The questions raised at the workshops sent some people back to the drawing board." Several public groups asked the EPA to postpone the formal hearings, scheduled for late August, to allow them more time to prepare testimony. In the meantime, the public held more workshops on its own under the sponsorship of the city of Tacoma and the Steelworker's Union. Many more questions were raised, and not only questions about pollution and health, but about other options as well, like diversifying the local economy. Yet the EPA was still taking the heat. Some comments bordered on the openly hostile, "I have seen studies which show that stress is the main source of cancer; the EPA is one main cause of stress."

By the time of the hearings in November, the EPA had clarified several scientific questions raised by the public's involvement. Significantly, its computer model estimating the amount of arsenic emissions had been wrong. Yet the corrected model still predicted a risk of one additional cancer death per year from arsenic, even after placement of the new hooding devices.

The workshops and hearings surprised the staff at the EPA. As Ruckelshaus put it, local citizens had shown that they were "capable of understanding [the problem of the smelter] in its complexities and dealing with it and coming back to us with rather sensible suggestions." In fact, "the public—the non-technical, unschooled public—came back with some very good suggestions as to how they could reduce the emissions of arsenic in the plant [and still keep it open]."

Perhaps of greater import, local people began to see the situation in a new light. Rather than view it solely as a conflict between jobs and health, many people began to see a new possibility: the diversification of the local economy. Although no one knew whether or not the plant would have to close in the near future, many could see that remaining so dependent on this one struggling industry was a bad idea.

No one, including Ruckelshaus, saw the new possibility at the start.[18] The idea of diversification, although obvious in retrospect, had not been part of anyone's mindset. The EPA, industry, labor, environmentalists, and local officials had been thinking in more narrow terms of emissions, health risks, and jobs. It took the noisy and conflictive process of public workshops, debates in the press, and the mobilization of neighborhoods to generate new ideas.

One year later, in June 1984, although Ruckelshaus had not yet come to a decision, Asarco announced that it would close the Tacoma plant the following year. Precipitated primarily by depressed copper prices and shortages of high-arsenic copper ore, Asarco nevertheless spread the blame for the shutdown to federal, state, and local environmental agencies for requiring it to install converter hoods costing $3 million by the end of that year. Furthermore, Asarco claimed that the EPA would require a great deal more investment in the future. Although this was not true, since Ruckelshaus had not yet made a final ruling, somebody would have to take the heat, and the EPA was the obvious lightning rod. As one worker told reporters, "I'll tell you something, it's the EPA's fault!"

Yet the community, however distressed, was also better prepared than it might have been. By the time the announcement came in 1984, the new goal had already been set: finding new jobs for the workers and attracting new industry to the region. When the plant closed in 1985, Tacoma and Ruston already had begun the task of diversifying its economy. People had come to the early workshops displaying buttons labeled either "Jobs" or "Health." By the final workshops, people were sporting buttons that said "BOTH."

In retrospect, nearly ten years later, Colin Conant, Executive Director of the Private Industry Council for Tacoma, looked back on the efforts of the Dislocated Workers Project for those laid off by Asarco.

> We created a model for re-training the workforce, and the community got behind it. We got many many people involved on advisory committees: the labor union, United Way, the Private Industry Council, Asarco, the Economic Development Board, employees, and the State Employment Security Department. People might do it that way now, but back then nobody was. The support made a big difference in how well people adjusted. It could have been much more psychologically disruptive. There were far fewer casualties than there might have been without so many people and organizations backing us up. Since Asarco's closing, there have been several more closings in the area and we basically applied the same model. We learned a lot from how we did it then.[19]

In addition to helping the workers adapt, the Asarco effort also served as a model in later years for resolving other environmental disputes in the Tacoma area. According to Doug Sutherland, Mayor of Tacoma during that time:

> It gave us substantial experience that has helped us in many other situations. For example, another major facility in the area is the Simpson Paper Mill, which had a problem with water pollution. Well, we modified the Asarco process, got all the relevant people involved, and it worked beautifully. No law suits. What really came out of this [Asarco effort] was a process and a group of people who were used to looking at an issue together without taking a litigative approach.[20]

Implications

Ruckelshaus recognized that the Asarco situation represented an adaptive challenge rather than a technical problem. Consequently, he resisted pressures from within the EPA and from the public to provide an authoritative solution. Instead, he chose to engage people in facing the challenge. By doing so, he placed an unusual problem in the laps of his own agency. The EPA had no real experience in orchestrating public deliberation. Public hearings routinely had been pro forma, with presentations of technical arguments by interested parties and little more. Hearings tended to focus on narrowly defined issues, without much creativity in exploring new possibilities like diversifying a local economy. Parties did not talk to one another; they presented testimony to a panel of EPA administrators and experts.

The EPA had never seen itself in the role of orchestrating public thinking on problems. In the public workshops in Tacoma, it quickly found itself "over its head" in problems about which its technical expertise meant little. What could pollution experts say about the value of jobs versus the value of health, or ways to cope with a risk-filled life, or paths to economic diversification?

Bearing the brunt of managing the tasks of informing and involving the public, the regional EPA office exhausted itself in the undertaking. Roughly thirty people devoted full time for four months to this one case. Was it worth it? According to one official, the whole "process proved terrifically costly and time-consuming." And in the end, the decision was still the EPA's to make.

Yet there were at least three significant benefits. First, within the EPA itself, the staff at headquarters began to appreciate what it meant to be on the frontlines. Because the regional staff had frequent contact with area groups, they knew better how to engage with the public. On arriving in Tacoma, staff from Washington, D.C., had quickly found themselves out of touch with the real-world import of scientific findings at the local level. As one regional staff member put it, "When they arrived in Tacoma and found themselves face-to-face with a well-informed and often angry public, they began to appreciate our problem a little better." Now, information relevant to public policymaking would flow up from the frontlines rather than just down from headquarters. That made policymaking better. Routine procedures to involve the community began to change. In following years, the EPA began to act as a frequent sponsor and forum for negotiation among stakeholders to resolve environmental disputes.[21] Furthermore, the agency began routinely to make use of the central distinction Ruckelshaus had made in Tacoma—between the science of assessing risk and the problem of managing the public implications of living with risk. The focus on risk management broadened the mission of the EPA, giving a larger context to its previously narrow scientific orientation.[22]

Second, the Tacoma experiment in public deliberation restored the credibility of the EPA, which in 1983 had just come out of two years mired in public scandal. The Reagan Administration, entering in 1981, had taken the extreme position that favoring industry meant opposing environmental protection. Anne Gorsuch Burford, Reagan's first appointee to head the EPA, had stymied every program to regulate business. She crusaded against the "excesses" of the environmentalists and polarized public debate by framing the issue starkly as a trade-off between jobs and the environment.[23] The result was a scandal-producing disregard for the mandate of the EPA to provide environmental protection. The White House was forced to retreat, and it did so by bringing back William Ruckelshaus. The EPA's first head administrator in 1970, he had established the agency's credibility with both environmentalists and the business community. Now he was back to restore it.

Less than four months after returning to the EPA, Ruckelshaus went to Tacoma. As we have seen, instead of being lauded, he was excoriated initially for shirking his responsibilities. Over time, however, the Tacoma effort at public involvement made big strides in terms of credibility. As a member of the Washington Environmental Council put it, the EPA's cooperation and openness went "a long way toward restoring trust and confidence in the agency here in the region." Even previous skeptics of public deliberation later praised the effort. Ruth Weiner of the Sierra Club, who had criticized Ruckelshaus earlier for "copping out," stated at the conclusion of her public testimony that the Clean Air Act "requires public involvement." "Moreover," she said, "in becoming involved, the public begins to appreciate the difficulty attendant on making regulatory decision, the ease with which EPA can be made a scapegoat because the agency's blunders are so readily magnified, and the inadequacy of simply identifying 'heroes' and 'villains' in environmental protection. It may have been hard work and a headache for all of us, but the public involvement is most certainly worth it."

Third, and perhaps most significantly, the communities of Tacoma and Ruston began seeing the need to adapt. Certain facts were now being faced. Asarco's use of outdated technology in its Ruston plant made it only sporadically competitive in the world copper market. The town's reliance on a single industry placed it in a precarious position of dependence. In addition, some people were paying the price of the plant in terms of health, yet without benefit from jobs or tax revenues.

With the advantage of hindsight, we can see these benefits of public engagement. However, when Ruckelshaus broke precedent by involving the public in solving its problem, he met resistance from every quarter: industry, environmental interests, labor, the press, and within the EPA itself. With problems as tough as jobs, health, and economic diversification, it is no wonder that everyone expects authority to make the decision. That seems our inclination—to look to someone or some agency to take the heat in choosing what to do. Ordinarily, these expectations act as constraints on people in authority, inhibiting them from exercising leadership. Yet Ruckelshaus cut against the grain when he insisted that the public realize that the job of regulating pollutants was not simply a technical matter of setting safe thresholds of emission. Trade-offs would have to be made that involved value conflicts not amenable to scientific analysis. And if those trade-offs between jobs and health were to be faced, then perhaps new adaptations might be achieved in the face of loss.[24]

Ruckelshaus insisted that these problems represented challenges to business-as-usual. At the very least, public attitudes toward living with risk had to change. Otherwise, agencies like the EPA would continue to be called upon to do the impossible, to provide fixes for what could not be fixed by fiat from above. Hard choices were necessary, requiring people to clarify and change their values. The EPA could stimulate those changes but it could not make them.

The technical experts within the EPA played a central role. They provided information regarding the conditions requiring an adaptive response. Their expertise was crucial in distinguishing the technical from the adaptive facets of the problem and for clarifying the choices. How much arsenic would be contained by a secondary hooding device, and how much would that reduce the risk of cancer? How did those estimates compare with other plant modifications?

How much income to the community would be lost if the plant closed? Framing and answering these and many other questions required technical expertise essential to the community's problem-solving. Surely in most situations, as in this one, experts are necessary to tease out the complex relationship between an adaptive problem and its technical components, but only if they see the difference.

Ruckelshaus did see the difference. He provoked an adaptive response, not only in Tacoma, and not only within the EPA, but in the nation. The events in Tacoma stimulated a national debate on how to manage environmental risk in which people began to learn about the enormous costs of "cleaning up" the environment. They had been pushed to face realities that would require all sorts of invention and adjustment. But the task of mobilizing an adaptive response was not easy. Nearly everyone resisted. After leaving the EPA, Ruckelshaus looked back on his experiment:

> Perhaps I underestimated how difficult it would be to get people to take responsibility, to educate themselves and one another about such a difficult issue. Probably not more than a relatively few citizens of Tacoma learned that for issues like this there is no "right" answer . . . They would have to decide what they wanted for their community. They would have to determine their own future. But even if a handful learned this lesson, then you have the basis for others learning it. You have the beginnings of a tradition of public deliberation about hard issues. And you also have all the other people in the country who watched what happened there in Tacoma, and indirectly learned the same lesson.[25]

The stories of both Barbara Parsons and William Ruckelshaus suggest a strategy of leadership consisting of several principles. I introduce them here and return to them shortly. First, they identified the adaptive challenge—the gap between aspirations and reality—and focused attention on the specific issues created by that gap. Recognizing that they were working with a problem that existing technical expertise could not solve satisfactorily, they shifted from giving authoritative solutions to a plan for managing people's adaptive problem-solving.

Second, they regulated the level of distress caused by confronting the issues. They paced the rate of challenge and gave structure to the process. This was not just a matter of planning and then implementing the plan by force of their authority. Ruckelshaus and Parsons had to improvise as each of their actions generated information about the capacity of people to engage the issues and learn.

Third, they kept attention focused on relevant issues. For Parsons, that meant a whole sequence of problems demanding attention. For Ruckelshaus, it meant focusing attention within the EPA on the need to manage risk, rather than merely assess it scientifically. It meant challenging the nation to come to terms with the realities of environmental risk, rather than imagine quixotically that risk could be eliminated altogether.

Finally, Parsons and Ruckelshaus devised a strategy that shifted responsibility for the problem to the primary stakeholders. In doing so, they had to change people's expectations of authority and basis of trust.

Both of these people had considerable resources with which to exercise leadership. Their authority not only constrained them but also provided them with several kinds of power. Our discussion so far has suggested some of the dimensions and applications of their power, but a fuller investigation of the resources of authority is essential. A person intent on leading must know the tools at her disposal.

5

Applying Power

To lead from a position of authority requires knowing how to tend and deploy the power that comes with the position. Authority can be divided into two forms: formal and informal. With formal authority come the various powers of the office, and with informal authority comes the power to influence attitude and behavior beyond compliance.[1] *Formal* authority is granted because the officeholder promises to meet a set of explicit expectations (job descriptions, legislated mandates), whereas *informal* authority comes from promising to meet expectations that are often left implicit (expectations of trustworthiness, ability, civility).

The relationship between these forms of authority is easily seen in the case of an elected official. Before her election, a candidate will focus on increasing her informal authority—the respect, admiration, and trust of prospective constituents. Her hope is to transform that trust into the formal authority of office. Yet even after she gains office and the powers that come with it, she still has to monitor her informal authority—her popularity—since it remains a critical source of her authority. It will determine not only her prospects for reelection but also her ability to influence fellow officials while still in office. If her colleagues see that she is weak, they can more easily ignore her.

So her informal authority derives not only from her popularity among her constituents but also from the respect, trust, admiration, and fear of her colleagues. Gaining power requires that she also gain informal authority from her political associates. Whether or not they pay her much mind depends on their own estimate of what she could do to them and for them. In large measure, she gains influence with them by extending her authority informally even to their constituents. If *they* think she is something special, then her colleagues will have to pay attention. They will listen because their own constituents are listening.[2]

Formal authorization brings with it the powers of an office, but informal authorization brings with it the subtle yet substantial power to extend one's reach way beyond the limits of the job description. Formal authority changes in quantum jumps at discrete moments in time when formal mandates for action are given: at swearing-in, hiring, firing, signing of legislation, issuance of a license. In contrast, informal authority changes constantly as one's popularity and professional reputation rise and fall.

For example, as a public manager, William Ruckelshaus had to meet the mandate of an EPA administrator set forth by Congress in order to protect his authority. If he were to violate that mandate, he would risk public humiliation and scandal, as had his predecessor, Anne Gorsuch Burford.

Ruckelshaus had to assure the public that he would meet their expectations as well. Without regaining the public's trust in the agency, he knew that he would have very little informal authority with which to get the interested parties to pay attention to the agency's findings and rulings and cooperate with them. Thus, his informal authority meant as much as formal authority from Congress. Without informal authority, he would be unsuccessful in addressing controversial issues.

The relationship between formal and informal authority is illustrated as well by the relationship of Barbara Parsons to her patients. By choosing her, patients agreed formally to an exchange of services for compensation. They authorized Parsons to be their physician. Surrounding and buttressing that formal transaction, the law set standards of medical care. If Parsons neglected her patients according to those standards, she would risk a malpractice suit. Were she to lose her license for failing to meet the expectations of the state licensing board, she would be forced to close her office.

Yet much of Parsons's power came from neither her formal arrangements with her patients nor the state licensing board. Her power to mobilize her patients to face hard problems came from the power of informal authority conferred by their trust. If her style or her recommendations disappointed that trust, her patients might leave her practice and find another doctor. Or, if leaving were too difficult because, for example, the costs of leaving Parsons's health maintenance organization were too high, they might ignore her prescriptions altogether.

Authority as a Resource for Leadership

Let's examine further the Buchanan and Tacoma cases to develop a framework for assessing strategic assets for mobilizing adaptive work. I summarize them in the context of the medical situation. In that case, Parsons's formal and informal authority gave her an array of capabilities.

First, her relationship with the Buchanans provided a *holding environment* for containing the stresses of their adaptive efforts. She was expected to offer a pair of arms that could help hold the burden. In turn, holding the burden enabled her to deploy the various other forms of power that came with her authority. The holding environment provided the foundation for everything else she did.

Second, Parsons could *command and direct attention.* The family looked to her for a diagnosis of the problem and a plan for addressing it.

Third, because she was expected to make decisions on direction, Parsons was given *access to information*—a vantage point from which to look into the family's lives. They revealed themselves to her.

Fourth, as a result of that privileged access, Parsons had some *control over the flow of information.* She could sequence facts about the illness or issues of dying based on her assessment of the family's resilience.

Fifth, attention and access to information brought her *the power to frame issues*—to influence the terms of the family's discussions among themselves. They looked to her for understanding.

Sixth, because she was expected to maintain order, she was given numerous means to *orchestrate conflict* and contain disorder. For example, she could structure family meetings to discuss contentious issues. And she could arbitrate disputes among her professional colleagues in a location distant from patients to keep these technical disagreements from distracting them.

Seventh, as a corollary to containing disorder, authority provided Parsons with the power to *choose the decisionmaking process* itself, be it consultative, autocratic, consensual, or some variation.

Her powers were limited, but these were the tools Parsons had to work with.

Managing the Holding Environment

The Buchanans gave Dr. Parsons the authority to hold them in a treatment process. Not only could she, in a literal sense, hold their hands but emotionally she could hold their attention. The Buchanans made her a key part of the holding environment within which to contain and channel the stresses they produced by their adaptive efforts.

The term "holding environment" originated in psychoanalysis to describe the relationship between the therapist and the patient. The therapist "holds" the patient in a process of developmental learning in a way that has some similarities to the way a mother and father hold their newborn and maturing children.[3] For a child, the holding environment serves as a containing vessel for the developmental steps, problems, crises, and stresses of growing up. Within the parental hold, the child's growth can be protected and guided. For the patient in psychotherapy, the therapist's relationship is a place to examine and make progress on hard problems. To be effective, therapists have to empathize and understand their patients' struggles so that the patients can begin to see more clearly the nature of their problems. That requires both technical knowledge and process expertise. In my terms, the therapist helps the patient transform Type III problems into more discrete and readily definable Type II problems. For example, a man who complains initially of being depressed about everything learns that he has specific reasons to be angry, frustrated, and sad.

For my purposes, I extend the use of the term "holding environment" beyond parental and therapeutic relationships. *A holding environment consists of any relationship in which one party has the power to hold the attention of another party and facilitate adaptive work.* I apply it to any relationship which has a developmental task or opportunity—including the relationships between politicians and their polities, nations and other nations, coaches and their teams, managers and subordinates, and even relationships between friends.

The holding environment can generate adaptive work because it contains and regulates the stresses that work generates. For example, a friend who listens with empathy to a painful story or who can tell a joke that fits the moment will provide respite and perspective that buffers distress. The friendship is a holding environment. Social structures and hopeful visions of the future during times of hardship reduce social distress: Franklin Roosevelt and the programs of the New Deal provided a holding environment for the nation during the Great Depression.

The holding environment of the doctor-patient relationship consists primarily of bonds of trust, but in other authority relationships it includes bonds of fear, mutual need, and brute force or its threat. The walls and bars of a prison, or the locked doors of a mental hospital, or the threat of international force all potentially provide holding environments to contain people and the stresses they generate and express. Even enemy relationships can generate holding environments. At the end of hostilities, the allies of World War II provided an extraordinary holding environment for the reconstruction of Germany and Japan. The American coalition during the Persian Gulf Crisis of 1990–91 set decisive limits on the means Iraq could use to solve its domestic problems of economic and social development. Invading Kuwait went too far. The relationships forged during the crisis helped structure a holding environment for postwar development and peacemaking in the Middle East.

Thus, holding environments formed initially by purely coercive means can provide a potent way to transform stresses into adaptive change. Sometimes they provide the only possible way. Other times, however, coercive relationships temporarily suppress unwanted behaviors without accomplishing the work of changing the attitudes, habits, and relationships that cause the behavior. They fail to develop into holding environments.

Indeed, the opportunity for adaptive work is often squandered within both noncoercive and coercive authority relationships. Charismatic authority relationships can degenerate into mutual dependencies that erode critical judgment on both sides. Doctors may hold the attention of their patients, yet neglect to raise important questions about patients' lifestyles. Prisoners held tightly behind bars sometimes face themselves and change, but many just harden further.[4] The victors in a war may leave the defeated to rot and fester, rather than address the causes of war.

Parsons's relationship with the Buchanans provided an essential holding environment that supplemented the family's support network. Steve and Connie Buchanan's psychological resilience was bolstered by a host of relationships, and by the daily routine of their lives. Regularity at home and at work helped make the new unpredictability of illness tolerable. Preparing the kids for school, arranging their after-school activities, shopping, cooking, earning a living all helped orient the family in a time of great confusion. Friends, colleagues, religious faith, and the demands of Steve's customers also helped keep the family from being paralyzed by the enormity of the challenge ahead. Having Dr. Parsons to trust and rely upon for information, guidance, perspective, and sympathy gave the Buchanans additional strength.

Of course, the point of the holding environment provided by Parsons and others was not to eliminate stress but to regulate and contain stress so that it did not overwhelm. People cannot learn new ways when they are overwhelmed. But eliminating the stress altogether eliminates the impetus for adaptive work. The strategic task is to maintain a level of tension that mobilizes people.

To return to our pressure-cooker metaphor, the cook regulates the pressure of the holding environment by turning the heat up or down, while the relief valve lets off steam to keep the pressure within a safe limit. If the pressure goes beyond the carrying capacity of the vessel, the pressure cooker can blow up. On the other hand, with no heat nothing cooks.

Parsons constructed a pressure cooker made from *relationships of informal authority derived primarily from trust*. If trust had been weak, she would have had to reduce the pressure, perhaps by delaying bad news. If trust were strong, she could afford to turn up the heat by introducing a tough problem. Trust provided a critical resource, and she had to tend to it fastidiously.

To build trust, we need to know what generates it. Trust in authority relationships is a matter of *predictability* along two dimensions: values and skill. Quite sensibly, people often expect consistent, predictable values and problem-solving skills from their authorities. Without a large measure of predictability in social life, civilization itself would not be possible. For social living to succeed, we all need to believe that our social structures and relationships will perform predictably in keeping with the norms to which we ourselves subscribe.

Numerous scientific and historical studies demonstrate the consequences of unpredictability.[5] In various animal and human experiments, unpredictable painful events are more distressing than predictable ones. They produce, for example, more ulcers and reports of anxiety.[6] In the history of southern Italy, the rise and strength of the mafia can be traced to the policies of the seventeenth-century Spanish throne, which destroyed the political and economic norms and structures of the region. By provoking feuds within the central regional government, encouraging payoffs within the justice system, and shattering norms of trust and cooperation in the marketplace, Spain extracted money in the short-term while setting in motion the economic collapse and the disintegration of a regional community that persists to this day. As one scholar describes, "Distrust percolates through the social ladder, and the unpredictability of sanctions generates uncertainty in agreements, stagnation in commerce and industry, and a general reluctance towards impersonal and extensive forms of cooperation. Sicilians—as everyone knows—do not trust the state: beyond the boundaries of limited clusters, they often end up distrusting each other as well."[7]

The trust that causes one individual to authorize another requires more than predictability alone, however. The victims of repeated extortion would find their local mayor predictable but untrustworthy. Authorities are expected to be competent in providing protection, direction, and order in the interests of their constituents. The trust that produces authorization requires predictability in the delivery of necessary services at an acceptable cost. Trust has two components: predictable values and predictable skills.

To trust Parsons, the Buchanan family needed to feel that she had their interests at heart and would not take advantage of them. She had to have the right values. They expected her not to abuse their vulnerability, for example, by introducing surprise increases in fees. That did not mean that they expected her to be self-sacrificing. Having a generous spirit did not preclude either gaining personal satisfaction or a good income from her doctoring. What mattered was not that she would forgo her own needs but that she cared about providing for theirs.

Tapping that source of trust was rarely problematic for Parsons. She enjoyed caring for her patients and making a good living. Of course, she drew limits to protect her own personal needs; she had to be clear about her limits so that patients could predict her unavailability. For example, she would not make herself available to her patients every night or every weekend. But if she accepted a patient into her practice—which meant that she accepted the patient's grant of authority—she took it as part of her trust to ensure when she was unavailable that another doctor would take her place, fully informed about the patient's specific situation.

With some patients, however, the stresses generated by illness sometimes made them demand more than Parsons would give. In those cases, Parsons had the difficult task of frustrating patients' demands without losing their trust. Usually, she could talk this through with them successfully. Often, these conversations provided an opportunity to help patients see that their anxieties were getting the best of them, that they were losing sight of their strengths and their ability to call other resources into action. For example, some patients would hesitate to call on family, friends, colleagues, and other professionals. Usually, given the limits of her knowledge and ability, Parsons could help arrange additional services or facilitate drawing on family and friends by calling them in herself and breaking the ice on a hard conversation.

On rare occasions, however, she could not foster her patients' abilities to mobilize their resources to contain distress, and they would demand more than she could give. In those cases, she lost their trust and the authority that went with it. The patients went elsewhere.

With the Buchanans, Parsons did not have the problem of "negotiating" how her caring would be perceived. Not only did her reputation precede her, but she had a history going back ten years with this family. Her availability fell within the range of their expectations, so that having access to her never became the prime indicator of her trustworthiness in their eyes. They respected that Parsons had a life of her own. They were willing to work with substitutes in her absence. They knew she cared.

But the basis of their trust was more complicated. Initially the Buchanans trusted Parsons partially for the wrong reasons. In her relationship with the family, trust depended not only on the perception that she cared but also on the perception that she could fix the problem, as she had arranged to do ten years earlier when Steve Buchanan had a kidney stone. She had to change that expectation subtly and slowly from "the doc will take care of this problem for us" to "the doc may not have all the answers, but she's on our side and she's helping us deal with the problem." Parsons's strategic dilemma, therefore, was strengthening trust when trust depended on meeting the unrealistic expectation of a cure.

How fast Parsons could change the expectations of her patients would have three broad determinants: (1) the severity of the adaptive challenge and the stress it generated, (2) the resilience of the patients and their support system, and (3) the strength of the holding environment her authority provided for containing and channeling the stress of the challenge.

Parsons regulated the level of stress by *pacing and sequencing* the flow of information about the illness and the adaptive tasks that she surmised would follow, and by *organizing* support services that would meet various specific needs (family, religious, and financial). The more they trusted her abilities (by reputation, prior acquaintance, and current association), the more of their distress she could contain within the doctor-patient relationship. Thus, a stronger professional relationship would permit her to push them faster to confront reality: its trade-offs, challenges, and uncertainties. *Pacing consisted of gauging the correlation between how much pressure the family could stand and how much pressure the next piece of adaptive work would generate.*

Starting from the time of her first encounter with the Buchanans after surgery, Parsons listened intently to assess Steve's and Connie's psychological resilience. She observed how family and friends gathered and talked. She looked for clues to the carrying capacity of the family and its network of support. When she began to broach the need for contingency plans in the event of death, she listened to their questions and responses, including the nature of their dreams at night, to gauge how much stress they could contain with the help of her holding. Her actions served two functions at once: they directed attention to the adaptive work issues, and they "tested the waters"— the current resilience of the system. If the family had balked at her questions, she would wonder if she was pushing too hard.

Part of the know-how Parsons required was inner discipline, *poise.* She had to have the emotional capacity to tolerate uncertainty, frustration, and pain.[8] She had to be able to raise questions about preparing for the possibility of death without getting too anxious herself. The Buchanans would carefully observe the nonverbal cues to Parsons's own emotional ability to deal with the issues she would ask them to address. If she were to communicate uneasiness in her body language or tone of voice, for example by fidgeting, stumbling for words, backing out of the conversation, or breaking into a sweat, she would communicate a lack of trustworthiness. If *she* could not carry on painful conversations with competence, then how could they?[9]

Tacoma. The Tacoma case illustrates the tasks of the holding environment in a political setting. As we have seen, Ruckelshaus came back in March 1983 to head an agency that had lost its public credibility. Ruckelshaus had to reconstruct the government's primary vessel for working on the country's conflicts over environmental issues. In 1981 he had said that "the role of the EPA Administrator in the 1980s should be that of an educator."[10] But education required trust. Only by restoring bonds of trust could he stimulate people to make hard choices between health and jobs. Only by restoring credibility in the agency could he make formal rulings and pronouncements that would stick. Otherwise, environmentalists, industry, and local citizens affected by pollution would make end runs around him to Congress, state legislatures, and other governmental offices to champion their causes. He would lose the capacity to moderate their conflicting claims.

Going to Tacoma with an open and public appeal to grapple with the complexities of arsenic pollution, health risks, and jobs, Ruckleshaus surprised and perhaps shocked local citizens and interest groups. They were not used to being included in decisionmaking except in a perfunctory way. Indeed, at first they did not trust or appreciate Ruckelshaus's actions. Disturbing people seemed a peculiar way to restore confidence in the EPA. Surely, it was a high-risk strategy.

Ruckelshaus used a variety of means to contain the distress generated by asking members of the public to face their problem. Foremost, he drew upon the informal authority he had gained as the EPA's first administrator. His reputation as an honest broker of public policy gave him the benefit of the doubt. People might be shocked by his action in Tacoma, but they would nevertheless pay attention. They knew where he had stood in the past. They might be highly skeptical, but not highly cynical. Moreover, Ruckelshaus could count on local reserves of credibility from having lived in the Tacoma area together with his earlier service as vice-president at Weyerhauser, the giant timber company nearby. He was no stranger from Washington, D.C.

In addition to relying on his reputation, Ruckelshaus took specific actions to increase trust. He went to Tacoma; people knew to whom they were talking. The government was not some amorphous and impersonal bureaucracy. People could feel more securely held amidst the controversy over the plant because they could actually *see* the person in charge. Furthermore, the EPA earned trust by reasoning with the public. The agency treated the public with respect by offering workshops to openly discuss the bases for decision. Even though the EPA challenged the community's reasoning, the officials in the regional offices showed themselves to be trustworthy because they responded undefensively to the scientific and human questions that the community raised in those workshops. Indeed, the EPA recalculated several scientific findings as a result of the public's critical response. No one could accuse the agency of trying to "pull a fast one." By insisting that the people themselves were in the best position to clarify these hard choices between jobs and health, the agency demonstrated respect and care for the people and earned their trust.

Unlike Parsons, however, Ruckelshaus did not rely solely on trust and respect to construct a holding environment. He also had formal powers derived from his authorization by Congress and the President with which to threaten recalcitrant factions with regulation. These coercive powers increased the public's concern and widened the interest in coming to meetings to engage in the process the EPA had designed. He could simply close down the factory, or, alternatively, let it dump its contents freely into the air and sea, at least until another public agency might intervene. His powers, held in restraint, helped keep people inside the pressure cooker.

Within the EPA itself, Ruckelshaus's reputation gave him enough credibility to contain the agency's own distress in being pushed to undertake a decision process with which it had little experience. For example, Ernesta Barnes, the EPA's administrator for the region that included Tacoma, disagreed with him on the role the government should play in problems like these. She felt that people elect and appoint officials to make and implement the tough decisions, not to refer them back to the public.[11] She was by no means alone in this opinion. Yet Barnes was also a close friend of Ruckelshaus and had trusted him over the years. She gave him the benefit of the doubt. Had she not trusted him, she might have done what many an official will do when facing a dubious directive from an untrusted superior: stall, dampen, and counteract the directive. Not only did Barnes go along but she devoted an enormous amount of her staff's energy and time to get it done right.

Of course, Ruckelshaus's formal authority within the EPA helped as well. He could and did order the agency to involve the public more fully in their rulemaking. His informal authority was a critical resource, but his formal powers provided necessary, decisive leverage.

During the proceedings, the public workshops served as a holding environment to contain highly charged discussions. These workshops provided structure; such details as time and location of meetings, placement of chairs, and size of the rooms all mattered. A few people in a big room may not feel sufficiently held to face conflictive points of view and to listen. Failing to set definite starting and stopping times for meetings may encourage people to wander in and out, rather than stay in place participating. Chairs set up in a circle encourages more participation than auditorium-style seating, where everyone is looking to the front of the room for guidance and answers. How to arrange chairs at each point in the problem-solving process, when to break up the large group into small groups, were among the detailed structural questions that had to be addressed by the EPA, with very little experience from which to draw. Although the staff had held numerous public hearings, they had never constructed *this* sort of holding environment before.[12] Yet they caught on fast. By breaking the workshop into small groups, they made the discussions easier to manage. By focusing on their scientific findings, they communicated their expertise in the field and earned respect. And by taking seriously the questions raised by the public, they demonstrated respect for the competence of the public and earned its trust.

Although constructing and managing holding environments for transforming stress into work is a central task of leadership from positions of authority, it is not the only task. Authority also provides resources to: (1) direct attention to the issues, (2) gather and test information—perform reality testing, (3) manage information and frame issues, (4) orchestrate conflicting perspectives, and (5) choose the decisionmaking process.

Directing Attention

Attention is the currency of leadership. Getting people to pay attention to tough issues rather than diversions is at the heart of strategy. Because the Buchanan family looked to Parsons for direction, she had the power to direct their attention to the questions she thought they needed to face. Furthermore, she could diminish the odds that they would distract themselves with peripheral issues. Being at the focal point of attention, of course, can also be dangerous. She could be scapegoated by a family—used as a distraction. A patient's family may say, "The problem is not the medical condition, the problem is that we have the wrong doctor."

Of course, the patient may be right. The doctor may be incompetent. Blaming the doctor is not always a form of work avoidance. But for people faced with harsh realities, the strong temptation to scapegoat authority may prevent critical thinking about the causes of the problem or the routes to meeting the challenge.

Given this dynamic, the authority's strategic task is to redirect attention from her person and role to the issues that are generating distress. Parsons accomplished this by shifting attention away from the technical issues of medical treatment and directing it toward the hard questions of adaptive change, at a rate the Buchanans could tolerate. This was a dynamic process. As their trust increased and her hold on them strengthened, Parsons's relationship with the family bolstered their resilience and accelerated the rate at which she could shift their attention.

Ruckelshaus faced a similar challenge. His authority gave him the power to command attention. He could make a public display and find the cameras whirring about him. The media covered him widely. His pronouncements captured people's thoughts because the powers that came with his formal authority and the influence that came with his informal authority made people look and listen.

By turning himself into a lightning rod of attention, however, he risked being electrocuted by the press, the public, and his own agency. No one liked the idea of turning the choice of jobs versus cancer back to the community. Consequently, Ruckelshaus faced a dilemma: if he applied the instruments of his office to provoke work, he would have to take the heat.

Yet taking the heat was part of the strategy. Without it, Ruckelshaus could not have made his point to the nation. Being the focal point of attention gave him the power to direct attention to the issue he framed: citizens had to make their own trade-offs between jobs and health, or discover an alternative. They could not look for a technical answer to an adaptive problem.

Reality Testing

People in authority positions are expected to provide answers to problems of direction, protection, and order because they are expected *to know*. They are expected to have or to mobilize the expertise to solve the particular problems at hand. The doctor is expected to examine and listen to the patient and conduct laboratory tests to determine the illness. Scientists of the Environmental Protection Agency are expected to investigate the production and toxicity of industrial pollutants, as well as the industry's role in the local economy and way of life.

Because authorities are expected to know, they are given *access to information.* The doctor is authorized to pry into the patient's private life, touch his body, and order tests that allow her to see inside. She is given license by the patient's family to ask questions of them as well. EPA officials may have a harder time getting access to industry, yet compliance with the agency's investigative authority is the rule rather than the exception.

Authority figures are supposed to be agents of reality testing: they are supposed to investigate problems more objectively than people in the problems' grasp. By virtue of their authority, they are given a special *vantage point* from which to survey and understand the situation. They can compare different sources of evidence. Yet being responsible for reality testing puts them at risk when their constituents do not want to know the facts or hear contrary points of view. Often people want to hear good news, and their resilience for hearing bad news will determine the rate at which an authority figure can challenge them with it.

Access to information, therefore, does not translate directly into latitude for taking action. An authority may be given wide access to diagnostic data without a clear authorization to communicate it. In leading, one has to communicate with subtlety, taking into account the particularities of the constituents, their networks of support, and the harshness of the news.

Managing Information and Framing Issues

Parsons was more than a conduit for information. Part of her job consisted of deciding which issues her patients were ready to face and then framing those issues so that her patients could proceed. Because patients sometimes raise issues in subtle, barely conscious ways, Parsons faced the major interpretive task of identifying which issues were close enough to the surface to warrant discussion and which were as yet unripe. Should she help surface the children's issue, the marital issues, the financial issue, or the professional issues?

Parsons would not be the only conduit and interpreter of information; there would be other sources in the system, including other health professionals. But while the Buchanans would gather information from other sources, professional and personal, Parsons's position as primary physician meant that her words would be given a special hearing.

Life for Ruckelshaus was not quite as simple. There were many sources of information from other organizations about environmental issues besides those within his domain at the EPA. Consequently, he had much less control than Parsons over the content and flow of information reaching his constituents. Yet by virtue of his position, people tended to look to him to frame the issues as they emerged in the public domain. He had some power to pick the issues that he thought were ripe or should ripen, and he had the power to frame those issues. To a significant degree, he could determine the direction of public debate. *The task was to frame issues so that people would comprehend the opportunity and challenge to them.* In going to Tacoma, he chose to ripen and frame the issue of community responsibility for living with risk, which he termed environmental risk management for the debate that ensued within the EPA itself.

The ripeness of an issue is determined primarily by identifying which issues are currently generating a widespread feeling of urgency. The central question is: Has the issue fastened in people's minds? The basic strategic logic is as follows: People are more likely to pay attention to arguments and perspectives about which they feel some urgency. Urgency, well framed, promotes adaptive work. If, as is often the case, there are several urgent issues in a community, then one has to weigh the competing issues to determine which should be tackled in what sequence. Unless there are compelling reasons to begin with an unripe issue, a person in authority would begin with those issues that have already fastened in people's minds. There is no science to this. In real-time, one makes an educated guess, tests how the issue is received, and then reassesses its appropriateness. If only a small faction is urgent about a problem, but one agrees from one's vantage point that the problem the faction sees should be confronted sooner than later, the strategic challenge will be to find ways to generate more generalized urgency, and thus ripen the issue. Of course, the most direct way to ripen the issue will be for the authority figure to take authoritative action on it, which draws immediate attention to it, but at the cost of attention to other issues.[13] By orchestrating nationwide publicity for his trip to Tacoma,

Ruckelshaus opened one issue at the expense of issues like acid rain and ozone depletion. If the person in authority is not prepared to limit his freedom to manage attention to a range of issues, he will either have to wait or find alternative ways to bring attention to the issue without placing himself at the focal point of attention. We return shortly to the implications of this logic.

President Clinton's first days in office illustrate, in part, the importance of gauging the ripeness of problems. With a wide agenda of issues, some of which were very ripe in the society (the budget deficit, a sluggish economy, health policy) and others for which urgency was not generalized (gays in the military), Clinton took action across the spectrum. Authoritative presidential action, of course, ripens issues quickly. When Clinton announced that by executive action he would lift the ban on gays in the military, it immediately became a national issue. But it also expended informal authority needed for other issues more challenging to Congress and the nation, such as raising taxes, closing defense industries, restructuring the health care system, and cutting federal benefits.[14]

Orchestrating Conflicting Perspectives

The leadership of adaptive work usually requires the orchestration of conflict, often multiparty conflict. Parsons's authority provided her with two key resources for resolving conflict: the right to mediate and the power to arbitrate. Among the family, her authority enabled her to play a mediating role. As a respected outsider, she had the power to call the family into her office and bring to the surface conflicting views about how they should respond to Steve's illness. When Connie and Steve disagreed about how to prepare the children for his death, Parsons was able to mediate between them, helping them air their worries in a way that avoided painful, ineffective arguments. They argued plenty, but Parsons's authority gave her the leverage to interrupt the argument, call a break, and provide perspective. In cases more problematic than the Buchanans', she could call in a professional counselor.

As an insider in the health care establishment, Parsons's authority gave her the power to arbitrate among her professional colleagues when conflicts arose. As the primary physician for the family, she had the power to call them into conferences to clarify and decide among the options for treatment. Although she did not have the authority to make all medical decisions for the family, she had the power to resolve professional differences about diagnosis and treatment. What she would communicate to the patient and family was a matter largely of her choosing. She might communicate the differences among the professionals or she might not; in either case, the health establishment by and large recognized her authority to decide.

For Ruckelshaus, orchestrating multiparty conflict was central to the challenge. Indeed, if there had been no competing values and perspectives at play, including his own perspectives given his personal biases and professional vantage point, the problem would have been straightforward: either close or protect the plant depending on what seemed right to everybody. Deciding what standards to set for the copper plant became problematic because one faction in the community primarily wanted to protect the plant's viability, while another faction primarily wanted to protect public health and the environment. The essence of the problem consisted of orchestrating these conflicting voices into some sort of harmony.

The task Ruckelshaus faced is typical of leadership in large social systems. By its nature, adaptive work does not often fall within the purview of established organizational and social structures. Pieces of the puzzle—information about the problem—lie scattered in the hands of stakeholders across divisions, interest groups, organizations, and communities. Not only is the information scattered, but the solution requires adjustments in the attitudes and behaviors of many people across boundaries. Hence, an authority who excludes stakeholders from defining and solving the problem risks developing an incomplete solution or a solution to the wrong problem. At a minimum, he must keep track of the missing perspectives and stakes when he leaves people out. Not only can lack of information undermine the quality of work, but the distress of exclusion can also cause people to sabotage the process and attack authority.

Groups that come together to address an adaptive problem generally consist of representatives from interested parties that act as factions. To exercise leadership in such a group, one needs to understand the constituent pressures on each of those representatives and the relationships among their organizations. A person who leads may identify the adaptive challenge, but the members, each representing a different faction, will define and break down the issues in their own ways. Each faction has its own grammar for analyzing a situation—a system of internal logic that defines the terms of problems and solutions in ways that make sense to its own group members. Shaped by tradition, power relationships, and interests, this internal language of problem-solving is used largely unconsciously, but members of the faction know intuitively when it is misused. To lead a group of factions, one has to sense the separate languages. For example, environmentalists in Tacoma spoke both in spiritual terms about the sanctity of the earth and in practical terms about public health. The Asarco workers spoke both about a family and community way of life going back one hundred years and about jobs. Leading these factions required engaging each in the perspective of the other. The task was to orchestrate the clash of views so that the factions learned from one another and, at a minimum, achieved a workable respect.

Thus, leading across boundaries requires permeating and reforming the boundaries. If one is to organize meetings with representatives of disputing groups, one must invade the normal boundaries and convince each decisionmaker to risk commitments to his or her "home" interests. In essence, one wishes to form a new coalition with these people, where the coalition entity has a purpose that redirects the previous purposes of the parent organizations. If successful, then the coalition will achieve a self-perceived boundary of identity and a cohesion of self-interest. That is the beginning. Then, each representative must lead his or her own faction in its own process of incorporating what the representatives learned in the coalition. Clearly, this is an iterative process in which individuals import and export perspectives across boundaries as their own constituents adjust their views.

Ruckelshaus worked across boundaries such as these. The first task was to stir up the conflict by raising the issue publicly and drawing competing perspectives out into the open. This was the easier part. He announced that a ruling was imminent and that the public would bear the weight of deliberating on it. That cast two coals into the fire at once: the issue itself—a ruling on arsenic emissions, and the process of decision—public participation rather than authoritative decisionmaking. Both features of his announcement aroused attention and engagement.

The second and more complex task for Ruckelshaus was to orchestrate the conflict he had unleashed between factions so that it would be resolved without getting out of hand, by degenerating into violence, for example. No one wanted to see a bomb go off at the Asarco plant by the hand of an enraged parent of a leukemic child. This second task took up the full-time energies of thirty staff members for four months.

To contain the level of disequilibrium, the staff used a variety of tools. Structure in the form of workshops went far to contain and direct the emotionalism of the debate. The workshops themselves were highly structured, actively facilitated by staff to ensure that no individual dominated the conversation. Staff recorders noted any questions remaining on the table and promised that they would be investigated further. The presence of EPA scientists bolstered the holding environment by providing an expert orienting perspective. Lay participants felt privy to discussions among competing industrial, environmental, and governmental experts. Including lay citizens in the decisionmaking both educated the public and diminished the public's feelings of distress and helplessness. As new workshops spontaneously emerged in the process, the EPA remained a presence, monitoring and listening to the debates. People felt that their continuing deliberations were being heard.

Nevertheless, the public debate was full of conflict and passionate argument, which are probably inevitable when a diverse community is facing a complex adaptive challenge. The workshops ensured that the various sides would hear one another, but the format did not attempt to smooth away the conflict.[15] Nor should it have.

With the formation of new coalitions of people—knitting together local business, big industry, labor, the United Way, state and local agencies, and city government—the community developed two new mechanisms for tackling ongoing problems. The Displaced Workers Project, created for Asarco, became a model for dealing with plant closings in the area. And the public involvement method used for Asarco to resolve industrial pollution issues came to serve, in modified form, as a means to handle other environmental disputes in the community. Ten years later, both of these continue to function.

By permeating old boundaries and creating new relationships across them, the Asarco experience strengthened the community's adaptive capacity.

Choosing the Decisionmaking Process

Authorities commonly have the power to choose the decisionmaking process. In essence, they must decide on the presence and relevance of conflict, and whether and how to unleash it. Deciding which process to use—autocratic, consultative, participative, or consensual—requires judgment based on several factors.[16] We have begun to introduce three of these factors already: the type of problem, the resilience of the social system, and the severity of the problem. To these we should add a fourth: the time frame for taking action. The first factor is relatively straightforward. In technical situations, where the authority has the expertise to define and solve the problem, people generally opt for autocratic or consultative decisionmaking. Anything else makes little sense, unless one is using a technical situation for training purposes. Otherwise, let the experts do their job.

Adaptive situations, however, tend to demand a more participative mode of operating to shift responsibility to the primary stakeholders. Because the problem lies largely in their attitudes, values, habits, or current relationships, the problem-solving has to take place in their hearts and minds. One produces progress on adaptive problems by working the conflicts within and between the parties. Yet when faced with an adaptive challenge, an authority might still choose a more autocratic mode as a result of other factors. First, the organization or community may have too little resilience to bear the stresses of adaptive work. Giving the work back to people may overwhelm them and run counter to prevailing norms. Low adaptive capacity may derive from lack of experience in conflict resolution, absence of shared orienting values, reluctance to endure short-term pain to obtain long-term benefit, or feeble bonds of identity and trust among the parties. There may be no familiarity with shared responsibility for common problems, no tradition of teamwork. The strategic challenge would be to use autocratic action to begin developing adaptive capacity. For example, a head of state might rid a judicial system of corruption to begin establishing a norm of trust; a public manager might order a group of bewildered subordinates to provide him with a strategic plan for an impending problem; or an executive might change the performance appraisal system to reward experimentation and teamwork rather than individual success alone.

Second, even in a highly resilient system, an authority may opt for autocratic action when confronted with an adaptive challenge so severe that it generates stress likely to overwhelm even that society. A participative process might further intensify friction among competing factions. In that case, authorities will have to bear more of the weight for defining and solving problems, even if their solutions will knowingly require a large degree of midcourse correction down the road. Foremost among priorities, the authority will have to reduce the level of disequilibrium, often by autocratic behavior, to bring the distress down into the range in which the factions in the society can begin working productively on the issues. For example, Franklin Roosevelt took hurried and autocratic action in 1933, and did so because calming the nation meant as much to the cause of economic recovery as any programmatic experiment.

Third, in a crisis situation, there may not be enough time to engage in a more participative process. A leader may have to take action knowing that he is guessing and will need to correct for it later. Roosevelt illustrates this as well. He immediately declared a bank holiday upon taking office, closing the nation's banks and stopping the widespread run that was driving many of them into bankruptcy. Autocratic action broke the momentum of the run and created time for a more deliberative process to develop a long-term bank policy.

These three factors can be distilled into the following rule of thumb: *One becomes more autocratic—exclusive—when the issue is likely to overwhelm the current resilience of the group or society given the time available for decision.*

In the case of the Buchanan family, Parsons made technical decisions about medical treatment on her own, seeking occasional consultation from other medical specialists. In mobilizing the family's adaptive work, Parsons shifted from an autocratic mode of problem-solving to a participative style over time as the Buchanans adjusted to the painful possibilities of their situation and developed the capacity to face them. She needed time. Although she took her cues from the family in gauging their readiness, she autocratically made decisions about how to frame and sequence the issues. In her judgment, they did not at first have the resilience to tolerate the distress of the illness. Their words early on gave her fairly clear indication. But as both the family and the holding environment grew stronger, as was evident when the Buchanans began to raise difficult questions themselves, Parsons gave more of the work back to them.

For Ruckelshaus, his formal authority gave him the power to decide how best to regulate the Asarco smelter. Indeed, the Clean Air Act required him to decide. But, in effect, by choosing the workshop process, he gave the decision away. When the plant decided on its own to close down, in June 1984, Ruckelshaus's decision was already five months overdue. His delay represented a decision to let the stakeholders do the deciding.

In light of his task, we can see why he might deliberately have refused to decide. Ruckelshaus's challenge was to mobilize people locally to tackle a tough adaptive problem. Given the persistent drop in copper prices, the need for economic diversification was becoming, on its own, more obvious and urgent. Not only did the owners of Asarco know it, but the workers and local beneficiaries of the plant were discovering it as well. The plant was no longer viable. In fact, it did not really matter what Ruckelshaus would rule. Yet had he made the decision when he was supposed to, in February 1984, he may well have provided a distracting focus of attention. The region might have attributed the plant closure to Ruckelshaus and his insensitivity to business. Rather than face the real problem, people likely would have scapegoated the EPA and deferred the adaptive process. As Ruckelshaus put it, "We had to allow them enough time to work it through. That work was not completed by February."[17] Indecision, in essence, forced the public to continue exploring the discovered challenge of economic diversification.

At the outset, however, no one knew that William Ruckelshaus would put off any decision, and neither did he. In response to *The New York Times* "Caesar" editorial, Ruckelshaus wrote, "The people of Tacoma are *not* being asked to make the decision; they *are* being asked for their informed opinion. They know that the right to be heard is not the same thing as the right to be heeded. The final decision is mine."[18] He publicly emphasized his authorization to make the decision. When Ernesta Barnes, the EPA's regional administrator, made her opening announcement on July 12th, she emphasized that Ruckelshaus would hold on to his prerogative to make the final decision. According to her, Ruckelshaus planned to weigh the public's comments heavily, but there would be no vote.

This, too, made sense as a tactic. Had he given away the power to decide, he would have given away a key mechanism to orient everyone involved in the debate and structure its process. Who would come to EPA workshops in which the EPA were playing a nondecisive role? People came because they thought that getting the EPA to listen would make a difference. But the audience that really mattered, according to Ruckelshaus, was the public itself. Various factions may have thought that they were lobbying the EPA, but in fact they were lobbying (and educating) one another under the EPA's auspices.

6

On a Razor's Edge

In spite of the resources that come with it, authority is also a strait jacket.[1] Constituents confer resources in exchange for services. Power is received in the promise of fulfilling expectations—people in authority, we insist, must provide direction, protection, and order. These expectations often make good sense. In technical situations, adequate preparations for the current problem have been made already. Procedures, lines of authority, role placements, and norms of operation have been established. People have a sufficiently clear idea about what needs to be done and how to go about doing it. Creativity and ingenuity may be needed, but only to devise variations on known themes, not new themes altogether.

Our expectations of authority figures become counterproductive when our organizations and communities face an adaptive challenge—when the application of known methods and procedures will not suffice. We continue to expect our authorities to restore equilibrium with dispatch. If they do not act quickly to reduce our feelings of urgency, we bring them down. Sometimes, we kill them.

That we sometimes call these situations "crises in leadership" is symptomatic of the problem of habitually blaming authority. Stymied by our expectation that authorities should provide in adaptive situations what they can and do provide routinely, we blame them for the persistence of frustrating problems that demand our own adaptive work. And so, predictably, our authorities supply us with fake remedies and diversions. We ask for it. If they want to maintain the authorization we give them, they have to deliver, or provide *promises* of deliverance. When we discover that our authorities have failed, too frequently we expiate our failures by scapegoating them and looking for someone with fresh promises.

When authorities do provide the quick fixes we repeatedly demand, they may be setting a course for crisis, both for themselves and their people. Maybe the storm that's brewing will hit on someone else's watch, and they will escape unscathed; maybe not. Many heads of state have fallen as problems fester into crises—recently: Duvalier in Haiti, Marcos in the Philippines, Ortega in Nicaragua, Honecker in East Germany, Ceauscescu in Romania, to name a few. Many heads of American businesses went the same route during the last decade by failing to mobilize adaptive responses to foreign competition.

Exercising leadership from a position of authority in adaptive situations means going against the grain. Rather than fulfilling the expectation for answers, one provides questions; rather than protecting people from outside threat, one lets people feel the threat in order to stimulate adaptation; instead of orienting people to their current roles, one disorients people so that new role relationships develop; rather than quelling conflict, one generates it; instead of maintaining norms, one challenges them.

Of course, real life is fluid. An authority figure, even in adaptive situations, will have to act differently to fulfill each of these social functions depending on several factors, as just mentioned: the severity of the problem, the resilience of the social system, the ripeness of the issue, and time. For example, in an organization one may have to act firmly to maintain norms and restore clear role assignments, while challenging people with questions and raising conflict about direction. But to make tactical decisions to move between technical and adaptive modes along each of these five dimensions, one first needs a clear conception of the differences. Table 2 outlines the shifts that adaptive situations require of authorities.

In adaptive situations, fulfilling the social functions of authority requires walking a razor's edge. Challenge people too fast, and they will push the authority figure over for failing their expectations for stability. But challenge people too slowly, and they will throw him down when they discover that no progress has been made. Ultimately, they will blame him for lack of progress. To stay balanced on the edge, one needs a strategic understanding of the specific tools and constraints that come with one's authority.

Yet in either case, an authority figure cuts his feet. When he is the focus of hopes and pains that are beyond his magic, or any magic, some people are bound to attack, at least in words. Even the most agile cannot dodge these attacks completely, nor shield himself, mentally and physically, from an assortment of wounds.

Leadership is a razor's edge because one has to oversee a sustained period of social disequilibrium during which people confront the contradictions in their lives and communities and adjust their values

Table 2. Leadership with Authority in Adaptive Situations

Social function	Situational type	
	Technical	Adaptive
Direction	Authority provides problem definition and solution	Authority identifies the adaptive challenge, provides diagnosis of condition, and produces questions about problem definitions and solutions
Protection	Authority protects from external threat	Authority discloses external threat
Role orientation	Authority orients	Authority disorients current roles, or resists pressure to orient people in new roles too quickly
Controlling conflict	Authority restores order	Authority exposes conflict, or lets it emerge
Norm maintenance	Authority maintains norms	Authority challenges norms, or allows them to be challenged

and behavior to accommodate new realities. We have begun to explore the resources that authority brings to directing this process. These tools can be organized according to five strategic principles of leadership:

1. *Identify the adaptive challenge.* Diagnose the situation in light of the values at stake, and unbundle the issues that come with it.
2. *Keep the level of distress within a tolerable range for doing adaptive work.* To use the pressure cooker analogy, keep the heat up without blowing up the vessel.
3. *Focus attention on ripening issues and not on stress-reducing distractions.* Identify which issues can currently engage attention; and while directing attention to them, counteract work avoidance mechanisms like denial, scapegoating, externalizing the enemy, pretending the problem is technical, or attacking individuals rather than issues.
4. *Give the work back to people, but at a rate they can stand.* Place and develop responsibility by putting the pressure on the people with the problem.
5. *Protect voices of leadership without authority.* Give cover to those who raise hard questions and generate distress—people who point to the internal contradictions of the society. These individuals often will have latitude to provoke rethinking that authorities do not have.

I have suggested that authority, formal and informal, is a key component of the holding environment—the containing vessel—for the stresses of change. In the short run, people in authority must regulate the stresses directly. They have to work within the vessel's current carrying capacity. In the medium term, the authority figure can reinforce his contribution to the holding environment by strengthening his own authority relationships within the community, and thus increase the community's resilience during his tenure.

For the long term, the vessel can be given enduring resilience so that it can tolerate the higher pressures that tougher issues generate, somewhat independent of the personal presence and power of the authority figure. People in authority can spur the development of civic associations that generate social networks of identification.[2]

They can increase the trustworthiness of authority structures and institutions.[3] They can create rituals that embody and strengthen shared orienting values. They can model norms of collaboration, responsibility-taking, and effective conflict resolution. They can authorize broadly.[4] And they can promote an ethos of learning and creativity. Over time, a community can become familiar with adaptive work, its pain and its profit.

The primary focus of this book is on the short-run task of making progress on an adaptive challenge. The long-term task of leadership—developing adaptive capacity—is largely beyond our current scope, although to some extent the long term is served by accumulating progress and capturing lessons from individual successes. In focusing on immediate problems, a person intent on leading must ask four practical and related questions: How can he identify an adaptive challenge, keep attention focused on the ripening issue, regulate stress to keep it within a productive range, and take action to promote social learning so that a new equilibrium is reached? The efforts in 1965 to secure voting rights for black Americans provides a testing ground for these questions; in this chapter, we focus on President Lyndon Johnson's strategy of leading from a position of authority.[5]

Prelude: The Ripening of the Issue

When Johnson assumed the presidency, he moved immediately to repair the containing vessel that had been weakened by Kennedy's assassination. He acted to reduce the public's disorientation and fear of being aboard a rudderless ship. In his first address to the nation, the new President sounded a clear and direct call to Congress for action. He introduced few, if any, of his personal ideas; instead he promised to carry on the work of his predecessor. By so doing, he reduced the distress of transition and established trust.

> And now the ideas and the ideals which [Kennedy] so nobly represented must and will be translated into effective action . . . In this critical moment, it is our duty, yours and mine, to do away with uncertainty and delay and doubt and to show that we are capable of decisive action; that from the brutal loss of our leader we will derive

not weakness but strength, that we can and will act and act now . . .
John Kennedy's death commands what his life conveyed—that America must move forward.

Presidents usually bring their own people into their administra-
tions. Yet in 1963, with only eleven months to prove himself before
the next presidential election, Johnson relied on Kennedy's Cabinet
and White House. Through continuity in personnel, Johnson again
buttressed the holding environment at the same time that he avoided
drawing attention to himself. With major initiatives ahead, he could
not afford to isolate himself on the point and increase his vulnerability to attack. "I constantly had before me the picture that Kennedy
had selected me as executor of his will, it was my duty to carry on
and this meant his people as well as his programs. They were part
of his legacy. I simply couldn't let the country think that I was all
alone."[6]

Even after he was elected President in his own right, Johnson kept
Kennedy men around him. Not only did he value their talent, but he
needed the ongoing support of their constituencies: media, Eastern-
ers, and intellectuals.[7] Thus, he continued to borrow Kennedy's
authority, shield his program with Kennedy's name, and deflect public attention from his own person. He had to strengthen the holding
environment to contain the pressures he planned to generate with
his policies.

Of his many initiatives, perhaps Johnson's most successful were in
civil rights.[8] At his best, Lyndon Johnson built for himself the opportunity for leadership by listening intently to the nation, identifying its internal contradictions, and transforming the dialogue of
competing interests into legislation and programs. He encouraged
Martin Luther King Jr.'s civil rights vision, and he encouraged what
he viewed as George Wallace's populist vision of economic justice.[9]
Progress would be made by pushing people to engage with one
another to adjust their views or reach compromises. The parties
would be made to do the work.

Indeed, in his legislative program Johnson routinely put the pressure on the people who asked him for help. Thus, Johnson put the
pressure on black leaders to persuade reluctant conservatives. The
key to success on civil rights, in Johnson's opinion, lay in the hands

of the minority party, the Republicans headed by Senator Everett Dirksen. Without their support, no new legislation could get past Senator Richard Russell and the block of Southern Democratic senators committed to its defeat. They would filibuster it to death, as they had done with nearly every civil rights bill for nearly a century.[10] Yet Johnson was not going to do the lobbying work alone. To win the Republicans over, Johnson called on Roy Wilkins, head of the National Association for the Advancement of Colored People (NAACP), as prelude to introducing the Civil Rights Act of that year. He placed the call on January 6, 1964, six weeks after assuming the presidency.

> Johnson: "When are you going to get down here and start civil righting?"
> Wilkins: "As soon as I get rid of my board of directors annual meeting."
> Johnson: "Well you tell them that I think they've got a mighty good man. I don't know of a better, fairer, or abler man in the United States. What I want you to do though is to get on this bill now. Because unless you get twenty-five Republicans you're not going to get cloture [to stop a filibuster]. Now you can't quote me on this, but Russell says he's already got enough commitments to prevent cloture. I think you are going to have to sit down with Dirksen and persuade him this is in the interest of the Republican party, and you think that if the Republicans go along with you on cloture, why you'll go along with them at elections. And let them know that you're going with the presidential candidate that offers you the best hope and the best chance of dignity and decency in this country, and you're going with a senatorial man who does the same thing. *I'm no magician.* Now I want to be with you, and I'm going to help you any way I can. But you're going to have to get these folks in here, and the quicker you get them the better. If we lose this fight we're going back ten years."

Indeed, the Senate went through seventy-five days of filibuster over the Civil Rights bill—the longest in its history. But on June 10, 1964, it was ready to vote on cloture. The key, as Johnson had said, was Dirksen. In response to Russell's protest that "the bill simply involves a political question and not a moral issue," Dirksen finally took his stand. Declaring "civil rights is an idea whose time has come . . . we are confronted with a moral issue," he had turned around.[11] Dirksen's priorities had shifted in the course of his conversations with Wilkins and others. The issue had been made to ripen. As Johnson later described the problem to his biographer Doris Kearns: "The challenge was to learn what it was that mattered to each of these men, understand which issues were critical to whom and why. Without that understanding nothing is possible. Knowing the leaders and understanding their organizational needs let me shape my legislative program to fit both their needs and mine." In pursuing domestic policies in general, Johnson sought to induce the relevant parties—business leaders, educators, labor, the media—to get involved with one another. Some authorities might concentrate on getting people to acquiesce to their commands. Johnson sought to educate people to cooperate with one another, respecting one another's goals. He corraled people into collaborative work. As he described it, "I wanted each of these men to participate in my administration in a dozen different ways. The key was to get men from different groups so involved with each other on so many committees and delegations covering so many issues that no one could afford to be uncompromising on any one issue alone."[12]

Johnson intended to mobilize the nation as a whole to work on issues that had been avoided for nearly two hundred years. Yet mobilizing the society to tackle hard problems and learn new ways required far more than fashioning deals in the legislature; it required public leadership. Johnson had to identify the adaptive challenges facing the nation, regulate the level of distress, counteract work-avoiding distractions, place responsibility where it belonged, and protect voices of leadership in the community. Nowhere did he illustrate this strategy of leadership better than during events in Selma, Alabama.

Selma—Eight Days in 1965

On Sunday, March 7, 1965, black Americans set out to march from Selma to the state capital at Montgomery in an all-out drive for voting rights. Selma, a city of about 29,000, had slightly more black people than white, but only 3 percent of the people on its voting rolls were black. Out of 15,000 black citizens, 325 were registered to vote.[13] The county had used time-worn methods to prevent black citizens from registering to vote, including lengthy written examinations and tricky oral questions like: Recite the Thirteenth Amendment to the Constitution, and what two rights does a citizen have after indictment by a grand jury? Governor Wallace of Alabama had declared during his campaign in 1962: "From this cradle of the Confederacy, this very heart of the great Anglo-Saxon Southland . . . , segregation now! Segregation tomorrow! Segregation forever!"[14]

In response to the voting rights march, Governor Wallace sent the state police against the 600 unarmed black people as they reached the city limits.[15] Americans throughout the country witnessed with shock and fury the televised scenes of black men, women, and children being beaten with billy clubs, stricken with tear gas, and bull-whipped by troopers on horseback. As loud as the screaming was the yelling of white onlookers, "Git 'em! Git 'em!"[16] In reaction, spontaneous demonstrations sprang up across the land as massive pressure focused on President Johnson to mobilize the national guard.[17]

Johnson, however, refused to move. In fact, he faced contrary pressures from Sunday's bloodshed, each with its own long history. On one hand, the outraged public called on the President to act forcefully at once to protect the marchers in Selma. People marched and sat-in at the White House; they marched and sat-in at the Justice Department; they berated him in the press nationwide. Dr. Martin Luther King Jr., "dismayed and discouraged," accused the federal government of "timidity."[18] On the other hand, many others wanted Johnson to keep out of the matter. They expressed great fear of federal interference in their own state affairs. White Southerners, among others in the nation, were tired of federal government intervention into their way of life and wanted to maintain local norms and control. Johnson was faced with a conflict between two different constituencies with two opposing values: states' rights, which represented white supremacy, and voting rights.

This conflict was nothing new. It dated back to the Civil War era. What should be the balance of power between local and central government in determining civil rights? No one knew better than Johnson, a long-time Texas politician, how sensitive this question remained in the South. And no one knew better than Johnson, as former Senate Majority Leader and Vice-President, that the balance of power between local and central governments had been shifting on the rights issue. The Supreme Court ruled in 1954 that segregated schools were illegal.[19] President Eisenhower felt obliged to back up that ruling in 1957 when he sent federal troops to Little Rock, Arkansas, to integrate Central High School. Five years later, in 1962, John F. Kennedy sent federal troops to protect James Meredith as he enrolled at the University of Mississippi. Just months before the march in Selma, Johnson and Congress had passed the historic Civil Rights Act of 1964, which further strengthened the power of the central government over local affairs. Black people could no longer be discriminated against in most places of public accommodation, like hotels, restaurants, and bathrooms. Employers and unions had to provide equal employment opportunities for minorities. Schools were given financial and technical assistance to speed desegregation.

The country had spent years deliberating and testing the issue and, by and large, had come down on the side of protecting civil rights against local transgression. But not fully. The previous year, Congress had been unable to agree on a voting rights provision for the 1964 Civil Rights Act. Johnson had floated the idea, but Congress rejected it. Too many white people found it hard enough to integrate restaurants and schools. They refused to give blacks political power. The Congressional stalemate on voting rights indicated that the country as a whole was not yet ready to enfranchise minorities. Urgency over the issue was far from widespread; voting rights had not yet fastened in people's minds. The steps taken in 1964 toward guaranteeing civil rights were as large as the public seemed able to take at that moment.

Legislators were not about to take pains unless constituents demanded it. Taking pains for a legislator meant making costly bargains with other legislators, giving in on one issue in exchange for support on another, and paying the price back home. These bargains were least painful and risky if the legislator had multiple goals with varying importance to his or her district. A minor goal could be traded away for an urgent one, particularly if other legislators had complementary priorities, without much cost. Such was the case with civil rights legislation. Until Selma, white citizens across the nation generally gave voting rights low priority. For instance, during the

Senate debate over the Civil Rights Bill of 1957, four liberal Western senators—Wayne Morse, Warren Magnuson, Mike Mansfield, and Jim Murray—agreed to support a greatly weakened bill in exchange for Southern support to finance the construction of the Hells Canyon Dam in Idaho. The dam would generate electrical power for the region. Although these Western senators would normally back civil rights, they were compelled to make trades because their districts cared more about the dam.[20]

In private meetings in early 1965, Johnson, knowing the constraints of his role, encouraged King in his plans to ripen the voting rights issue. Although he hoped there would be no violence, he thought public pressure might set the stage for legislative action.[21] As did King. By generating nationwide urgency, the civil rights movement aimed to change the public's priorities and throw Congress into motion. King and his strategists had learned through decades of effort that the federal government would protect the rights of black Americans when public pressure forced it to.[22] So the civil rights movement would turn up the heat. Through the carefully scripted presence of television reporters, the brutality of racism would be transmitted into living rooms throughout the land. Demonstrations would force the nation to pay attention. On Sunday, March 7, after the televised beatings in Selma, Dr. King announced:

> In the vicious maltreatment of defenseless citizens of Selma, where old women and young children were gassed and clubbed at random, we have witnessed an eruption of the disease of racism which seeks to destroy all of America . . . The people of Selma will struggle for the soul of the Nation, but it is fitting that all Americans help to bear the burden. I call, therefore, on clergy of all faiths, representative of every part of the country to join me in Selma for a minister's march on Montgomery Tuesday morning.[23]

In anticipation of Tuesday's march, the pressure on Johnson grew enormously. Marches and demonstrations proliferated across the country. Busloads and planeloads of priests, ministers, rabbis, nuns, and lay people descended on Selma.[24] In Washington, D.C., sit-ins at the Justice Department continued to block Attorney General Katzenbach's office. The White House was deluged with telegrams and calls to take action. A group of demonstrators sat-in during a White

House tour, yelling angry epithets at whoever passed by. Clearly, the public did not relish the prospect of more televised beatings, this time with King and the nation's clergy at the forefront. The public looked to President Johnson to restore order. As he described it, "Everywhere I looked I was being denounced for my 'unbelievable lack of action.'"[25]

On Monday afternoon, King's lawyers appealed to the federal court in Montgomery for an injunction forbidding local and state authorities from interfering with Tuesday's march.[26] Instead, Judge Frank Johnson issued a restraining order to delay the march entirely for a few days until proper safety precautions could be made. In light of this order, President Johnson felt compelled to step in. He quietly sent LeRoy Collins from the Justice Department aboard Air Force One to negotiate a middle path with King that would keep the public pressure on without going farther than any President could legally allow. At the very last minute, on Tuesday morning as the march itself was moving, they made a deal. King avoided clashing with local and State police, and with the federal court, and turned the march back after a dramatic moment of prayer at the site of Sunday's violence.[27] The nation held its breath as it lived through the encounter on television. And though momentarily relieved, the acute level of tension remained very high. Dr. King insisted that the full three-day march to Montgomery still lay ahead.

Johnson continued to hold steady. He neither quelled nor inflamed the situation. Rather than take dramatic public action or a clear stand, Johnson issued a luke-warm statement Tuesday afternoon deploring the brutality in Selma and urging leaders on all sides to "approach this tense situation with calmness, reasonableness, and respect for law and order."[28] He added that he would be sending a voting rights bill to Congress by the weekend. Privately, however, after seeing the televised beatings and judging their public impact, he called in the Justice Department and asked them to draft the strongest bill that would have any chance of surviving a constitutional challenge.[29]

On Tuesday night, Reverend James J. Reeb, a white Unitarian minister from Boston, was beaten badly by a group of white people in Selma; he died two days later. His was the second death. Jimmy Lee Jackson, a seventeen year-old black man, had been shot by state troopers two weeks before while marching in nearby Marion, Alabama.[30] Reverend Reeb's fatal beating added more fuel to the demonstrations and the urgency. "But," as Kearns described it, "Johnson refused to be pushed. Pickets surrounded the White House, carrying placards calculated to shame him into action: 'LBJ, open your eyes, see the sickness of the South, see the horrors of your homeland.' Telegrams and letters demanding action streamed into the President's office."[31] Still, Johnson held steady through Tuesday night, Wednesday, Thursday, and Friday. At one point, a presidential aide interjected, "We have to do something." Johnson replied, "We will. Keep the pressure on. Make it clear we're not going to give an inch. Now that Wallace . . . it's his ox that's in the ditch, let's see how he gets him out."[32]

Finally, on Friday, Wallace asked to meet with the President, and Johnson granted the request at once. As Johnson understood the situation, Wallace had national aspirations. He had run briefly for President in 1964. He could ill afford more bloodshed broadcast nationwide from his state. As much as he hated to give in on civil rights, Wallace also had to maintain law and order. Thus, Johnson had something Wallace needed. He could help Wallace back out of his corner because he, Johnson, had refused to back into one himself. "On Saturday, in the Oval Office, they discussed the question of troops. Johnson appealed to the large ambition and the populist strain that he perceived in Wallace: How could there be any fixed limits, he suggested, to the political career of the first Southern governor to combine economic and social reform with racial harmony? Why not Wallace?"[33]

The meeting resulted in an arrangement. Johnson would rescue Wallace from his obligations to maintain the law and protect innocent black people, for which he would have paid dearly with his own white constituents, but Wallace would have to ask Johnson publicly to mobilize the national guard.[34] Following the meeting, Johnson took Wallace into a prearranged press conference where he made sure that Wallace was still publicly on the hook, that is, accountable for protecting all citizens, black and white. Johnson announced: "If local authorities are unable to function, the federal government will completely meet its responsibilities."[35]

The next day, Sunday, while 15,000 demonstrators outside the

White House sang "We shall overcome," and chanted: "LBJ, just you wait, See what happens in '68," Johnson solicited an invitation to appear before a joint session of Congress the next evening, Monday, March 15, and he began to prepare for his now historic speech.[36]

Principles of Leadership

Before reviewing the speech that served as the climax to these events, we should analyze Johnson's strategy of leadership. As events in Selma unfolded, Johnson would have had to ask himself several questions in making his assessment. Of course, one cannot say with any certainty how Lyndon Johnson thought his way through this crisis or whether his leadership actions were reflective or instinctive. Even Johnson himself could not tell us completely because our human minds work faster than we can recall, and many of our calculations are made unconsciously. Also, Johnson was very good at telling history the way he wanted it told. Nevertheless, we can pose the strategic questions without knowing the extent to which Johnson may have done so himself. This analysis may not explain Johnson as much as it illustrates a conception of leadership.

Identifying the Adaptive Challenge. Johnson immediately confronted two questions already familiar to him: (1) What issues were represented by this conflict—what were people really fighting about? and (2) Did the issues constitute a technical problem for which an authoritative response would suffice, or did the situation require adaptive change? In many situations, the answers to these questions are not obvious, but in this situation they were readily apparent. The country had been working on these questions for years. The issue was a conflict over values: Would the values of freedom and equality or the values of traditional, local white cultures prevail? Stated simply, either white people had to make room, or black people had to accept their place. Johnson could not solve this dilemma. No authoritative presidential decision would "fix" this kind of problem. This problem existed in the minds and hearts of citizens, and only adjustments *there* would resolve the value conflict. What the President could do was animate and prod people across the nation to address the internal contradiction between the values of freedom and equality they espoused and the mode of suppression they lived or permitted. Although laws, political stands, and programs could not mandate adaptive change, they could fix attention on the need for adjustment. They could begin to change institutions to create new norms and set new limits on behavior.[37] As Johnson commented after passage the previous year of the Civil Rights Act, "I understand that a law doesn't change people's feeling. But it's a beginning. It shows the way."[38]

Johnson wanted to know, given the limits and constraints of his authority, how he could make it possible for people to learn new attitudes and habits of behavior. How could he change people's feelings at least sufficiently to generate the political will for legislation that would then set a new standard and norm for the society? These questions are the kind that politicians and activists need to keep asking throughout their careers. Johnson did not have the final answers. But his responses to Selma illustrate at least four conditions for stimulating adaptive change after the challenge has been identified: *managed stress,* disciplined by *attention to the issues,* with *pressure* on those who need to take responsibility for the changes in their midst, and *protective cover* for threatened leadership voices.

Regulating Distress. In the midst of crisis, the first priority is to evaluate the level of social distress, and, if it is too high, take action to bring it into a productive range. Confronted by overwhelming distress, a society and its factions may fall back on extreme measures to restore direction, protection, and order: authoritarian rule, suppression of dissent, fragmentation into smaller identity groups (ethnic, religious, regional), and war (civil and otherwise). Thus, Johnson had to assess the level of disequilibrium in the society in order to determine whether or not emergency actions were called for, like sending in the National Guard. Could the nation sustain the storm without breaking apart? Were the bonds that held people together (political and civic institutions, economic interdependencies, cultural norms, shared values, patriotic identifications) sufficiently resilient to withstand the stresses?[39] Was the nation overwhelmed for other reasons (a depressed economy or war)?

These questions defined the upper limits of tolerance, and Johnson's answers were clear: The nation *as a whole* could take it.

Americans had withstood much more. The bonds holding the nation together were not breaking. Political institutions were operating. Particular cultural and political norms were being challenged, as were critical values, but many of society's other norms and values were functioning as before to provide meaning, orientation, and structure to people's lives. People were still going about their business. The Vietnam build-up was not capturing very much attention. The economy was functioning smoothly. Many people questioned deeply the contradictions within the nation, but relatively few seemed to give up their patriotism. To be sure, civil rights activists were being brutally injured and killed, and that might itself be cause for immediate action, but the nation itself was not apparently at risk—as it had been one hundred years before. Johnson could afford to hold steady for a time.

Crises provide authority figures with more power because people look to them to provide resolution. Distress enhances their visibility and impact. Thus, in times of distress, people around the country scrutinize a President's every response—precisely because he is the nation's central figure of authority. They search for indications of how worried *they* should be about the situation. If *he* appears alarmed, then their fears will rise.

Hence, a President's immediate mechanism to contain distress during a crisis is to contain himself. If he indicates through his calm demeanor that the situation, serious as it is, is no cause for panic, he reduces the possibility of one. He can regulate the level of disequilibrium in the society by the cues he gives, even by the pitch and tone of his voice. Of course, he can go too far; when he denies for too long the difficulty people experience, they will get angry.

However, people look to authority not only for cues but also for action. Action itself can reduce the experience of disequilibrium because it shifts the appearance of responsibility for the problem onto the shoulders of the one taking action. Action suggests that "*He* will show us the way." People can relax their attention because someone in authority is paying attention. Thus, authoritative action will tend to reduce stress, while inaction will increase it. This may be true regardless of the content of the action. Action itself communicates. For example, it is quite conceivable that what mattered most in reducing the sense of crisis during Franklin Roosevelt's first one hundred days was not his specific actions but his activism.[40]

How did Johnson regulate the level of distress? In this case, events beyond his own immediate doing had provoked the distress. Southern blacks and Southern whites had caused it, albeit with Johnson's tacit encouragement. As the central authority figure for the nation, Johnson had the presence of mind, or the instincts, to use it as opportunity. King and his organizers turned up the heat, but Johnson let the stew simmer. By his calm demeanor and lukewarm statements, Johnson communicated that the crisis was no emergency. But by inaction, Johnson raised the level of tension so that people could no longer ignore their own responsibility for the harsh reality of black people being beaten for requesting an equal right to vote.

Directing Disciplined Attention to the Issues. By having waited over a week to make a move, Johnson allowed television images of racial brutality to settle into the public consciousness. He prevented premature closure. When he finally announced during his press conference with Wallace that, if necessary, he would take decisive action, he merely relieved the immediate source of distress. The underlying issue had now fastened in people's minds, where it would continue to generate dissonance. Dissonance would call for more action. The issue would ripen: people would come to see the issue as a public priority. And therein lay the opportunity. Johnson waited to seize that moment when he could address the issue of racial justice rather than merely diffuse the dissonance. He took the event and gave it meaning that would have been lost before.

Had Johnson intervened as the nation demanded, by mobilizing the National Guard, he would surely have reduced the public's distress over police brutality against black Americans. Johnson's action would have directed the nation's attention to a side issue: protecting the marchers' right to express their demands. Yet as Johnson unbundled the issues, the point was not the right to march; the point was the right to vote. Had Johnson intervened immediately, the issue might have been understood the wrong way—the easy way.

Worse, his intervention would also have diverted the nation's attention from the issue of racism to the issue of state's rights. Johnson, the Southern politician, knew better than to let that happen.

> If I just send in federal troops with their big black boots and rifles, it'll look like Reconstruction all over again. I'll lose every moderate,

and not just in Alabama but all over the South. Most southern people don't like this violence; they know, deep in their hearts, that things are going to change. And they'll accommodate. They may not like it, but they'll accommodate. But not if it looks like the Civil War all over again. That'll force them right into the arms of extremists, and make a martyr out of Wallace. And that's not going to help the Negroes . . . I may have to send in troops. But not until I have to, not until everyone can see I had no other choice.[41]

Had he intervened immediately, Johnson would probably have survived quite well, personally. As a Southerner intervening with federal troops to protect innocent black people, he would likely have gained considerable popularity throughout much of the nation. There were good precedents for federal interference into racial disturbances: Kennedy in Mississippi, Eisenhower in Arkansas. And *they* were Northerners.

Stepping in decisively to resolve the crisis, however, would have interrupted the work being done in the polity. By letting the distress persist for over a week, Johnson provided the nation with no choice but to face the issue of racism itself. The appalled public would not permit Southern whites to frame the issue as states' rights. Furthermore, voters throughout the nation had witnessed from their own living rooms that the marchers longed for the right to vote, not the right to march. The issue would not be mistaken as states' rights or the right of black people to march. By refusing to be pushed by the public, Johnson pushed people to face the internal contradictions of *their* society, embodied in the sights they could not avoid watching on television.

Giving the Work Back to People. Johnson's long experience taught him to be wary of the trap that Wallace had set—shifting all responsibility to the highest authority. By stepping in with troops, Johnson would have presented himself and his office as a receptacle for blame or credit. Either would be a diversion from working on the problem of equality. The solution to the crisis would have become "Johnson's solution," framed as federal interference in states' affairs, or federal protection of the right to march. Instead, Johnson did nothing to divert responsibility until the public's will had crystallized.[42] He let the people with the problem bear weight. He let blacks carry the major responsibility for provoking change. He waited for Wallace to request federal troops. And he waited until voters across the nation had done enough work to reveal to themselves, and to him, the outlines of a solution—their solution. As Kearns described it, "When Johnson finally sent troops to Alabama [two weeks after the crisis began], the act was generally regarded, not as an imperious imposition of federal power, but as a necessary measure to prevent further violence. By waiting out his critics and letting the TV clips make their own impression on the country, he had succeeded in persuading most of the country that he had acted reluctantly and out of necessity, not because he was anxious to use federal power against a guilty South."[43]

The civil rights movement had focused attention and ripened the issue. Johnson's task was to restrain himself from absorbing the attention and responsibility. The tactic of holding steady shifted the feeling of necessity to the public so that it would face the issue with its costs and its gains. The public and its representatives were made to do the work of changing their attitudes and priorities about justice.

Thus, by keeping the spotlight on the persons embodying the issues, Johnson gave the work of adjustment back to the people with the problem: the civil rights activists, George Wallace, Congress, and the general public. For example, he encouraged King in private meetings to arouse public attention. Animated constituents would generate the political will and leeway for legislative action. Moreover, he let Wallace stew for awhile, appealing to him at the White House in his moment of distress to adjust his own view of himself. To paraphrase Johnson: "Wallace could be a statesman, not just for Alabama, but for the nation. He could help his people adjust to the demands for economic and social reform. Social justice might make sense to a populist like Wallace in the context of economic justice."[44] Johnson's authority as President gave him a grip on Wallace, but only because he had refrained from stealing the limelight and shifting the responsibility for law and order away from the governor. When Wallace finally asked for federal assistance (on the grounds that Alabama could not afford the cost of protecting the marchers), Johnson let everyone know that he was acting on Wallace's initiative.[45] He made sure that the debate remained focused on civil rights and not on states' rights, and that Wallace had borne the burden. As

Johnson put it publicly, "It is not a welcome duty for the federal government to ever assume a state government's own responsibility for assuring the protection of citizens in the exercise of their constitutional rights."[46]

Protecting Voices of Leadership in the Community. Johnson provided protection to King and his colleagues in the form of encouragement, guidance, and warning. But this was not without its risks. For example, a police attack on Dr. King and his national entourage of clergy during Tuesday's march would have been a very big blow to his presidency. As a Southerner, how could he have recaptured the high ground? Who would believe that his was just a tactical error? When a federal court issued a restraining order to delay the march for a few days, Johnson knew that a limit had been reached. Although King had tactically violated local and state law previously to make his point, he relied on *national* values, politics, and opinion to hold the states and cities in a process of change. Breaching a federal court order would have violated the national structure of authority—the final containing vessel. And Johnson sat atop that structure. Neither Johnson nor King, nor the civil rights cause itself, could afford damaging a fundamental trust for legal process. To avoid a confrontation between King and the federal government, Johnson tried to dissuade King from marching that day; King insisted, however, and they reached a compromise. In essence, Johnson made clear to King the limits of the cover he could provide. The march went on in truncated form, and Johnson held steady through it.[47]

The pressure on Johnson to "take control of the situation" was enormous. Presidents are expected to control internal conflict, which often means supressing dissonant voices. But by and large, Johnson stayed out of King's way and let the tension grow. By so doing, he risked losing trust, and thus the basis of his authority. Yet by protecting King, Wilkins, and others, Johnson let the issues surface and ripen, and kept his hands free to orchestrate the ensuing debate.

The Speech

By waiting, Johnson raised the stakes, not only for the nation but for himself. If, as President, he failed to act decisively after what seemed so prolonged a time of crisis, the public would hold him accountable. Public expectations constrained him. As with any person in a position of senior authority, a President eventually has to provide a clear focal point to restore a sense of direction and order. Johnson did that eight days after the crisis in Selma had begun. By that time, the nation looked to Johnson with ever heightened anticipation. But by that time, the nation was ready to hear what it needed to hear, and not just what it wanted to hear. Johnson spoke before a joint session of Congress during prime evening television. The speech, excerpted at length, captures Johnson's strategy.

I speak tonight for the dignity of man and the destiny of democracy . . . At times history and fate meet at a single time in a single place to shape a turning point in man's unending search for freedom. So it was at Lexington and Concord. So it was at Appomattox. So it was last week in Selma, Alabama . . . There is no cause for pride in what has happened in Selma. There is no cause for self-satisfaction in the long denial of equal rights of millions of Americans. But there is cause for hope and for faith in our democracy in what is happening here tonight.

For the cries of pain, the hymns and protest of oppressed people, have summoned into convocation all the majesty of this great government . . . In our time we have come to live with moments of great crisis . . . But rarely in any time does an issue lay bare the secret heart of America itself . . . a challenge, not to our growth or abundance, our welfare or our security, but to the values and the purposes and the meaning of our nation.

The issue of equal rights for American Negroes is such an issue, and should we defeat every enemy, double our wealth, conquer the stars, and still be unequal to this issue, then we will have failed as a people and a nation. For with a country as with a person, "What shall it profit a man, if he shall gain the whole world, and lose his own soul?" . . . There is no issue of states' rights or national rights. There is only the struggle for human rights . . .

Last time a President sent a civil rights bill to Congress it contained a provision to protect voting rights. That bill was passed after eight long months of debate. And when that bill came to my desk for signature, the heart of the voting provision had been eliminated. This time, on this issue, there must be no delay, no hesitation, no compromise with our purpose . . . And we ought not, and we cannot, and we must not wait another eight months before we get a bill. We have already waited 100 years and more. And the time for waiting is gone.

So I ask you to join me in working long hours, nights and weekends if necessary to pass this bill. And I don't make the request lightly. For from the window where I sit with the problems of our country, I recognize that outside this chamber is the outraged conscience of the Nation, the grave concern of many nations—and the harsh judgment of history on our acts.

But even if we pass this bill, the battle will not be over. What happened in Selma is part of a far larger movement which reaches into every section and state of America. It is the effort of American Negroes to secure for themselves the full blessings of American life. Their cause must be our cause too. It is not just Negroes, but all of us, who must overcome the crippling legacy of bigotry and injustice. *And we shall overcome.* As a man whose roots go into Southern soil I know how agonizing racial feelings are. I know how difficult it is to reshape attitudes and the structure of society . . . I say to all of you here and to all in the Nation tonight, that those who ask you to hold on to the past do so at the cost of denying you your future.

This great, rich, restless country can offer opportunity and education to all—black and white, North and South, sharecropper and city dweller. These are the enemies—poverty and ignorance—and not our fellow man. And these too shall be overcome. Let no one, in any section, look with prideful righteousness on the troubles of his neighbors. There is no part of America where the promise of equality has been fully kept. In Buffalo as well as Birmingham, in Philadelphia as well as Selma, Americans are struggling for the fruits of freedom. This is one nation. What happens in Selma or in Cincinnati is a matter of legitimate concern to every citizen. But let each of us look within our own communities and our own hearts, and root out injustice there . . .

The real hero of this struggle is the American Negro. His actions and protests—his courage to risk safety and even life—have awakened the conscience of the Nation. His demonstrations have been designed to call attention to injustice, to provoke change and stir reform. He has called upon us to make good the promise of America. And who among us can say we would have made the same progress were it not for his persistent bravery, and his faith in American democracy. For at the heart of battle for equality is a belief in the democratic process.[48]

Historic in its sweep and claim, this speech inspired much of the country. It also demonstrates and helps summarize our principles of leadership. First, Johnson spoke clearly to the orienting values of the nation, the values that had made it one nation: freedom, equality, and democracy. The issue of civil rights was to be seen in that context. He identified the adaptive challenge by identifying the discrepancy between our values and behavior. Indeed, he identified the next adaptive challenge as well: poverty.

Second, by speaking in so dramatic a fashion—before a joint session of Congress—Johnson tried to maintain the level of urgency at the same time that he addressed its causes. Taking charge might have reduced the pressure had Johnson not demanded immediate Congressional action. Moreover, Johnson pointed out that Congress had failed to complete its work on voting rights in the earlier civil rights legislation. These acts kept the pressure on.

Third, Johnson kept attention focused on the issue by cautioning the public to stay clear of the likely work avoidance mechanisms that might arise: (1) viewing the events in Selma as an issue of states' rights rather than national values, (2) viewing voting rights legislation as a technical fix after which people could relax their attention, (3) holding onto the past, and (4) scapegoating the white people of Selma by a "prideful righteousness" that would deny the presence of racism throughout the land.

Fourth, Johnson told people that the challenge of civil rights would require adaptive and ongoing work: the attitudes and the structure of society would have to change. He acknowledged how difficult that would be. In large part, the work belonged to the general public. Voting rights legislation was no final remedy; it was simply a catalytic step. Yet Congress would not be off the hook either. By challenging its members so publicly to spend sleepless nights, he made them bear the weight as well. He put all of their names on the line (including his own) by expecting rapid passage of the bill he would submit in two days.[49]

Finally, Johnson exercised leadership in one of the few ways that authority figures can—by protecting the voices of those who lead with little authority, even though such voices often will be both deviant and annoying. He credited the civil rights movement for provoking the nation to face the large gap between what we stood for and the way we lived.

In exercising leadership on civil rights, was Johnson advancing his own vision for the country? Not really. As a Southern congressman since 1937 and senator since 1949, Johnson came out in favor of civil rights only in 1956 when he saw the issue ripening and saw himself as a national contender.[50] For nearly twenty years he had voted against every civil rights bill before Congress—laws to end the poll tax, segregation in the armed services, and lynching.[51] In 1960 he opposed liberal proposals for federal voting registrars in favor of the middle-of-the-road proposal for voting referees, which had not worked. As Vice-President, he had decided against liberalizing Senate rules, which distressed civil rights advocates.[52] During the debate over the Civil Rights Act of 1964, he backed a moderate conception for a voting rights clause. When Congress seemed unready even for that, he did not push it.

It seems then that the civil rights movement and the events in Selma had their impact on Johnson's conscience, as well as that of the nation. As he described in his memoirs, "Nothing makes a man come to grips more directly with his conscience than the Presidency. Sitting in that chair involves making decisions that draw out a man's fundamental commitments. The burden of his responsibility literally opens up his soul. No longer can he accept matters as given: no longer can he write off hopes and needs as impossible. In that house of decision, the White House, a man becomes his commitments. He understands who he really is. He learns what he genuinely wants to be."[53]

We often think that leadership means having a clear vision and the capacity to persuade people to make it real. In this case, Johnson had authored no vision. Events acted on him to shape the vision to which he then gave powerful articulation. He *identified the nation's vision* and put it into words. As the nation clarified its values, so did he. Johnson's leadership lay in his wherewithal to give meaning to the crisis and avoid the common pitfall of restoring order prematurely. He let the heat remain high. He kept people's attention on the issues generating the heat. He shifted responsibility to those with the problem. He let the dissident voices be heard. Along with the nation, he wrestled with its fundamental orienting values. He gave those values the power of his voice and his presence.[54] And he seized the moment to turn the nation's emerging values into potent legislation.[55]

Johnson signed the Voting Rights Act into law on August 6, 1965. Within one week, federal registrars set up shop; six months later, 9,000 black people were registered to vote in Selma.[56]

7

Falling Off the Edge

Lyndon Johnson's successes on domestic issues contrast sharply with his failure on Vietnam. In foreign affairs, Johnson took the stance that leaders lead and followers follow. This provided the wrong footing for leading the key stakeholders in developing policy and for calculating the political consequences of his decisions. Autocratic decisionmaking assumes that authorities have little to learn, and in Johnson's case, it limited his ability to test basic substantive, political, and moral assumptions.

Substantive flaws in policy reasoning were manifold. In setting Vietnam policy, Johnson and his advisers drew inapt historical analogies with Munich 1938, the British suppression of the Burmese insurgency after World War II, the Korean War, and the French Indochina War.[1] In addition, they accepted as truth the domino theory—if one country falls to communism, others will fall like dominoes—rather than considering it a hypothesis requiring scrutiny.[2] Furthermore, they made poor and untested assumptions about the history and psychology of the Vietnamese, both North and South, their wars and authorities, and the resilience of indigenous guerilla warfare.[3]

Deficiencies in the process of policy development arose from failing systematically to answer critical policy questions that were being raised by individual advisers and the President. Many of these questions were either left in the air or answered impressionistically. For example, would the North Vietnamese be inclined to bargain?[4] Did the American people have the will to prosecute a long war in Asia? Would the Viet Cong fight the kind of conventional war Americans knew how to fight, or would they rely on guerilla tactics? Was it ethical to fight this war? The key questions were asked, yet no structured process provided a means fully to investigate and analyze the answers.[5]

Finally, Johnson miscalculated the political risks of going to war. Fearing the loss of ground on his domestic agenda, the Great Society, he made highly optimistic estimates of how easily he could bring Ho Chi Minh to the bargaining table. He succeeded in the short term in rallying Congress and public opinion, but failed to gauge the likely effects of prolonged military involvement on both his career and domestic agenda.[6]

In formulating foreign policy, Johnson seems to have ignored the lessons of his domestic policy successes. What he seemed to know in his bones about domestic affairs he seemed to forget in the arena of foreign policy. In setting and implementing Vietnam policy, Johnson made fatal mistakes by acting the part of the lone warrior and by creeping up in stealth not only on his enemy but also on his own constituents. In terms of the principles illustrated by Johnson's civil rights leadership, he failed to face the nation with the adaptive challenge of Vietnam, to keep the level of distress within a productive range, to discipline attention, to distribute responsibility, and to use dissent as a source of insight and options. What might have seemed in his mind an effort to pace the work became instead an act of misleading the nation.

"Johnson's War"

After Kennedy's death, Johnson pledged, "Let us continue." Yet in addition to inheriting civil rights legislation, antipoverty initiatives, and other domestic policies that he understood and believed in, he inherited a crisis in Vietnam that had reached the boiling point in the aftermath of the U.S.-backed overthrow of Ngo Dinh Diem, South Vietnam's President, in early November 1963. According to his advisers, South Vietnam would fall to the Communists unless bolstered by a quantum leap in American military involvement.

With his eye on the Great Society and his own election the following November, Johnson hedged and delayed, trying to avoid a decisive commitment. Instead, he found small ways to bolster the South Vietnamese government. He reaffirmed America's commitment to the new and shaky regime by increasing the number of "advisers" from 16,300 to 23,300 and expanding economic aid by 50 million dollars. He also approved a new program of covert operations against the North Vietnamese.[7] At the same time, Johnson's policy advisers prepared plans radically changing the nature of U.S. involvement by bombing the North and sending large numbers of American ground troops into the South. These included secret drafts of legislation authorizing war.[8]

Although Johnson's advisers planned to escalate the war sometime after the election, Johnson himself denied any plan to move to a larger war, both to voters during the election campaign and in private discussions with members of Congress. Johnson depicted Barry Goldwater, his Republican opponent, as a "hawk" on Vietnam and a reckless warmaker. Johnson told Americans that U.S. involvement would be limited to training and logistical support. He repeated that promise in campaign speeches: "There are those that say you ought to go north and drop bombs, to try to wipe out the supply lines, and they think that would escalate the war. We don't want our American boys to do the fighting for Asian boys. We don't want to get . . . tied down in a land war in Asia."[9]

On August 4th, during the campaign, the North Vietnamese allegedly executed a "wholly unprovoked" attack on two U.S. destroyers in the Gulf of Tonkin.[10] Two days later, Johnson sent the already prepared legislation to Congress, asking it urgently "to approve and support the determination of the President as Commander-in-Chief to take all the necessary measures to repel any armed attack against the forces of the United States to prevent further aggression . . . [and] to take all necessary steps, including the use of armed force, to assist any member or protocol state of the Southeast Asia Collective Defense Treaty [SEATO] requesting assistance in defense of its freedom."[11] Only two senators dissented. In the House, the vote was unanimous, 416 to 0. In the Gulf of Tonkin Resolution, Congress gave Johnson all the authorization he would need to go to war.[12]

Had the United States really been attacked in the Gulf of Tonkin? Was our bombing of North Vietnam in retaliation based solely upon a radar finding? No enemy ship had been seen, and no wreckage had been found. Secretary of Defense Robert McNamara and others knew of the lack of evidence for the attack, but neither he nor the President were about to cast doubts before Congress or the nation. With the memories of Pearl Harbor still fresh, an *unprovoked* attack on U.S. ships could be used to ratchet up the expectations of Congress and the public for more fighting. "Hell, boys," Johnson said later in private conversation, "for all I know they could have been shooting at whales out there."[13] Yet even had the attacks taken place, they were certainly not unprovoked. The ships in the Gulf of Tonkin were engaged in electronic espionage against North Vietnam.[14] American soldiers and sailors had been placed in harm's way; indeed, they had been fighting alongside the South Vietnamese army for years, and performing covert operations along the North Vietnamese coast for months.

In bombing North Vietnam in retaliation, Johnson told Congress and the public that this was meant to be a one-shot operation and not the start of more extensive involvement. "Our response, for the present, will be limited and fitting. We Americans know, although others appear to forget, the risks of spreading conflict. We still seek no wider war." Yet the Gulf of Tonkin Resolution had been written with sufficient ambiguity to give Johnson the power to escalate the war in the future. Apparently, McNamara was delighted that the administration's blank check had been signed.[15]

After his November landslide victory, accompanied by Democratic Party majorities in both houses of Congress, Johnson saw an almost clear road ahead for the enactment of the Great Society's profusion of domestic initiatives. As Johnson saw it, Vietnam posed the stumbling block. There the situation kept deteriorating badly. Many American soldiers were killed and wounded in Viet Cong attacks on U.S. installations in September, November, and then on Christmas eve 1964, and an increasing sense of urgency began to take hold in Washington. Although Johnson held back from retaliating, the military heightened their preparations for bombing North Vietnam and for sending in ground troops. In a meeting on January 22, however, Johnson told Congressional leaders that "more U.S. forces are not needed in South Vietnam short of a decision to go to full-scale war. The war must be fought by the South Vietnamese. We cannot control everything that they do, and we have to count on their fighting their war."[16] Congress itself was baffled about what to do. The State Department reported to Johnson that "the great majority of congressmen are neither satisfied nor dissatisfied; their thoughts are fragmented and they are genuinely perplexed. In this state, they are willing to go along with the people who have the direct responsibility, the experts in the Executive Branch."[17]

On February 7, 1965, the Viet Cong attacked the U.S. barracks and helicopter field at Pleiku—killing 9, wounding 126, and destroying 22 helicopters and aircraft—the heaviest Communist assault so far on Americans. The United States was clearly becoming more exposed each day. Facts were being created on the ground. The U.S. presence created vulnerabilities requiring in turn a greater presence to defend the soldiers already there.

In response, Johnson retaliated by bombing the North, but with a difference. He shifted to a policy of sustained bombing, called Operation Rolling Thunder. The public viewed the strikes favorably. In a Gallup Poll, 67 percent approved, 15 percent disapproved, and 18 percent had no opinion. A Harris Poll showed an increase in Johnson's ratings from 41 percent before the retaliation to 60 percent after. However, telegrams to the White House, presumably from those who felt most strongly one way or the other, ran twelve-to-one against retaliation. Indeed, the polls showed that the public was far from galvanized for war. Only 6 percent thought the fighting was "very important," 69 percent thought it "not very important," and 20 percent "moderately" so.[18]

As the air war expanded, military pressure grew for sending in ground troops. Initially, two battalions of Marines were sent to protect American bases, but in early April 1965, as the situation continued to worsen, the task shifted from the protection of bases to engaging in offensive operations. General William Westmoreland, head of U.S. forces in Vietnam, later wrote, "The adage that a good offense is the best defense was as applicable in Vietnam as it had been elsewhere throughout history."[19] Publicly, however, Johnson denied any change in mission and gave the instruction that "premature publicity be avoided by all possible precautions."[20] He had no intention of distracting Congress and the public from the Great Society, which included, among other things, the new Voting Rights

Bill. By June, 72,000 American soldiers were in Vietnam, but their impact on the stability of the South Vietnamese government and its capacity to fight the war appeared totally insufficient to hold back defeat.

Indeed, it seemed as though the American presence only heightened North Vietnam's determination to speed toward victory. By July, it looked like South Vietnam would fall soon. With its demise predicted within months, Johnson felt inexorably drawn toward full-scale Americanization of the war. Advised that it would require 425,000 to 600,000 troops by mid-1966, 8–12 billion dollars in 1966 alone, and five years to win, Johnson, on July 28, made the fateful decision to move forward. He authorized 200,000 troops for Vietnam by year's end.[21]

Rather than focus public attention on the decision, Johnson placed his announcement in a midday press conference taken up with other noteworthy events—the nominations of Abe Fortas to the Supreme Court and John Chancellor as head of the United States Information Agency. Deliberately minimizing the significance of the escalation in Vietnam, he reported an increase to 125,000 troops, and merely hinted at more. "I have asked the Commanding General, General Westmoreland, what more he needs to meet this mounting aggression. He has told me. We will meet his needs."[22] The true expected costs, in terms of men, time, and money, were concealed.

The Sources of Autocratic Action

As a political calculation, Johnson felt compelled to bear the weight alone and deceive the nation. He believed that he could not afford to offer his policies up for debate, as some of his advisers suggested. McNamara and the Joint Chiefs of Staff argued that implementing a policy to stop the guerilla insurgency and shore up the South Vietnamese government required clear and unequivocal national commitment.[23] They advocated an open process that would engage Congress and the public in facing immediately the costs of the war: raising taxes, placing the economy on a wartime footing, and mobilizing 235,000 reservists.[24] On February 7, 1965, just after the Viet Cong attack at Pleiku, but before Johnson's decision to initiate sustained bombing of the North, McGeorge Bundy, Johnson's National Security Adviser, wrote from Saigon:

> *At its very best, the struggle in Vietnam will be long.* It seems to us important that this fundamental fact be made clear to our people and to the people of Vietnam. Too often in the past we have conveyed the impression that we expect an early solution when those who live with this war know that no early solution is possible. It is our own belief that the people of the United States have the necessary will to accept and to execute a policy that rests upon the reality that there is no short cut to success in South Vietnam.[25]

Far better than his advisers, Johnson understood that getting a commitment for prolonged fighting would probably have large costs in terms of Congressional and public time and attention, and his own informal authority—his professional reputation and his public prestige. All of these resources would be spent at the expense of support and funding for Great Society programs. Yet for Johnson, the great opportunity of his presidency lay in achieving social and economic justice at home, and Vietnam stood in the way of that opportunity. The nation could hardly be expected to take on both, knowingly. Johnson, however, wanted both, and autocratic action and deception—keeping policy development out of the Congressional and public arenas—seemed the only ways to get both. He could neither accept risking the Great Society nor imagine letting South Vietnam fall.[26]

Johnson's political miscalculation was not just a personal error or failure of character; it required a permissive context. Congress ceded responsibility to the President even during the critical decisions of July 1965 to deploy U.S. soldiers in a ground war. Indeed, Congress avoided responsibility for policy design and decision by colluding in Johnson's deception. With the exception of Senate Majority Leader Mike Mansfield, the other heads of Congress—Senators Dirksen, Hickenlooper, Kuckel, Long, and Smathers, and Representatives McCormack, Albert, Arends, Boggs, and Ford—all agreed that the President should send in U.S. forces by executive decision *without* stirring up a big debate in the Congress. They let Johnson bear the burden.[27]

Autocratic action would have been inconceivable had it not been for historical trends favoring presidential autonomy in making war. The Constitution was sufficiently ambiguous about foreign affairs to provide Presidents with much greater freedom to make decisions than in the checks and balances of domestic policymaking.[28] And during two centuries, Presidents had taken advantage of that ambiguity, steadily expanding their powers. For example, if a President could not start a war legally, he could place American troops in a position where they were likely to be attacked and then fight a defensive war. Such was Polk's strategy in the 1846 war over Texas with Mexico, a war recognized, but not declared, by Congress.[29] By the twentieth century, Presidents were taking quite a few matters into their own hands. Before leaving office in 1909, Theodore Roosevelt put it this way: "The biggest matters, such as the Portsmouth peace, the acquisition of Panama, and sending the fleet around the world, I managed without consultation with anyone; for when a matter is of capital importance, it is well to have it handled by one man only."[30]

In Lyndon Johnson's day, Presidents relied increasingly on their status as commanders-in-chief to exercise greatly expanded authority.[31] World War II and the Cold War had turned the United States into not only a superpower but the head of the free world. Though the total war had ended, the sense of emergency remained. When Truman decided to enter Korea, he opted not even to ask Congress for a resolution supporting his effort. He stood alone, and Congress let him. By doing so, Truman and Congress broadened prevailing assumptions about presidential autonomy. Indeed, they set a precedent by which Congressional debate began to be seen as an aid and comfort to the enemy.[32] Communist aggression appeared to threaten American values and interests worldwide, creating the demand for an implacable visage and a huge standing army with military bases and security arrangements around the globe. The prevailing wisdom held that only a strong executive could provide such a visage and control such an apparatus. The United States saw itself in a perpetual state of crisis, and in the time-compressed era of nuclear weapons, crisis would require one man to decide whether or not to preempt or retaliate.[33]

The trend in presidential decisionmaking in foreign policy, beginning with the nation's founding and greatly accelerating in the twentieth century, led Presidents to hold decisions tightly and involve Congress and the public only when they felt compelled to do so. Congress and the public reinforced this trend.[34] They often dissented or consented (usually the latter) after the fact, and without contributing much to the formation of policy. They looked to Presidents to carry the burden of foreign affairs, and some even assumed that Presidents always had.

By the 1960s, a prevailing view in Washington claimed that Presidents for two centuries had made as many as 150 "small wars" on their own.[35] This claim, however, was historically inaccurate, as the vast majority of these so-called wars were minor efforts to curb piracy and protect American citizens abroad during local disorder. Indeed, Congress had rebelled in the past against presidential aggrandizement of Congress's Constitutional authority to make war, but these efforts, some of which Lyndon Johnson would have remembered, backfired badly and reinforced the trend toward autonomous presidential action. The most salient case occurred in the wake of World War I, when Congress enacted neutrality legislation that later prevented Roosevelt from taking action to strengthen the allies against the Nazis when there may still have been time to prevent World War II. According to Arthur Schlesinger Jr., "No one for a long time after would trust Congress with basic foreign policy. Congress did not even trust itself."[36]

Some legislators believed that the Cold War required the President to carry the load, and others saw political advantage in insulating themselves from American foreign policy decisions, and debacles.[37] In 1955, when Eisenhower asked for a blank check to defend Formosa and "related positions and territories of that area," the Congress overwhelmingly approved. Lyndon Johnson, the Senate majority leader at the time, declared, "We are not going to take the responsibility out of the hands of the constitutional leader and try to arrogate it to ourselves."[38]

Thus, for President Johnson to have approached much differently his decisionmaking responsibility in Vietnam would have required either a sea change in the prevailing conception of the President's responsibilities in foreign affairs, or a very innovative helmsman. An innovator in the politics of domestic policy, Johnson approached foreign policy in customary ways. In formulating Vietnam policy,

Johnson let historical trends convince him of his exclusive, personal responsibility for the conduct and outcome of the war. Consider the personalized language of his reasoning:

Everything I knew about history told me that if I got out of Vietnam and let Ho Chi Minh run through the streets of Saigon, then I'd be doing what Chamberlain did in World War II. I'd be giving a big fat reward to aggression. And I knew that if we let Communist aggression succeed in taking over South Vietnam, there would follow in this country an endless national debate—a mean and destructive debate—that would shatter my Presidency, kill my administration, and damage our democracy.[39]

And again,

Either way I went it was a terrible situation. I knew that if I ran out . . . I'd be the first American President to ignore our commitments, turn tail and run, and leave our allies in a lurch after all the commitments Eisenhower had made, and all that SEATO had made, and all that the Congress had made, and all that the Tonkin Gulf [Resolution] said, and all the statements that Kennedy had made, and Bobby Kennedy had made . . . I'd be the first American President to put my tail between my legs and run out because I didn't have the courage to stand up and support a treaty and support the policy of two other Presidents.[40]

Technical Reasons for Autocratic Action

The presidential trend toward autocratic behavior was based in part on the various requirements of making foreign policy. First, as the unfolding of Vietnam policy demonstrated by 1967, dealing abroad with both friends and foe can be severely compromised by lack of unity behind the President. A public that is predisposed to defer to authority and that knows little about the costs of U.S. foreign policy can be expected to rally around the President. Second, military crisis requires dispatch. Only a clear chain of command can implement complex strategy in short order. Third, the intricacies of foreign affairs require the substantive expertise of experienced professionals. Only the President and his political and military advisers, immersed in the technical details, can be trusted to know what is best. Fourth, negotiations require decisiveness. International law demands of each nation a single point of responsible authority.[41] Finally, the President sits at the hub of military and diplomatic channels of information, some of which are secret. He needs to be able to maintain that secrecy. As the framers of the Constitution recognized, practical foreign policy may require autocratic decisionmaking distant from the turbulence of public debate and legislative politics. Even Thomas Jefferson, who felt more strongly than most about the dangers of presidential authority, said in 1790 while serving as George Washington's Secretary of State, "The transaction of business with foreign nations is Executive altogether."[42]

Thus, autocratic action makes some sense given the complexities of foreign affairs. Clearly, as Johnson felt, the President and his advisers must do the work, and others must follow. Kearns describes Johnson's reasoning:

> As the Democratic Majority Leader under a Republican President, Johnson had supported Eisenhower on most matters of foreign policy. He had preached and practiced bipartisanship. Now he was the President, and he expected the same deference from *his* Congress. After all, partisanship and public debate were enemies of a sound foreign policy. It was in the public's best interest—given its tendency every now and then to "go off on a jag in one crazy direction or another"— to leave complicated questions of international affairs in the hands of the President. The public, Johnson reasoned, would only hurt itself by knowing too much. Democracy demanded good results for the people, not big debates.[43]

Surely, Johnson's view of himself as the solitary decisionmaker, the sole provider of direction, protection, and order would be appropriate in a routine problem situation and in those foreign policymaking situations where unity, dispatch, expertise, negotiating authority, and secrecy are dominant requirements. But in the case of Vietnam, these requirements were either unachievable or did not apply. First, sustained unity could not be achieved through autocratic action. Rallying around the President provides him at best with a short-term advantage. The American public has never been deferential in enduring a prolonged war without being convinced of its necessity. And there was little if any evidence to suggest in 1965 that the Vietnam War would resolve quickly. Furthermore, in the age of television, the public would not remain ignorant for long. Sustainable unity in response to the North Vietnamese required ripening the issue and building consensus, not unilateral decision.

Second, Vietnam policy did not require split-second decisionmaking. There was time for deliberation. Perhaps, as one senator lamented, "the United States, still new to its world role, was unable to distinguish between genuine emergencies and situations that only seem to require urgent action. As a result, Congress had acted with undue haste, assuming, quite wrongly, that it would somehow be unpatriotic to question the President's judgment in a moment of assumed emergency."[44]

Third, though the technical complexities of Vietnam policy required expert and systematic analysis—of international politics, the resilience and strategy of the South and North Vietnamese governments, battlefield policy, troop requirements, and the like—the basic questions of values and priorities were political and not technical. Only a political process could effectively uncover the values by which America would judge its President and his policy, and send its children to war.

Fourth, the necessity in international negotiations for a single point of responsible authority does not reduce the negotiator's need for support. The negotiator still needs the backing of his multiple constituencies. Vociferous dissent at home, when it emerged in 1967, obviously weakened the President's leverage at peace talks. Engaging early on in a broad-based debate within the nation would not have diminished Johnson's *formal* authorization to represent the United States in negotiations—he was still the President—but it might have clarified his mandate. Without a mandate, the image of the United States as a united enemy became an easily exposed charade.

Finally, the questions posed by the Vietnam War were not the kind that required secrecy. Was the Vietnam War a just war? Was it worth the costs? Addressing these issues would hardly have called for breaches in security. Indeed, analysts and policymakers privy to secret information could surely have sanitized it for legislative and public use.

Thus, the rationale for developing foreign policy by autocratic means did not pertain to this case. Vietnam policy required major investments, trade-offs, losses, and the working out of differing conceptions of America's role on the world stage. Whether America chose to go to war or chose to let South Vietnam fall, many Americans would have to change their priorities, attitudes, beliefs, and behavior. War could not be sustained without conviction.

Franklin Roosevelt faced a similar dilemma in the summer of 1940 when Britain alone fought off the Nazis. Although Roosevelt felt the urgent need to fight beside Britain, as one of his New Dealers describes, "Woodrow Wilson had taught him the terrible responsibility of bringing a divided nation into war. He was going to be sure, very sure, that, if the United States had to enter the war, it would enter as far as humanly possible a united nation."[45] Even Roosevelt's lend-lease exchange of American destroyers for British bases before the election in 1940 came amid extensive consultation and debate within the executive branch, between the administration and Congress, across party lines, and with the press. After the election, Roosevelt put his policy, embodied in the Lend-Lease Bill and other legislation, through an "arduous, exacting, and uninhibited" Congressional process.[46] Roosevelt identified the adaptive work and prodded the nation to face and do it. Although he lied during his 1940 campaign about his intention to enter the war, he did not hide his actions as he prepared for it.[47] Roosevelt paced the challenge, but unlike Johnson, he did not shield Congress and the public from the work that only they could do.

By treating Vietnam in a manner appropriate to technical problems, Johnson failed to do what he had done so successfully in domestic affairs—create a holding environment for getting others to share responsibility for tough issues, and for protecting voices of dissent. For example, he bullied the prescient Mike Mansfield, the Senate Majority Leader, and J. William Fulbright, Chairman of the Senate Foreign Relations Committee. Both had grave doubts about Americanizing the war and predicted trouble with the public. Johnson, still popular, sarcastically criticized Fulbright in 1965: "Well, Bill, what have you been doing today to damage the Republic? You say you've got a bad stomach. Well, that's because you're so anti-Johnson, lately. I told you that it's bad for you to take out after me. Now you tell your wife that I love her and I am sorry you're so damned cranky and grouchy all the time."[48]

By suppressing people like Fulbright and Mansfield, Johnson deterred those who might usefully have provoked debate. By taking the part of the lone warrior who knows best, Johnson sacrificed the political tools at his disposal to reality-test his policy. Momentarily, he may have eased systemic stress and made more room for Great Society legislation; but he also set the nation and his presidency on a disastrous course. He failed to recognize that by taking a firm policy position on a problem in a place about which few people knew or cared, he squandered his unique position as orchestrator of the policymaking process. By 1967 he could not manage attention because attention fastened on him. He could not regulate distress because he appeared to be the source of distress. Vietnam became "Johnson's War," not Congress's and not the nation's.[49]

When Pacing the Work Becomes Work Avoidance

There may be several good reasons to avoid or delay the distress, conflict, and learning required to do adaptive work. First, if the issue does not represent an immediate threat, delay may permit giving priority to more important issues. Second, if the challenge overwhelms the society's ability to adapt, delay may not only reduce destructive disequilibrium but may also provide time to strengthen the society's problem-solving abilities. The former reason, more relevant in the case of Vietnam, played a role in Johnson's thinking.

Hoping to bring Ho Chi Minh quickly to the bargaining table, Johnson thought he might find an early solution and avoid altogether turning the issue into an adaptive challenge for the nation. At a minimum, he thought he could delay the day of reckoning and create time for Great Society legislation. As he described later, "I was determined to keep that war from shattering that dream, which meant I simply had no choice but to keep my foreign policy in the wings."[50]

Tragically, he assumed too much. Ho Chi Minh was not another senator who could be brought to terms by the proper sequence of sticks and carrots. And success on the Great Society required more than legislation passed before the closing of a window of opportunity. A plethora of domestic legislation was no substitute for changing public values, attitudes, and behavior toward long-term domestic problems. Johnson's programs demanded ongoing public and admin-

istrative leadership.[51] By becoming consumed as the personal embodiment of Vietnam policy, Johnson lost his concentration and his
power to move that agenda forward beyond legislation. Ironically,
by hiding his war policy decisions from Congress and the public to
protect the domestic agenda, Johnson presented them with a war
that eventually thwarted work on that agenda.

Vietnam policymaking unwittingly created more disequilibrium
than the public could tolerate. Along with changes wrought by the
civil rights movement and the sexual revolution of the 1960s, the
distress took many forms, including splintered families, universities,
and communities, riots and repressive policing measures, and work
avoidance of various sorts (drug abuse, dropping out, and vilifying
all structures of authority). The trust in authority so necessary to
regulate distress had been spent.

Any President wrestling with a multiplicity of issues at once must
highlight some issues in relation to others in an attempt to pace the
work of the nation on its full assortment of issues, domestic and
foreign. Some issues have to be put on hold, or glossed over. In this
sense, presidential leadership must always pace and sequence issues
according to value and ripeness.[52] Undoubtedly, Johnson was trying
to organize the work of the nation by focusing public attention on
domestic issues rather than foreign. But wars, once begun, galvanize
attention. The pain they generate cannot be hidden. By 1967 the
public had begun to work the issue on its own, in opposition to the
President, in an explosive and deafening debate uncontained and
unorchestrated by presidential authority. By losing the public's trust
and by letting it become *his war,* Johnson had sabotaged his own
capacity to lead the nation in its conflict.

In directing attention to one set of issues and not another, Johnson
attempted to sequence the multiple issues facing the nation. But he
did not seem to have a strategy to pace the adaptive work on
Vietnam, per se. Pacing is a means to prepare people for tackling
hard questions, a tactic used in a larger strategy of facing the issues.
Pacing might resemble work avoidance because both can involve
deception. But the deception associated with pacing is a temporary
tactic while seeking opportunities to turn parts of the work over to
people as they demonstrate their readiness. Johnson, however, had
no strategy to strengthen their readiness or to direct Congress and

the nation to work the issue of Vietnam when conditions allowed. Indeed, as the war dragged on, he suppressed conflict and remained the sole decisionmaker. His was not a tactic but a strategy of circumvention.

Having to Know the Answers

Johnson had said that democracy demanded results and not debates. From his domestic policy experience, he knew better. He knew how to make democracy work precisely because he knew how to orchestrate conflicting points of view on the challenges facing people. As he put it, "The task of responsible leadership . . . is to avoid irreconcilable positions."[53] According to Joseph Califano, his aide for domestic affairs, Johnson "was a political and intellectual baker, kneading with those enormous hands until every aspect of the proposal was explored; once confident of that, he would put the bread in the oven."[54]

At home, Johnson had been a master of the politics of inclusion. He found (and invented) ways to get people involved in testing propositions and solving problems. Like the conductor of a symphony, he would mobilize people to work the issues and play their part. That way, he kept his hands on the baton. He could step back and lead the process, sensing its ebbs and flows, identifying which issues needed developing, which were ready to play, and what ensemble could be brought together.

But Johnson viewed foreign policy as a job for technical experts, not as a proper realm for the politics of inclusion. Forsaking his political strengths in turning Congress and the nation to face problems instead of running from them, Johnson allowed himself to be swept along in the vortex of exaggerated expectations about the role of the chief executive. Furthermore, his strong personal need to dominate most situations, which had been disciplined by legislative politics into exceptional mastery of the participative process, now stood untethered in an unfamiliar context with traditions and norms that reinforced dominance.[55] As President, he was supposed to dominate foreign affairs.

The coupling of these two factors—his personal need to dominate and the prevailing trends in foreign policymaking—sharply limited

Johnson's freedom to raise hard questions and prevented him from engaging in a mode of learning with his political colleagues and with the nation. Indeed, for Johnson to stand before the nation and present the facts as he knew them seemed an unthinkable form of political suicide. To throw an open question to the public or Congress would easily be seen either as weak or as a dereliction of presidential duty.

In fact, many participants and observers of these events have asked themselves, years later, what sort of speech might they have written for Johnson. By and large, they come up blank.[56] The reason, I think, is telling. Even in retrospect, analysts seem to assume that Johnson's tasks would be, first, to find a policy solution and, second, to persuade the public. This assumption reflects the constraint on leading from a position of authority. Even in our retrospective analyses, we cannot imagine a President raising hard questions to which he has no decisive answers.

Placing Oneself

Any authority figure must decide where to place himself in relation to an issue.[57] In general, he has three strategic options: (1) circumvention, with the risk of backing into a potential crisis; (2) frontal challenge—getting out in front and becoming the "bearer of bad tidings" by introducing the crisis; or (3) riding the wave—staying just in front of the crisis, anticipating the wave and trying to direct its power as it breaks.

On the issue of civil rights, Johnson took the third option. He saw the wave. He had seen it coming ever since the Supreme Court ruled in 1954 to desegregate schools. Rather than back into the crisis and fall behind the issue, and rather than get out in front of the issue by making public declarations on behalf of civil rights, he worked behind the scenes as President to prepare for and shape the distress. When the wave hit, he was ready. Not only were his speechwriters prepared but so was his Justice Department, which was responsible for drafting civil rights legislation, and so was Congress.

Yet on Vietnam Johnson used the first strategy, circumvention. He backed into the crisis. When the nation discovered that it was in an unexpected and costly war, people felt tricked, betrayed, misled. He neither prepared behind the scenes for the crisis, as he had with civil rights, nor did he get out in front early on to prepare the nation at large, as Ruckelshaus had in Tacoma. Either course of action seemed to jeopardize the domestic programs Johnson held dear.

Had Johnson exercised leadership in Vietnam, he may still have suffered defeat. Leadership is no guarantee of survival. Quite the opposite. But in situations demanding adaptive work, the exercise of leadership may increase the odds of survival. At least that is the hope. What would leadership in Johnson's situation have looked like? A few speculations seem in order.

Rather than circumvent Congress and the public, Johnson might have used variations of the other two strategies. One frontal strategy might have taken the form of a major address, shortly after his election in 1964, laying out the problem to Congress and the public: the pros and cons of involvement in Vietnam, the probabilities and the costs, in terms of war, American foreign policy, and the domestic agenda. Johnson would have taken a lot of heat, perhaps quite a bit more than Ruckelshaus, who took plenty of heat for going out to Tacoma. But after his major electoral victory, Johnson would have had time to recover from a possible setback in popularity. Had he held steady, refusing to be pushed until the issue had ripened, he may have found himself with a sufficient consensus for a policy the nation could live with. Of course, the policy may not have conformed to the expert opinion of his advisers, but adaptive work often requires giving up a measure of "expert" control over the outcome. Indeed, what is clear in retrospect about Johnson's Vietnam strategy is that the outcome may have been better if Johnson's own questions, and the questions raised by some of his policy advisers, had been wrestled more fully to the mat.

Such a strategy, however, would very likely have cost Johnson in just the currency he hated most to pay: legislative attention to the Great Society. To face the country with the trade-offs it would take, Johnson would have needed to face and accept at least the partial loss of his own grand aspiration—a daunting personal task for anyone so determined as he.

Another frontal strategy, perhaps far more protective of his domestic agenda, might have used the campaign of 1964 to construct a mandate to get out of the war: to "let Asian boys fight an Asian war." As it was, public opinion was not very strong in either direction. In the spring of 1964, more than two thirds of Americans said they paid little or no attention to events in Vietnam.[58] Thus, Johnson probably had the opportunity to frame and ripen the issue in these terms, particularly with so hawkish a foil as Barry Goldwater. Indeed, Johnson had appealed successfully to antiwar sentiment in attacking Goldwater. But instead of following through on that appeal, Johnson felt pulled by Goldwater's position toward taking a more aggressive stance; hence, the timing of the Gulf of Tonkin incident three months before the election.

Ironically, a political campaign ought to be just the proper time to engage the public in issues of public policy; that's when people are paying attention. Yet in trying to meet the multiple expectations of multiple constituents, candidates tend to downplay the hard issues, telling voters what they want to hear rather than challenging them to face the need for adjustments in their lives and hard trade-offs in their candidates. No doubt, constructing a mandate against the war might have lost Johnson some votes, but every poll and indicator at the time suggested that Johnson was way ahead of Goldwater and had a wide margin of safety—indeed, a landslide margin. He had the opening to get himself a mandate that would provide some protection in the future for his domestic agenda if and when South Vietnam might fall.[59] Johnson's fear of giving up any vote, hawkish or otherwise, prevented him from using the campaign to build a consensus, however. After losing and winning elections by a hair during his career, Johnson did not take chances.[60] And he wanted to be as popular as his predecessor, whose cruel death stirred immense, retroactive popularity.

Losses accompanied this strategy, as well. To get the nation to face the likely fall of South Vietnam, Johnson would have had to face that loss himself, something he and most of his advisers were unwilling to do. It was one thing for France to be defeated by Ho Chi Minh's movement; it was another thing altogether for the free world superpower to leave in humiliation. On June 28, 1965, for example, Undersecretary of State George Ball wrote Johnson a memorandum that provided a basis for getting out. It was initially titled, "A Plan for Cutting our Losses in South Viet-Nam." Militarily, Ball asserted, "the terrain in south Viet-Nam could not be worse . . . This is clearly

what General de Gaulle described to me as a 'rotten country' . . .
Politically, South Viet-Nam is a lost cause. The country is bled white
from twenty years of war and the people are sick of it . . . South
Viet-Nam is a country with an army and no government." But the
next day Johnson's advisers assailed the memorandum as too extreme, causing Ball to shift his emphasis from withdrawal to negotiation, and to resubmit his new, less alarming memorandum with
the new title "A Compromise Solution."[61] The loss was unthinkable.

Adopting the third strategic option—riding the wave—might also
have allowed Johnson to stay ahead of the crisis, but by *externalizing
the conflict*. To prevent its becoming "Johnson's War," Johnson
might have gone behind the scenes to stimulate conflictive work on
Vietnam without being at its center. He might have encouraged
hawks and doves in Congress to generate a debate, sweating over
the trade-offs. Given his political dexterity, Johnson could probably
have orchestrated such a debate to provide himself both with cover
and with options not to be found with his small team of policy
experts operating in relative isolation. He might have engineered a
serious discussion even before the Gulf of Tonkin incident, weighing
the costs and benefits of various courses of action. Given the information and military projections at the time, Congress could have
decided to commit itself to prosecute the war fully to its conclusion,
to pull out entirely before its Americanization, or to take a middle
road. A debate might have brought people to share responsibility for
choosing an option. In this manner, Johnson might have let Congress
introduce the issue and take some of the heat. This would have
followed in the vein of his political experience. As Johnson told Jim
Rowe, a long-time political friend and adviser, "Just remember our
old friend [Texas Congressman] Maury Maverick isn't here any
more. Maury got too far ahead of his people, and I'm not going to
do that."[62]

All of these options would have required Johnson to face loss and
to prepare others for it. The unthinkable had to be thought. Something had to give. To varying degrees, each strategy would likely have
its costs in terms of both the Great Society and American conceptions
of role and foreign interest. But if the nation could not find it within
itself to render a commitment to a potentially protracted war, it
would have been better for Johnson to have known early on.

On Vietnam policy, Johnson fell off the razor's edge because he acted authoritatively when no authoritative decision was appropriate. By making the President the decisionmaker instead of the leader of the nation's problem-solving, Johnson lost his vantage point and his leverage over the holding environment.[63] He could not regulate distress, direct attention, or distribute responsibility. He could not protect voices of leadership without authority because, by coupling his own authority to the issue, each dissident voice became a threat to his power. By giving Vietnam policy questions low priority—half hidden from the public and Congress—he unwittingly let them ripen by the natural chaotic processes of emergency and crisis. Having lost his ability to direct the heat and attention the war unleashed, Johnson took all the heat and sacrificed his presidency.

The Fall of Richard Nixon

Johnson's successor also lost his presidency in the context of Vietnam.[64] The same trends toward autocratic action that shaped Johnson's foreign policymaking shaped Richard Nixon's as well. Indeed, the pressures on Nixon were worse. Johnson bequeathed a nation divided and distressed, which could only have increased the pressures on Nixon to come up authoritatively with *his* solution to the Vietnam War. He would achieve peace with honor. He would end the war so that it would not have been in vain. Both pro-war and anti-war factions could unite behind this goal. And though perhaps no President could achieve it, Nixon would try.

During the first several months of his presidency, Nixon repeatedly expressed his desire to pull the country together. "His would be a government of national unity."[65] But unity at home required peace in Vietnam. Using the classical model—I'm the leader here; leave it to me!—Nixon entered the White House thinking he knew better than Johnson the way to bring Ho Chi Minh to the bargaining table. After all, Nixon was far more expert on matters of foreign policy than Johnson had been. With massive, secret, and unauthorized bombing of North Vietnamese sanctuaries in neutral Cambodia (which Johnson had not allowed), bold threats of "measures of great consequence and force," and secret diplomacy, Nixon expected to deliver a rapid peace.[66] He had said during the election, "How do

you bring a war to a conclusion? I'll tell you how Korea was ended
. . . Eisenhower let the word go out—let the word go out diplomati-
cally—to the Chinese and the North [Koreans]—that he would not
tolerate this continual ground war of attrition. And within a matter
of months they negotiated."[67]

Nixon set a deadline of November 1969 for a breakthrough on
the war. But when his efforts to end it seemed only to produce an
expanded war in Cambodia, domestic opposition intensified. Demonstrations multiplied across the land. Hundreds of thousands
marched in Washington. Nixon, in turn, attempted to turn the po-
larity to his political advantage. The politics of unity gave way to
the politics of division. Vice-President Spiro Agnew called it "positive
polarization."[68] On November 3, 1969, in his speech to the "silent
majority," Nixon claimed to represent the orienting values of America against a misguided but vocal minority trying to "impose" its
values by "mounting demonstrations in the streets."[69]

Viewing domestic opposition as an enemy, Nixon tried to suppress
it. Against his public opposition, he intensified domestic surveillance
by the FBI and the CIA.[70] And in the face of Congressional opposition, he instructed his staff that there would be no more "screwing
around." "Don't worry about divisiveness. Having drawn the sword,
don't take it out—stick it in hard."[71]

By 1972 President Nixon, his advisers, the press, and numerous
political factions in America had developed an "us versus them"
model as a basis for analyzing events and making decisions. As
Nixon's speechwriter tells it:

The election of 1968, and the reaction to the events of the first half
of Nixon's first term, confirmed in the minds of the President and his
most trusted advisers that: 1. "We" would never have an appeal to
"them," and it was a waste of time trying to win them over or appease
them. 2. "They" could be useful to "us," as the villain, the object
against which all of our supporters, as well as those who might
become our supporters, could be rallied. 3. Our forum was the Presidency, and their forum was the Eastern Establishment press, and since
they "managed" the news we would be better off discrediting the news
media. 4. "We" were on the side of the right, representing the will of
the people in a democracy, and majoritarians had the duty to identify

and overcome the anti-democratic elitists. There was disagreement within the Administration about all of these theses, particularly about the intensity with which we should fight the press, but there was little dissent on the assumption that lay beneath all of them: that it was "them" against "us" on nearly everything.[72]

Nixon would render the differences vivid between "us" and "them" by emphasizing that only *he* could have done the things he would do. Only *he* could accomplish breakthroughs with both Red China and the Soviet Union. Only Nixon had the know-how to do the work facing the nation. Nixon would dazzle the country with his virtuoso performances. According to his speechwriter, "'Only Nixon Could Have' came up again in memos Nixon stimulated Haldeman to write, paving the way for dealings with the Soviets on SALT with a minimum of reaction from the far right, which might have presented a President of more liberal mien with a considerable problem . . . Nixon's ability to bring along the right-wing, grumbling but with 'no place else to go,' was seen to be one of his greatest strengths."[73]

However, Nixon's defensive and imperious conduct eventually alienated even his political allies in Washington. "I believe in the battle, whether it's the battle of a campaign or the battle of this office . . . It's always there wherever you go. I, perhaps, carry it more than others because that's my way."[74] Secretive behavior reinforced the public's latent fears that Nixon could not be trusted, dating from his earliest years in politics. Nixon's distrust generated distrust, which reinforced his own and perpetuated the vicious cycle. As one of his aides later described, "Gradually, as we drew the circle closer around us, the ranks of 'them' began to swell."[75]

Watergate was the culmination of autocratic behavior gone awry. The events are well known. A group of White House spies and operatives, acting in the main against anti-Vietnam War protesters like Daniel Ellsberg, who had leaked the Pentagon Papers in June 1971, turned its efforts toward Nixon's reelection campaign in the winter of 1972.[76] With neither economic nor war-related good news to tell, Nixon's popularity had fallen badly. In January, the polls were showing him running neck and neck against Senator Edmund Muskie at 41 percent each.[77] To try to reverse this trend, Nixon's men sabotaged Muskie's campaign and later, in June, burglarized Democratic Party headquarters located in the Watergate Hotel and Office Complex in Washington, D.C. Within a week of the burglary, Nixon signed on to covering it up. At first the cover-up succeeded; the burglary did not interfere with Nixon's landslide reelection victory. Within a little more than two years, however, as the story unraveled and the facts became known, the House of Representatives drew up articles of impeachment and Nixon resigned.[78]

The Costs of Going It Alone

President Nixon violated a trust: he lied to the public, blatantly, out of self-interest, and was found out. A cover-up might be justifiable in times of war for purposes of national security, but not for stealing campaign secrets. Nixon sabotaged not only the Democratic Party, but also the very basis of his formal presidential authority: representing the law of the land.[79] Most significantly, he added greatly to Johnson's damage of the institution of the presidency itself, and therefore to a vital component of the national holding environment for doing adaptive work in the future. The institution lost credibility, weakening the network of informal authority relations based on trust between the citizens and their government. Instead of providing a backstop of cohesion in a land already frayed by war and acute social change, the presidency got drawn into the division. The damaged institution could no longer provide a key source of reliability to a troubled people so that they might continue to work on the country's most difficult problems. Held more weakly, the nation fled from this work. Indeed, it seems inconceivable that anyone could begin to analyze the successes and failures of America during the last twenty years without accounting for the impact of this damage. The Los Angeles riots of 1992 are but one symptom of work long avoided.

Operating by the lone warrior model of leadership, Nixon circumvented Congress, the public, and even his own advisers in the executive branch.[80] Nixon believed that he could, if left alone, solve the problem in Vietnam and usher in an era of more peaceful coexistence with communist nations. He understood that the rift between the Soviets and the Chinese provided an opportunity to play one off against the other. He also knew that a nation with a quarter of the world's population could not remain unrecognized. And he knew that secrecy was critical to managing these relationships, for neither the Chinese nor the Soviets would enter into serious negotiations without trusting that the American government could maintain secrecy.[81]

But did the need for secrecy preclude all options for getting the public to come to terms with a changing view of communist countries, or its investment and losses in Vietnam? Did the President have no role to play in the public's adaptive work on foreign affairs? Nixon had cause for pride in his technical mastery of foreign policy—the opening to China and détente with the Soviet Union. But ultimately the success of his foreign policy would rest on domestic opinion. Détente and arms control with the Soviets would rest on the capacity of the public and Congress to make sense out of these apparent reversals. After all, how was the country supposed to react to presidential friendlinesses with the Chinese and the Soviets when two generations of Americans had learned to hate and fear the communists and thousands of their children were now dying for the cause of anticommunism in Southeast Asia? Television pictures all at once showing scenes of war in Vietnam along with President Nixon smiling and toasting Mao Zedong and Leonid Brezhnev posed a first order challenge to our values, attitudes, and behavior. To view foreign policymaking as work directed abroad discounted badly the seriousness of the adaptive work required at home.

Changing American attitudes would have required at least some appreciation for the public's debate. But Nixon viewed public debate as a threat. He preferred "silent" majorities. Viewing the public's unrest as a menace, rather than as an opportunity for adaptive work, Nixon responded defensively. And from a technical point of view, he was right: division at home did provide aid and comfort to the enemy. Ironically, however, his "us versus them" defensiveness may well have strengthened the North Vietnamese conviction that America would remain a house divided and could be defeated. Unwittingly, he may have added fuel to the conflict.

Nixon adopted an "us versus them" outlook not only as a product of his character, although that was critical. Us versus them described the social and emotional currents of the Cold War. Bumper stickers across the nation read: "America: Love It or Leave It." Nearly everyone seemed up in arms during the Vietnam era. The dissension within the nation had already brought down one President. Nixon's personality and public life fell in quite naturally with this polarizing trend.[82]

Thus, two powerful forces reinforced Nixon's predilection toward autocratic behavior: the polarizing trends of the Vietnam years and the historical trends toward presidential autonomy in foreign affairs heightened during the Cold War. The mesh of these forces with Nixon's insular style produced imperial behavior that cut consistently across foreign and domestic policy.[83]

Hence, ascribing Nixon's downfall solely to character is too easy. Nixon's leadership philosophy—leaders lead and followers follow—was not much different from Lyndon Johnson's leadership strategy in foreign affairs. Both Presidents acted like technicians. Both identified leadership with giving answers, treating Vietnam as a technical problem that foreign policy and military expertise could solve with the help of some political manipulation. Both took the work on their own shoulders rather than shift the burden of grappling with the issues to Congress. Both fell into the trap of isolating themselves on the point and ignoring the adaptive work of their relevant publics. Both viewed contention as an impediment rather than as a sign of a society contending with an adaptive challenge. By isolating themselves from the political process, both lost critical opportunities to reality-test their technical, political, and moral assessments of war policy in Vietnam and, for Nixon, in Cambodia as well. Neither of them used their capacity as President to dominate public attention in a strategy to coordinate the public's engagement with the issues, or stimulate, enrich, and advance the public argument. Both squandered the holding environment of the presidency, and thus their power to regulate distress. Neither treated political leadership on Vietnam policy as the politics of inclusion. Nixon was simply more consistent.

Nixon used a variation of Johnson's circumvention strategy—trying to subvert and control the crisis—in the hope of arranging a grand technical fix, sooner than later. Instead, he might have embraced the public unrest, claimed it as a sign of democracy, and used his office to moderate its intensity and clarify the issues. Rather than isolate himself from the public debate, taking the attacks personally and defensively, Nixon might have reached out to the public and to Congress. For example, he could have moderated a presidential series of discussions on nationwide television between heads of prowar and antiwar factions on the practicalities of the war in the context of emerging trends in Soviet and Chinese affairs, or on the moral dilemmas posed by the war. He could have raised his own questions and offered perspectives given his expertise and vantage point as President. Or he might have challenged Congress to give him a clear mandate, one way or another—to share policymaking responsibility. By claiming democracy rather than defending himself against it, Nixon might have sent more coherent international messages about America. Instead, he demonized the conflict and played to the uninvolved.[84]

Using his office to coordinate the public debate on Vietnam would have required going against the grain of both his personal inclination and prevailing presidential trends toward seizing control, but it also might have provided Nixon with better options than those he and Kissinger invented, despite their considerable prowess. Such a public debate also might have clarified the domestic viability of their policies. Would America be willing to leave soldiers in Vietnam to enforce a treaty? When South Vietnam began to fall within a year of Nixon's resignation, America balked, and not simply because the people had lost its faith in government after Watergate. Rather, the people had also lost their interest in fighting the war. They wanted to cut their losses. Having been unprepared from the beginning and misled repeatedly during the war about its costs, the nation had had enough. Peace was barely at hand and never in the bag.[85] Nixon had done little to prepare people for the sustained commitment that "peace with honor" would require, even if it were attainable.

The tragedy of Nixon's downfall is not only the tragedy of one man. The tragedy is the work neglected.[86] Political ousters sometimes function in part as avoidance mechanisms, providing society with a false or incomplete diagnosis (it was all the "leader's" fault) and a diversion from its own adaptive work still to be faced. Anti-Nixon fervor was not all avoidance. Watergate represented the outcome of an imperial trend in the presidency that had taken over not just foreign policy but also domestic affairs. That trend and the abuses of power that came with it had to be stopped, if possible. The

Watergate hearings were Congress's mechanism for reasserting its relevance and its Constitutional authority. Yet the hearings not only attempted to reverse a trend, they also served to deflect attention—probably unwittingly—from the domestic demands of foreign affairs, including the wounds of the war. For example, in 1973 and 1974, while the nation sat transfixed at the spectacle of the Watergate hearings on television, tens of thousands of soldiers returned unwelcomed from Vietnam, beginning years of neglect and inner torment.[87] Rather than face these men and the reality of our first major lost war, many of us watched Congress's gladiator fight. This is not to suggest that the hearings themselves were at fault or that they should have been conducted differently. Americans might have looked anywhere for a diversion from the issues embodied by the soldiers' returning. As a columnist noted in late 1975, "Today it is almost as though the war never happened. Americans have somehow blocked it out of their consciousness. They don't talk about it. They don't talk about its consequences."[88] Vietnam was barely mentioned in the presidential campaign of 1976.[89] It took us nearly a decade before we even began to face the sacrifices, mistakes, and costs of the Vietnam War, before we began to build monuments, make documentaries and films, embrace the soldiers who fought the war, and capture its lessons.

Presidential Leadership

The framers of the Constitution had in mind the transformation of executive authority from an imperial monarchy to a constrained presidency. By forcing the President to share powers with the legislature and the courts and by rendering his officeholding contingent on public opinion, they intended to force his attention to the views of others. Presidential action, it was hoped, would pay high regard in its synthesis to the conflicting values, priorities, beliefs, and behaviors of a diverse nation facing adaptive hurdles everyday.

In a sense, the presidency as an institution embodied a revolutionary conception of executive leadership. And no wonder; it emerged from the antiauthoritarian sentiment of the new and rebellious nation. No longer were people to look up to the solitary silverback—the monarch—for decisive answers to the problems of direction, protection, orientation, conflict, and the care of norms. The colonists had grown tired of being misled by rulers whose visions came from within. They wanted public officials whose visions were derived or shaped from without. Presidential perspectives had to be reality-tested against a multiplicity of views. Presidential action would require collaboration.

Ironically, with the emergence of America's dominant role in twentieth-century world affairs and the domestic stresses generated by that role, the presidency reverted, in varying degrees, to the imperial mode.[90] Under the Cold War pressures to provide a more traditional kind of leadership, Truman, Eisenhower, and Kennedy took on more autocratic styles of behavior in foreign policy.[91] Congress and the public as a whole expected technical expertise and autocratic policymaking in the guise of leadership, and that is what they got. In a time of prolonged distress, our gaze became fastened on authority, shaping both the actions and selection of Presidents. By the time Johnson and Nixon came on the scene, the stage was set for tragedy.

The Constitutional design for presidential leadership seemed eminently suited to a nation facing adaptive work, yet the renewal of that design now became in its own right an adaptive challenge. Following Watergate, Jimmy Carter tried, in some ways, to meet that challenge. His presidency offers a complex picture of an authority still operating too much like the technician, yet trying to move toward a more honest encounter with the public.

On one hand, Jimmy Carter saw himself as the provider of well-engineered policy answers. His very education as an engineer may have left him ill-prepared to understand the adaptive requirements of policies, and therefore the need for collaboration and pacing. Having campaigned for President as an anti-Washington outsider, he began and remained a President with a weak set of relationships with members of Congress. He did not understand their role in public problem-solving or their ways. In his first months in the White House, he launched a slew of major policy initiatives toward a Congress not eager, after Watergate, to take orders from anybody, and ill-equipped to digest so much so fast.[92]

On the other hand, Carter tried, without great skill but courageously, to challenge the nation to face problems of both values and habits. On July 15, 1979, during the revolution in Iran, he gave his address on oil policy. In it he challenged Americans to face their "moral and spiritual crisis" in which self-indulgence and consumption endangered the values of family, community, and faith. In our society, he suggested, "human identity is no longer defined by what one does but by what one owns." Yet "owning things and consuming things do not satisfy our longing for meaning." Later in the speech, he discussed the oil crisis and became more concrete in his proposals. He asked Americans "to take no unnecessary trips, to use car pools or public transportation whenever you can, to park your car one extra day per week, to obey the speed limit, and to set your thermostats to save fuel."[93] Both messages seemed to go over badly.[94] Journalists branded it the "malaise" speech. Although Carter may have spent months thinking about these issues, feeling them through, with the benefit of a final ten-day retreat at Camp David with scholars and politicians, he neglected to lead the public through a similar learning process by which its views and sense of responsibility would change. Instead, Carter merely delivered the answers.

But perhaps it was less his surprising speech than his subsequent actions which caused further erosion of the public's perception of his leadership ability. The day after his speech, Carter asked for the resignation of his entire Cabinet and senior White House staff, an event unseen since President Tyler's day in the 1840s. By doing so, he followed one distressing event with another. After challenging the nation in its values and its pocketbooks, the President created chaos and confusion at the top of the government. The chaos at the top deflected the public's attention away from the problems addressed in his speech and onto the ineptness, once again, in post-Watergate Washington. Unwittingly, Carter weakened an already injured holding environment. He tacitly communicated that the authority structure, the containing vessel, had not done its job, and worse, that he had made serious errors of executive judgment in choosing whom to authorize. Carter needed to look ahead to maintaining a steady course after delivering a disturbing speech that pressed people to examine their consumerism and extravagance as factors in the energy shortages. He needed to give people time to incorporate the challenge. As Johnson demonstrated in his response to a distressed nation during events in Selma, in the midst of a teaching moment one has to hold steady. Disorder at the top is perhaps the last thing people want to see when the distress of change compels them to seek greater reliability in their authorities.

President Carter may have believed in facing people with hard problems, but he seemed not to know how. That was not entirely his fault: strategies for orchestrating adaptive work—even if modeled in some ways by Franklin Roosevelt or Lyndon Johnson—had never become part of conventional wisdom on leadership, or even a major focus of research.[95]

Authority constrains leadership because in times of distress people expect too much. They form inappropriate dependencies that isolate their authorities behind a mask of knowing. And then everyone rationalizes the dependency. As some senators put it during the Vietnam era, democracy is awkward in an age of crisis.[96] And in our time of global change, everything ends up feeling like a crisis, even when it is not. As a result, doubt, the exchange of ideas, weighing contrary values, collaborative work, the testing of vision against competing views, changing one's mind, seem like unaffordable luxuries. Raise hard questions and one risks getting cut down, even if the questions are important for moving forward on the problem. Thus, the need for leadership from people in authority becomes ever more critical during periods of disequilibrium, when people's urgency for answers increases. Yet that role is played badly if authorities reinforce dependency and delude themselves into thinking that they have to have the answers when they do not. Feeling pressured to know, they will surely come up with an answer, even if poorly tested, misleading, and wrong.

Part III

Leading Without Authority

8

Creative Deviance on the Frontline

We see leadership too rarely exercised from high office, and the constraints that come with authority go far to explain why. In public life, people generally look to their authorities to solve problems with a minimum of pain, and where pain must be endured, they often expect their officials to find somebody else to bear the costs. In the 1990s, we hear across the country, "Cut the deficit—but don't raise my taxes, raise his." "Cut military spending, but don't close my factory or my army base." Many of us want change, "but not in my back yard," a syndrome so common that it has a name: NIMBY.[1] Our politicians find it very hard to raise tough questions at election time because their constituents insist on protection. When we do elect activists, we want them to change the thinking and behavior of other people, rarely our own. We can hardly blame our public officials for giving us what we ask for.

The scarcity of leadership from people in authority, however, makes it all the more critical to the adaptive successes of a polity that leadership be exercised by people without authority. These people—perceived as entrepreneurs and deviants, organizers and trouble-makers—provide the capacity within the system to see through the blind spots of the dominant viewpoint.[2] Often they remain relatively unknown, like Marie Foster or Bernard Lafayette, key activists in 1960s Selma; and sometimes they begin with no authority and eventually gain broad informal authority, as did Martin Luther King Jr., Mohandas K. Gandhi, and Margaret Sanger. People such as these

183

push us to clarify our values, face hard realities, and seize new possibilities, however frightening change may be. Of course, if they have no means to compensate for their own blind spots, they can mislead us just as badly as anyone in authority.

Because we are not used to distinguishing between leadership and authority, the idea of leadership without authority is new and perplexing. As a result, the person without authority gets few relevant pointers from scholarship. Analysts have generally neglected the distinctive problems and opportunities of mobilizing work from positions of little or no authority. Thus, nearly all studies of leadership, in addition to many histories, focus primarily on figures of authority. Just as social systems organize themselves in relation to a structure of authority, focusing attention at the head of the table, our social commentators do so as well. Leadership may more often emerge from the foot of the table, but that is not where we spend most of our time looking. We study the lives and characteristics of heads of state and CEOs of corporations, assuming all the while that we are studying leaders and not simply authority figures who serve the social functions of direction, protection, and order, sometimes in adaptive situations that demand their leadership, and sometimes in routine situations that do not.

That I use the metaphor of the table, with the head traditionally a man and the foot characteristically a woman is no accident. Leadership without authority has been the domain to which women have been restricted for ages. Even today, Congress remains over 90 percent men, and we are only beginning to imagine seriously the election of a woman President in our time. Having been denied formal authority roles in most societies, some women have learned strategies for leading without authority, and some have learned not to try leading at all. The same can be said of many disempowered groups. Women who have managed to carve out roles of authority were likely to be ignored by traditional historical and social science scholarship, which focused on the activities of men. In the United States, for example, women have headed social reform movements dating back more than 150 years, but only recently, with the emergence of women's history as an established academic field, have their accomplishments been chronicled. Perhaps recognizing the *category* of leadership without authority will increase our awareness of women's leadership at the same time that we learn to authorize women to public positions from which to lead with formal authority.

The question, however, remains, "Can someone exercise leadership from the foot of the table, or even from outside the family—without any authority, formal or informal?" I think the answer is yes, and in several ways. Some people, like Gandhi, lead societies without holding formal office of any kind. More frequently, people have a base of formal authority within their own subgroup, like Lech Walesa as head of Solidarity in Communist Poland, Martin Luther King Jr. as founder of the Southern Christian Leadership Conference, or Margaret Sanger as head of what became Planned Parenthood. In addition, they have a wide network of informal authority in the community at large, as did Gandhi. But these people lead not only within the boundaries of the communities that authorize them, formally and informally, but also across those boundaries, reaching to communities where their words and actions have influence despite having no authorization. In segments of the larger community that these leaders influence, they lack both kinds of authority. In a sense, they lead across two boundaries: the boundary of their formal organization, if they have one, and the boundary defined by the wider network of people with whom they have gained informal authority (trust, respect, moral persuasion).

In fact, many people daily go beyond both their job description and the informal expectations they carry within their organization and do what they are not authorized to do. At a minimum, these people exercise leadership momentarily by impressing upon a group, sometimes by powerfully articulating an idea that strikes a resonant chord, the need to pay attention to a missing point of view. A staff assistant will speak up at a meeting even though she has no authority to do so. Or someone will run an unauthorized experiment and later announce the results. Or in the early hours of a disaster, some people will step forward and mobilize others to face and respond to the crisis. On a public level, a Rachel Carson will publish a *Silent Spring*.

In U.S. history, furthermore, many people have engaged in various forms of civil disobedience to mobilize adaptive work among communities that were indifferent or hostile. Those they led across formal and informal boundaries gave them no authority whatsoever, certainly not in the early stages of their efforts. The people they led learned and changed their ways grudgingly. In the past two centuries Samuel Adams, Henry David Thoreau, Elizabeth Cady Stanton, and Susan B. Anthony are but a few.

At an extreme, war has been used as a means to mobilize adaptive work. When Abraham Lincoln went to war with the South, he clearly had no authority, formal or informal, in the eyes of seceding Southerners. Indeed, in ten states he won no popular votes in 1860 because he was not even put on the ballot. He led across the newly formed boundary, challenging Southerners to solve rather than flee from the problems of reconciling differences within a union that their recent forebears had played dominant roles in producing.[3]

Thus, when we speak of leadership without authority, we are referring to a very large set of stances, from the person operating from the margins of society even to the senior authority figure who leads beyond his pale of authority, challenging either his own constituents' expectations or engaging people across the boundary of his organization who would ordinarily or preferably pay him no mind.

Over time, a person who begins without authority or who leads beyond whatever authority she has may have to construct, strengthen, and sometimes broaden her base of informal authority in order to get more leverage. She may find that an initial, rebellious leadership action puts her in an informal authority position that requires trust, respect, and moral force in order to sustain progress. Such were the beginnings of King, Gandhi, and Sanger. An emerging leader may need a base from which to speak to hard issues without being ignored or cast out altogether. Furthermore, to involve the relevant factions in the community, she may need people across boundaries to believe that she represents something significant, that she embodies a perspective that merits attention. When that happens, she has to respect both the resources and constraints that come with authority, formally from her own group, and informally from beyond. Just as leading with authority requires protecting voices of dissent, a leader without authority will have to "take counsel" from her adversaries, incorporating in her strategy whatever wisdom of theirs connects to her central thesis.[4]

As she seeks informal authority from those across organizational or factional boundaries, she has to place her cause in the context of the values of her opposition. In addition, she may have to learn from her antagonists in order to correct for the possible narrowness of her own views. She is not just teaching; she is being taught. Thus, King, Stanton, Anthony, Gandhi, and Sanger placed and came to understand their struggles in the context of the day's dominant values and concerns. King spoke of equality and freedom, and learned the workings of the legal, political, and economic systems controlled by white society in building a national movement to combat racism. Stanton and Anthony both invoked the Declaration of Independence in demanding equal rights for women, and assimilated the militance, defiance, and toughness of male society in building a tradition for women to defend themselves against domination. Gandhi spoke of liberty and self-determination, and discovered techniques for invoking the force and brutality of the British Army to weaken Britain's stronghold on India. Sanger put birth control in the setting of poverty, unchecked population growth, and family health, and absorbed politics, contraceptive medicine, and law in advancing what seemed to her obvious birth-control rights requiring no legal or medical justification.

Just as Parsons, Ruckelshaus, and Lyndon Johnson had to strengthen bonds of trust to bolster their formal authority and hold people's attention, people who begin without any authority often have to place their contributions within an on-going tradition or organization that provides a vessel of trust to hold the distress they generate. Since they have less leverage to shape the holding environment, they must make use of the vessel that is there.

The Benefits of Leading Without Authority

Leadership, as used here, means engaging people to make progress on the adaptive problems they face. Because making progress on adaptive problems requires learning, the task of leadership consists of choreographing and directing learning processes in an organization or community. Progress often demands new ideas and innovation. As well, it often demands changes in people's attitudes and behaviors. Adaptive work consists of the process of discovering and making those changes. Leadership, with or without authority, requires an educative strategy.[5]

Senior authority generally includes the power to manage the holding environment, direct attention, gather and influence the flow of information, frame the terms of debate, distribute responsibility, regulate conflict and distress, and structure decision processes. Yet the constraints of authority suggest that there may also be advantages to leading without it. First, the absence of authority enables one to deviate from the norms of authoritative decisionmaking. Instead of providing answers that soothe, one can more readily raise questions that disturb. One does not have to keep the ship on an even keel. One has more *latitude for creative deviance*. Second, leading without or beyond one's authority permits focusing hard on a single issue. One does not have to contend so fully with meeting the multiple expectations of multiple constituencies and providing the holding environment for everybody. One can have an *issue focus*. Third, operating with little or no authority places one closer to the detailed experiences of some of the stakeholders in the situation. One may lose the larger perspective but gain the fine grain of people's hopes, pains, values, habits, and history. One has *frontline information*.

For example, in terms of latitude, King had the leeway to dramatize issues in ways that Johnson could not. King could stage demonstrations or disobey local law as a means of bringing the brutality of racism into people's living rooms. Imagine for a moment that Johnson had gone to Selma to march instead of King. It is doubtful that the police would have been so brutal with the President at the head of the line. Most likely, the local and state police would have "loved Johnson to defeat" in the same way that the more strategically minded police in Albany, Georgia, had "loved King to defeat" during his demonstrations there in late 1961. In the same vein, King also had the latitude to use himself as an *embodiment* of the issue. By going to jail, he used his own person to dramatize racist suppression. By writing his "Letter from Birmingham Jail," he became a living example of the inequities he battled.[6] Imprisonment served as another metaphor and opportunity to address the nation's conflict in values.

In terms of issue focus, Johnson had to concern himself with being "the President of all the people." Leading from authority, he could not afford to embody a single issue without jeopardizing that authority and his capacity to lead on many others. He had to make trade-offs between issues, dilute issues, and sometimes accept the lowest common denominator. In contrast, King could focus on civil rights. Indeed, as long as he maintained that focus, he could reach out to a large and varied constituency of Americans, black and white, with diverse views on many other issues. For example, King did not have to risk splitting his supporters by antagonizing those who felt strongly for or against communism. When President Kennedy and Attorney General Robert Kennedy, pressed by J. Edgar Hoover, told King to distance himself from his closest associates, who were leftists, King went far to comply.[7] This went quite against his own values, but communism was not his issue. Yet King was not as single-minded in maintaining his focus as he might have been. Having gained widespread moral authority, he felt compelled to speak out on the Vietnam War. Whether this helped his cause is a question beyond our scope, but one has to consider the possibility that his mantle of informal authority became, in part, a constraint on his ability to focus on the single issue of civil rights.

In terms of frontline information, King knew intimately the habits and attitudes of his community in ways that Johnson could only imagine at a distance. He knew the humiliation, the fear, the rage, and the fatigue. He knew what moved people and who moved people. To be sure, Johnson had his own advantages in regard to information, but these complemented King's advantage without superseding it.

The following three cases of leadership illustrate these benefits more fully.

Mohandas K. Gandhi in India

King took his lessons from India's Gandhi, who in turn took his lessons from the Bhagavad Gita, Jesus, Thoreau, and Tolstoy, to name a few.[8] Gandhi developed and refined the technique of nonviolent civil disobedience to illustrate to the British public the moral contradictions of its colonial policies. Massive demonstrations, brutal beatings, nationwide strikes, hunger fasts, and years in jail all were meant to dramatize to the British the gap between their espoused values—justice and self-determination—and their behavior—subjugation. Gandhi tried to force attention upon that to which very few in Britain wanted to pay attention. He identified the adaptive challenge and he used various methods of creative deviance to get people to face it.

Gandhi gained informal authority from much of the Indian population and led India using the resources of that informal authority. At the same time, he also generated adaptive work among the British over whom he did not exercise even the least informal authority. The British did not ask him to represent *their* internal contradictions. If he later gained moral authority in some of their eyes, that was an outcome of his activism, not a precondition. For much of his career, he led the British as a provocateur.

Lacking authority with the British, Gandhi used himself to dramatize the issues. He embodied the British values he demanded the British live by. When he fasted for justice, people began to pay attention, not because another person was about to die of starvation but because Gandhi practiced what he preached. If he and his constituents were ready to make a personal sacrifice for the values that those in Britain held dear, then perhaps the cotton mill workers in Lancashire, England, would do so as well.[9]

Fundamentally, Gandhi used a strategy to provoke learning targeted at the values, attitudes, and habits of his adversary. He did this as well with the Indian people. India had its own large measure of adaptive work to do, although not all of his collaborators recognized that the problems facing the two nations were nontechnical. Many "Home Rule" activists in Indian politics considered colonialism a Type I problem—clearly defined with a clear-cut solution. The British should leave, period, end of story. Gandhi saw beneath the surface of the problem. Colonialism was a way of life not only to Britain but to India. Breaking up that way of life would require enormous adaptive work. The British could just leave India, as eventually they did, but getting them ready to leave and getting India ready to rule herself were adaptive challenges of the first magnitude. Britain would have to face the loss of empire and wealth, requiring the reconstruction of identity based on other values, the reconstruction of economy based on other means. India would have to construct a national identity (Hindu or Muslim or both), a national government (democratic or socialist), and an effective economy (industrial or agricultural, protectionist or open, planned or market-driven). There was nothing clear-cut about the learning required by the parties with a stake in this predicament.[10]

It took Gandhi a long lifetime, more than fifty adult years, to mobilize action and opinion in Britain, India, and South Africa. During all those years, he held no formal authority. Indeed, he shunned taking office in either the dominant political party, the Congress Party, or the new government itself when it finally formed in 1947. He thought he had more latitude for action without formal authority. He could challenge the people in ways that might be difficult for an official whose primary concerns must turn to holding the party and government together, to seeking an equilibrium.

Yet Gandhi gained extraordinary *informal* authority. People throughout India looked to him with great awe, trust, fear, and occasional dread. They called him Mahatma—The Great One. More than the formal authorities in India, Gandhi operated at the focal point of the nation's attention. His fasting mattered because, over the course of thirty years he had become the singular embodiment of the nation's hopes and pains. Indians and non-Indians granted him moral authority, not only because he used his own person to represent the issues but because he had the strategic ability to dramatize over and over again that the aspirations of his people were consonant with the moral underpinnings of the West.

He used this informal authority with consummate skill. With it, he regulated the levels of social disequilibrium generated by the political movement for independence. He would call for a demonstration and then quell it when he thought that the tensions unleashed were becoming destructive. For example, in 1921, on the eve of his first effort at mass civil disobedience—which he limited to one city instead of extending it nationwide, as his political colleagues demanded—an Indian mob murdered a group of British policemen. In response, Gandhi called the whole strike off. To him, the outbreak was symptomatic of public unreadiness for a nonviolent campaign, and more violence would impede progress.[11] The special personalized relationship that he developed with the general public gave him the power to frame and focus attention on the issues, move people to action, and slow them down.[12] It also gave him dominant influence with the senior Indian politicians in the movement for independence, who could not help but respond to Gandhi's widespread reputation.

He could orchestrate and address conflict, not only between the Indians and the British but among the factions within India as well—militant and nonviolent, Muslim and Hindu. To be sure, the formal authority of the British gave them a great deal more power to regulate disequilibrium. Within wide limits, they controlled how the system responded: with carrots, sticks, and structure; they had been doing so for centuries. But Gandhi's informal authority gave him pivotal control over how the system would be challenged, and how fast and hard.

Gandhi did not always have informal authority even with his own people. In various campaigns for justice, both in India and in his earlier years in South Africa, Gandhi was a nobody speaking up and raising hard questions and often failing. His lack of authority gave him more room to experiment with deviating from the norms. He gained informal authority only over time as his strategy, through trial and error, began to work. As he made small gains, he accrued respect, trust, and attention, which became tools to apply to the next campaign. Informal authority came as a useful by-product of his leadership strategy, waxing and waning with tactical gains and losses, but mostly rising over time and providing him with resources for broader and more sustained leadership activity.

When Gandhi returned to India on January 9, 1915, after twenty years of struggle in South Africa, he returned triumphant after his publicized and successful use of nonviolent civil disobedience to change repressive laws against South Africans of Indian decent. But rather than parlay his success in South Africa in exchange for authority within the indigenous political structures emerging in India, Gandhi, on the strong recommendation of his mentor, Professor Gokhale, set out to rediscover India at the grassroots, the India of villages. Why? By staying close to the frontline of life in India, Gandhi learned about the nature and enormity of the work facing his country. He learned about the values of his people, the economic arrangements, the ingrained habits of servitude and poverty, the brutal prejudices among them, the ignorance, and the pain.[13]

Formal authorities, in contrast, operate at a distance from the frontline. Although having their own special vantage point with access across a whole region of organization, community, or social system, authority figures are beholden to their subordinates for information. The advantage of formal positions of authority is breadth. The disadvantage is distance from raw and relevant detail.[14]

The American presidency illustrates this information dilemma. As Richard Neustadt suggests, "It is not information of a general sort that helps a President . . . not summaries, not surveys, not the bland amalgams. Rather it is the odds and ends of tangible detail that, pieced together in his mind, illuminate the underside of issues put before him . . . To help himself, he must reach out as widely as he can for every scrap of fact, opinion, gossip, bearing on his interests and relationships as President. He must become his own director of his own central intelligence."[15]

Gandhi understood that adaptive work required an intimate understanding of Indian society—of the strengths upon which a future self-reliant India could be built, and the weaknesses that hampered change. For example, Gandhi's nonviolence, fundamentally an Indian idea, struck a responsive chord throughout the countryside because the idea itself had its roots there. That Christianity also espoused some degree of nonviolence enabled Gandhi to connect Indian and British values and turn one into a means to move the other. The link gave him a strategy. Yet these shared values also highlighted weaknesses in India as well. As Gandhi saw it, a political movement based upon the principle of justice and dignity for all could not sanction the traditional caste system, or prejudice between Muslim and Hindu. As his biographer summarized from his first speeches to the Indian National Congress: "The British might go, but would that help the fifty to sixty million outcast untouchables, victims of cruel Hindu discrimination? Independence must mean more than Indian office-holders in the places and palaces of British office-holders."[16] For Gandhi to challenge these ways of life demanded knowing them deeply, by experience, by operating close to the frontline, where the stakeholders of India lived. Gandhi could speak to people, to their hopes, fears, weaknesses, and needs because he spent time knowing them. He could touch and inspire people because they touched and inspired him.

Had Gandhi taken political office, even at the end of his career, he might have traded away these benefits. As President or Prime Minister of India, two offices easily within reach, Gandhi would have taken up the center. At the center, he would then have become the repository of all the conflicting strains within the country expecting him to meet their needs and reduce distress. Inevitably, he would have felt the constraints of a role that would have compelled him to become a sort of "vector sum" of conflicting forces walking a middle path. Outside the center, Gandhi had the freedom to present a focused and coherent message, and to embody it. He had only to meet the expectations of those who, believing in him already, provided a base for his challenge to the nation and to Britain.

Margaret Sanger in the United States

Perhaps more than anyone else in this century, Margaret Sanger mobilized people in the United States and abroad to face the relationship between poverty, population, the status of women, and the need for women to have the freedom to plan and limit the size of their families.[17] Starting her career as a nurse at the turn of the twentieth century, Sanger saw firsthand the plight of women on New York's Lower East Side as they struggled with more children than they could financially or emotionally care for, exhausted themselves, endangered their lives having illegal abortions, or died in childbirth. She had seen her own overworked mother dying young while tending to eleven children. In her day, many women in America were desperate for a safe means of contraception, yet birth control of any sort was illegal. Indeed, even writing about birth control fell under state and federal laws against obscenity.

As Sanger told the story, her awakening came while caring for a young Jewish immigrant named Sadie Sachs in her Lower East Side tenement. Mrs. Sachs was suffering from infection after a self-induced abortion, and her doctor had responded to her plea for reliable contraception by advising her to tell her husband, Jake, "to sleep on the roof." Sanger told Mrs. Sachs about condoms and coitus interruptus, since these were the commonplace contraceptives of the day, though Sanger found them unacceptable because they ceded the power of birth control to men. When she returned three months later to find Mrs. Sachs dying of widespread infection, she resolved to leave "the palliative career of nursing in pursuit of fundamental social change."[18]

She began her public career in 1910 giving speeches in small socialist circles about the lives of poor immigrant women and writing columns on sex education and health for *The Call,* the popular socialist daily. In 1914 she started her own magazine provocatively called *The Woman Rebel,* in which she continued to challenge Victorian prohibitions against discussing the role of women and the use of contraceptive methods under a woman's control. In August 1914, after but a handful of issues of the *Rebel,* she was arrested for sending "indecent" materials through the mail. Rather than prepare for trial, however, she wrote *Family Limitation,* a pamphlet that explained in a plain and simple way the common forms of contraception. Although millions of Americans were already using these methods in secret, the taboo against discussing them kept women in a state of enforced ignorance about proper use. After preparing the pamphlet for publication, Sanger fled the country to Europe. From aboard ship, she cabled her New Jersey printer to release 100,000 copies of the pamphlet, which had been readied for distribution.

While she was a fugitive abroad, the police arrested Sanger's husband in their New York apartment for handing out a copy of *Family Limitation.* The three Sanger children were taken care of by friends and relatives while he spent thirty days in prison. The judged ruled: "Your crime is not only a violation of the laws of man, but of the law of God as well, in your scheme to prevent motherhood. Too many persons have the idea that it is wrong to have children. Some women are so selfish that they do not want to be bothered with them. If some persons would go around and urge Christian women to bear children, instead of wasting their time on woman suffrage, this city and society would be better off."[19] When Sanger heard of her husband's fate, she came home to stand trial.

The escape to Europe, the pamphlet, her husband's imprisonment, and the court's clear verdict all served to bring public attention for the first time to the issue of birth control. Suddenly, reputable newspapers and magazines were writing stories on the subject. In 1914 *The New York Times* carried only three articles about birth control, in 1915 it carried fourteen, and in the following two years, ninety. As the issue began to generate a much wider base of support, Sanger shed her radical rhetoric and began to frame the debate in ways far more understandable to a broader audience. She sought broad informal authority. She made an absolute distinction between contraception and abortion, advocating only the former, and she separated herself from a host of other issues about which she had an interest, from pacifism in the face of World War I to the broad socialist agenda. As she now more tamely put it, giving women control over their own fertility held "the key to personal fulfillment through marriage, motherhood, and independent self-realization . . . Women would make themselves the instruments of social regeneration . . . They would reconstitute the family, that fundamental unit of collective life, in a manner consistent with the rigor and discipline the modern world demanded in all dimensions of human activity."[20] This was not, however, a cynical strategy; Sanger's own views grew as she began to engage other points of view seriously and, in turn, was taken seriously herself. Apparently, she learned from engaging a wider audience. And she made the strategic decision to devote her efforts singularly to birth control. Operating without authority, she could afford to focus.

By the time of her trial in February 1916, public opinion had begun to shift. Sanger, wearing lace, posed for photographs with her two sons to offset her image as a radical; and an orchestrated campaign of supportive letters swamped the desks of judges and legislators. Indeed, a distinguished list of British intellectuals whom Sanger had befriended during her fugitive year, including the already famous H.G. Wells, wrote to President Woodrow Wilson. The public mood probably had its effect, for the charges were dropped. Sanger's victory led to publicity and speechmaking across the country.

Immediately, she started the nation's first birth control clinic in a storefront tenement in Brooklyn, modeled after the clinic system she had seen in Holland. She evidently wanted to create an example for America. Unable to secure a physician as medical director, she asked her sister, Ethel Byrne, a registered nurse, to run the clinic. But within weeks they were both arrested and put in jail.

Sanger seized the opportunities of the new crisis. Ethel went on a hunger strike, which generated more useful publicity and attracted the governor's attention. And after serving their sentences, Sanger appealed their convictions in the hope of obtaining a court ruling that would affirm at least the right of physicians to prescribe contraception in case of medical need. Doctors might then define the patient's need quite broadly as a matter of their own professional judgment. Sanger and her lawyer saw this as the only potential gap in the law that might enable them to establish birth control clinics legally across the country. On January 8, 1918, they got what they needed. The New York State Court of Appeals upheld Sanger's conviction under the state's obscenity law prohibiting lay men and women from distributing contraceptive information, but it offered an interpretation that granted specific license to physicians to prescribe contraceptive devices.

Seeking a partnership with the male medical profession, however, seemed a big mistake to some of Sanger's activist colleagues. The American Medical Association was a staunch supporter of the laws that made discussions about contraception illegal. Doctors, by and large, had been an impediment. Sanger and other experienced women probably knew more about techniques of birth control than American physicians at that time. Yet to Sanger, drawing in the medical profession and letting them play the expert role was a necessary tactical concession to the authority structure of the society. It enabled the legal establishment of clinics without first having to change any laws. Furthermore, Sanger agreed with some of the key orienting values of the medical profession. She wanted to place birth control on as scientific a footing as possible, while promoting research into new methods that might prove safer, more reliable, and more readily accessible.

From then on, enlisting the support of physicians would be central to her efforts. In 1921, as she established her national organization of family planning clinics, which later became the International Planned Parenthood Federation, she insisted that physicians be hired as medical directors for the clinics. Yet even her concessions to the medical profession and the legal victory that made it possible for doctors to get involved did not make it easy to gain their official support. Sanger had to find ways to engage the attention of the profession. The chairman of the American Gynecological Society, Dr. Robert Latou Dickenson, had decried Sanger's efforts to start birth control clinics. But when Sanger hired her first physician in 1923, Dr. Dorothy Bocker, Dickenson took notice, checked up on the clinic and its new medical director, and criticized the quality of her research in the *American Journal of Obstetrics and Gynecology*. Sanger had piqued his professional interest. She then asked Dickenson what it would take to have *him* work with the clinic in the design of its research, to which he made several demands, including Bocker's replacement. Sanger acceded, and though Dickenson did not officially join Sanger's Birth Control Clinical Research Bureau until several years later, in 1931, he gradually became a strong supporter of her work and a major advocate within established medical circles for birth control use and research. Sanger sought allies among other physicians as well, and after several years of effort, Dickenson and these other allies succeeded in getting the American Medical Association to reverse itself and endorse contraception. In 1937 it set a new standard for itself: "Voluntary family limitation is dependent largely on the judgment and wishes of individual patients."[21]

Through the decades of the twenties, thirties, forties, and much of the fifties, Sanger doggedly reached out to every constituency that might count—mobilizing women around the world and men with authority not only in the medical sciences but in politics, business, and labor. By writing, traveling, and speaking virtually nonstop at a frenzied pace for years at a time, she educated, provoked, and organized women and men to see the causal connections between poverty, population growth, the health of families, and a woman's status and ability to determine the size of her family. She demanded public candor about an aspect of life heretofore unspeakable yet undeniably critical to our existence.

Sanger's life had been full of both despair and achievement. For years at a time, she felt stymied. The Great Depression and World War II put many of her efforts on hold. Even Roosevelt's experimental approach to the New Deal had little room for this issue. He could not afford to offend the Catholic Church. As well, some reputable economists attributed the Depression to the steady decline in population, and urged against birth control. Yet she did not stop. Sanger used these years to build an international network and to solidify her American organization. Finally, in the late 1950s, for reasons that included a growing appreciation of the link between population and poverty, and the development of the birth control pill—funded with support that Sanger arranged—family planning became an accepted idea. Sanger lived just long enough to see the Supreme Court guarantee protection for the private use of contraceptives in the 1965 case of *Griswold v. Connecticut*.

Margaret Sanger identified an adaptive challenge—an internal contradiction in America. Millions of people were using birth control by the turn of the century, yet the laws prohibited its discussion, research, and prescription. A nation that valued self-reliance and autonomy rendered half of its population dependent and out of control. A nation in which women were entering the work force by the millions refused to face the necessary trade-offs and adjustments in family size. A nation committed to reducing domestic and international poverty did nothing to limit population growth. By exposing these internal contradictions between values and behavior, Sanger gained leverage over people's attention and sentiments.

Over decades Sanger built a wide network of informal authority relationships with feminists and sympathizers around the world. She used this authority to set strategy, direct attention, frame the issues, and orchestrate conflict within the movement. But most of the people she led gave her no informal authority whatsoever. To them, she was a persistent nuisance. Indeed, social change on an issue so intimate and basic as the structure of families and women's autonomy over childbearing challenged nearly everybody in authority: the courts, politicians, businessmen, the Catholic Church, and the medical profession. Sanger had the latitude to speak to the issues because no one had asked her to. Asking generates expectations, and expectations create limits. The courts were constrained by law, politicians by the sentiments of their constituents, businessmen by their associates and customers, Catholic officials by Rome, and doctors by their guild. Sanger was not constrained. She had the latitude to break and discuss taboos.

Yet to change primary norms and rules, Sanger had to broaden her base of support and find allies among these authorities. She could not afford to isolate herself on the point, to let the conflict be cast as if it were essentially a dispute between a monolithic structure and a few rebellious women. Mobilizing the many divisions of society for change meant kindling internal political tensions within each one. Each would then, on its own, generate new ideas and policies in its natural attempt to rectify internal dissonance. By fostering allies within each segment of society, the latent conflict between opposing factions in each segment would come alive. Debate would be fostered. The issue would ripen. Dickenson and his allies would become advocates persuading other doctors; religious authorities would provoke other religious authorities; business allies would engage other businessmen; and political allies would deal with other politicians.

In essence, Sanger used an educative strategy—to move both elites and public opinion. Thus, establishing a nationwide network of clinics not only provided medical and educational services to those in need, it also touched the general public. In her view, efforts to change laws, largely futile in themselves, only made sense if they provoked public engagement with the issues. Changing laws was an outcome of social learning. When she wrote, went to jail, lobbied in Congress, or traveled to meet Gandhi, Sanger aimed to stimulate public debate.[22] By creative deviance, she prodded those in authority to continue the debate. And like Gandhi and King, she became expert at using the press. She always traveled with her typewriter.

Sanger focused on a single issue. She gained informal authority because she knew one issue totally and had the discipline to stay away from distracting arguments about the major problems of the day, including war, peace, and communism. Though she cared deeply and had strong opinions about them, she stayed the course, speaking to the other problems only as they might connect to hers. In that way, she provided a clear context for her actions and became increasingly understandable to a wider group of people. Indeed, she became perhaps too adept at framing the issue of birth control in light of the concerns and values of whatever audience she happened to be reaching. In speaking to social policymakers, she talked about the alleviation of poverty; with conservative men and women, she focused on the need to strengthen overburdened families by giving them the resources to plan their families according to their capacities; with progressive women, she spoke openly about the satisfaction to be had from taking control over their own bodies; but with many intellectuals who, pre-Hitler, saw eugenics as a means to improve the human race, she spoke of the need for birth control among the poor and unfit, even while disavowing racism.

Despite her celebrity status and globe-trotting efforts, Sanger operated at the frontline. From the start as a nurse, through years running the Birth Control Clinical Research Bureau in Manhattan—the prototypic family planning clinic—until old age when she received and responded to a vast number of letters from women in all walks of life, Sanger touched intimately the life experiences of women. She knew them, worked with them, and never forgot that they were her primary constituency.

Two Lieutenants in Vietnam

Lack of authority may provide special assets and opportunities for leadership, but only for those who recognize and seize them. The following two stories illustrate a kind of challenge that many of us face every day in our organizations: confronting customary habits and procedures that obstruct adaptive work.[23]

As the war in Vietnam reached its peak, bombing missions over North Vietnam became routine. Yet Air Force Lieutenant Chuck Adams, a bomber pilot, began to notice a strange pattern of lost planes. Every so often a bomber would blow up in the sky while still high above the reach of antiaircraft fire. Adams deduced the possible cause. Since no high-altitude losses of aircraft had taken place in the two years preceding the introduction of a new type of bomb designed to explode at a preprogrammed altitude, Adams reasoned that the bombs were faulty. He discussed this theory with his ordinance officer and fellow pilots. The ordinance officer brushed the theory aside, but the pilots flying the planes thought it made some sense—at least enough sense to call a halt to using the new bombs until an investigation could be conducted. They took their case to the commanding officer, who first asked the ordinance specialist for his view. Finding no authoritative backing for the theory, the commander dismissed the pilots' case and ordered them to fly.

Adams and his fellow pilots were facing what subordinates in tightly managed organizations often face: resistance from authority, for understandable reasons. All the way up the chain of command, people with varying degrees of authority were expected to meet a set of performance expectations, on schedule. Adams's commanding officer was no different. Were he to deviate from the bombing plan based on the hunch of his pilots and without the support of his weapons expert, he would have subjected himself to ridicule from above. He had a mission to accomplish and a schedule to keep in fighting a difficult adversary, and changing or delaying that mission would not be taken lightly.

Adams understood that his commanding officer was constrained by expectations that accompanied his office. Adams himself had to address conflicting expectations associated with his own position of authority.[24] His flight crew looked to him to protect them from unnecessary danger. Were Adams to follow orders, he would be risking the lives of his men for reasons that would be hard to justify, given his hunch. That went against the grain of the informal authority his crew gave him. If Adams didn't do something, given their earnest suspicions of danger, he would diminish his crew's trust just as the commanding officer had diminished his trust.

Yet if Adams failed to follow orders, he would jeopardize his formal authority as a military officer—his job and chances for promotion. Should he buckle under, or commit insubordination based on a hunch? Adams felt stuck in the middle between his superior officer and his men, and he could find no middle option. As he saw it, the choice was clear: follow or disobey. He saw no room for deviance. He saw no options for leadership. All Adams had was the vantage point of someone at the frontline seeing things more sharply than those farther away, and he did not think that was enough.

When told to fly, he flew, and prayed. Adams blamed the commanding officer for making him fly, which reduced the loss of his crew's informal authorization. And they were lucky. But another plane, not so lucky, blew up within months. Only then did the commanding officer order a halt to the use of the new bombs, pending an investigation back in California at the site of the production plant. As it turns out, the bombs were indeed defective.

Reviewing the situation twenty years later, Adams, now a colonel, could see in retrospect a whole range of options for leadership in between obedience and insubordination. He might have pushed his group of fellow pilots and their crews for ideas on how to make the case against the faulty bombs. They might have found a way to push their commander, respectfully but forcefully, to pay closer attention to the evidence behind their hunch. For example, after reassuring the commander that ultimately they would obey his orders, they might have told him that they were not inclined to leave his office until they felt sure that he had fully weighed the evidence against the suspected triggering mechanism. They might have asked him to investigate up the chain of command whether any other hunches of this sort had been filing in. With more humor, they might have wheeled a bomb into his office to dramatize the issue. They also might have asked him to find out whether the mission plan for that week was critical: Was there room for postponement until more reliable bombs could be had? How long would that take? Was there anything they could do to speed up bringing in trustworthy bombs?

In retrospect, it is hard to know if such a conversation would have gone anywhere. But if Adams had orchestrated a work process among his fellows and with his senior, they might have discovered a way out of the dilemma. Adams, however, did not see the option of organizing the work, even when his own life was at stake. He did not exercise leadership because he saw no middle way at the time to challenge authority, respectfully.

Consider another soldier in Vietnam. Army lieutenant John Richards found himself charged in the closing days of the war with dangerous daily assignments to search out and destroy the enemy. Yet he and his platoon were fighting at a time when most American troops had already been withdrawn and the soldiers on the ground could see that the war, as a strategy of foreign policy, had been lost.

To Richards, this was an insane period of months. Following orders meant likely death for some of his men, for no apparent reason. Unlike some other lieutenants who, on patrol surrounding American bases, could fight for the purpose of protecting other soldiers, Richards could find little justification for risking the lives of his men. The challenge now in the face of strategic defeat was to cut American losses.

Richards thus faced sharply conflicting expectations. His formal authorization from his commanding officers required him to continue his dangerous assignments. His informal authorization from his men required him to protect them from unnecessary risk.

Richards weighed the problem and discussed it openly with his troops. One option was to disobey orders. They knew they could do so in subtle ways without incurring the risk of court martial. But for several soldiers, including Richards, disobeying orders was not an acceptable option. Military organizations required discipline, and respect for the chain of command was crucial to the long-term integrity of the institution to which Richards and others were committed. A soldier joined the army knowing that the whole was greater than the parts and that individual sacrifices of the highest order would be required, not only by military necessity but also by incompetence and mistake. However, some men, primarily draftees, had no interest in risking their lives for the sake of the institution and its code.

Richards, through hard and impassioned discussion with his men, found a way to accommodate both obedience and insubordination, to lead beyond his formal authority. He allowed his platoon to break into two groups, one that felt committed to the military and honored its norms, and one that did not. The committed group, headed by Richards, continued to fight and to risk their lives. The uncommitted group, *with the help of those fighting,* stayed out of combat as best they could. Each group respected the choice of the other. And most of them came home.

Adams and Richards shared somewhat similar situations. The two lieutenants had both formal and informal authority, and in both cases the authorizations were partially in conflict. The sources of their formal authority—the chain of command—wanted the mission accomplished. The sources of their informal authority—the bomber crew and the infantry soldiers—wanted protection from going out on a flawed assignment. In both cases, the lieutenants had frontline information that called the assignment into question. The challenge they identified required a change in norms and procedures.

However, the situations were structurally different. Adams would have had to exercise leadership up the chain of command, whereas Richards out in the field could shield his platoon from above, although at some risk. Perhaps this made it less difficult for Richards to see the possibility of leadership beyond his authority. Adams followed orders because he could not envision a way to challenge senior authority with both strength and respect. The two seemed mutually exclusive. At the time, he neither saw the leadership option nor mobilized his fellows to invent one. In contrast, Richards saw the possibility. By working the toughest of issues with his platoon and valuing conflicting perspectives within it, he generated a solution that honored institutional loyalty and, at the same time, individual differences. Adams and Richards both had frontline information and a clear issue. The difference between them lay in seeing and seizing the opportunity for creative deviance.

Establishing the Norm of Leadership Without Authority

Over the span of a career, Gandhi and Sanger gained informal authority, but both spent many years leading without it, mobilizing audiences who had no interest in paying attention to them. Indeed, large segments of the audiences they wished to engage were antagonistic. When they did gain informal authority from some of these audiences, it was not a precondition for leading but a product of leading. Though providing tools, the authority gained also acted as a constraint. In turn, the constraints served both as a limit and as a prod toward creativity. As they became prominent sources of meaning within their societies, Gandhi and Sanger began to carry the overlapping but conflicting expectations of mixed constituencies, pressuring them toward compromise and innovation. Gandhi innovated the strategy of nonviolent civil disobedience to speak to the British with moral authority. Sanger created a system of medically staffed clinics that would serve women while speaking to the medical profession. Both created authority for themselves starting with none.

The Vietnam officers Adams and Richards faced specific adaptive problems at one moment in time rather than the ongoing challenge of social adaptation. Yet, as with Gandhi and Sanger, the opportunity for leadership required going beyond their authority—particularly, their formal authority. In doing so, Richards faced grave risks, not only to his career but also to his platoon. Competing expectations drove him toward innovation. But his innovation might have been wrong; it might have resulted in increases rather than decreases in loss of men. He had to bear that uncertainty without the support of his superiors.

Distinguishing leadership and authority is more than an analytic and strategic tool. It is also a means to describe the personal experience of leading. As we often experience it in real-time, leadership means taking responsibility for hard problems beyond anyone's expectations. Ironically, many people wait until they gain authority, formal or informal, to begin leading. They see authority as a prerequisite. Yet those who do lead usually feel that they are taking action beyond whatever authority they have. How did leadership feel to Gandhi, Sanger, and Richards, even after gaining informal authority from certain constituents—Indian nationalists, anticolonial sympathizers, feminists, or members of the platoon? I suspect that they continued to experience leadership as an activity performed without authority, beyond expectations. They were not waiting for the coach's call.

9

Modulating the Provocation

The principles of leadership that we have discussed—identifying the adaptive challenge, keeping distress within a productive range, directing attention to ripening issues and not diversions, giving the work back to the people, and protecting voices of leadership in the community—apply to leaders with or without authority. However, because the benefits and constraints differ, those who lead without authority must adopt strategies and tactics that are at once more bold and subtle.

First, without authority, one has very little control over the holding environment. One can shape the stimulus, but one cannot manage the response: one cannot institute an organizing structure, pick a temporizing side issue, secure a new norm, or provide a calming presence. A leader without authority can spark debate, but he cannot orchestrate it. Without authority, a leader must regulate distress by modulating the provocation.

Furthermore, without authority one may have a frontline feel for a single issue in depth, but not as broad a sense of the multiplicity of challenges facing the community which affect its stance on any particular issue. This may render the leader without authority less aware of the other crucial problems confronting the society and the ripeness of his issue in relation to other pressing issues that may need to take priority.

In monitoring levels of distress, any leader has to find indicators for knowing both when to promote an unripe issue and whether the stress generated by an intervention falls within the productive range for that social system at that time. Different organizations and societies will have different sources and levels of resilience, and each social system requires serious analysis. But as a general rule, the leader operating without authority can read the authority figure as a barometer of issue ripeness and systemic stress because social systems generally charge authority figures with the particular job of resolving ripe issues.[1]

Second, in attracting and directing attention to an issue, a leader without authority has to take into account the special vulnerability of becoming a lightning rod. Rather than orchestrating the debate among competing factions, one becomes a faction readily targeted for attack. Of course, authority figures frequently get attacked as well, but the resources at their disposal for deflecting attention and letting others take the heat are often unavailable to leaders without authority.

Third, just as people look to authority to solve problems, leaders without authority commonly make the mistake of assuming that only authority figures have the power to affect change. As a result, there is a strong temptation to identify the authority figure as the audience for action: "If only we could bring *him* around, everyone else would move in the right direction." In general, however, people in power change their ways when the sources of their authority change the expectations. Their behavior is an expression of the community that authorizes them. Thus, a strategy that mobilizes the stakeholders in the community may be quite a bit more likely to get work done than the strategy of "challenging authority."

Selma, 1965

We have seen the story of Selma from the perspective of President Johnson's leading from high office. Now consider the same story from the perspective of those who led from the frontline.[2]

The first stirring of the Selma voting rights movement occurred in 1961, when Reverend Fred Reese, a science teacher at Hudson High School and newly elected president of the local black teachers' organization, read a statement to a meeting of all local teachers and administrators urging black teachers to attempt to register to vote in Dallas County. Fearful of recriminations, few black teachers heeded Reese. However, the seeds had been planted in Selma's black middle class for a voting rights movement.

By January 1963, when approximately 125 blacks were registered to vote in the County, Marie Foster, a dental hygienist, began to feel that something should be done to correct the low Negro voter registration rate. Her dental office was just above the small Dallas County Voters League, the only black civil rights organization in town (since the NAACP had been banned in Alabama), and she came into contact daily with Sam and Amelia Boynton, the former NAACP activists who ran it. With their encouragement, Foster spent nearly ten years trying to register, always failing "one or more pertinent questions," as the rejection form said, before gaining the vote.[3] Energized, she wanted to do more. As she describes:

I was just sitting around my house one day when I became angry because Negroes didn't seem to be getting anywhere in Selma. Only one hundred and twenty-something-odd were registered in the entire county at that time. Selma is just the largest city in the county. But there were a lot of Negroes in other parts of the county. And every time one of us went down to the courthouse to register, the registrar would be out to lunch or he would say it was closed for the day or would quiz you on something he knew you couldn't answer. One of their favorite questions was "How many bubbles are there in a bar of soap?"

So I was thinking about all of this and getting angrier by the moment. So I called my friend, Amelia Boynton, who is now Amelia Billips. She was active in the civil rights movement so I asked her what could be done about it. We ended up talking about what was going on around here. We didn't have any kind of movement then or any major registration effort. It took them years to register me, but Mrs. Boynton and I were both registered at that time, which had to have been the winter of 1963. Anyway, we discussed conducting a class to teach black folks how to fill out the application and how to act once they got down to the courthouse. You see, attitude could make a difference. They had to register a Negro every now and then so the ones they did register had the right attitudes. So it was stuff like that we wanted the people to know.

By February of 1963 Marie Foster had begun to conduct a voter registration class. She kept a daily roster of who attended classes and who passed the tests she and the other instructors gave. In the summer of 1963 she met Assistant Attorney General John Doar, head of the Civil Rights Division in the U.S. Department of Justice, who was working on a voting suit against Dallas County. At Doar's request, she allowed him to take her roster to Washington. She explained, "He wanted to let the folks in Washington know that things were being done in the voting area in certain places in Alabama." Still, the registration drive proceeded slowly: in two years of work, only 175 more blacks were registered in the county.

The same February that Foster had started voter registration classes, 22-year-old Bernard Lafayette, a college student and Freedom Rider, came to Selma, buoyed by Foster's efforts to organize. Lafayette represented the Student Non-Violent Coordinating Committee (SNCC)—an offshoot of King's organization, the Southern Christian Leadership Conference (SCLC), in Atlanta. In a serious, unimposing, and methodical manner, Lafayette spent months talking with blacks from all ranks of Selma society. But, according to J. L. Chestnut, the only black lawyer in Selma at the time, "Bernard would strike out with most of the preachers, the teachers, the middle class. In theory, these would be the very persons who would lead and staff a voter registration effort. But the ties they had to the white ruling hierarchy—the ties that established them as leaders—made them the least likely group of all to become involved. They had the most—the best jobs, the largest homes, the most prestige—and therefore the most to lose." As J. H. Owens, the president of all-black Selma University put it, "You can't go around walking in the face of white people one day and then beg them the next day to donate money to your school." A well-regarded high school teacher held Lafayette's efforts in similar low regard: "It's nothing but a mess. That boy ought to go home. He's gonna get the white people all stirred up, then he'll run back to Atlanta and we'll be picking up the pieces."[4]

For months, Lafayette was unable to generate even one mass meeting. Making little headway with adults, Lafayette then turned to organizing the students, believing that the parents would get involved when they saw their kids on the line. King's organization was successfully employing the same tactic in Birmingham that same spring, where a frightened and lethargic black community had come alive when Bull Connor, the infamous police chief, turned the fire hoses on its children and sent them off to jail. Lafayette, a young man himself, had a way with younger people. And they were ready to act. As Chestnut pointed out, "They didn't have jobs, houses, mortgages, or ties with the white power structure."

In early May 1963 Sam Boynton—the stalwart NAACP organizer and president of the Voters League—died. Lafayette seized his memorial service as the occasion to hold the first mass voter registration rally. Three-hundred and fifty people came, two thirds of them teenagers and students, along with the local press, Sheriff Clark, and several deputies. James Forman, head of SNCC, arrived from Atlanta and gave an earthy, bold, and provocative speech about "what black people were sick and tired of taking at the hands of the white man," and telling them "to come out in the open with their views on freedom and get themselves down to the registration office the next week to hasten the day of reckoning." People shouted, "Say it!" and "Amen." Now, both black and white people of Selma were alerted.[5]

One month later, on June 12, the night after Wallace's stand in the "schoolhouse door" at the University of Alabama, two white men attacked and beat Lafayette with the butt of a rifle. With eyes and face swollen and bruised, and with blood caked-up on his T-shirt, Lafayette saw another opportunity. "This is the symbol we need," he said. He spent weeks wearing that T-shirt, which became, as Chestnut recalls, "a sort of turning point in terms of public sympathy in Black Selma. Even the blacks who were most apprehensive about him couldn't help but respect his commitment and courage, and they damn sure didn't go for anybody beating him. People were impressed that he didn't leave town."[6]

After Lafayette returned to college Marie Foster, Fred Reese, Amelia Boynton, and other black activists in Selma's Voters League continued the mass meetings. A replacement from SNCC helped in the effort. Marie Foster recalls what went on during the meetings:

Sheriff Jim Clark and his deputies would come to just about all of our meetings to observe and to so-called keep the order. In a way we did not want them there, being as how they tried to degrade us. In another way, we were glad they came because we could involve them and speak to them. The organizers would ask me to bring up a topic in black history every night, you know, to make the black man know that he was somebody, and that he had just cause to hold up his head . . . I would stand up in the pulpit and I would tell them, "You know I thought white people were supposed to have a lot of sense"—and I'd be looking right at Clark or his men—"but it seems that Selma white folks don't have much sense. I am sick of going into these stores running up two and three hundred dollar bills. You mean to tell me that our money is good but we are not good enough to be called MR. Brown or MISS Johnson." And the crowds would go wild clapping and cheering in agreement.

Finally, in July of 1964, the authorities stepped in. Dallas County Sheriff Jim Clark persuaded Alabama Circuit Court Judge James Hare to prohibit Selma's black citizens from meeting in groups of more than five.[7] After a while Selma's blacks began to meet secretly, and soon decided that the injunction would have to be broken. In late summer 1964 they contacted Dr. King at the national headquarters of the SCLC in Atlanta, Georgia.[8] He and his staff had been discussing the possibility of conducting a voting rights campaign. They knew that in the wake of the Civil Rights Act of 1964, the issue of voting rights was not yet ripe. President Johnson had told them that it would take a few years before anybody would be ready to pass more civil rights legislation.[9] But the movement was not about to stop pressing. On the contrary, the victories of that year strengthened their resolve to fight for the right to vote. If the issue was not yet ripe, they would ripen it. No more waiting. King explained their attitude in his "Letter from Birmingham Jail" the year before. In response to eight white clergyman who had published a statement decrying King's "unwise and untimely" activities, and who asked King to wait and give the new city government in Birmingham a chance, King wrote,

> Perhaps it is easy for those who have never felt the stinging darts of segregation to say, "Wait." But when you have seen vicious mobs lynch your mothers and fathers at will and drown your sisters and brothers at whim; when you have seen hate-filled policemen curse, kick and even kill your black brothers and sisters; when you see the

vast majority of your twenty million Negro brothers smothering in an airtight cage of poverty in the midst of an affluent society; when you suddenly find your tongue twisted and your speech stammering as you seek to explain to your six-year-old daughter why she can't go to the public amusement park that has just been advertised on television, and see tears welling up in her eyes when she is told that Funtown is closed to colored children, and see ominous clouds of inferiority beginning to form in her little mental sky, and see her beginning to distort her personality by developing an unconscious bitterness toward white people; when you have to concoct an answer for a five-year-old son who is asking: "Daddy, why do white people treat colored people so mean?"; when you take a cross-country drive and find it necessary to sleep night after night in the uncomfortable corners of your automobile because no hotel will accept you; when you are humiliated day in and day out by nagging signs reading "white" and "colored"; when your first name becomes "nigger," your middle name becomes "boy" (however old you are) and your last name becomes "John," and your wife and mother are never given the respected title "Mrs."; when you are harried by day and haunted by night by the fact that you are a Negro, living constantly at tiptoe stance, never quite knowing what to expect next, and are plagued with inner fears and outer resentments; when you are forever fighting a degenerating sense of "nobodiness"—then you will understand why we find it difficult to wait.[10]

To King and his colleagues, the country had to face its own internal contradiction: the gap between what it said and what it did. Would it live according to its professed value of equal opportunity?

King's strategic challenge was to dramatize that question on a nationwide scale. If the movement could find a way to get people countrywide to face that contradiction, perhaps policies would change. As they saw it, they would have to expose more fully the hidden brutalities of racism. To compel the country to pay attention, they would disturb the daily equilibrium of people's lives and jar people into focusing on the ruthless cost of racist voting policies. But letters and words alone would not do it.

At the time of the call from Selma, King and his strategists had already decided to take action and had been searching the South for cities likely to react brutally to peaceful black demonstrations. Now, with this call, Selma seemed like the right place. In Jim Clark, Dallas County had just the right kind of sheriff. In George Wallace, Alabama had just the right kind of governor. And black Selma was ready to take action. Ralph Abernathy, cofounder of the SCLC, described the thinking of the organizers.

> We had been circling around Selma, trying to decide whether or not we could stir up enough trouble to force the federal government to act on the persistent denial of voting rights to blacks in the South. For several reasons [Selma] seemed like a . . . good place to make our stand. First, the local authorities were unreasonable and intransigent . . . they were unwilling to make any compromises and seemed likely to respond with oppressive measures if challenged. Sheriff Clark . . . had a temper that could get him into trouble, a temper we were counting on, because when he was angry, he could use his power with . . . ruthless abandon. So we would get our confrontation on television, the kind of visual conflict that would best define for the viewing public what we were up against. Second, the local black churches were powerful, and there were several leaders on whom we could rely for support . . . Third, the voting issue itself required emphasis at this particular stage of the movement and no community so clearly [as Selma] reflected the need for intervention in this matter.[11]

They announced that the campaign would be launched on January 1, 1965, one hundred and two years after Lincoln's Emancipation Proclamation had taken effect.

City and county officials in Selma reacted to the news by trying to maintain the status quo, but their efforts were complicated by a split in their authority structure. Selma was the county seat for Dallas County, Alabama, and voting registration took place within the county courthouse which sat in the middle of town. That meant that the county police had jurisdiction over the courthouse itself, while the city police had jurisdiction over the rest of the city. They shared the same end in response to the demonstrations, but had sharply divergent strategies. County officials reflexively tried to suppress the protest; city officials tried to accommodate it.

Selma had just elected a new mayor, Joe Smitherman, an appliance salesman who had ousted the incumbent with a pledge to bring in new industry, which also meant preserving the city's peace and stability. That meant no displays of public violence such as those that brought notoriety to Birmingham and its police chief. Consequently, Smitherman appointed the relatively progressive Wilson Baker to head the police department. Baker, who had taught law enforcement for six years at the University of Alabama and had studied the last decade's interaction between the civil rights movement and police, hoped to defuse any protests by quietly meeting some of the protester's demands: "If you give a little, you won't have to give a lot," he counseled. "Let 'em march and it'll peter out."[12] In late November, as soon as he heard of King's plan to march in Selma, he flew to Washington to persuade the Justice department to get King to delay the march six months, by which time he said he would get the County Board of Registrars quietly to register black people in larger numbers.[13]

The Justice Department in Washington saw in Baker's plan a way to prevent more civil rights disorder. The Department had lived through years of unrest and quite courageously had repeatedly protected civil rights activists in the South. They were not eager for more turbulence. Burke Marshall, head of the Civil Rights Division, was persuaded by Baker, who was nothing like the defiant and bullying lawmen he had occasionally known in the South. So Marshall called Dr. King in Atlanta and made the request. But King refused. "The die is cast," said Marshall. "They're coming to Selma in January." Then, as Baker prepared to leave, Robert Kennedy, the outgoing Attorney General who had been sitting in on the meetings, spoke up. "You know," he said to Baker, "if you're smart enough, you can beat him [King] at his own game."[14]

Baker was smart enough. His strategy of pacification was simple. He knew that a demonstration would draw little attention unless it was resisted. And Baker did not plan to resist. Indeed, he planned to protect the marchers from any disturbance that might be caused by angry white citizens. Baker would maintain equilibrium by letting the demonstrators wear themselves out. As long as the city's response was peaceful, he would win. There might be arrests for violating Hare's injunction, but no spectacles.

Baker's formal authority, however, was limited by his jurisdiction.

He could not control what might occur at the county courthouse itself or on the other side of the Edmund Pettus Bridge, past the city line. Baker's problem was not only Selma's angry white citizens but also Sheriff Jim Clark of the county police and Colonel Al Lingo of the Alabama state troopers. They would brook no disobedience of the law by black people. In the spirit of Bull Connor, "The only way to stop 'em is to stop 'em."[15] Clark and Lingo meant to keep blacks in their place—at any cost.

At first, Baker seemed to be winning the contest of wills. He repeatedly defused the daily civil rights demonstrations of January and early February by maintaining civility. King countered by taking more dramatic measures to galvanize attention. He got himself put in jail and wrote to *The New York Times*: "This is Selma, Alabama. There are more Negroes in jail with me than there are on the voting rolls."[16] But the message did not quite get across because Baker prevented violence and thus staved off notoriety. Baker, quick on his feet, kept both Clark and King largely outmaneuvered. Indeed, by February King and his strategists began to doubt the usefulness of Selma to demonstrate the issue of voting rights.

But then, on February 18, state troopers broke up a registration march in neighboring Marion, Alabama. One of the troopers began clubbing an older woman, and when her seventeen-year-old grandson, Jimmee Lee Jackson, intervened to shield her, the trooper shot Jackson through the stomach.[17] Jackson died four days later, and people at the funeral began saying, "Damn it, we ought to carry his body over to George Wallace in Montgomery."[18]

King seized this idea and tragedy as a way to escalate the campaign. They would move across the city line. He announced plans to march from Selma to the state capitol at Montgomery fifty miles away. King intended to go around Baker and challenge the county and state. The strategy worked. On Sunday morning, March 7, as the marchers crossed the city line, they came under the jurisdiction of Sheriff Clark and Colonel Lingo. After two months of pent up frustration, not only with the civil rights activists but also with Wilson Baker's success at quarantining them, Clark and Lingo unleashed their horses, tear gas, and billy clubs while the nation watched in horror. At once, Baker, Clark, and Lingo had lost. King and the demonstrators had won.[19]

Operating Beyond One's Authority

The people who first exercised leadership in Selma had no authority to organize for voting rights. Fred Reese, head of the black teachers' association, had formal authority for matters related to schools, but no formal authority over matters pertaining to voter registration. His pleas to black teachers went largely ignored. His informal authority as clergyman, teacher, and member of the black middle class in Selma gave him the minimum resources for leadership: some place from which to stand and intervene. Yet his informal authority did not take him far since it did not apply to matters of civil rights; he had no track record. He was trusted and respected as a clergyman and teacher, not as a lawyer or political activist. Reverend Reese spoke up beyond his authority, formal and informal. Most preachers in Selma did not. And though few listened immediately to Reese, he planted seeds that sprouted. As they sprouted, he began to accrue informal authority and its power. When black teachers finally came around to join the demonstrations, the mobilization of black Selma took a quantum leap forward.

Marie Foster, like Reverend Reese, also led without authority. A dental hygienist, she had no formal authority in the black community in the arena of civil rights. Her informal authority consisted of the respect that came from being a middle class black professional. That gave her membership in the community and a place to stand, but nothing more. The community did not look to her to speak up, yet she did. Challenging a way of life endured for over one hundred years, she pushed her people to live in the new discomfort and danger zone of overt defiance. They were hardly eager to incur public humiliation, the loss of jobs, and lynching. When she questioned the black community's aspirations and commitment, she put herself and her community at risk.

She began, quite naturally, by turning to someone with some informal authority in civil rights, Amelia Boynton. Together they started educating black citizens in registering to vote. Leadership would require learning, not just by whites but by black people as well. The education campaign gave Foster and Boynton a new constituency, and because they spoke to aspirations long suppressed and deeply felt, they gathered informal authority. Black people in Selma began to look to them for direction, protection, and order in organizing for voting rights.

Bernard Lafayette set his sights on Selma because he had seen the dedication of Reese, Foster, Boynton, and their small operation, the Voters League. He gained their support, which provided a small measure of informal authority, and he had his base of formal authority, SNCC, which could provide tactical advice and moral encouragement. SNCC, however, meant little if anything to anybody in Selma, and few people were heeding the advice of the Voters League. For the most part, Lafayette engaged in thoroughly unauthorized activities, speaking twenty hours a day with people who paid him very little mind. Yet he laid the groundwork with both adults and youth. When Sam Boynton died, Lafayette saw the opportunity to turn the death of one of Selma's most prominent activists into a catalytic event. And when he turned his own beaten body into a walking illustration of the issue, he provoked a change in black thinking and acquired the power that comes of respect. Mass meetings started happening weekly.

Unlike the activists in Selma, King had a great deal of authority. While he had a small base of formal authority as head of the SCLC, most of King's authority was informal. Since the Montgomery bus boycott of 1956, he had become the singular repository for the aspirations and pains of the black community, particularly in the South. He had gained their admiration and trust because of his courage and skill in mobilizing them. They provided his primary source of power. Yet perhaps just as significant was the esteem in which millions of sympathetic white Americans held him. He spoke and represented their values in action, even if they had not yet begun to bring their behavior into harmony with those values. He moved them, and they gave him informal authority—moral authority. Indeed, in 1964 the white world had given him the Nobel Prize for Peace.

King's informal authority, like Gandhi's, gave him major resources: attention, the power to frame the issues, and some power to pace the work, to turn up the heat or lower it. People everywhere paid attention to him because he represented either a threat or a worthy challenge. The activists in Selma were counting on the attention he would bring in order to contain local hostility: brutality avoids the limelight. At the same time, the attention King could bring might force a more measured expression of brutality into the limelight, where local norms would be subject to scrutiny by the larger society, and racism would be seen for what it was. Moreover, King's informal authority gave him the power to set the context for action, whether it was integrated buses or voting rights. Setting the terms of the debate enabled him to focus attention on the issues he thought were ripe, and frame them in a way that made them understandable to a wide public audience. He gave meaning to events. When whites began to give in a little and blacks in Selma wanted to accept the offer and back off on the demonstrations, he had the authority to remind them "to keep [their] eyes on the prize: This movement [is] about winning citizenship for black people in America, not about having a march in Selma."[20] He was able to keep up the heat.

King's power, however, was by no means absolute. After Selma, once black anguish and aspirations had been unleashed, not even King had the informal authority to provide the necessary holding environment and direct them productively. This became clear six months later in August 1965 when Los Angeles erupted in the Watts riots, only weeks after passage of the Voting Rights Act. King surely had considerable power. He could call forth and control demonstrations, as he did in Selma, but even his authority within the black community had sharp limits.

Reading the Authority Figure as a Barometer

When he demonstrated in Selma, King perturbed the nation. Millions of Americans were forced to confront their own complicity with the hard realities of racism. But because he led people who had not asked to be led, going beyond whatever authority some Americans had given him, King had no control over the system's resilience. He could adjust the level of challenge, but he could not increase the system's capacity to tolerate it. In leading people who gave him no authority, his success and survival depended on his own sensitivity to the severity of the stress he generated and the pace at which he did so. His interventions had to take into account the level of distress the larger system could withstand.

A leader needs indicators. But because he is inclined to focus on a single issue, one who leads beyond his authority will often have little information about the other sources of stress in the system. He may challenge the system too far and too fast and invite his own suppression. He has to understand, therefore, the response patterns of the community into which he intervenes. Inevitably, he gains this understanding through trial and error in action, by analyzing the sources of his wounds as he gets them. But are there other, better ways for leaders operating beyond their authority to know when they have gone too far? What, for example, should the Chinese students have known in Tiananmen Square before they pushed the government so far in the spring of 1989 that it smashed them and avoided the issues they exposed?[21]

One barometer of systemic distress is the behavior of people in senior positions of authority. Connected into the many issues facing the whole community, senior authorities tend to respond as a sum of the forces at play. They are called into action as the stressed community gazes upward for direction, protection, and order. They often react to these appeals by taking action to restore equilibrium, and that reaction indicates when the community has reached the limits of its tolerance—at least in the view of the persons in authority.

Of course, in the same positions of authority, different people will act in different ways. They will each have their own distinct, personal styles; and while some will encourage their constituents to confront change, others will cling to old realities. But if authorities do not always lead, they almost always act at some point to reduce stress, which they are adept at perceiving. In general, authorities are exquisitely sensitive to the fears and expectations of those who authorize them, as they must be in order to keep their jobs. Authorities are at least partly reactive: they may be puppets as much as puppeteers, and, as puppets, may provide useful cues to those who lead without authority.

Thus, King had to keep his eyes on Johnson, and the local activists in Selma had to keep their eyes on Joe Smitherman, Wilson Baker, Jim Clark, and George Wallace. The movement's strategy and tactics had to account for these personalities and the pressures of their positions and constituencies. Attacks by authority would be symptomatic of systemic distress. Leading without authority, therefore, became a sort of modern ballet—somewhat choreographed, somewhat improvised—in response to those in authority, with the wider public as the audience.

As the level of black aspiration and rhetoric rose in Selma, white people began to feel challenged. Sheriff Clark started showing up at black meetings. His attendance at these meetings was a measure of the stress they provoked. When he then arranged a year later for a court order prohibiting meetings of more than five people, he provided a further signal of intensifying stress in the white community. The authority system had gone into action to restore equilibrium.

That meant that the strategic decisions for the activists would begin to involve much higher stakes. In the past, civil rights workers had often backed down at this point in the process for fear of being brutally suppressed. The local white community, stressed beyond its limit of tolerance, was expected to recoil in the harshest way. Indeed, had Selma been left to its own devices without the presence of federal and media attention, it would surely have beaten down the black challenge.

But Selma was not alone. By 1965 civil rights activists had learned over decades how to use the federal government to contain the local disequilibrium they generated. Thus, the strategic decision for Reese, Foster, and Boynton was whether or not to move the issue into the national arena, using media attention and federal authority to prevent a brutal "quick fix" restoration of local order by local authorities.

They decided to push Selma past the breaking point, and that meant that the nation and the federal government would have to provide the holding environment. It also meant that people might die. As much as possible, national attention and federal force would have to contain and control the distress in Selma and its potential for violence. Reese, Foster, and Boynton called on King to turn Selma into a national symbol of injustice.

Now the strategic challenge was King's. He and his strategists would have to monitor the level of distress they would generate. At the local level, they aimed to move beyond the limit of tolerance in order to provoke the kind of brutal work avoidance that would awaken the national conscience. But at the national level, they would have to keep the distress within the proper range—above the threshold for stimulating public and political engagement with the issue, but below the breaking point. At all costs, they wanted to avert work avoidance on a national scale, which might occur if people had an excuse 'for rationalizing away racism and police brutality. Consequently, King's organization, the SCLC, tried very hard to restrain the militant forces within the black community. When Malcolm X came to Selma in early February, King's strategists did everything they could to maintain their control over the demonstrations, even though, as it turned out, Malcolm X did nothing incendiary.[22] Were the nation to feel threatened above its limit of tolerance, King and his movement might lose the whole campaign.

King and the SCLC monitored how hard they could push the nation by monitoring the actions of the President. As senior authority figure for the nation, President Johnson's responses would indicate how well the public at large could tolerate the adaptive challenge issuing from Selma. As the issue began to heat up, everything looked good. In his State of the Union address in mid-January, Johnson spoke briefly of the need for a new law to protect the voting rights of black people. In early February, while King briefly sat in a Selma jail, Johnson issued a statement reiterating his support for voting rights. Within the Justice Department, Johnson reactivated plans to draft a voting rights bill. Then King, after his release from jail, requested a meeting at the White House with Johnson and left feeling encouraged about the President's intention to submit strong voting rights legislation.[23] So far, Johnson did not seem alarmed by the demonstrations. Yet Johnson continued to voice doubt about the timing. The nation and Congress did not seem ready to pass a bill with real potency that would give federal officials control over voter registration.

So King turned up the heat on February 22, announcing his plan for the fifty-mile march to Montgomery. By early March, Congress began to soften. On March 2 Everett Dirksen came out in favor of voting rights legislation. But on the next day, the Senate Rules Committee voted not to recommend a change in the Senate's cloture rules, which made passage of strong legislation much less likely. As a result, King held steady with his plans for the march. On Friday, March 5, King met with President Johnson once again. Apparently, Johnson said nothing to King to discourage the demonstrations.[24] Yet he also could not promise that the voting rights bill would contain the clauses that King thought were crucial to its success: the use of federal registrars in those counties that denied the vote to black people. If King were reading Johnson as a barometer on how hard to push, King was pushing just the right amount: not too much, but not too little. Johnson was neither unduly disturbed nor ready to act.

The march took place on Sunday, March 7. After the brutality of that day, the level of national disequilibrium rose steeply. The media called it Bloody Sunday. Suddenly, thousands of people cared about this issue. White people were demonstrating in major cities across the country, and millions seemed to be calling on Johnson and the Congress to take action.[25] People were learning. King held firm, and, fortunately, so did Johnson. On Sunday evening, King announced another march for Tuesday and invited clergy from all denominations across the nation to join with him.

But behind the scenes, as the level of distress reached its peak, the negotiating began. On Monday, March 8, lawyers from the SCLC appealed to Federal Judge Frank Johnson Jr. for a temporary restraining order to prevent Clark and Lingo from interfering with Tuesday's march. King and Abernathy thought that enough blood had been shed to make the point to the nation. Jimmee Lee Jackson had been the first person ever killed in an SCLC campaign.[26] The civil rights movement did not need another brutal beating or more deaths to get its point across. It simply needed to keep the nation's attention focused on the issue.

Although sympathetic to the cause of civil rights, Judge Johnson disliked the idea of a massive march so soon after Sunday. Instead of restraining Clark and Lingo, he asked the activists to delay their demonstration until he could hear the State's case on Thursday, March 11. Perhaps the Judge sympathized with widespread public dismay over the prospect of a poorly planned fifty-mile march, with no real safeguards against violence. Even a federal restraining order could not really guarantee a safe journey. Judge Johnson saw no need to rush.[27]

King, however, rebuffed the Judge's request for delay. He wanted to maintain momentum. In response, the Judge turned his request into an order.[28] Now, a *federal* judge had drawn the line. He enjoined SCLC not to march until after Thursday's hearing. That meant that the demonstration would violate not only state law but federal law as well. King was coming up against the nation's boundary—its limit of tolerance. Breaking federal law would not be so easily accepted by Congress and the public.

On Monday night President Johnson sent a mediator aboard Air Force One to negotiate with King to delay the march. This indicated clearly that King had reached President Johnson's limit. If Tuesday's demonstration turned into another bloody spectacle, the nation would blame President Johnson, and not just state and local officials, for failing to step in. Furthermore, Johnson could not sit passively by in the face of a federal court order. King would go too far if he marched again, unleashing violence. By Monday evening King and Abernathy were not sure what to do. Thousands of people had traveled to Selma that day to march with them on Tuesday. Could they simply call the whole thing off? And if they could, would doing so take all the pressure off Congress and the nation?

LeRoy Collins, President Johnson's emissary as the new head of the Justice Department's Community Relations Service, woke up King and Abernathy early in the morning on Tuesday to work out a deal. Instead of undertaking the march to Montgomery, he suggested that they make a symbolic journey, retracing the route on Bloody Sunday and stopping at the point on the Edmund Pettus Bridge where the beatings had taken place. Collins said he would get Clark and Lingo to agree.

For King and Abernathy, leadership meant keeping the disturbance within a range that Johnson could tolerate. So they marched with thousands singing, "Ain't Gonna Let Nobody Turn Me Round." And when they reached the middle of the bridge, King and Abernathy stopped, held a prayer, and then turned around. The point had been made. Distress had reached the limit of tolerance, and the pressure had been maintained just below that limit as the nation watched the procession and held its breath.

Becoming a Lightning Rod of Attention

Attention has its costs and benefits. Authority figures, like silverback gorillas in mountain forests, draw attention by virtue of their height and position. For them, being the center of attention is not necessarily dangerous. Groups are inclined to protect their authority figures for quite a while, out of habit as much as fear of the disorientation that might follow their dismissal. It takes a prolonged period of disappointment for a community to turn on its authorities.

But without authority, a leader stands relatively naked before the people, often appearing to be not only the identifier of a distressing problem but also the source of the distress itself. All eyes turn to the person who raises disturbing questions, and some of those eyes are hostile. Groups can avoid problems, at least temporarily, by shooting the messenger. Thus, although attention is a major tool of leadership, it also makes one a likely target of attack. If a person lacks authority, people take issue not only with the substance of his point of view but with his right to raise it. Indeed, they often attack the right and ignore the substance.

The mechanisms for killing the messenger are varied and subtle depending on the culture, the organization, and the problem. Yet attacks often follow a general pattern: first, a person or faction raises a difficult question that generates some distress by pointing to a potential conflict over values and purpose, norms and organizational relationships, power, or strategy. Second, in response, the disquieted members of the system will turn their gaze to a senior authority figure, expecting him to restore equilibrium. Finally, the authority figure, pressed by these expectations to reduce distress, feeling emotionally compelled to act, neutralizes or silences the "problem" faction, directly or indirectly. These moves happen fast. The authority figure may not even be aware of the way others have gotten him to perform the role of executioner on their behalf.

A major challenge of leadership, therefore, is to draw attention and then deflect it to the questions and issues that need to be faced. To do so, *one has to provide a context for action.* The audience needs to readily comprehend the purpose of unusual or deviant behavior so that it focuses less on the behavior itself, or the person, and more on its meaning.

Martin Luther King Jr. became the lightning rod of attention on civil rights. His every move and behavior became subject to scrutiny, not simply by the media and the public but also by the authority structure. Just as Sheriff Clark sat in on the early voting rights meetings in Selma, FBI Director J. Edgar Hoover tapped King's daily phone conversations, gathering data that would discredit him if made public.

King knew of the wiretaps; he knew of the dangers he ran by

operating at the focal point. Always, he was at risk for making mistakes—both personal mistakes, like sexual indiscretions, and tactical mistakes, of which there were many.[29] King repeatedly ran the risk of public exposure and humiliation. The slightest error could be used against him. Being the lightning rod of attention meant that many people would find a humiliating downfall entertaining.

But he could not hide from scrutiny and still maintain pressure on the nation's conscience. The solution for King, both sincere and strategic, was to become a living embodiment of the issue to which he wanted to draw attention. King turned the dilemma of becoming a lightning rod to his advantage. The attention inevitably directed toward him would then be directed toward the issues of civil rights. Personal events were given larger meanings.

Bernard Lafayette made the same choice when he spent three weeks walking around in a blood-stained T-shirt. So did Gandhi by spinning cotton each day and by wearing his traditional loincloth and homespun shawl, even to Buckingham Palace to visit the King.[30] So did Sanger when civic authorities in Boston refused her the right to speak in 1929. She stood silent before a crowd at Ford Hall Forum with a band of tape plastered across her mouth while the Harvard historian Arthur Schlesinger Sr. read a brief statement: "As a pioneer fighting for a cause, I believe in free speech. As a propagandist, I see immense advantages in being gagged. It silences me, but it makes millions of others talk and think about the cause in which I live."[31]

King, as well, would have to embody personally the issue he stood for. That meant that he would have to struggle constantly with himself to live according to a very high set of standards. In the wake of the events in Selma, Reese, Foster, and Boynton had the same hard personal challenge. All became objects of idealization and scrutiny. Their leadership could not take place behind the scenes—like President Johnson's leadership on voting rights. Thus, King had to use his person as a dramatic tool. Indeed, Abernathy and others deliberately placed him at the focal point in his early days of the 1956 bus boycott in Montgomery because King, a newcomer to town, was willing to take the heat and had the rhetorical skill to use it.

Yet however much King embodied civil rights, *he* never became the issue. The distinction is important. King only *represented* the issue, and most people, I think, could tell the difference. The context of his activity was clear. Few people thought King was the source of the civil rights perspective, even if they knew him as chief spokesman and strategist. When he put himself in jail, the import was plainly symbolic. When he was killed, few thought the cause of civil rights was dead, even if it was strategically at an impasse. Indeed, even after his death he continued to represent civil rights because the cause was alive in others.

President Johnson's behavior illustrates the other side of the distinction. Johnson went way beyond representing the cause of the Vietnam War. By virtue of taking on the role of solitary decision-maker, he *became* the issue—his judgment, dishonesty, and style. It became Johnson's War because there was no other obvious way to make sense of events except to attribute them to him. Consequently, when Johnson withdrew in March 1968 from running again for President, many people thought the war was over. They failed to see that he had been a puppet as much as puppeteer. The continuation of the war represented not simply the actions of the President but potent trends and conflicting perspectives within the American polity. Rather than orchestrate these conflicts, Johnson had stood alone, making it appear that he alone was the issue. In contrast, on civil rights, as with much of his domestic program, Johnson gave adaptive work back to the society.

And so did King when he produced the spectacle of the police beating the marchers for the watching eyes of national television. Cynical commentators might try to portray the marching blacks as the witless puppets of the manipulative King. But such a contortion of facts would not explain away the television images of state troopers and policemen beating defenseless people who asked for the right to vote. By dramatizing forcefully the contradictions within the nation, King made people feel the contradictions in their own attitudes. In this way, he deflected attention from himself to the issues and spread responsibility for working them through. The nation could not easily attribute its contradictions to King.

Mobilizing the Stakeholders

Leaders without authority—deviants, as they often are perceived—have to think hard about where they direct their challenge. Indeed, the better the quality of their argument, the more likely it will touch on an internal contradiction in the community and thus arouse or aggravate conflicts, which then call forth authoritative efforts to restore order. Hence, a leader who pushes the authority figure in an attempt to solve important problems should expect the authority figure to strike back, not necessarily from personal motivations but from the community's pressure on him to maintain equilibrium.

Authority's rejection of challenge represents a complex dynamic. A leader without authority can easily oversimplify the complexity of the situation by interpreting the rejection as an indication of a flawed presentation, an inadequate argument, or the personal bias of the authority figure. Certainly, there may be some truth here and important lessons to draw in devising the next move. However, the rejection generally originates with the community of stakeholders that resist a disturbance of their equilibrium. The authority is their proxy. Indeed, the authority may be personally sympathetic but may see no options, given the expectations he carries. Thus, returning to the authority figure with an "improved version" of the presentation that takes his biases into account often leads nowhere.[32]

Any challenge must mobilize the real stakeholders, not just their proxies. One begins with four questions: Who are the primary stakeholders in this issue, and how might they need to change their ways? What expectations do they have of their authority? How could the authority figure begin to reshape those expectations to provide himself with latitude to take action? And what could one do, leading without authority, to reshape those expectations to pave his way?

The events in Selma illustrate the principle of mobilizing the stakeholders. Fred Reese, Marie Foster, Amelia Boynton, and Bernard Lafayette did not take on the authority system in Selma directly. They took on their own relevant public—black citizens whose compliance with the system helped to keep it in place. No awakening of white citizens could precede awakening black people to stand behind their own aspirations. Had any one of these four activists staged a lone demonstration on the steps of the courthouse, Sheriff Clark would have disposed of them easily, while both white and black citizens watched, many with glee, many with despair, at the futility of the act.

Similarly, Abernathy and King did not take on the President directly. Abernathy describes their moment of reckoning on Tuesday morning after praying on the Edmund Pettus Bridge.

> When I finally finished [the prayer] and lifted my head, I turned around. The troopers were gone. They had retreated to one side and left before us an empty highway, a straight shot to Montgomery, the asphalt glistening as brightly as the Yellow Brick Road. It was as if I had prayed them out of our way.
>
> I looked at Martin [Luther King] and he looked at me. For an instant I'm sure he must have been tempted to plunge forward into that gap, with troopers on both sides of the road. Maybe that's what George Wallace and Jim Clark wanted us to do. Had we broken our word and violated the injunction, we would have been fair game. They could have arrested all of us—or as many as they could haul away—and we would have been discredited by everyone in authority. Even Lyndon Johnson could not have defended our actions, if indeed he had wanted to. And we could never again have looked Collins in the eye.[33]

Abernathy and King avoided the trap of directing their challenge at the top authority figure. Instead, they targeted the nation and, indirectly, Congress. The President would be expected to act on civil rights only insofar as his constituents gave him leeway. The best the President might do would be to hold steady while the pressure on the nation and on Congress increased—while the issue became a public priority. Then the President's latitude would widen and he could shepherd new civil rights legislation through Congress. The behavior of authority would be changed as social sentiment changed.

In fact, this had been the civil rights leaders' general strategy for several years. They had used it before. Following sustained demonstrations in Birmingham and in preparation for the March on Washington in August 1963 to push for civil rights legislation, for example, King and his colleagues had targeted the public, not President Kennedy. As a result, Kennedy had the latitude to get behind them in his hastily arranged but formal and dramatic speech on civil rights in June 1963.[34] To be sure, King and Abernathy lobbied and monitored those in authority, but they aimed their actions toward the larger relevant publics: black communities needing encouragement, discipline, and organization, and white communities across the land, many of which could be persuaded to promote civil rights—if forced to acknowledge that their legal system betrayed the values the law was supposed to represent. King explained the strategy in his "Letter from Birmingham Jail" in April 1963:

> You may well ask: "Why direct action? Why sit-ins, marches and so forth? Isn't negotiation a better path?" You are quite right in calling for negotiation. Indeed, this is the very purpose of direct action. Nonviolent direct action seeks to create such a crisis and foster such a tension that a community which has constantly refused to negotiate is forced to confront the issue. It seeks so to dramatize the issue that it can no longer be ignored. My citing the creation of tension as part of the work of the nonviolent-resister may sound rather shocking. But I must confess that I am not afraid of the word "tension." I have earnestly opposed violent tension, but there is a type of constructive, nonviolent tension which is necessary for growth.[35]

To use this strategy, King and his collaborators had to become masters in the use of the media for public communication. However improvised their tactics, they were dramatists in the shaping of teaching moments for each of their audiences, be it rallies, sermons, sit-ins, marches, boycotts, letters from prison, or freedom rides. At the end of the day, some people might have to take a beating or die, but learning took place. Attitudes and habits changed. Values were clarified and behaviors became more consonant with them. Selma lawyer J. L. Chestnut describes in retrospect his reaction to the fact that 9,000 black people had registered to vote in just six months:

> To say I was impressed would be an understatement. I was beside myself. These were people who'd been told for generations that voting is white folk's business, stay away from the courthouse, don't antagonize white people. We came from nowhere to somewhere in an awfully short period of time. A voteless, hopeless people had moved in a matter of months to a position of almost being able to elect our own leaders, to govern ourselves . . . This was a monumental achievement and Selma couldn't be the same again.
>
> After centuries of ducking and dodging, black people had come out of the closet—and they liked the air. Folk still were concerned for their jobs, their mortgages and bank loans, but the blanket fear of

upsetting anybody white was lifting. The reign of terror was over . . . That's what America is all about—freedom to breathe, freedom from fear. That was fundamental. King often said, "The vote is not the ball game, but it gets you inside the ballpark." That's where we were at the end of 1965. We had gotten into the ballpark. Now we had to learn to play the game.[36]

Part IV

Staying Alive

10

Assassination

Leadership is dangerous, with or without authority, because the stresses of adaptive work can be severe. Ask a white man or woman in Selma to give up the only way of life they have known, handed down to them by their parents, reinforced through school and friendships, and you ask them to undergo a sustained period of disorientation and distress. Severe distress can make people cruel; empathy, compassion, and flexibility of mind are sacrificed to the desperate desire for order.

People who lead frequently bear scars from their efforts to bring about adaptive change. Often they are silenced. On occasion, they are killed. If leadership must always demand great personal sacrifice, then our communities and organizations must wait for the occasional hero. And many of us are indeed waiting. Unfortunately, the adaptive pressures on us wait for no one. If we want to generate more leadership in our society, we have two options. We can embolden a greater number of people toward heroic effort, and we can investigate ways to lead that reduce the likelihood of personal injury, even to the hero, so that more people can step into the fray. Although these avenues are not mutually exclusive, we follow the second route here. To do this, we first investigate the question, Why is leading dangerous?

Leaders are always failing somebody. With or without authority, someone exercising leadership will be shouldering the pains and aspirations of a community and frustrating at least some people within it. Adaptive work often demands loss. Even a bright new innovation or scientific discovery will meet resistance from those that feel threatened. At the very best, the loss will be temporary and more a matter of perception than reality. The future may be better, but some must bear the risk.[1] The black teachers of Selma, representing the small black middle class, strongly resisted joining in the civil rights demonstrations in 1965 for fear that they would lose the measure of respect, authority, and security they had worked hard to achieve. In the end, they did not have to sustain that loss, but at the moment of decision, to join in or stay away, the perceived risk of loss powerfully shaped their behavior. Indeed, overcoming that fear of loss required heroic efforts on the part of a few activist teachers and movement organizers. They did not gainsay the risk, but they did buffer the perception of risk by explaining to teachers why the movement's strategy might work, and they inspired and mobilized teachers to take risks by speaking to their anger, frustrations, and hopes, if not for themselves, then for the young people in their classrooms.

Often, however, the loss is real and sustained; adaptation for some people means accepting the loss, defining and solving problems emerging from the loss, and making the best of it by finding the next opportunity. The losses to Steve Buchanan and his family are obvious. Only a little less stark were the losses of Asarco copper plant workers in Tacoma. They lost their jobs; they had to pick up and find new work. For some, that meant uprooting their homes and families. The white people in Selma, Alabama, faced losses in terms of identity, social structure, and political power. Civil rights meant a change in their way of life.

Leaders and authority figures get attacked, dismissed, silenced, and sometimes assassinated because they come to represent loss, real or perceived, to those members of the community who feel that they have gotten, or might get, the bad end of a bargain. Even if people hope for a positive-sum outcome, fear provokes defense, particularly if the stakes are high. At these times, taking authority itself is risky, whether or not one exercises leadership with it. One risks job, reputation, and perhaps life.

To describe the risks of authority (with or without leadership), I turn back to the distinction between authority and leadership.

Authority figures become repositories of hope by virtue of taking office. As long as they meet expectations, perhaps by changing those expectations as did Parsons and Ruckelshaus, authorities retain the good will of their constituents. But they also become repositories of frustration to those whose expectations they have failed. In relatively stable periods of time, these failures may not be of much significance and passion, and an authority figure can survive without too much wear and tear. Humming along on routine problems, people can operate according to well-understood procedures without much disappointment.

In unstable times, however, when norms and procedures break down, adaptive pressures are high, and disequilibrium is rising, the expectations and frustrations with authority build as well. At those times, an authority figure, even one who does not exercise leadership—someone who colludes with his community in avoiding adaptive work in an effort to restore equilibrium—will risk attack and loss of office. As the passions in the society mount, and as the mechanisms being used to restore equilibrium fail, the authority figure becomes the likely scapegoat. Minimally, people expect him to maintain equilibrium in turbulent times. Failing that, he comes to represent the loss of stability.

In these times, exercising leadership may be the authority figure's most likely route to staying alive. If the adaptive challenge cannot persistently be avoided—by using a denial, a diversion, a scapegoat, an external enemy, or the like—then the authority figure will pay the consequences for having failed to prepare the society for the current crisis. He will be blamed and, quite often, brought down. Much less subject to scrutiny by the society is the degree to which the authority figure had been colluding, sometimes unwittingly, with its avoidance of festering problems. His popularity is based on his collusion. But members of society do not blame themselves. The authority figure takes the blame.

This scapegoating of the authority figure is surely unfair. Communities often give authority to an individual to provide direction, protection, and order, yet they resist the kind of leadership on the part of people in authority that would put the challenge of adaptive change back on themselves. The authority figure is placed in a double bind, a Catch-22. Upon meeting up with adaptive problems, the authority figure, still bearing expectations for direction, is pressured *not* to provide direction that generates the pain or loss which tend to accompany adaptation. He is expected to protect, but not if protection means challenge.

Scapegoating authority is also unproductive. The dynamic reinforces the social tendency in times of distress to shirk broad responsibility for doing adaptive work. As long as the society continues to place the burden on the back of authority, neglecting to face the need for change, then it may slowly deteriorate, as may be the case in some of our communities, or spiral into a series of revolutions in which one dictator is replaced by another, each looking quite different as he institutes a "new order"; but the political culture of dependency does not change.[2]

Not uncommonly, the authority's downfall takes on a sacred air. Corazon Aquino described the casting out of Ferdinand Marcos as "indeed a miracle . . . a symbol of God's love and the task he set us to do."[3] Overthrowing Marcos made the crimes he committed extraordinarily important. They were not always so. During more stable times, his corruption had very little power to attract attention or diminish his appeal; it was later, in times of festering adaptive pressures, that his sins required atonement. As a historian of religion describes, the sacrifice "is an attempt to make a fresh start by driving away the accumulation of evil that hinders divine beneficence."[4]

Yet the redemptive power of sacrifice is often illusory. Continuing to operate *as if* the crisis comprised only a technical problem, people look for a technical solution—deposing the authority figure. But when he is gone, the problems remain. The new savior who replaces him is bound to disappoint. (In his time Marcos had been viewed as a savior as well.)[5]

The accumulation of evil never resides in one person at the top because no one gets to the top without representing the interests of the dominant factions in the system. The evil, if it is evil at all, lives in the routine ways in which people throughout the system collude in maintaining a dysfunctional status quo. Changing the status quo will always require more than simply changing the person of the authority figure. Adaptive work requires adjustments, learning, and compromise on the part of many among the dominant, complacent, and beleaguered. Changing the authority figure may well usher in a new era, but only to the extent that she cuts against the grain and exercises leadership, or she represents the *outcome* of an adaptive process and her selection embodies a change in the orientation of the community to its problems.

In times of distress, people are often of mixed minds about change. They passionately want their lives to change and they look to figures of authority to take bold action to direct the change. Yet they also want the change to take place with a minimum of loss to them, and they look to authority for protection. As a consequence, an authority in Aquino's position faces a major dilemma: she has to meet the public expectation for dramatic action, while taking action that would cause real change. Genuine change requires frustrating people's expectation that new heroic authority can deliver a new age miraculously without widespread pain. So we have competing principles at work: maintaining the holding power of one's authority, which requires meeting expectations for bold action as well as protection, and promoting adaptive work, which requires anticipated or real hardship.

The common resolution of this strategic dilemma is to couple boldness with protection—for example, by acting boldly on side issues while restoring order. In the short run that seems a less risky solution because it presents the desired image without causing much dismay. Adaptive success over time, however, demands coupling boldness with challenge, more than protection—risking one source of informal authority to gain another in the form of productive results. In Aquino's case, she might have acted boldly to institute economic and social policies avoided during the Marcos regime but well-tested in several newly industrialized countries: the need to reduce the highly unequal distribution of wealth through land reform and other means, the opening of the economy to international competition, and the reduction of corruption and personal influence as the primary currencies of power.[6]

The Politics of Inclusion

The politics of inclusion are not faint-hearted efforts at making everybody happy enough. Inclusion means more than taking people's views into account in defining the problem.[7] Inclusion may mean challenging people, hard and steadily, to face new perspectives on familiar problems, to let go of old ideas and ways of life long held sacred. Thus, inclusion does not mean that each party will get its way. Even the most well-crafted efforts at inclusion can rarely prevent the experience of loss by some. As a result, one often cannot shield oneself from the outrage of those parties who must face loss and are unwilling to change.

Furthermore, from a strategic standpoint, some parties often must be excluded from the problem-solving process. They generate more disruption than can be contained effectively by the holding environment—the network of cohesive bonds and authority relationships among members of the community. This is one of the trials of leadership. Sometimes one excludes people and puts aside their perspectives, regardless of their validity. One silences them, actively or by complicity. In a sense, as it will often be experienced by those whose voices are not to be heard, one performs multiple little assassinations, if not physical, then of character or capability.

Consider the formation of the U.S. Constitution during the Federal Convention of 1787 and the issue of slavery. During that summer, many divisive issues had to be resolved by the framers, who represented very different perspectives on the nature of government and the balance needed between liberty and order, local and national control, and the division and sharing of powers. To prevent fragmentation into North and South, the framers made a quite deliberate decision to avoid a strong stand on the institution of slavery. They felt that the whole tapestry would unravel and no union would form if slavery's future were decided then.[8]

This decision, however cruel in its effects, made sense even to some who abhorred slavery. The union mattered more to them, and when slavery finally was abolished, the union tested by war was strong enough to survive. But the experience of the Civil War also illustrates the principle that an issue placed on the shelf for too long can explode. Though it may well go away temporarily, a leader has to keep track of the issue because it can generate a future crisis. From a strategic perspective, a tactical decision to avoid an issue or exclude an interested party on the basis of the holding environment's carrying capacity often results in a temporary reduction in stress that can lull people into a false sense of security.

Running that risk may be necessary. But when the adaptive capacity has been increased, and the enterprise successfully addresses its initial set of problems, a leader must consider reintroducing the neglected issues. Perhaps had politicians done so more vigorously and effectively in the first decades of this nation, and before cotton became so central to the South's economy and social and cultural life, the Civil War could have been averted. By Abraham Lincoln's day, the politics of inclusion meant going to war. The Constitution had no escape clause; differences were supposed to be worked out within the framework of the union. The South would be included by force. But leading the nation to meet this challenge represented such enormous loss that doing so cost Lincoln his life.

Pacing the Work

Clearly, challenging people to face harsh realities can be brutal work. When King and Gandhi asked people to go into the streets at the risk of getting beaten by police, they made brutal requests. When Ruckelshaus asked Asarco workers to choose between a way of life and a case of leukemia per year, he outlined a brutal demand. Asking Americans to choose between fighting or getting out of Vietnam would have pushed a brutal outcome, either way, into the body politic. Any politician in the 1990s who goes home to tell people the "good news" about the end of the Cold War and its effects on their jobs and way of life will be asking them to face bittersweet truths. Telling people to face pain can feel like cruelty, particularly when one has no answer to give, only questions, perspectives, and some hard facts.

The pains of change deserve respect. People can only sustain so much loss at any one time. Leadership demands respect for people's basic need for direction, protection, and order in times of distress. Leadership requires compassion for the distress of adaptive change, both because compassion is its own virtue, and because it can improve one's sense of timing. Knowing how hard to push and when to let up are central to leadership.

There are numerous methods to pace the work, and we have already seen them in operation in various contexts. Strengthening the holding environment indirectly affects pacing because it increases the community's tolerance for stress. Thus, creating a trustworthy set of relationships, as we saw in the Buchanan and Tacoma cases, both between authority figures and stakeholders and among emerging coalitions, increases people's adaptive capacity. Deciding what issues to focus attention on, how to frame them, and how to manage the flow of information are all direct mechanisms of pacing. Another method is to exclude voices representing issues that are too provocative, such as the voices of slaves in 1787. Finally, choosing the decisionmaking process provides a means to pace the work because it determines both the breadth of participation and where the weight of responsibility falls. An autocratic or consultative process gives less of the burden to people than a delegative or consensual mode of operating.

Thus, the questions one would ask in pacing the work derive from familiar concerns. First, how stressful is the question or problem being raised? How much loss does it involve? Second, how resilient are the people being challenged? Are they accustomed to learning or are they likely to reach quickly for an avoidance mechanism with which to restore equilibrium? Third, how strong are the bonds of authority that give one the power to hold people's attention to brutally hard questions?

In each society and organization, people will have different tolerances for the stresses of adaptive work, and different situations will generate different levels and symptoms of distress. Leadership requires knowing the social system well enough to predict how stressful the challenge facing it will be and how capably it will absorb the stress. If the organization has lived in a stable environment for thirty years, with a stable authority structure headed by the same person, an event like a transition in authority may provoke a moderate to high level of stress. If the transition is sudden, then the stress will be greater. If the transition has been long in coming and well prepared for, then the stress will be lower. If a political and economic revolution, as in Central and Eastern Europe, drastically changes the operating environment, the stress will be severe.[9]

Leadership operates within particular worlds and requires an experimental mindset—the willingness to work by trial and error—where the community's reactions at each stage provide the basis for planning future actions. Research about each particular context is crucially important, but no analysis or catalogue can substitute for a leader's improvisational skills. Thus, a leader stays alive not by "playing it safe" but by taking deliberate risks based on his ongoing assessment of the territory, knowing that corrective action will almost always be necessary. He takes the risk of challenging people, directly or indirectly, slow or fast, soft or hard, guided by his comprehension of and sensitivity to the changes people have to make in their lives as they take account of the questions he raises. As Martin Luther King Jr. explained to his outraged black constituents, the civil rights movement needed to have compassion even toward racist white people. He saw no point in frightening them beyond their limit of tolerance. Had the movement provoked a rigid posture of defense against change among whites, it may not have accomplished any change for blacks. To the degree that unleashing black aspirations and outrage overwhelmed the nation's adaptive capacity during the summer riots of those years, the civil rights cause was probably set back.

Yet compassion, as King described it, is rarely soft. The respect required in leadership is often the limit-setting love that gives people little leeway for turning their eyes from difficult work. But toughness is not the same thing as the gleeful abuse of power, or vengeful delight. When Lyndon Johnson challenged his white Southern colleagues and constituents to come to terms with civil rights, he had no interest in humiliating them. His tactics worked because he knew their defenses and respected them at the same time that he challenged them.

In pacing the work, a leader has to take account of the strength of his hold on people's attention and commitments. If he has authority in the social system, then he has some leverage over the holding environment. He can reduce the distress by being an authoritative and hopeful presence, providing clear direction and protection, orienting people with the reasons for undergoing hardship, adding internal structures, controlling conflict, and framing the debate in less challenging ways. Conversely, he elevates distress when he puts pressure on stakeholders, unleashes conflict, includes provocative voices, and frames the debate more starkly. Thus, a leader must monitor repeatedly his own informal authority in the community as it fluctuates. With a strong hold, he can generate more productive stress and move faster. With a weak hold, he has to move more slowly.

For example, Lyndon Johnson may have had enough informal authority before and after the election of 1964 to use a more challenging frontal approach to the nation on the issue of Vietnam. William Ruckelshaus returned to the EPA in 1983 in the role of savior, which gave him enough informal authority to run the Tacoma experiment in public deliberation. Barbara Parsons drew upon a ten-year relationship with the Buchanan family when she began to hold their attention to the adaptive work facing them. And Corazon Aquino, with an extraordinary public mandate, might have had enough leverage initially to reform the Philippine elite rather than primarily challenge the vestiges of Marcos.

In contrast, when a leader has little or no authority in the system, she can only control the severity of her challenge. She cannot contain the distress by structuring the process, corralling stakeholders into a meeting, or issuing calming statements. Civil rights strategists, for example, ratcheted up the stress they generated as the society seemed to move and respond to their efforts. They did not take on the more disturbing issue of voting rights first; they took on access to education and the freedom to ride in public buses without discrimination. Only after the nation had tackled those problems and several others, and had become familiar with challenges such as these, did the civil rights movement directly confront the distribution of political power.

A leader must take the risk of action when the appropriate level and duration of distress are uncertain. Even the pacing must be improvised. Will nations like Poland, Russia, and China, for example, learn better by sustaining severe pain for a short time, or moderate pain over a longer time?[10] When Watts began to burn in August of 1965, weeks after passage of the Voting Rights Act, Johnson, as Califano describes it, "was forced to face the fact that he might be losing his race against the ticking clock of expectations that the promise of his own legislative achievements and rhetoric had wound up."[11]

Unlike rote learning situations in which the answer is supplied, though paced, by the teacher, adaptive learning situations demand that people discover, invent, and take responsibility. Leadership is a special sort of educating in which the teacher raises problems, questions, options, interpretations, and perspectives, often without answers, gauging all the while when to push through and when to hold steady.

Socrates illustrates this kind of teaching and the pitfall of pacing the work too quickly. Socrates challenged people in the marketplace, asking questions of those who thought they had wisdom. He educated through inquiry, and he upset people. As far as we know from his pupil Plato, Socrates aimed his questions at the blindspots of his community. He did not presume to have the answers or to have a fix on the truth. But he also did not assume that people had broad wisdom or knowledge simply because they were considered experts in one specialized field. A skilled physician might know little about emotional matters of the heart. Socrates, in his irreverence for certainty in a world that craved it, challenged people to live with doubt.

In 399 B.C., an Athenian jury of 501, by a margin of 30, convicted him of corrupting Athenian children through his teachings. The jury then sentenced Socrates to death by poison.[12] Could Socrates have succeeded in his task without causing his own demise? Perhaps. According to Plato's dramatization at least, Socrates had enormous respect for argument and logical inquiry, but he seems to have had less respect for the normal human defenses, emotional defenses, that protect the equilibrium people try so hard to create in their organizations and systems of belief. Socrates paced his challenge less on the basis of what his opponents could digest emotionally than on the basis of how quickly logic could carry him in the argument.[13] If the logical connections of the argument were long and tedious, then so would be the pace of the discussion. If Socrates could make the connections more quickly, then the argument would move swiftly.

As a model of leadership, this neglects human truths. The learning required to accomplish adaptive work is not simply conceptual. Logical argument is rarely sufficient. Sifting through the old and fashioning something new takes emotional work. To move at the pace of logic alone, people would need an unusually high level of rationality and intellectual freedom from habit, tradition, and pride. The leader as educator has to engage the parties in a process of inquiry that accounts for their fear or pain, if learning is to be produced. By not pacing his presentation to the comprehension of his audience, Socrates encouraged people to focus attention on *him* rather than on the questions he posed.

Again, Johnson put it succinctly: "Congress is like a whiskey drinker. You can put an awful lot of whiskey into a man if you just let him sip it. But if you try to force the whole bottle down his throat at one time, he'll throw it up." Johnson the legislator understood the principle, but, tragically, Johnson the President set the pace less by the nation's adaptability than by his own urgent drive to accomplish so much. Limitless aspiration, unleashed by gaining the presidency, ran wild. As Califano describes: "His own singular capacity to enact so many laws and programs led him to overestimate the capacity of the government to administer and the nation to absorb so much so fast."[14]

The Temptation of Martyrdom

In exercising leadership, people often are drawn to taking courageous stands. Indeed, leadership may require the willingness to die. Sometimes, however, people confuse courage with the temptation of martyrdom. Martyrdom may promise permanence for one's words, or one may imagine that steadfastness will inspire following generations. In particular, martyrdom has a powerful allure for people with grand aspirations invested with the dreams and suffering of others, particularly when facing unyielding resistance and when previous hard-won gains slip away.

Martyrdom does not arise from the nature of the martyr's person or acts alone. It derives from the meaning people give to him and his acts. Martyrdom is a role created by the community. Thus, heroes who die in a dangerous enterprise may not become martyrs. Millions of soldiers have died heroically in wars for their nation but are not normally called martyrs. The people for whom they have died create no such role for them. Contrary to common usage, an individual cannot "martyr" himself, even though he sacrifices his life, unless the group makes him into a martyr. Most commonly, martyrdom is a role reserved for charismatic authorities who are assassinated in the service of their cause.

As we have seen, communities generate charismatic authority during times of distress when people search desperately for someone to relieve their pains. A powerful authorizing relationship, often left informal, results when an individual steps forward with great promise. The charisma derives not only from the person's skills, personality, and devotion but also from the community's investment. As in Hollywood, the star steps into a role that the audience has made. Until people's unrealized dreams and aches attach to the aspiring actress, she is merely another talented individual with private hopes.[15]

The long-term challenge of leadership is to develop people's adaptive capacity for tackling an ongoing stream of hard problems. The point is not to foster dependency but to counteract the inappropriate dependency on authority that distress tends to produce in adaptive situations. Yet in the actual exercise of leadership, dependency must wax and wane. People need to rest the weight of their burden on someone's shoulders. How many of us manage without the hope of being protected or rescued in times of distress? Leadership requires carrying that burden, containing the distress, for a time, sometimes a long time, while people adapt sufficiently to take it back.

Particularly at the early stages of an adaptive process, charismatic authority is a very great resource for leadership. Witness Roosevelt at the start of his presidency, Churchill at the start of the war, or King during the civil rights movement. Charisma can provide a very strong hold over people's attention while they undergo a period of sustained distress, mobilization, creativity, and change.

The pitfall of charisma, however, is unresolved dependency. People can fail to move on, to discover their own "magic," their own capacity for responsibility. They may not grow to realize their capability for self-governance. Rather than establish new norms, understandings, and authorizing structures, they may focus their sights and energies on the single charismatic individual. No one else can compare to him. The charismatic and his constituents develop a relationship in which promises insulate against the distress of facing problems. For the charismatic, it feels good to be idealized. For his constituents, it feels good to have someone who assures deliverance in the long-run, and in the short-run provides direction, protection, orientation, the control of conflict, and clear norms.[16]

Sometimes for a long period of time, these charismatic bonds may be all that hold a community together in its effort to face major change. If no charismatic emerges, people may be truly bereft and lost in a sea of forces and pressures beyond their adaptive capacity. The society may die. If someone does emerge, the people may understandably attribute his rise to "divine grace." Indeed, if he exercises leadership, he may well save his community and help it to renew itself. First, he binds people together by powerfully articulating their values, hopes, and pains. Second, he weaves these hopes into some image of the future. And third, he provides energy, strategy, and faith that the vision can be realized. In mobilizing his community, his confidence and strength fosters a necessary dependency that only over time can be dismantled. Yet to sustain adaptive change, the community has eventually to discover and develop its own capacity for doing work, including the capacity to authorize other citizens without expecting magic.

What happens, then, when the charismatic authority is murdered? Sometimes the martyr can serve as a model, a continuing source of inspiration, cemented in memory by the price he paid. But it may also be that the process of developing self-governing capability stops, perhaps for a long time. We hear from the bereaved, "If only *he* were still alive!" as if the adaptive strength of a community depended fundamentally on one individual. The charismatic may be held in place for perpetuity while the act of murder itself takes on a magical aura, drawing people to its scene for generations to renew the connection.[17] Thus, in 1991 the Civil Rights Museum opened its doors on the site of King's assassination. Or people may await the return of the martyr in a future incarnation. The event of his death may come to mean more than his life.

Martyrdom can keep people hanging on. If one's aim is to immortalize oneself in the memory and culture of a community, then martyrdom is the right strategy. But martyrdom can entrap the people who need to be mobilized. Living words become rigid canon. And therein lies its potential futility. Over time, a leader has to help people let go. When a charismatic authority is killed, that process of letting go may stop.

The personal temptation to martyrdom becomes particularly strong when the problem comes into its full complexity, swamping the capacity of the charismatic to maintain the illusion that he has the answers. At that moment, the wish to escape the torment produced by carrying people's aspirations, but not being able to fulfill them, grows. Years of fatigue add to the wish. Yet the option of simply stepping down, passing the mantle, goes against the grain both of the charismatic's own grandiosity and the group's clinging dependency.

Martin Luther King Jr. sensed his death and referred to it in a speech the night before his assassination in 1968. Ironically, he had wanted that year to take a sabbatical. He felt a despondency produced by doubts about the efficacy of the civil rights movement, violent rioting that he could not control, sharpening divisions within the black community, and diminishing national attention. But he felt constrained by the dependency of his constituents, who expected him to continue bearing the cross. Andrew Young and Coretta Scott King called the idea of a sabbatical "impossible." As King's biographer David Garrow put it, "The role in which he was caught up would not allow him to jettison the responsibility that lay on his shoulders."[18] Yet giving in to these pressures may have been a mistake, not only because it led to his death but also because it discouraged self-reliance in the community. If King had viewed himself as a barometer of these pressures, his despondency may have provided valid evidence suggesting that the dependency had grown too strong—and felt overwhelming—and he needed to make room for others. A long sabbatical might have been a very useful tactic. King might have said: "I've had enough. I've taken you as far as I know how. We've gone far together, but there is much farther to go. We have many gifted leaders, so I'm going home for a good while. The rest is up to you."

11

The Personal Challenge

Why is it lonely on the point? Because those who lead take responsibility for the holding environment of the enterprise. They themselves are not expected to be held. They do the holding, often quite alone. They run the risks of moral regret. Max Weber described this ethic of responsibility at the conclusion of World War I in a speech at Munich University: "It is immensely moving when a *mature* man—no matter whether old or young in years—is aware of a responsibility for the consequences of his conduct and really feels such responsibility with heart and soul. He then acts by following an ethic of responsibility and somewhere he reaches the point where he says: 'Here I stand; I can do no other.'"[1]

Yet the ethic of responsibility frequently goes awry. Years ago, soon after medical school, I worked as a physician examining top corporate executives in an elegant medical clinic in New York City. As part of their benefits package, these executives were given an annual medical exam; and I was one of the six or seven doctors on staff. Not surprisingly, more than half of the hundreds of people I examined seemed burdened by the stresses they were carrying. Stress manifested itself in various ways, from habitual smoking and drinking to ulcers, heart disease, bad nutrition, and family problems. Why were they stressed? For the most part, these people carried the weight of other people's worries, frustrations, and desires. They were not allowed to have their own crises of confidence; they were supposed to know what they were doing. They nearly always hid their fears from others and quite often from themselves. They tended to have little insight into their own investment in carrying the load, although in the confidence of a doctor's office they often began to disclose the burden. Indeed, they talked readily, which indicated the pent-up urgency of their misgivings. But they did not talk outside. The boundaries between their colleagues (members of the board, senior staff, top management) and them were nearly impermeable to emotions of doubt.[2]

The myth of leadership is the myth of the lone warrior: the solitary individual whose heroism and brilliance enable him to lead the way. This notion reinforces the isolation. From the perspective of the individual who leads with authority, constituents confer power in exchange for being relieved of problems. If he shows reluctance or weakness in shouldering the burden, they will often feel betrayed, and he will be diminished in their eyes. When President Carter collapsed from heat exhaustion while running a race the month following his "malaise" speech, the visual images broadcast nationwide reinforced many people's suspicions that Carter was insufficiently in control of public affairs. When President Bush fell ill at dinner at the climax of his 1991 trip to Japan, he felt quite a bit of pressure to convey an image of strength and resilience the following day, even though everybody else with the flu that season seemed to stay in bed for a week.[3] And if, as some physicians suspected, it was not the flu but a fainting spell, could the President say so? When President Reagan was shot in the chest in 1981, his poise and good humor both before and after surgery not only calmed a nation that cared but gave people the image of spunk that they wanted. During the crippling depression of the 1930s, Franklin Roosevelt's mastery of polio symbolized the recovery and vigor the nation craved.

The strategic challenge is to give the work back to people without abandoning them. Overload them and they will avoid learning. Underload them and they will grow too dependent, or complacent. Thus, an authority has to bear the weight of problems, for a time. That is a very real burden. Unloading that weight on people unprepared to respond would be negligent. Shouldering the pains and uncertainties of an institution particularly in times of distress comes with the job of authority. It can only be avoided at the institution's peril.

Those who lead without authority also must bear a heavy weight. While authority figures become repositories of hope by virtue of taking office, people who lead without authority shoulder what they perceive as the needs and opportunities of a community because they take personal responsibility for framing hard questions about purposes and possibilities. Identifying themselves with those questions, they often invest their own love, pain, and outrage. Their lives would be less stressful if they did not care. Then, as they build a constituency and become known, they gain informal and sometimes formal authority and begin to carry other people's aspirations and passions as well. As they begin to disturb people beyond the bounds of their sympathetic constituency, they generate stress in the larger system. They have to stomach the repercussions of that distress at the same time that they provoke it. They cannot expect to be properly valued by the authorities in the system they challenge, at least not in the short-term. They cannot expect to be held.

To lead and yet sustain the personal stresses that come with leading requires inner discipline. So far, we have focused on a strategy for managing the social environment. In concluding our study, we briefly address the equally critical capacity to manage oneself. What follows, then, are seven practical suggestions for bearing the responsibility that comes with leadership without losing one's effectiveness or collapsing under the strain. They are: (1) get on the balcony, (2) distinguish self from role, (3) externalize the conflict, (4) use partners, (5) listen, using oneself as data, (6) find a sanctuary, and (7) preserve a sense of purpose.[4]

Getting on the Balcony

Leadership is both active and reflective. One has to alternate between participating and observing. Walt Whitman described it as being "both in and out of the game." For example, Magic Johnson's greatness in leading his basketball team came in part from his ability to play hard while keeping in mind the whole game situation, as if he stood in the stands. Bobby Orr played hockey in the same way.[5]

Although the principle may be easy to grasp, the practice is not. Rather than maintain perspective on the events that surround and involve us, we often get swept up by them. Consider the experience of dancing on a dance floor in contrast with standing on a balcony and watching other people dance. Engaged in the dance, it is nearly impossible to get a sense of the patterns made by everyone on the floor. Motion makes observation difficult. Indeed, we often get carried away by the dance. Our attention is captured by the music, our partner, and the need to sense the dancing space of others nearby to stay off their toes. To discern the larger patterns on the dance floor—to see who is dancing with whom, in what groups, in what location, and who is sitting out which kind of dance—we have to stop moving and get to the balcony.

What allowed Lyndon Johnson to manage the crisis in Selma successfully was his ability to get to the balcony. He understood intimately what the crisis was about. He maintained perspective on the dynamics of the social system as it contended with a tough issue. He recognized efforts to seduce him, the central authority, into supplying a quick fix, and he knew by virtue of his experience that the demand for an authoritative solution was a trap. Mobilizing the national guard in Alabama would have let Wallace and the nation escape from responsibility. The balcony enabled Johnson to interpret the trends that would otherwise have swept him away.

But in waging the Vietnam War, Johnson got caught up in the unfamiliar dance of foreign policy and never got to the balcony. Besieged by expectations—his own, Washington's, and the American public's—Johnson engaged in the nation's conflict without ever leading it. Instead, he managed the substantive and politically technical problems of making war. Johnson seemed to lack a conscious philosophy of leadership—a set of clearly articulated guiding principles and questions. When he succeeded on civil rights, he succeeded by virtue of experience turned political instinct. When his experience failed him, as it did in Vietnam, he seemed to have no method of gaining perspective. In the absence of familiar reference points, and without a framework of principles and questions, his instincts led him astray.

How can one get to the balcony, particularly in an unfamiliar situation, when fast music is sweeping everyone up in the dance? Although no framework can substitute for the kind of intimate knowledge that Johnson had of southern politics, the right questions can help one get far enough above the fray to see the key patterns.

The following diagnostic framework summarizes the reasoning behind the strategic principles of leadership we have explored: identifying the adaptive challenge, regulating distress, directing disciplined
attention to the issues, and giving the work back to people.

Identifying the Adaptive Challenge. As we have seen, an adaptive
challenge consists of a gap between the shared values people hold
and the reality of their lives, or of a conflict among people in a
community over values or strategy. In both cases, these internal
contradictions are likely to generate distress. Thus, we can offer the
diagnostic principle that distress itself, if it cannot be alleviated
through the application of technical know-how and existing procedures, provides a clue to what the adaptive challenge is. Although
some people might suggest that distress may in some situations be
more a matter of perception than of reality, as Fred Reese and his
colleagues discovered in mobilizing the fearful black middle class in
Selma, the testing and changing of perceptions is often at the heart
of adaptive change.

The problem causing the distress frequently will not be on the
surface. Although the superficial conflict may be over procedures,
power, schedule, structure, and lines of authority, these seemingly
technical issues often act as proxies for underlying conflicts in ways
of life. The conflict between George Wallace and Lyndon Johnson
over the Constitutional question of states' rights, for example, represented a fundamental conflict over sharply competing images of
the American community and its values.

This idea reverses the more common notion that substantive issues
are really proxies for conflicts over power. Frequently, when we see
two people butting heads, we interpret the conflict as a personal
power struggle and lose sight of the perspectives each represents on
the issues.[6] Although gaining advantage in a power conflict may
motivate some individuals to take particular stands on an issue, from
a systems view, a person's power interests can only be realized if he
represents the sentiments and perspectives of a faction in the community. As a diagnostic matter, that an individual sees personal
advantage in espousing a particular substantive point of view indicates support in the community for that point of view. Thus, diagnosing a conflict in terms primarily of power stakes among

individuals will miss the underlying issue conflict among factions in the community.

In meeting with Wallace in the oval office, Johnson appreciated keenly the interests Wallace represented for his local constituents, as well as the values of the larger American constituency for which Wallace might wish to speak, given his national political ambitions, in the near future. Negotiating over power required knowing the issue dynamics in the community that underlay personal interest.

Undoubtedly, a person's individual personality shapes enormously his actions. Yet, as with power motives, individual actions themselves are shaped powerfully by the social context and its pressures and incentives. Indeed, personality diagnoses in general have little practical value unless one also identifies the issues that person represents in his organizational role and the forces acting on him as a result. Jumping to personality explanations, like jumping to power explanations, will often overlook the systemic causes of the problem.

For example, I have frequently heard the diagnosis, "The problem is that Jack is burned out," or "The problem is that Jack is drinking too much"; yet those who make these off-the-cuff assessments frequently do not analyze the organizational stresses that accentuate Jack's exhaustion or drinking. What stresses does he incur because of the role he plays and the perspective he represents on difficult issues in the organization? Jack's behavior is often a symptom not only of the stresses in his personal life but also of systemic problems in the enterprise.

Building on the principle that people represent issues, that interpersonal conflicts among people with formal or informal authority represent issue conflicts among their constituents, we can further propose that problems in working effectively within an organization will often mirror the problems in the larger community that the organization aims to solve. Internal rivalries, misunderstandings, and patterns of disrespect will mimic patterns in the social environment. It is as if the doctor takes on the problems of the patient. Thus, at Harvard University, for example, each professional school unwittingly takes on the strengths and weaknesses of the professional community it aims to improve. The organizational dynamics within the Business School look similar to those of the business community, the resolution of disputes within the Law School mimic those of the legal profession, and so forth for the schools of divinity, education, design, medicine, public health, and government. The success of these schools in improving their professions is largely contingent on their capacity to take notice and correct for these patterns rather than fall prey to repetition.

The mechanism of repetition in any organization is somewhat straightforward. Members either informally identify with or explicitly represent a faction of the community outside. In part, these personal identifications may have been what drew them initially to a job in their organization.[7] As well, working in the organization over time elicits each member's own predilection to identify with some aspects of the issues and not others, some factions in the external environment and not others. Resonating with an outside faction's particular perspective, each member then imports it into the organization.[8] As a consequence, the maladaptive patterns of behavior inside may derive from work issues and work avoidances outside. The organization will dramatize the external dynamics often quite unwittingly.

This mirroring, inexact as it might be, provides diagnostic clues for comprehending the dysfunctions and impediments in the outside community that the organization needs to address. Indeed, if one can get on the balcony instead of getting caught up in recreating the problem internally, one can seize the opportunity of using the organization as a case in point—a laboratory—for identifying challenges and inventing options for taking action outside, which was the organization's original aim.[9] Consider the following story.

When Kevin Jackson, a junior at Yale, was invited to represent his college at the annual conference of the Council on Higher Education in America, he felt honored and full of anticipation.[10] Jackson, a black youth from Harlem, was the star of his family. No one in the family had graduated from college before, and they were all extremely proud of his success. When he left for the conference, held that year in California, he felt everything was going his way. But by the time the conference ended he felt so battered that he experienced crushing headaches even at the memory of the conference for years afterward.

The conference was divided into work groups with separate assignments due by the end of the four-day gathering. Jackson's group was supposed to examine a variety of issues, including affirmative action. For the first three days everything went smoothly in Jackson's group; in fact he once again took up his "star" role. The designated chair was a black woman, but Jackson quickly gained informal authority for directing the discussion. Although he felt some tension developing within the group, he disregarded its importance. On the fourth and final working day, however, a severe confrontation developed between three white students and him. The topic of discussion had finally turned to affirmative action, and Jackson was the only student voicing support for it. The confrontation began on an intellectual level, gradually became less intellectual, and ultimately degenerated into personal attacks. Jackson finally fled the scene.

In his bruised state of mind Jackson concluded that he had been the victim of a racially motivated committee-room lynching. Over time, however, he began to acknowledge that there had been other people in the room, including some black students. Jackson had to wonder why the rest of the group, including the black members, had, in effect, colluded in what had happened to him.

In retrospect, Jackson realized that as the informal authority in the group, he had become the lightning rod for the tensions that built up. What were these tensions? To Jackson, the group seemed particularly passive in letting him define the agenda. Jackson, for his part, misinterpreted the passivity as a vote of confidence. He had not probed for the origins of the long silences at the beginning of the meetings. Perhaps the members of the group were ambivalent about letting Jackson play a dominant role but felt they could not challenge a black man.

These tensions may not have surfaced had the group not been assigned the special task of discussing affirmative action. But given that task, the group apparently turned Jackson into a personal embodiment of the issue: Did Jackson merit being at Yale, or leading the group's discussion? Rather than diagnose the difficulties of addressing affirmative action in a racially mixed society, the group dramatized them. No one had the presence of mind to analyze and use the tensions. Instead, they let Jackson take the heat and suffer the conflict over the issue.

A more experienced Jackson might have observed from the balcony that both the conference staff and his own reticent group had selected black authority figures, and now the group was erupting on the issue of affirmative action. Perhaps the staff and the group had acted out their own form of affirmative action by their choices, or were concerned about the perception that they had done so. Rather than take it personally, Jackson might have interpreted the "lynching" as a sign of how taxing both the group and the society found it to work this issue. He might have provided a context for their difficulties by suggesting that the group learn from its own conflict in order to capture lessons about the dynamics of the issue in the larger society.[11] For example, he might have said, "Hey, wait a minute. Some of us are getting very passionate about this issue and for good reason: we care a lot about the values at stake. Each of us is a living example of these values. We take pride in our individual accomplishments, while we also care about social justice. Obviously, we're not going to do anybody any good to repeat in here the problem the nation has had in working this conflict. What can we learn from our own struggle discussing the issue? What recomendations might we make not only about the substance of the issue of affirmative action, but also about the impediments people face in working the issue and the process they might use to do it better?"

Our analysis of Jackson's case illustrates these various diagnostic principles at work. We can distill them into a set of basic questions for gaining a balcony perspective:

1. What's causing the distress?
2. What internal contradictions does the distress represent?
3. What are the histories of these contradictions?
4. What perspectives and interests have I and others come to represent to various segments of the community that are now in conflict?
5. In what ways are we in the organization or working group mirroring the problem dynamics in the community?

Regulating Distress. We have explored the principle that the distress generated by an adaptive challenge must be contained within limits in order to produce progress, and I have described the holding environment as a vessel within which people facing adaptive work can accomplish the necessary learning. The containing vessel is made up of various sorts of glue: an authority structure, shared purposes, common identifications, civic associations, trustworthy institutions, and other bonds of community. As we have seen in the early 1990s, particularly in the former Soviet bloc, when high levels of distress overwhelm the sources of cohesion, people often attempt to restore a semblance of personal and social equilibrium by narrowing their affiliation to a smaller but more certain identity group faction and fighting for resources with other newly bolstered factions as the society as a whole breaks apart. Clearly, this is not all bad. Progress by anybody's account may sometimes take the form of divorce. Such was the American Declaration of Independence from England. However, disintegrative forces can also lead to chronic chaos and entrenched, self-perpetuating conflict and trauma, as well as the death or stagnation of a community or institution.

Thus, of vital importance in mobilizing people to meet an adaptive challenge is the job of regulating, to the extent possible, the level of disequilibrium. From an authority position, this will mean using the powers and influence given formally and accrued informally to strategically frame the issues, orchestrate conflict, develop structures and processes, provide a measure of orientation and protection, and maintain those norms that should endure. In short, one has to pace the work. Operating without authority, one has to gauge when and how hard to press people to pay attention to issues they might otherwise avoid.

Every community and culture will have its own particular sources of cohesion and limits of tolerance for productive distress, and each will have its own distinctive methods of modulating distress and restoring equilibrium. Thus, to keep people within a productive discomfort zone, one clearly has to know the local symptoms of distress and the local habits of response. One must know the local history of problem-solving.

To identify the tolerable range of distress and discern how to regulate its level within a particular setting, we add a further set of questions to the framework:

6. What are the characteristic responses of the community to disequilibrium—to confusion about future direction, the presence of an external threat, disorientation in regard to role relationships, internal conflict, or the breaking up of norms?

7. When in the past has the distress appeared to reach a break-

ing point—where the social system began to engage in self-destructive behavior, like civil war or political assassination?

8. What actions by senior authorities traditionally have restored equilibrium? What mechanisms to regulate distress are currently within my control, given my authority?

Directing Disciplined Attention to the Issues. We have examined the principle that social systems frequently try to restore equilibrium by reducing the overt manifestations of their internal tensions. Initially, they will try to apply their current problem-solving methods. When these do not seem to work and the disequilibrium persists, the system often will use work avoidance mechanisms to reduce generalized distress. The work avoidance, if effective, diverts attention enough to make people forget temporarily about the real problems that gave rise to the disequilibrium in the first place.

Thus, a key diagnostic task from the balcony is to identify patterns of work avoidance so that, when resuming action, one can redirect attention to the issues. In so doing, it is useful to assume that people's efforts to restore equilibrium at the cost of facing hard problems are often not conscious or deliberate. Often, they are convenient misdiagnoses of the situation. For example, when people say to themselves, "If only we had the right leader our problems would be solved," they are not *intending* to avoid work. They often believe that statement because it fits their way of understanding the cause of problems.[12]

Moreover, if we propose that work avoidance and destructive conflict are symptoms of people contending, however ineffectively, with an adaptive challenge, then the task is both to counteract these behaviors at the same time that one affirms the significance of the issues and stakes. For example, instead of saying, "We are avoiding the issues here," which would annoy people to no end, one might say, "We are working, perhaps too indirectly, on a difficult issue; let's address it more directly," which affirms the effort.

If work avoidance is symptomatic of an adaptive challenge, then work avoidance patterns can provide clues to the work issue itself. When a leopard moves through the forest after a rain, a biologist can spot its trail more easily than she can spot the leopard. Similarly, when work avoidance takes the form of scapegoating, for example, the faction or person being scapegoated provides clues about the work issue. The question is: What distressing perspective does the faction or person represent in the organization?[13]

Furthermore, we have proposed that authority figures are barometers, that they too provide clues to the issues. If one can use them as data, or use one's own reactions to situations as data when in the authority position, then the actions of an authority figure, even in work avoidance, may indicate the intensity and the nature of the issues causing distress. For example, in a meeting one might ask oneself what issue was on the table when the authority figure stepped in and stifled someone's report, or halted the conversation by calling a break before the set time?

Just as every community and culture will have its own distinctive responses to distress, so also will it have its own patterns of work avoidance. Some will be more inclined to externalize the enemy, while others may tend to perpetually reorganize in the hope of a structural fix, blame authority, scapegoat, or the like. Obviously, one has to become familiar with the specific patterns by which a community sacrifices problem-solving to restore equilibrium.

The dance within organizations and communities is made more complex because there are usually several adaptive problems at once challenging the system. It is as if several bands were playing dance music at the same time. Consequently, another key diagnostic task is to distinguish ripe from unripe issues. Each requires a different strategy. Ripe issues have already galvanized attention and generated urgency in a critical proportion of the community. The challenge then is to keep attention focused on the dimensions of the problem requiring adaptive work by the interested parties. An unripe issue, however, usually captures the attention of a small minority in the community, and the task for them is to draw attention to the issue, often in the face of resistance by the larger community having other concerns. We have seen the process of ripening play out in the case of voting rights.

In order to identify the issues that need attending and to counteract patterns of work avoidance, we ask the following additional questions:

9. What are the work and work avoidance patterns particular to this community?
10. What does the current pattern of work avoidance indicate

about the nature and difficulty of the present adaptive challenge and the various work issues that it comprises?

11. What clues do the authority figures provide?
12. Which of these issues are ripe? What are the options for tackling the ripe issues, or for ripening an issue that has not fastened in people's minds?

Giving the Work Back to People. I have proposed that a community can fail to adapt when its people look too hard to their authorities to meet challenges that require changes in their own ways. Indeed, the higher and more persistent distresses accompanying adaptive problems accentuate the dependency dynamic. And authority figures often respond by employing or colluding with work avoidances that shield people from responsibility and pain.

Thus, what one observes from the balcony has to take into account one's own placement on the dance floor in terms of formal and informal authority. One has to assess the pressures that can unwittingly dominate one's behavior. Because leadership will often require cutting against the grain of expectations, one has to become sharply aware of what those expectations are in order to set strategy. If one is in a position of authority, what are the likely seductions? If one is operating without or beyond authority, what kinds of diversions might one generate, for example, by engaging in a direct contest with authority figures or when becoming a lightning rod?

We have examined the principle that giving the work back to people frequently takes the form of orchestrating conflict. Adaptive work often requires the engagement of parties with competing interests, and in leading the community of interests one has to comprehend the stakes and potential losses within it. In essence, identifying the issues consists of recognizing the kinds of changes that various people may have to make in order to make joint progress. Developing a strategy to get them to accomplish change, and perhaps realize losses or create mutually beneficial solutions, requires knowing with some intimacy the texture of interests in people's lives.

In order to identify the relevant parties, the nature of their adaptive work, and the pitfalls of shielding them from responsibility, we ask these questions:

13. Changes in whose values, beliefs, or behaviors would allow progress on these issues?
14. What are the losses involved?
15. Given my role, how am I likely to be drawn into work avoidance?

Without undertaking an analysis from the balcony, one becomes all too quickly a subject of the dance floor. Yet, however important the balcony may be, it is not a place to retreat. Diagnosis is meant to enable action. Midcourse assessment enables midcourse correction. In viewing social processes from the balcony, one becomes merely a temporary observer before the next round. In practice, this transition back and forth between analysis and action is no easy task. It involves skills that often do not come naturally. There are a number of common human impediments to appreciate. What follows is a discussion of some of these skills and impediments.

The Role/Self Distinction

Exercising leadership and bearing personal responsibility requires seeing the difference between oneself and one's role. A person who leads must interpret people's responses to his actions as responses to the role he plays and the perspective he represents. For example, most parents know that when their teenage son slams the door in their faces, he is working on the task of separation that accompanies growing up. Though they may be upset with his behavior, they will usually know better than to take it personally. Their son is angry less with them as individuals than with the role they play as parents. Indeed, many parents of teenagers face a similar anger, though perhaps in a different idiom. If the parents do take the anger personally, their response will likely be off the mark. They may scream back, sulk, or wall themselves off. Based on a misinterpretation of their son's behavior (He is angry with *us*), they will not be able to give what their son needs next.

Distinguishing role from self is not a prescription for keeping emotions—values and passions—at a distance and disingenuously playing a role. But it enables an individual not to be misled by his emotions into taking statements and events personally that may have little to do with him. Kevin Jackson's reaction to his working group on affirmative action provides an example. Here is another.

In October 1962 the world avoided nuclear war in part because President John F. Kennedy had the capacity to distinguish role from self during the Cuban missile crisis. When McGeorge Bundy, his National Security Adviser, first came to him to report that offensive Soviet missiles had been sighted in Cuba, Kennedy took it personally. He had repeatedly gone on the record, as recently as one month before Bundy's report, stating that he would not allow the placement of offensive weapons in Cuba, and Khrushchev had assured him repeatedly that no such thing would happen. As a result, Kennedy felt personally betrayed and personally on the line. With the Bay of Pigs operation only eighteen months past and Congressional elections less than a month away, he could ill-afford another foreign policy fiasco.

Outraged, Kennedy was immediately inclined to order an air raid on Cuba to destroy the missiles, and he called on his top advisers to determine the feasibility of doing just that.[14] But his advisers felt less personally outraged, and thinking more dispassionately about the crisis, began to weigh a series of alternatives to an air strike, including a quarantine of Soviet ships carrying military equipment to Cuba. They tried to figure out why Khrushchev had placed the missiles, and of course no one believed that it had anything to do with Kennedy as a person. Even if the Soviets had wanted to shame and embarrass Kennedy, which probably was not the case, that would have constituted a strategic move given Kennedy's role and not a personal attack.[15]

During the crisis, Kennedy quickly regained his perspective. Indeed, as the situation heated up, the ability to distinguish self from role gave him the psychological flexibility to imagine himself in Khrushchev's shoes as Premier, which then enabled him to interpret and respond more realistically to Khrushchev's behavior without aggravating the crisis. At the peak of tension, Kennedy received two very different letters, both from Khrushchev, within the span of twenty-four hours. The first sounded passionate and tormented, yet sane in its willingness to bargain and yield. The second letter sounded rigid and official. The contrast produced quite a lot of consternation among Kennedy's advisers. How should they respond? In sorting it out, Kennedy, with the insight of his brother Robert, made the crucial assumption that the second letter was the product of bureaucratic politics and pressures on Khrushchev as Premier. Kennedy, as a politician, knew well about such pressures. On the other hand, he assumed that the first letter, the passionate one, expressed Khrushchev's personal sentiments. So Kennedy chose to ignore the bureaucratic letter. He responded to the first in kind, personal in tone and willing to bargain. And it worked. A deal was struck. The crisis resolved.[16]

Externalizing the Conflict

When conflicting criticisms seem to damn whatever one does, the distinction between role and self can be life saving.[17] Making the distinction enables one to externalize the conflict, thereby focusing attention on the issues and giving the conflict back to its rightful owners. As we have seen, when President Johnson felt he had no options on Vietnam, he might have proceeded to deliberately externalize the conflict. Instead, he internalized it, making it his own. At the small group level, he failed to make sure that his policy advisers systematically listened to one another. As a result, the arguments were never hammered out fully before the President. He allowed more powerful personalities with greater institutional authority to dominate the rest.[18] At the institutional level, he generated a pseudo-consensus in Congress by "emergency" passage of the Gulf of Tonkin Resolution. The lack of debate unwittingly shielded members of Congress from grappling with the issues facing the nation. Johnson put the issues beyond their reach; he minimized external conflict and manipulated acceptance of his personal decisions. At the national level, the public, not having the facts, could not confront the realities shaping its destiny. By choosing to make the decisions and then persuade the nation, Johnson invited people against the war to focus their dissent on him.

In contrast, Martin Luther King Jr. externalized the civil rights conflict. His strategy did not prevent his assassination, but during his life it kept the public's attention where it belonged. King repeatedly reinforced the message that the conflict was not between white Americans and him, nor even between black and white Americans. It was a conflict between American values and American reality. Ruckelshaus did something similar in pushing the environmental conflict back into the communities of Ruston and Tacoma and re-fusing to base his decision on the technical expertise of the EPA. So did Sanger when she created allies within authoritative institutions, like medicine, and provoked conflict among its members on the medical treatment of women.

Internalizing the conflict causes serious difficulties. It leads to a misdiagnosis. The issue readily becomes personalized and gets inter-preted as a personal problem even when it is not. Furthermore, it produces work avoidance because it allows people to deflect their attention from the issue to the person, and to shift responsibility to him. Moreover, the person taking the heat of a personalized conflict often feels compelled to react with a personal defense, which can perpetuate the dynamic.

When the press began to attack the 1984 vice-presidential candi-date Geraldine Ferraro for her husband's financial dealings, she in-ternalized the conflict. Responding with a personal defense, she held a very lengthy news conference in which she opened all the books and answered any and all questions.[19] By doing so, she hoped to put an end to the attacks on her family. But answering detailed questions raised more questions. The very personal defense gave the charges heightened interest and revealed further vulnerabilities, and the stories about her and her husband continued. Yet the on-slaught was not essentially personal. After all, the media had a market for reports about her only because she was a candidate. The attacks were not on the person of the candidate, but on the role she played.

In retrospect, one way to interpret her press coverage is to see it as the handiwork of the media anxious to find any prominent can-didate guilty of something shameful. The stories might also be blamed on negative research by the opposition. Yet as we know from the days of Ronald Reagan's teflon coating, not all mud sticks. When it does, it suggests there is an audience for it, that people are looking for reasons to confirm their suspicions. In Ferraro's case, what might she have seen from the balcony?

In order to distinguish self from role, Ferraro might have asked: What challenge do I represent to people that generates enough dis-comfort in them so that discrediting me generates news interest? The answer to that question was obvious, above all to her. Ferraro was a *woman* seeking the nation's penultimate role of political authority.

That fact posed a major adaptive challenge to men and women throughout the land.

Having identified the real problem, Ferraro might have chosen from a variety of appropriate responses. One kind of response would have been to redirect attention to the issues. Ferraro might have engaged people in examining their attitudes toward a woman's role and point of view. Obviously, this would have been difficult. At every opportunity, she would have had to deflect the attention focused on her person and family back onto the underlying questions. "Of course, our financial books are open for all to see. But that's not the real issue." The attacks may not have stopped, but she could have framed the debate so as to give context to her candidacy.

In essence, the nation placed her in the role of representing a woman's ability and perspective. She could not escape that role. She could only internalize or externalize the issue conflicts represented by that role. For most of the campaign, she did the former, either defending herself or speaking to the "national" issues (the nuclear arms race, jobs, education) at arm's length from questions about a woman's capacity for authority and the particular views on national issues that she, as a woman, would bring to the White House.

Only in the final four days of the campaign did Ferraro get behind "herself," or, more accurately, articulate steadfastly the challenge she represented in her unique role. In a last-ditch effort to gain women's votes, she finally spoke directly to the issues she embodied. Instead of holding them close in, she put them back out into the public arena.

> We can win Olympic gold medals *and* we can coach our daughters' soccer teams. We can walk in space *and* help our children take their first steps. We can negotiate trade agreements *and* manage family budgets. We can be corporate executives and also wives and mothers. We can be doctors and also bake cookies with our six-year-old future scientists. The choices are unlimited. We can be all these things. But we don't have to be any of them . . . My candidacy is not just for me, it's for everyone. It's not just a symbol. It's a breakthrough. It's not just a statement. It's a bond between women all over America. My candidacy says America believes in equality. And the time for that equality is now.[20]

Thus, externalizing the conflict for Ferraro would have meant two things: redirecting attention from her person to the issues she represented in the role the public gave her as candidate, and framing the conflict so that people would understand it not merely as a conflict between their perspectives and hers but between competing perspectives within the polity. Do women have the capacity to exercise leadership and authority? Should women work primarily in the home? What do we mean by equality? Ferraro's task was educative; to consider her candidacy seriously, Americans clearly needed to think hard about these questions.

To educate, Ferraro had to speak in a way that affirmed the different views even as she questioned them. Martin Luther King Jr. illustrated this as well. While affirming traditional ideals—freedom and equality—he questioned their realization. By doing so, he gained authority in the eyes of those he challenged, which then increased his capacity to raise questions. Externalizing the conflict enabled him to keep his hands free to lead the public debate toward a new synthesis. Ferraro, as we have seen, did this to an extent finally at campaign's end. She spoke to the American ideals of equality, fair play, and individual expression; the historic fight against prejudice; and the fact that women take authority in jobs and families every day.

Getting a strategic perspective is critical to staying alive longer. But how can one distinguish self from role and externalize the conflict in the midst of the storm, when thrown overboard, threatened by sharks, and about to go under? One needs partners.

Partners

Even if the weight of carrying people's hopes and pains may fall mainly, for a time, on one person's shoulders, leadership cannot be exercised alone. The lone-warrior model of leadership is heroic suicide. Each of us has blind spots that require the vision of others. Each of us has passions that need to be contained by others. Anyone can lose the capacity to get on the balcony, particularly when the pressures mount. Every person who leads needs help in distinguishing self from role and identifying the underlying issues that generate attack.[21]

Partners come in two general types: the confidant and the ally. The confidant is the person to whom one can cry out and complain. A confidant can provide a holding environment for someone who is busy holding everybody else. People attempting to lead need partners who can put them back together again at the end of the day. These partners, often friends, spouses, lovers, or close colleagues, provide perspective. They help one climb back up to the balcony to understand what has happened. They help ask questions like, "What's going on here? What's the distress about? What can be learned from the mistake? What are the options for corrective action?"

John Kennedy had that kind of partner in his brother Robert. At the beginning of the Cuban Missile Crisis, Robert got President Kennedy to pause and reflect by passing him a note: "I know now how Tojo felt when he was planning Pearl Harbor." Robert had no interest in seeing his brother go down in history as another Tojo—acting without warning, and risking the start of war.[22] And when the two letters arrived from Khrushchev, Robert helped his brother get to the balcony to view himself from Khrushchev's role.

The second general type of partner is an ally. The ally is a partner usually operating across a line of authority or organizational boundary. Although allies will share a value or point of view and will often confide in each other about specific strategic questions, the presence of a boundary will limit the information flowing between them.[23]

Alliances operate in at least three basic ways: across different organizations and, within an organization, from junior authority looking up and from senior authority looking down. Across different organizations, one of the allies may have senior, equivalent, or junior authority, but most significantly the allies have no direct authority over one another. Their alliance is shaped not by the strong forces that affect authority relationships within an organizational unit but by an often more malleable indirect authority relationship defined by each's standing in his own organization and the relationship between their organizations. Clearly, these kinds of alliances are very common in government, between government and political movements and interest groups, and across divisions within large corporations where shared and overlapping tasks require the engagement of people in different places. For example, William Ruckelshaus had allies not only within the EPA but also in industry and the Sierra Club. On domestic issues, Lyndon Johnson had allies across every conceivable boundary.

Alliances are not necessarily explicit. Leaders often work across an authority or organizational boundary covertly because making an overt alliance might create a diversion from the work at hand. For example, President Johnson's phone call to Roy Wilkins, encouraging him to start lobbying Congress, was confidential. As a result, Wilkins had more power with senators and congressmen because they viewed Wilkins appropriately as a representative of black interests, without confusing Wilkins's efforts with Johnson's interests. Johnson could best play his part behind the scenes.

Forming alliances with various authority figures from a position of little or no authority played a central role in the strategies of Gandhi, Sanger, and King. In contrast, Chuck Adams found no way to push further with his superiors the question of faulty bombs in Vietnam. A leader from below or outside the authority structure needs protection, encouragement, and warning. He must seek senior allies, yet he will unnecessarily feel frustrated and betrayed if he forgets that the more authoritative ally has to contend with a larger circle of expectations and pressures.

As we saw with Johnson in Selma, a leader operating from above needs allies close to the frontline. People there see challenges that senior people cannot see. Furthermore, they may have more latitude for raising hard questions. Moreover, their participation is often necessary to defining and solving the problem. Not only will they have information and perspectives that need to be taken into account for framing the problem, but the solution will often consist of changes that they must implement.

Clearly, junior allies may not agree with the perspective of senior authority. Even when in open disagreement, however, junior allies can take some of the weight off the senior's back and prevent premature closure on the issues. From a senior position within an organization, backing and protecting deviations in the lower ranks (whether or not one agrees with the deviant position) may keep alive productive conflict. Indeed, one might deploy a maverick junior to a committee for such a purpose.

This is consonant with the principle that those who lead from senior positions must protect voices of leadership without authority. Yet, how can a person in authority recognize these voices? I suggest a counter-intuitive rule of thumb. Because the pressures on authority are to restore equilibrium, one's emotional impulse will often be to squash those in the community who raise disturbing questions. Consequently, an authority should protect those whom he wants to silence. Annoyance is often a signal of opportunity. By restraining himself and examining the potential value of getting people to address the provocative questions being raised, he can look past the person's style. What perspective does the annoying person represent? Deviants may be the senior's best sources of leadership.

Listening: Using Oneself as Data

Not only is the balcony a psychological vantage point from which to observe others, it is also a vantage point from which to observe oneself and the way one listens. To interpret events, a person who leads needs to understand his own ways of processing and distorting what he hears. To sustain the stresses of leadership, he needs to know enough about his own biases to compensate for them. If he reacts automatically to reject advice when it is given in a way that appears condescending, for example, he needs to become sufficiently acquainted with that reflex that he can listen and respond flexibly, according to the needs of the situation. Compensation requires the inner discipline to step back and test the accuracy of one's own perceptions and the appropriateness of one's reaction. Listening is a trial-and-error process of making an interpretation, seeing where it falls short, and revising it. To listen, one has to live with doubt.

Learning about the tuning of one's own harpstrings, how one is inclined to resonate more with certain themes than with others, is an ongoing process. Even the most intense programs of self-examination do not provide full self-understanding. More likely, if successful, such a program provides the skills and courage to continue learning over time. When Socrates described himself, he drew a crucial distinction between wisdom and a passion for wisdom. Having a passion for wisdom surpassed the attainment of wisdom. Curiosity was a virtue. Indeed, he considered only a life of ongoing examination worth living.

How do people maintain an adequate level of self-examination? Though different people may need different methods, two general principles apply. First, we learn by reflecting on daily actions, successes and failures, of ourselves and others. In particular, we can learn from those habits that repeatedly get us into trouble and from those behaviors that surprise us. They often provide clues to our own peculiar mesh of internal drives and social forces. We can ask ourselves, "What drew me to behave inappropriately in this situation?" Or, "Where did *that* behavior come from?"[24] Second, we can use partners as a hedge against self-deception. They may be formal partners hired for the purpose, like a consultant, coach, or therapist. More often, they will be informal partners who, when permitted to do the job of debriefing us, can promote reflection because they are the people to whom we ordinarily can talk openly.

In adaptive situations, where improvisation is the norm, listening and intervening go hand in hand. Each action ought to be viewed as an experiment. Improvisation demands ongoing assessment. In practice, a person who leads must intervene and then hold steady, listening for the effects of the intervention. She must move from balcony to dance floor, back and forth. She has to allow for silence. Holding steady gives the system time to react to her intervention. It also gives her time to listen. By listening, she refines her interpretation of events and takes corrective action. Based on what she hears, she intervenes again. By this approach, interventions are not simply proposed solutions; interventions are ways to test the waters and gather information to refine the strategy.

If she knows herself, she can listen by using herself as an instrument. As a member of the social system, she inevitably resonates with various issues, trends, and themes in the community. She can pretend to be a solo player, but she can never actually become one. By virtue of taking a role, she becomes subject to social forces and expectations. At best, she can intermittently transcend the influences by getting to the balcony.

Even from the balcony, however, people who lead never really get an objective picture because they never entirely dispense with the filters through which they perceive events. Nor can they ever be entirely free of the community's force field. But they can learn about their own filters and biases and factor them into their interpretations. They can then listen to themselves for clues to what may be going on around them. Resonating with the social system, their own thoughts and feelings indicate at once something not only about themselves but also about the environment.[25]

For example, Carol Lewis, the computer company manager, routinely felt annoyed whenever a particular person would speak up at weekly staff meetings. He always spoke too emotionally, and he seemed to revel in acting and dressing differently. She often felt compelled to silence him, and for months she did. But upon reflection she noticed that the longer she silenced him, the more emotionally and untimely were his outbursts. Furthermore, this person seemed always to represent a different perspective from the rest of the group. With some probing during the meetings, she began to see that, though his perspectives conflicted with the dominant trends in her department, they were sometimes quite germane to its tasks. Rather than being a cue to restore equilibrium, her annoyance gradually became a clue in her search for conflicting perspectives to test against dominant trends. Getting annoyed signaled the need to listen.

Similarly, when John Kennedy felt outrage and betrayal at learning of Soviet missiles in Cuba, his feelings provided a clue to the likely feelings Americans in general would have when finding out about them. His strategy had to be responsive to those sentiments in the community. He would have to express the outrage, through words and action, strategically and not reactively, given the stakes.

Finding a Sanctuary

Listening to oneself requires a place where one can hear oneself think. Working amidst the cacophony of a multiple-band dance floor, one needs a sanctuary to restore one's sense of purpose, put issues in perspective, and regain courage and heart. When serving as the repository of many conflicting aspirations, a person can lose himself in the role by failing to distinguish his inner voice from the voices that clamor for attention outside. Partners can help greatly, as can a run, a quiet walk, or a prayer to break the spell cast by the frenzy on the floor. We need sanctuaries.

To exercise leadership, one has to expect to get swept up in the music. One has to plan for it and develop scheduled opportunities that anticipate the need to regain perspective. Just as leadership demands a strategy of mobilizing people, it also requires a strategy of deploying and restoring one's own spiritual resources.

Preserving a Sense of Purpose

Leadership oftentimes is a passionate and consuming activity. People need inspiration and drive to step out into a void which only later is recognized as a place of creativity and development. So strong are the emotions of leadership, they can overwhelm the person who has not developed a sufficiently broad sense of purpose. We have analyzed in this study the job of leadership and strategies to surmount its obstacles and sustain its pains. Yet the practice of leadership requires, perhaps first and foremost, a sense of purpose—the capacity to find the values that make risk-taking meaningful. That is where this book began, with an inquiry into the values that orient one who leads.

A sense of purpose is not the same as a clearly defined purpose. A sense of purpose generates defined purposes within any given context by asking these simple questions: What is the opportunity now? What should our purpose be? Organizations and societies are full of well-defined purposes, and these are essential. Defined purposes are the single most important source of orientation in doing both technical and adaptive work, like a ship's compass heading at sea. But even more precious than any defined purpose is a sense of purpose that can enable one to step back and review, perhaps with doubt, perhaps with delight, the orienting values embedded in any particular mission.

Over time, specific purposes may no longer capture current reality or account for the way values have evolved. For example, the Constitutional value of ensuring domestic tranquility has remained the same over the course of two-hundred years, but programmatic purposes have changed in light of experiences that have clarified the application of this value in light of other precious values. Before the Civil War, ensuring domestic tranquility meant returning escaped slaves to their owners; in 1957, it meant using federal troops to integrate the high school in Little Rock.

These changes are perhaps most apparent these days in business, where companies with long histories and well-honed purposes face markets that no longer support them. Many companies are flocking to retreat centers to reformulate their purposes which, having been etched in stone for decades, have lost their vibrancy and relevance. Somehow, in the previous market environment, a sense of purpose was lost, only to be regained from hard experience. Instead of maintaining a spirit of inquiry that, with one eye on the reality of the market and another on the values of the institution, would generate ongoing adaptive change, complacency set in.

Adaptive change becomes a high-risk enterprise, however, when we postpone it so long that a revolution becomes necessary. Companies may die instead. Societies may degenerate. One look toward Russia and its neighbors should make us wary of any firm belief that adaptive work has to be a discontinuous process. The cases we have examined here demonstrate how progress can indeed be evolutionary and incremental. The fulcrum, however, is a sense of purpose that keeps people asking the question, particularly in times of plenty, "What's our next adaptive challenge?"

Preserving a sense of purpose helps one take setbacks and failures in stride. Leadership requires the courage to face failures daily. Otherwise, one cannot take corrective action. Moreover, a sense of purpose helps generate the freedom to change venues for leading when, after repeated trial, one sees no options for further action. Sometimes one has to give up entirely on an organizational or political situation. Without the personal freedom to change, however, the loss of a prized and familiar job and direction can lead to disorientation and despair. Often, to avoid the loss, we limit our sights instead and, staying in place, give up leading. The accumulation of wounds narrows our scope. In the short run, a personal equilibrium is restored, but over time a corrosion of spirit can set in as people lose the inspiration that comes from setting their lives in a larger frame. A sense of purpose provides the ongoing capacity to generate new possibilities.

Leadership takes place every day. It is neither the traits of the few, a rare event, or a once-in-a-lifetime opportunity. In our world, in our politics and businesses, we face adaptive challenges all the time. Every time we face a conflict among competing values, or encounter a gap between our shared values and the way we live, we face the need to learn new ways. When a public official is asked to square conflicting aspirations, he and his constituents face the need to question dearly held assumptions. When an executive sees a solution to a problem, technical in many respects except that it requires changes in the attitudes and habits of subordinates, she faces an educative task. When a subordinate close to the frontline sees a gap between the objectives he is told to implement and the facts he sees in light of the organization's purpose, he faces the risks and opportunity of leading without authority.

Leadership, seen in this light, requires a learning strategy. A leader has to engage people in facing the challenge, adjusting their values, changing perspectives, and developing new habits of behavior. To an authoritative person who prides himself on his ability to tackle hard problems, this may come as a rude awakening. But it should also ease the burden of having to know the answers and bear the uncertainty. To the person who waits to receive either "the vision" to lead or the coach's call, this may also seem a mixture of good and bad news. The adaptive demands of our societies require leadership that takes responsibility without waiting for revelation or request. One may lead perhaps with no more than a question in hand.

Notes
Acknowledgments
Index

Notes

Introduction

1. According to estimates, the New York City draft riots of 1863 were the worst in U.S. history, killing more than 100 people in a city of about one million. The 1943 race riots in Detroit were more destructive per capita, but less in overall terms. Eric Monkkonen, "The Past and the Riot," *The Urban History Newsletter,* October 1992, p. 13; personal communication, Eric Monkonnen, Professor of History, UCLA, February 27, 1993.
2. "2 of 4 Officers Found Guilty in Los Angeles Beating: Tension Eases as Residents Hail the Verdict," *The New York Times,* April 18, 1993, p. A1.
3. As Bush put it, "What we saw last night and the night before in Los Angeles is not about civil rights. It's not about the great cause of equality that all Americans must uphold. It's not a message of protest. It's been the brutality of mob, pure and simple." "Excerpts from Bush's Speech on Los Angeles Riots: 'Need to Restore Order,'" *The New York Times,* May 2, 1992, p. A8; also see Robert Dallek, "Post-Riot Rhetoric Has a 60's Ring: Now, as Then, There's No Instant Cure-all," *The Boston Globe,* May 10, 1992, p. 73.
4. Richard Leakey and Roger Lewin, *Origins: What New Discoveries Reveal about the Emergence of Our Species and Its Possible Future* (New York: Dutton, 1982).
5. Personal communication, Nicholas Brady, November 17, 1992.
6. These kinds of silence are not formal categories in music. I offer these merely as examples.
7. Plato, *The Republic,* trans. Cornford (New York: Oxford University Press, 1941), p. 240.
8. For a discussion of the importance and difficulties of generating practical

theory from data, see Barney G. Glaser and Anselm L. Strauss, *The Discovery of Grounded Theory: Strategies for Qualitative Research* (Chicago: Aldine, 1967).

1. Values in Leadership

1. Most of the 100 top executives in education, business, and politics with whom I worked through the Instituto FES de Liderazgo in Colombia, 1991–1992, insisted that Escobar was a "real leader," even though they reviled his behavior.

2. "After Waco, the Focus Shifts to Other Cults," *The Boston Globe,* April 30, 1993, p. A1; "Growing Up under Koresh: Cult Children Tell of Abuses," *The New York Times,* May 4, 1993, p. A1.

3. As long as scholars allow the contradictions and confusion of common cultural assumptions to define how we conceive and study leadership, then our body of research will reflect the confusion rather than resolve it. Calder makes this point by suggesting that our scholarly research on leadership has been dominated by everyday assumptions, thereby failing to generate "higher-order" abstractions. Instead of examining common attributions about leadership as phenomena indicative of cultural patterns, scholars have limited their field of view by letting these attributions serve as the frame of reference. *"The paradox of leadership research is resolved by the realization that what has been attempted is not the development of scientific theory but the systematic and consistent use of everyday thought."* Bobby J. Calder, "An Attribution Theory of Leadership," in Barry M. Staw and Gerald R. Salancik, eds., *New Directions in Organizational Behavior* (Chicago: St. Clair, 1977), p. 182, italics in the original.

4. Among the most prominent connotations: (1) Leadership is the process of influence between a leader and followers to attain organizational objectives. (2) Leadership is the ability to provide the managerial functions associated with positions of senior authority. (3) Leadership means having a vision and getting people to realize it. (4) Leadership is the ability to influence others, particularly by noncoercive means. See Joseph C. Rost, *Leadership for the Twenty-First Century* (New York: Praeger, 1991), pp. 38–44.

5. See Calder, "An Attribution Theory of Leadership," for a discussion of how people commonly attribute social causation to the personal capacities of individuals, and then call those capacities leadership. Wildavsky suggests that people routinely interpret their problems in a characteristic way: "for or against existing authority." See Aaron Wildavsky, "A Cultural Theory of Leadership," in Bryan D. Jones, ed., *Leadership and Politics: New Perspectives in Political Science* (Lawrence: University Press of Kansas, 1989), pp. 98–100.

6. For some examples, see Elliott Jaques, *Requisite Organization: The CEO's Guide to Creative Structure and Leadership* (Arlington, VA: Cason Hall, 1989), p. 121; and John P. Kotter, *The Leadership Factor* (New York: Free Press, 1988). Kotter goes farther than many business scholars in his view that vision is not only the product of the CEO alone, but the CEO's effort to identify and articulate the long-term interests of the parties involved. Like Jaques, he also provides a normative conception of process.

7. "Indo-European Roots," in William Morris, ed., *The American Heritage Dictionary of the English Language* (Boston: Houghton Mifflin, 1969), p. 1526.

8. See Howard T. Prince and Associates, eds., *Leadership in Organizations,* third edition (West Point, NY: United States Military Academy, 1985).

9. The following overview simplifies a rich and varied literature on leadership. The taxonomy is based on Edwin P. Hollander, "Leadership and Power," in Gordon Lindzey and Elliot Aronson, eds., *The Handbook of Social Psychology,* third edition (New York: Random House, 1985), pp. 485–537. For the reader interested in other surveys and typologies of the leadership literature, the following are helpful. For a view taken largely from social psychology and management studies, see Cecil A. Gibb, "Leadership," in Gardner Lindzey and Elliot Aronson, eds., *The Handbook of Social Psychology,* second edition (Reading, MA: Addison-Wesley, 1969), vol. 4, pp. 205–282; and Bernard M. Bass's survey of over 7,500 studies of leadership in *Bass and Stogdill's Handbook of Leadership,* third edition (New York: Free Press, 1990). For a political science view, see Glenn D. Paige, *The Scientific Study of Political Leadership* (New York: Free Press, 1977), chaps. 2–4. For normative views, see Robert Terry, *Authentic Leadership: Courage in Action* (San Francisco: Jossey-Bass, 1993); and Rost, *Leadership for the Twenty-First Century,* chaps. 1–4. For views from across a range of disciplines, see Barbara Kellerman, ed., *Leadership: Multidisciplinary Perspectives* (Englewood Cliffs, NJ: Prentice-Hall, 1984).

10. For example, Barbara Kellerman in her edited volume *Political Leadership: A Source Book* (Pittsburgh: University of Pittsburgh Press, 1986), pp. ix–xi, organizes her selection of primary sources with the following questions: "Do leaders change history? Why do leaders lead? Why do followers follow? What are the types of leaders? How do leaders and followers relate? Is there a leadership for all seasons?" In the same vein, Jean Blondel asks, "What are the origins of [a leader's] power? What are the instruments by which this power is exercised? What difference do leaders make?" Jean Blondel, *Political Leadership: Towards a General Analysis* (Beverly Hills, CA: Sage, 1987), p. 4.

11. Most dictionaries define leadership as "the ability to lead," i.e., as a set of personality traits. Following this cultural preference, research on leadership has focused at various times on identifying these traits. Yet the hypothesis

that there are generic abilities to be identified or developed remains somewhat confused in the leadership literature because the frame of reference for leadership shifts in different studies. Conflicting definitional frames of reference are used to select whom to analyze. Attempts have even been made to lump together different trait studies to see which traits are found across a variety of them, yet the studies themselves often select for different things: position, informal following, and function. For example, if we select a group of CEOs to identify their common characteristics, we implicitly equate leadership with holding high positions of authority, or the ability to get them. If we define leadership in terms of a set of functions or the presence of an informal following, then the people we select to study will be different, and the characteristics we identify will differ. For an introduction to this methodological quandary and a review of the critical literature on *trait theory,* see Bass, *Bass and Stogdill's Handbook of Leadership,* chaps. 4 and 5. For specific analyses, see Ralph M. Stogdill, "Personal Factors Associated with Leadership: A Survey of the Literature," *Journal of Psychology,* vol. 25, 1948, pp. 35–71; Charles Bird, *Social Psychology* (New York: Appleton-Century, 1940), pp. 369–395; and William O. Jenkins, "A Review of Leadership Studies with Particular Reference to Military Problems," *Psychological Bulletin,* vol. 44, 1947, pp. 54–79.

12. For an analysis of these trends, see "Leadership Definitions: The 1980s," in Rost, *Leadership for the Twenty-First Century,* chap. 4.

13. See Thomas Carlyle, *On Heroes, Hero-Worship, and the Heroic in History,* written in 1841 (Boston: Houghton Mifflin, 1907); William James, "Great Men, Great Thoughts and Their Environment," *Atlantic Monthly,* vol. 46, October 1880, pp. 441–459; Frederick M. Thrasher, *The Gang: A Study of 1,313 Gangs in Chicago,* second revised edition (Chicago: University of Chicago Press, 1936); and Sidney Hook, *The Hero in History: A Study in Limitation and Possibility* (New York: John Day, 1943). James, Thrasher, and Hook, coming long after Carlyle, take serious account of situational variables as well as traits. For a critique of Hook's distinction, see Robert C. Tucker, *Politics as Leadership* (Columbia: University of Missouri Press, 1981), pp. 27–30, who argues that all actors give meaning to events, framing them according to their values. Different actors may give the same event different meanings and, as a result, engage with it differently, but all actors are responsive to events. For an illustrative study of characteristics believed to be associated with leadership, see W. H. Cowley, "The Traits of Face-to-Face Leaders," *Journal of Abnormal Psychology,* vol. 26, 1931, pp. 304–313. Early perspectives on a hereditary basis for leadership include: Frederick Adams Woods, M.D., *The Influence of Monarchs: Steps in a New Science of History* (New York: MacMillan, 1913); and Albert

E. Wiggam, "The Biology of Leadership," in Henry C. Metcalf, ed., *Business Leadership* (New York: Pitman, 1931), pp. 13–32.

14. James Madison, for example, exercised leadership brilliantly as congressman and as key framer of the Constitution, but performed far less brilliantly, some say poorly, as President. John Quincy Adams, as diplomat and Secretary of State, "must rank among the greatest this nation has produced, yet as President was a disappointment." Richard Ellis and Aaron Wildavsky, "'Greatness' Revisited: Evaluating the Performance of Early American Presidents in Terms of Cultural Dilemmas," *Presidential Studies Quarterly,* vol. 21, winter 1991, p. 31.

15. John K. Hemphill, *Situational Factors in Leadership* (Columbus: Ohio State University Bureau of Educational Research, 1949), p. v, italics added. Also see Herbert Spencer, *The Study of Sociology* (New York: D. A. Appleton, 1884); Fillmore H. Sanford, *Authoritarianism and Leadership: A Study of the Follower's Orientation to Authority* (Philadelphia: Institute for Research in Human Relations, 1950); and Alvin W. Gouldner, ed., *Studies in Leadership* (New York: Harper and Brothers, 1950). A large body of work within political science investigates the institutional constraints on individual action. This tradition lies in dynamic tension with the biographical tradition, which asserts that individual action impacts events and institutions significantly. Fred Greenstein seems to have found common ground by suggesting that "the impact of an individual's actions varies with (1) the degree to which the actions take place in an environment which admits of restructuring, (2) the location of the actor in that environment, and (3) the actor's peculiar strengths or weaknesses." Fred I. Greenstein, "The Impact of Personality on Politics: An Attempt to Clear Away Underbrush," *American Political Science Review,* vol. 61, 1967, pp. 633–634. For a review of these arguments, see Bryan D. Jones, ed., *Leadership and Politics: New Perspectives in Political Science* (Lawrence, KS: University Press of Kansas, 1989); Dankwart Rustow, "Introduction to the Issue 'Philosophers and Kings: Studies in Leadership,'" *Daedalus,* vol. 97, summer 1968, pp. 683–694; and Jameson W. Doig and Erwin C. Hargrove, "'Leadership' and Political Analysis," in Jameson W. Doig and Erwin C. Hargrove, eds., *Leadership and Innovation: A Biographical Perspective on Entrepreneurs in Government* (Baltimore: Johns Hopkins University Press, 1987), chap. 1. Also see Tucker, *Politics as Leadership,* pp. 27–30; James Q. Wilson, "The Politics of Regulation," in James Q. Wilson, ed., *The Politics of Regulation* (New York: Basic, 1980), pp. 357–394; Blondel, *Political Leadership,* chap. 5; and Norman Frohlich, Joe A. Oppenheimer, and Oran R. Young, *Political Leadership and Collective Goods* (Princeton: Princeton University Press, 1971), pp. 3–11.

16. For the original study distinguishing autocratic and democratic styles of

authority, see Kurt Lewin and Ronald Lippitt, "An Experimental Approach to the Study of Autocracy and Democracy: A Preliminary Note," *Sociometry,* vol. 1, 1938, pp. 292–300. Also see "Leadership as a Function of Regime," in Aaron Wildavsky, *The Nursing Father: Moses as a Political Leader* (Alabama: University of Alabama Press, 1984), pp. 182–216, for a framework of political development and the challenges of leadership appropriate to it. For other analyses of the mesh between leadership style and various situational contingencies, see Fred E. Fiedler, *A Theory of Leadership Effectiveness* (New York: McGraw Hill, 1967); Victor Vroom and Philip W. Yetton, *Leadership and Decision-Making* (Pittsburgh: University of Pittsburgh Press, 1973); Paul Hersey and Kenneth Blanchard, *Management of Organizational Behavior: Utilizing Human Resources* (Englewood Cliffs, NJ: Prentice-Hall, 1977); and Gary A. Yukl, *Leadership in Organizations,* second edition (Englewood Cliffs, NJ: Prentice-Hall, 1989).

17. See Edward E. Jones, Kenneth J. Gergen, and Robert E. Jones, "Tactics of Ingratiation among Leaders and Subordinates in a Status Hierarchy," *Psychological Monographs,* vol. 77, 1963, pp. 1–20; Edwin P. Hollander, *Leadership Dynamics: A Practical Guide to Effective Relationships* (New York: Free Press, 1978); and Morris P. Fiorina and Kenneth A. Shepsle, "Formal Theories of Leadership: Agents, Agenda Setters, and Entrepreneurs," in Jones, ed., *Leadership and Politics,* pp. 17–40.

18. This approach overlaps with the situational perspective, which places emphasis on the institutional forces that influence leadership behavior. The difference is perhaps a matter of balance. Are patterns of influence a matter of mutual transaction, or is influence primarily "in the hands" of institutions that determine the behavior of actors? See "The Nature of Leadership," in David B. Truman, *The Governmental Process* (New York: Knopf, 1951), pp. 188–193; "The Ambiguity of Leadership," in Robert A. Dahl, *Who Governs?* (New Haven: Yale University Press, 1961), pp. 89–103; and Bruce J. Crowe, Stephen Bochner and Alfred W. Clark, "The Effects of Subordinates' Behavior on Managerial Style," *Human Relations,* vol. 25, July 1972, pp. 215–237. Cecil Gibb, who calls the transactional approach interaction theory, describes it this way: "Followers subordinate themselves not to an individual who is utterly different but to a member of their group who has superiority at this time and who is fundamentally the same as they are, and who at other times is prepared to be a follower just as they are . . . The leader inevitably embodies many of the qualities of the followers. Any individual's personality at a given point in time reflects the field forces with which it is interacting." Cecil A. Gibb, ed., *Leadership* (Middlesex, England: Penguin, 1969), p. 210.

19. Hollander, *Leadership Dynamics.*

20. Richard E. Neustadt, *Presidential Power and the Modern Presidents: The Politics of Leadership from Roosevelt to Reagan,* third edition (New York: Free Press, 1990), pp. 40–49.

21. Glenn Paige grapples with this problem explicitly in his comparison of Hitler and Gandhi along various dimensions. His eighteen dimensions of analysis (e.g., coercion, consensus, technicity, creativity, and morality) generate normative assessments and predictions. However, Paige joins with nearly all political scientists in *defining* leadership in "value-free" terms: the behavior of people in positions of political authority, and their competitors. Thus, both Gandhi and Hitler are considered leaders. See Glenn D. Paige, *The Scientific Study of Political Leadership* (New York: Free Press, 1977), pp. 1 and 139–149.

22. Fred E. Fiedler, *A Theory of Leadership Effectiveness* (New York: McGraw Hill, 1967). Other major theorists of contingency theory, like Vroom and his collaborators, place value on "organizational effectiveness," and not simply the ability to maintain control or power. Organizational effectiveness means the accomplishment of organizational objectives. The hypothesis is that some situations call for autocratic decisionmaking while others call for various forms of consultation and participation. The decisionmaker should decide which mode of decisionmaking is most effective given the nature of the situation. For example, one should engage the participation of subordinates whenever one thinks their perspectives are necessary either to the decision itself, or to their commitment to the decision. See Victor Vroom and Philip W. Yetton, *Leadership and Decision-Making* (New York: Wiley, 1974); and Victor Vroom and Arthur Jago, *The New Leadership: Managing Participation in Organizations* (Englewood-Cliffs, NJ: Prentice-Hall, 1988).

23. One might ask: Could transactional and political theorists correct the problem of the consumption of their "value-free" theories as normative values by simply clarifying that they are speaking about means and not ends? In theory, perhaps. But in practice, I do not think people will internalize the distinction as long as the word leadership is used. The term, in my experience, is already firmly attached to the orienting values and self-images of young adults and working people. See Ronald A. Heifetz, Riley M. Sinder, Alice Jones, Lynn M. Hodge, and Keith A. Rowley, "Teaching and Assessing Leadership Courses at the John F. Kennedy School of Government," *Journal of Policy Analysis and Management,* vol. 8, summer 1989, pp. 536–562. Under the direction of Dr. Sharon Parks, the Lilly Endowment has sponsored a more full description and evaluation of these courses to determine, in part, their impact on the construction of values.

24. Operating in a descriptive tradition, many leadership scholars assume that the task of scholarship is to identify, describe, and analyze what leadership

is. Yet, as others before me have suggested, this has been difficult because there are no clear cultural agreements defining the term. "The existing literatures do not 'add up' (Argyris, 1979) partly for the reason that diverse phenomena have been studied in the name of leadership." (Hosking and Morley [p. 89], cited in Rost [p. 6]). Consequently, scholars have studied a variety of things under the rubric of leadership, and, in addition, have frequently left the value dimensions implicit. In this regard, Joseph Rost stands out for his recent effort to define his terms and analyze why he chooses them. Yet even Rost seems to offer a normative definition of leadership in a classical mode when he complains that "leadership scholars still have no clear understanding of what leadership is" (p. 14), and then proceeds to offer his value-infused perspective in the spirit of a truth, as if it were the nature and essence of leadership. It seems to me that scholars might usefully consider that leadership is less an "is" than a "should be," and that our arguments might center not around who has most accurately described objective reality (or perhaps prevailing cultural assumptions) but around what image we can usefully offer to people who in part shape their self-images by our conceptions. That may be quite a hard task from the point of view of research methodology, but at least we will be wrestling with the problem before us. See Rost, *Leadership for the Twenty-First Century;* Dian-Marie Hosking and Ian E. Morley, "The Skills of Leadership," in James G. Hunt, B. Rajaram Baliga, H. Peter Dachler, and Chester A. Schriesheim, eds., *Emerging Leadership Vistas* (Lexington, MA: Lexington Books, 1988), pp. 89–106; and Chris Argyris, "How Normal Science Methodology Makes Leadership Research Less Additive and Less Applicable," in James G. Hunt and Lars L. Larson, eds., *Crosscurrents in Leadership* (Carbondale: Southern Illinois University Press, 1979).

25. I prefer the term "orienting values" over "end values" because I think "end values" function by orienting people's choices of instruments. They are "where people come from," and not where they are going, as the term "end" suggests. For example, in decisionmaking about one's children, one is oriented by the value love. Love serves not as an end or a goal, but as a source of daily orientation.

26. Political scientists have tended to conceive of politics using powers and influence as the units of analysis. Yet there is a school of political thought, going back at least as far as Plato, that uses the polity's direction and work as the frame of reference. See Tucker, *Politics as Leadership,* pp. 4–9. Carl Friedrich put it this way, "To differentiate the leadership of a Luther from the leadership of a Hitler is crucial for a political science that is to 'make sense'; if a political science is incapable of that, it is pseudo-science, because the knowledge it imparts is corrupting and not guiding." Carl J. Friedrich, "Political Leadership and the Problem of the Charismatic Power," *Journal of Politics,* vol. 24, February 1961, p. 19.

27. I owe this idea to Thomas C. Schelling.

28. As suggested, this idea is analyzed by Vroom, Yetton, and Jago. Their focus is on decisionmaking processes by authority figures within organizations rather than, as in this study, problem-defining and problem-solving processes in complex political environments, or leadership without authority. See Vroom and Yetton, *Leadership and Decision-Making;* and Vroom and Jago, *The New Leadership: Managing Participation in Organizations.*

29. Tucker makes this point from a purely analytic perspective: "In the final analysis, the strength of leadership as an influencing relation rests upon its effectiveness as activity." Tucker, *Politics as Leadership,* p. 25. Preceding this perspective is a research approach established in the 1950s in social psychology and organizational behavior in which researchers began to examine behavior instead of personality. Specifically, they focused on two behaviors of people in positions of organizational authority: consideration for the satisfaction of subordinates and the initiation of structure (defining the task, initiating and organizing the work process, and maintaining standards). Most researchers have assumed that different situations will demand different balances between these two behaviors, and they have studied the contingencies distinguishing them. In contrast, some have advocated an all-seasons approach. In particular, Robert R. Blake and Jane S. Mouton, in *The Managerial Grid III* (Houston: Gulf Publishing Company, 1985), recommend both a high concern for people and a high concern for production as a generic approach to leadership. In general, these studies focus on the behavior of those with organizational authority. For the classic description of this work, see Ralph M. Stogdill and Alvin E. Coons, eds., *Leader Behavior: Its Description and Measurement* (Columbus: Ohio State University Bureau of Business Research, 1957). For a review, see "Consideration, Initiating Structure, and Related Factors for Describing the Behavior of Leaders," in Bass, *Bass and Stogdill's Handbook of Leadership,* chap. 24.

30. Many researchers and training organizations spend a great deal of time reinforcing the personalistic view of leadership by administering batteries of personality tests as a core element of leadership development. Although the tests may be of great use in generating reflection and insight among the people tested, which may be important skills of leadership, they are often unhinged from any clear operational conception of leadership. Lacking a basis in a conceptual framework of leadership strategy, they do not tell people enough about the effective use of their skills in the practice of leadership. For the pioneering efforts in this area of inquiry, see the various publications of the Center for Creative Leadership, Greensboro, North Carolina.

31. For a discussion of pathological personality structures and their mesh with institutional roles of authority, see Otto F. Kernberg, "Regression in Or-

ganizational Leadership," in Arthur D. Colman and Marvin H. Geller, eds., *Group Relations Reader 2* (Washington, DC: A. K. Rice Institute, 1985), pp. 96–106.

32. Pierre M. Turquet describes this dynamic in "Leadership: The Individual and the Group," in Colman and Geller, eds., *Group Relations Reader 2*, p. 85. There is little doubt in my mind that talented individuals have much to learn to lead effectively. To use an analogy, even the most gifted young violinist is ruined by poor training. To become a great violinist requires both talent and great training. Furthermore, quite average children with fine training make excellent musicians. All too often, terms like talent and character suggest something immutable after an early age. Indeed, following the influence of Freud's theory of human development, many scholars of leadership and politics make the assumption that inclinations and preferences are fixed in early childhood. In contrast, Dankwart Rustow stresses the importance of "conceiving of the leader's personality, not as fixed, but as changing; to consider, in turn, the character traits that he may display in long years of waiting for his opportunity, the new resources of personality that he brings to bear as he assumes his role as leader, and the decline which his personality may undergo as his historic task is accomplished." Rustow draws on Albert Hirschman's notion of "reform-mongering" in his study of economic development in Latin America to suggest that the "reform-monger or the charismatic leader is likely to emerge as the teacher in such a process, but to teach others he must first learn himself." (Rustow, "Introduction," pp. 690 and 683–694.) Rustow is not being naive about adult learning capacity. Erik Erikson, Robert Kegan, Elliott Jaques, and others have studied and persuasively argued that people continue to learn and develop through adolescent and adult years beyond merely the acquisition of information, but in profound ways. See Erik Erikson, *Young Man Luther: A Study in Psychoanalysis and History* (New York: Norton, 1958); Robert Kegan, *The Evolving Self* (Cambridge: Harvard University Press, 1982); and "Cognitive Processes: How They Work and How They Mature," in Elliott Jaques, *Requisite Organization: The CEO's Guide to Creative Structure and Leadership* (Arlington, VA: Cason Hall, 1989), sect. 5.

33. See "The Power of Leadership," in James MacGregor Burns, *Leadership* (New York: Harper Colophon, 1978), chap. 1.

34. "The Structure of Moral Leadership," in Burns, *Leadership,* chap. 2. Other organizational and political theorists have modified and elaborated Burns' concept of transformational leadership by converting it into a nonnormative framework. See Bernard M. Bass, *Leadership and Performance beyond Expectations;* and Erwin C. Hargrove, "Two Conceptions of Institutional Leadership," in Jones, ed., *Leadership and Politics,* pp. 57–83. Both conceive of transformation, not in Burns' sense of elevating the

moral functioning of a polity but in the sense of inspiration, intellectual stimulation, and personal consideration (Bass), or altering the basic normative principles that guide an institution (Hargrove, p. 66).

35. See Tucker, *Politics as Leadership,* pp. 77–79, for his discussion of non-constituted leaders.

36. See Max Weber, "Politics as a Vocation," in Gerth and Mills, eds., *From Max Weber,* pp. 77–128. Professor Michael O'Hare at the University of California, Berkeley, provided the articulation of this idea.

37. See Vroom and Jago, *The New Leadership: Managing Participation in Organizations.*

38. Burns, *Leadership,* pp. 42–43; and Tucker, *Politics as Leadership,* pp. 98–105. For a review of the leadership literature in regard to conflict, its sources and management, see "Conflict and Legitimacy in the Leadership Role," in Bass, *Bass and Stogdill's Handbook of Leadership,* chap. 15.

39. Robert C. Tucker follows a similar logic, although he stops short of a normative conception. By building on Cecil Gibb's statement that "leadership flourishes in a problem situation," Tucker orients leadership by the activities of problem definition, policy formulation, and policy implementation. His emphasis on problem definition points us in the direction of reality testing as a key instrumental value in leadership. See Tucker, *Politics as Leadership,* pp. 18–19; and Cecil A. Gibb, "The Principles and Traits of Leadership," in Gibb, ed., *Leadership,* p. 211.

40. Selznick provides an elegant analysis of the role of organizational leadership in shaping the orienting values of an institution, in Philip Selznick, *Leadership in Administration: A Sociological Interpretation* (New York: Harper and Row, 1957). Also Drath and Palus at the Center for Creative Leadership have been working on a conception of leadership (based on Robert Kegan's work) as "meaning making in collective experience," which points us toward the task of giving people a way to make sense of their situation. Wilfred Drath and Charles Palus, "Leadership as Meaning Making in Collective Experience" (Greensboro: Center for Creative Leadership, 1993).

41. Collins and Porras divide vision into two components: purpose (a statement of orienting values) and mission (a medium-term practical goal that accounts for current reality). See James C. Collins and Jerry I. Porras, "Organizational Vision and Visionary Organizations," *California Management Review,* vol. 34, fall 1991, pp. 30–52.

42. See Neustadt's analysis of Truman's mishandling of the Korean War in *Presidential Power,* pp. 103–122, in which he analyzes the President's role as teacher in taking events and giving them meaning. His analysis could be used to support Tucker's critique of Sidney Hook's distinction between eventful and event-making men, as described in note 13, above.

43. Quoted in Arthur M. Schlesinger Jr., "A Clinton Report Card, So Far,"

The New York Times, April 11, 1993, Section 4, p. 13. Schlesinger suggests, "Except for the part about admitting failure frankly, that was the story of Roosevelt's New Deal." For examples of improvisation in other contexts, see "War Is the Domain of Uncertainty," in Major General Baron Hugo von Freytag-Loringhoven, "The Power of Personality in War," *Roots of Strategy: 3 Military Classics,* Book 3 (Harrisburg, PA: Stackpole, 1991), chap. 4, pp. 252–289; Michael Cohen and James March, *Leadership and Ambiguity: The American College President,* second edition (Boston: Harvard Business School Press, 1986); and Robert D. Behn, *Leadership Counts: Lessons for Public Managers* (Cambridge: Harvard University Press, 1991).

44. Burns, *Leadership,* chap. 1.
45. For a discussion of Hitler's faulty diagnoses, see Tucker, *Politics as Leadership,* pp. 89–96. For an analysis of the domestic causes of war, with implications for the genesis of World War II, see Jack S. Levy, "Domestic Politics and War," in Robert I. Rotberg and Theodore K. Rabb, eds., *The Origin and Prevention of Major Wars* (Cambridge: Cambridge University Press, 1989).
46. In the postwar years, Jasper Shannon wrote, "Perhaps a more realistic, not to say more scientific age will look upon our belief in leaders who can solve our social ills by political magic as absurd as we regard the divine power attributed to monarchs in the healing of bodily ills." "The Study of Political Leadership," in Jasper B. Shannon, ed., *The Study of Comparative Government* (New York: Greenwood, 1949); cited also in Paige, *The Scientific Study of Political Leadership,* p. 42.
47. In the U.S. system, reality testing takes both analytic and political forms as each political faction sends its own policy analysts to work, and where open deliberation about the differences among them is often the norm. See, for example, Charles E. Lindblom, *The Policy-Making Process* (Englewood Cliffs, NJ: Prentice-Hall, 1968).
48. A diagnostic error, made consciously, is also immoral. Because a common tendency in human societies is to flee bad news, seek simplifying solutions, or cluster around old ones, we become vulnerable to charlatans who mislead us through misdiagnosis.
49. Other scholars have tackled this normative problem in a way somewhat similar to mine, yet with formulations that seem to me less useful to the practitioner. For example, ethicist Robert Terry, formerly director of the Reflective Leadership Center at the Hubert H. Humphrey School of Public Affairs, University of Minnesota, offers this definition: "Leadership is the courage to bring forth and let come forth authentic action in the commons." His use of "authentic action" is akin to what I mean by reality-testing. See Terry, *Authentic Leadership.* Joseph Rost offers this definition: "Leadership is an influence relationship among leaders and followers who

intend real changes that reflect their mutual purposes." By "real changes," Rost is again tracking the idea of adaptive work. See Rost, *Leadership for the Twenty-First Century,* p. 102.

50. For an analysis of conspiracy theories used historically by people to explain their predicaments, see Franz Neumann, "Anxiety and Politics," in *The Democratic and the Authoritarian State: Essays in Political and Legal Theory* (New York: Free Press of Glencoe, 1957), pp. 283–287. Neumann suggests that "just as the masses hope for their deliverance from distress through absolute oneness with a person [a charismatic figure], so they ascribe their distress to certain persons who brought this distress into the world through a conspiracy . . . Hatred, resentment, dread, created by great upheavals, are concentrated on certain persons who are denounced as devilish conspirators" (p. 279); cited also in Robert C. Tucker, "The Theory of Charismatic Leadership," *Daedalus,* vol. 97, summer 1968, p. 752. For a view of scapegoating from object relations theory, see Leonard Horwitz, "Projective Identification in Dyads and Groups," in Colman and Geller, eds., *Group Relations Reader 2,* pp. 28–30.

51. See Eric J. Miller, "Organizational Development and Industrial Democracy: A Current Case-Study," in Colman and Geller, eds., *Group Relations Reader 2,* p. 245.

2. To Lead or Mislead?

1. The word "stress" has physiological and psychological significance. Scientists use the term as a metaphor to describe more vividly ecological systems in disequilibrium, even though these systems do not "experience" stress.

2. The equilibria of nature are often dynamic, not static. The specific balance will change over time as conditions change and perturb the system. A new balance is reached, however temporary it too may be. For example, one species dies out and another takes up its ecological niche.

3. See "An Analysis of the Concept of Natural Selection," in Ernst Mayr, *Toward a New Philosophy of Biology: Observations of an Evolutionist* (Cambridge: Belknap/Harvard University Press, 1988), pp. 95–115.

4. John A. Moore, *Science as a Way of Knowing: The Foundations of Modern Biology* (Cambridge, MA: Harvard University Press, 1993), pp. 163–164.

5. Roger D. Masters, *The Nature of Politics* (New Haven: Yale University Press, 1989), p. 129.

6. For a study of Moses leading the slaves through various stages of political development and transforming them into a nation, see Aaron Wildavsky, *The Nursing Father: Moses as a Political Leader* (Alabama: University of Alabama Press, 1984).

7. For an introduction to the literature of organizational learning and culture change, see Chris Argyris and Donald Schön, *Organizational Learning: A*

Theory of Action Perspective (Reading, MA: Addison-Wesley, 1978); Terrence E. Deal and Allan A. Kennedy, *Corporate Cultures: The Rites and Rituals of Corporate Life* (Reading, MA: Addison-Wesley, 1982); Rosabeth Moss Kanter, *The Change Masters* (New York: Simon and Schuster, 1983); Edward Schein, *Organizational Culture and Leadership: A Dynamic View* (San Francisco: Jossey-Bass, 1985); Ralph H. Kilmann, Mary J. Saxton, Roy Serpa, and Associates, *Gaining Control of the Corporate Culture* (San Francisco: Jossey-Bass, 1985); James M. Kouzes and Barry Z. Posner, *The Leadership Challenge: How to Get Extraordinary Things Done in Organizations* (San Francisco: Jossey-Bass, 1987); and Peter M. Senge, *The Fifth Discipline: The Art and Practice of the Learning Organization* (New York: Doubleday, 1990). Also see Talcott Parsons, *The Evolution of Societies* (Englewood-Cliffs, NJ: Prentice-Hall, 1977), for an effort to identify the elements of a social system that increase its general adaptive capacity.

8. For the classic description of how mindsets shape the collection and interpretation of data, see Thomas Kuhn, *The Structure of Scientific Revolutions,* second edition (Chicago: University of Chicago Press, 1970).

9. This is not an argument for the notion that all reality is relative and in the eyes of the beholder. Although the analysis of problems is fundamentally affected by values, which are relative, that is not to say that "what is" is simply a matter of opinion. Diagnosing a problem, *within* a particular value orientation, proceeds quite usefully according to scientific principles that enable one to distinguish reality from fantasy.

10. This story is presented as allegory, not history, because it is based on archeologists' speculations about the settlement and decline of Easter Island. For an introduction to the archeological literature on Easter Island, see Jo Anne Van Tilburg, "HMS Topaze on Easter Island" (London: British Museum Occasional Paper #73, 1992). Also see Jo Anne Van Tilburg, "Pseudoscience and Commodification in the Pacific: Selling Easter Island as Myth, Mystery, and Metaphor," Paper delivered at the Annual Meeting, Society for American Archeology, Pittsburgh, PA, March 1992.

11. Personal communication, Dr. Jo Anne Van Tilburg, Institute of Archeology, UCLA, April 1992.

12. Jo Anne Van Tilburg, "HMS Topaze on Easter Island," p. 90.

13. I frequently use the term *norms* in this study inclusively to mean conventions, habits, generally accepted values, and, at times, formal rules and procedures that govern behavior in an organization or community. (My apologies to the anthropologists and sociologists.)

14. See "The Equilibrium of Institutionalized Groups," in David B. Truman, *The Governmental Process* (New York: Knopf, 1951), pp. 27–33.

15. See Albert O. Hirschman, *The Strategy of Economic Development* (New Haven: Yale University Press, 1958), pp. 47–49, in which he applies a learning model to economic development. Not surprisingly, the "price of

development is a high one in terms of human suffering, social tensions, forced abandonment of tradition and values, etc." (p. 48).

16. I conceive of urgency as an indicator of stress both in its rate of increase as well as its severity. For example, a sudden increase in stress may produce more urgency than a slowly increasing level that plateaus, even if the plateau is higher than the level reached suddenly. These are questions for empirical research that go beyond the classic experiments with boiling frogs. (Drop a frog in boiling water and it will jump out; slowly heat the water to a boil and the frog will remain in the water and die.) For example, we need to understand the variables by which different organizations and societies tolerate better a fast jolt to their system (e.g., Poland's economic policies of the 1990s), or a gradual and sustained challenge.

17. For example, in its motto *kaizen*—continuous improvement—the Toyota Corporation established a set of organizational values and norms oriented by the ongoing need to learn and adapt.

18. For analyses of both the adaptive and self-defeating aspects of defensive behavior at the individual level, see Anna Freud, *The Ego and the Mechanisms of Defense,* revised edition (New York: International Universities Press, 1966); and George E. Vaillant, *The Wisdom of the Ego* (Cambridge: Harvard University Press, 1993), chap. 1. At the group and organizational levels, see Wilfred R. Bion, *Experiences in Groups* (New York: Basic, 1961); Chris Argyris, *Strategy, Change, and Defensive Routines* (Boston: Pitman, 1985), and *Overcoming Organizational Defenses: Facilitating Organizational Learning* (Boston: Allyn and Bacon, 1990); Larry Hirschhorn, *The Workplace Within: Psychodynamics of Organizational Life* (Cambridge: MIT Press, 1988); and Irving Janis and Leon Mann, *Decision Making: A Psychological Analysis of Conflict, Choice, and Commitment* (New York: Free Press, 1977).

19. The father's own vulnerability to experiencing intolerable distress in response to the child is a more complex psychological process than summarized here. See Edward R. Shapiro and A. Wesley Carr, *Lost in Familiar Places* (New Haven: Yale University Press, 1991), pp. 13–14.

20. Craig Snyder, ed., *The Strategic Defense Debate* (Philadelphia: University of Pennsylvania Press, 1966), p. 220.

21. Strobe Talbott, "SDI During the Reagan Years," in Joseph S. Nye and James S. Schear, eds., *On the Defensive: The Future of SDI* (Lanham, MD: University Press of American, 1988), p. 16.

22. William Broad, "Long Streams of People Led to Stars Wars Speech," *The New York Times,* March 4, 1985, p. A1.

23. Talbott, "SDI During the Reagan Years."

24. See Ronald Reagan, *An American Life* (New York: Simon and Schuster, 1990), chap. 70.

25. See Ashton Carter and David Schwartz, eds., *Ballistic Missile Defense*

(Washington, DC: Brookings Institution, 1984); and Thomas C. Schelling, "What Went Wrong with Arms Control?" *Foreign Affairs,* vol. 64, winter 1985/86, pp. 219–233.

26. Robert McNamara, "Reducing the Risk of Nuclear War," in Snyder, *The Strategic Defense Debate,* p. 124.

27. Talbott, "SDI During the Reagan Years."

28. By a margin of 3 to 2, many Americans were seeing "the Soviet Union as a growing threat as well as an immediate danger." By an even larger margin, 2 to 1, 64 percent of Americans favored a mutual freeze compared with 25 percent who favored an arms buildup. "Poll Finds Doubt over Responses to Soviet Threat," *The New York Times,* April 15, 1983, p. A1. (Although the poll was taken two weeks after the President's March 23 speech, the poll did not refer to SDI, which had not yet come alive in the public debate.)

29. According to Talbott's account, Assistant Secretary of Defense for International Security Policy Richard Perle championed the cause of SDI as a weapons system to protect U.S. silos, while Secretary of State George Shultz and his special advisor for arms control, Paul Nitze, saw SDI as a bargaining chip. Talbott, "SDI During the Reagan Years."

30. None of us can get inside the mind and recreate the thought process of President Reagan. His memoirs are not of much help in fathoming the unreality of SDI as he packaged it for the nation. In them, he seems not to notice the inconsistency of his vision of impenetrable defense with the reality of the limits of SDI, even if it were to work as planned. Reagan seemed unusually capable of commitment to his central convictions, be it lower taxes or SDI, and uncaring about the "details" that might temper those convictions. I believe it had more to do with his capacity to live in dreams than with any cynical strategy of deceit. See Richard E. Neustadt, *Presidential Power and the Modern Presidents* (New York: Free Press, 1991), pp. 276–279.

31. Colin Gray, "Deterrence and Strategic Defense," in Snyder, *The Strategic Defense Debate,* p. 175. In the case of SDI, this included the problem of relating to American allies in Europe, who were incensed by Reagan's failure to consult with them before presenting his idea. As Francis Pym, former Foreign Secretary of State of Great Britain for Foreign and Commonwealth Affairs, put it, "The bedrock of our security is the positive acceptance of our peoples of an effective strategy for both defense and disarmament. To obtain that acceptance and support is among the top priorities for all politicians and statesmen in the West. What is required is a continuous process of presentation and explanation of what the issues are—presentations that analyze the problems fully, frankly, and fairly, and that expose the options available. It is not a question of 'selling' SDI; it is

a question of taking people into your confidence." Francis Pym, "A European View," in Snyder, *The Strategic Defense Debate,* p. 136.

32. Michael Vlahos, "Perceptions of Power," in Snyder, *The Strategic Defense Debate,* pp. 80–81. According to the panel President Reagan convened to create a plan for SDI, chaired by Dr. James C. Fletcher, strategic defenses could only be effective if "sized" to Soviet offensive forces. To be effective, SDI would have to be linked to arms control in order to avoid simply escalating the arms race into new domains. Even SDI required relating. See Alex Gliksman, "The Strategic Defense Environment," in Snyder, *The Strategic Defense Debate,* pp. 199–200.

33. One expression of this resistance was the Jackson-Vanik Amendment of 1973, which derailed Nixon's efforts at détente. See Henry Kissinger, *Years of Upheaval* (Boston: Little, Brown, 1982), pp. 986–998.

34. Gregory F. Treverton, "'Foreign' Assessment," Discussion Paper Series #148D (Cambridge: John F. Kennedy School of Government, Harvard University, 1986).

35. James G. Blight and David A. Welch, *On the Brink: Americans and Soviets Reexamine the Cuban Missile Crisis* (New York: Hill and Wang, 1989), pp. 29, 238, 258, 294–295, and 302.

36. Carter and Schwartz, *Ballistic Missile Defense,* p. 1.

37. According to a *Washington Post* poll, 55 percent of Americans favored a system that would "guarantee protection of the nation against nuclear attack regardless of cost." "Poll Shows Public Optimism on Arms Cuts," *The Washington Post,* November 17, 1985, p. A27. In other polls the same week, a *Time Magazine* poll suggested that 68 percent of the public believed that SDI was likely to work; in a *New York Times*/CBS poll, 58 percent of respondents felt the same optimism. In a Gallup survey, 61 percent wanted to "see the U.S. go ahead with the development of SDI." These three polls are reported in "US public opinion generally favors 'Star Wars,'" *The Christian Science Monitor,* November 21, 1985, p. 3.

38. See Ashton B. Carter, "Directed Energy Missile Defense in Space," Background paper prepared for the Office of Technology Assessment, Congress, Washington, DC, April 1984.

39. Perhaps this gives away too much to FDR, but I don't think so. His campaign strategy was shaped by isolationist public opinion, which in turn shaped the antiwar democratic platform and the charges of war-mongering by Wendell Wilkie, his Republican opponent. Surely, Roosevelt misled the public on his stand toward entering the Nazi War to get reelected. Reelection politics indicated to him the rate at which the country seemed ready to tackle the problem posed by a potential Nazi takeover of Europe. Getting elected was not only an end unto itself, it was also a means to pursue the foreign policy that Roosevelt saw as necessary.

40. Johnson's decisions to escalate the war in Vietnam, as I discuss in Chapter

7, may also have involved self-deception in the form of overly optimistic forecasting.

41. By collusion, I mean a deliberate or unconscious collaboration, usually the latter.

42. Leon Wieseltier, "Traditional Deterrence," in Snyder, *The Strategic Defense Debate*.

43. As McGeorge Bundy, et al., put it, "We believe the President's initiative to be a classic case of good intentions that will have bad results because they do not respect reality." In McGeorge Bundy, George Kennan, Robert McNamara, and Gerard Smith, "The President's Choice: Star Wars or Arms Control," *Foreign Affairs*, vol. 63, winter 1984/85, pp. 264–278.

3. The Roots of Authority

1. See Allan Mazur, "A Cross-Species Comparison of Status in Small Established Groups," *American Sociological Review*, vol. 38, October 1973, pp. 513–530. Mazur describes in his cross-species studies the critical role of deference behavior. Apparently, the emergence of deference behavior correlates in higher primates (macaques, baboons, chimpanzees, and gorillas) with the presence of control and service behaviors by dominant individuals. In these primates, the deferring individual will avoid confrontation and allow the dominant individual the right-of-way. In contrast, in primates genetically more distant from humans (shrews and squirrel monkeys), dominance is maintained through threat, chase, or attack, not active deference, and in these species, we do not see service and control behaviors.

2. See Muzafer Sherif, *An Outline of Social Psychology* (New York: Harper, 1948); David A. Easton, *A Systems Analysis of Political Life* (New York: Wiley, 1965), pp. 205–207 and 215–217; Robert A. Dahl, *After the Revolution?—Authority in a Good Society* (New Haven: Yale, 1970); and Richard Sennett, *Authority* (New York: Knopf, 1980). For an analysis of the ways in which U.S. Presidents have dealt with the antiauthority bias of American political culture dating from the nation's rebellious beginning, see Richard Ellis and Aaron Wildavsky, "'Greatness' Revisited: Evaluating the Performance of Early American Presidents in Terms of Cultural Dilemmas," *Presidential Studies Quarterly*, vol. 21, winter 1991, pp. 15–34.

3. Of course, our primate ancestors no longer exist. Current primates have undergone evolutionary change over time as have humans, and therefore investigating current primates gives us a glimpse into likely ancestral behavior, but not an exact portrayal.

4. See "Evolution of Grouping Patterns," in Robin I. M. Dunbar, *Primate Social Systems* (New York: Comstock/Cornell University Press, 1988), chap. 7; and Edward O. Wilson, *Sociobiology*, abridged edition (Cambridge: Harvard University Press, 1980), chap. 3.

5. Economists and political theorists who work on the problems of coordination, cooperation, and collective action may easily recognize the discussion in this study. Although the language differs, this study is centrally concerned with the social functions of authority systems, their relationship to other cultural constructs (for example, common identifications, shared norms and values), and the role of leadership in raising the quality of collective performance in the face of complex problems that generate divisiveness. Perhaps the central difference between this study and the tradition of Mancur Olson, Robert Axelrod, Douglass North, Elinor Ostrom, Robert Putnam, and others is the unit of analysis: the individual actor changing institutions versus the nature and design of institutions per se. See Mancur Olson, *The Logic of Collective Action* (New York: Cambridge University Press, 1965); Robert Axelrod, *The Evolution of Cooperation* (New York: Basic, 1984); Douglass C. North, *Institutions, Institutional Change, and Economic Performance* (New York: Cambridge University Press, 1990); Elinor Ostrom, *Governing the Commons: The Evolution of Institutions for Collective Action* (New York: Cambridge University Press, 1990); and Robert D. Putnam, *Making Democracy Work: Civic Traditions in Modern Italy* (Princeton: Princeton University Press, 1993).

6. See Marshall Sahlins, *The Use and Abuse of Biology: An Anthropological Critique of Sociobiology* (Ann Arbor: University of Michigan Press, 1976); and Stephen Jay Gould, *The Mismeasure of Man* (New York: Norton, 1981), chap. 7.

7. Michael R. A. Chance and Clifford J. Jolly, *Social Groups of Monkeys, Apes, and Men* (New York: Dutton, 1970).

8. George B. Schaller, *The Mountain Gorilla: Ecology and Behavior* (Chicago: University of Chicago Press, 1963), p. 243.

9. Kelly J. Stewart and Alexander H. Harcourt, "Gorillas: Variations in Female Relationships," in Barbara B. Smuts, Dorothy L. Cheney, Robert M. Seyfarth, Richard W. Wrangham, and Thomas T. Struhsaker, eds., *Primate Societies* (Chicago: University of Chicago Press, 1987), pp. 158, 163; Richard W. Wrangham, "Evolution of Social Structure," in *Primate Societies*, p. 293; and George B. Schaller, *The Year of the Gorilla* (Chicago: University of Chicago Press, 1964), p. 133.

10. Schaller, *The Mountain Gorilla* and *The Year of the Gorilla*; Dian Fossey, *Gorillas in the Mist* (Boston: Houghton Mifflin, 1983). Unless otherwise noted, all information about gorillas in the following paragraphs is taken from these sources.

11. Terry L. Maple and Michael P. Hoff, *Gorilla Behavior* (New York: Van Nostrand Reinhold, 1982), p. 54.

12. Stewart and Harcourt, "Gorillas: Variations in Female Relationships," in *Primate Societies*, pp. 158–159.

13. Schaller, *The Year of the Gorilla*, p. 132.

14. See Frans De Waal, *Chimpanzee Politics: Power and Sex among the Apes* (New York: Harper Colophon, 1982); and Frans De Waal *Peacemaking among Primates* (Cambridge: Harvard University Press, 1989).

15. Jane Goodall, *The Chimpanzees of Gombe: Patterns of Behavior* (Cambridge: Belknap/Harvard University Press, 1986), p. 208. See also Toshisada Nishida and Mariko Hiraiwa-Hasegawa, "Chimpanzees and Bonobos: Cooperative Relationships among Males," in *Primate Societies*, p. 167. De Waal, in *Chimpanzee Politics*, p. 47, provides a graphic example of the role of dominant individuals in controlling conflict in the context of the Arnhem Zoo.

16. Nishida and Hiraiwa-Hasegawa, "Chimpanzees and Bonobos," in *Primate Societies*, p. 175.

17. Goodall, *The Chimpanzees of Gombe*, pp. 525–528. In 1971, the Gombe community of chimpanzees split when the male population reached a level of fifteen adults. The former beta became the new community's alpha male; and a six-year "war" ensued, with invasions, killing, and eventually the death (or dispersal) of the new community. The dominant males "prosecuted the war," actively patrolling the territory, attacking and killing estranged females and their young, and invading across the border to kill dominant males. Goodall, *The Chimpanzees of Gombe*, pp. 503–534.

18. Frans De Waal, *Chimpanzee Politics,* section 2.

19. There are also differences in style within species, even when inhabiting the same environment; this appears due, in part, to personality differences among dominant animals. Personal communication, Professor Marc Hauser, Department of Biological Anthropology, Harvard University, April 1993.

20. Natural law theory is not social Darwinism, even though it has been invoked occasionally on its behalf. For a summary of the origins of natural law theory, see Michael Lessnoff, *Social Contract* (London: MacMillan, 1986), pp. 20–27. See Gould, *The Mismeasure of Man*, for a discussion of biological potentiality.

21. Sarah Hrdy, *The Woman That Never Evolved* (Cambridge: Harvard University Press, 1981), pp. 190–191.

22. See Sigmund Freud, *Civilization and Its Discontents*, written in 1930, trans. Strachey (New York: Norton, 1961), chaps. 5–8. Freud puts it succinctly in describing what civilization must contend with in human nature, "*Homo homini lupus* [Man is a wolf to man]" (p. 65).

23. Gould, *The Mismeasure of Man*, chap. 7.

24. Rona Abramovitch, "The Relation of Attention and Proximity to Rank in Preschool Children," in Michael R. A. Chance and Ray R. Larsen, eds., *The Social Structure of Attention* (London: Wiley and Sons, 1976), pp. 153–176.

25. K. Toki, "Führer-Gefolgschaftsstruktur in der Schulklasse" [Leader-Follower Structure in School Classes], *Japanese Journal of Psychology,* vol. 10, 1935, pp. 27–56; cited in Bass, *Bass and Stogdill's Handbook of Leadership,* p. 600.

26. Barbara C. L. Hold, "Attention Structure and Rank Specific Behavior in Preschool Children," in Chance and Larsen, eds., *The Social Structure of Attention,* pp. 177–201.

27. Donald R. Omark and Murray S. Edelman, "The Development of Attention Structures in Young Children," in Chance and Larsen, eds., *The Social Structure of Attention,* pp. 119–151.

28. Sherwood L. Washburn and David A. Hamburg, "The Implications of Primate Research," in Irvin DeVore, ed., *Primate Behavior: Field Studies of Monkeys and Apes* (New York: Holt, Rinehart and Winston, 1965), p. 613; also see Donald R. Omark, "The Umwelt and Cognitive Development," in Donald R. Omark, F. F. Strayer, and Daniel G. Freedman, eds., *Dominance Relations* (New York: Garland STPM Press, 1980), pp. 231–258.

29. For an introduction to the literature on small group behavior and leadership, see Robert F. Bales, "The Equilibrium Problem in Small Groups," in Talcott Parsons, Robert F. Bales, and Edward Shils, eds., *Working Papers in the Theory of Action* (New York: Free Press, 1953), pp. 111–161; Wilfred R. Bion, *Experiences in Groups* (New York: Basic Books, 1961); Bruce Tuckman, "Developmental Sequence in Small Groups," *Psychological Bulletin,* vol. 63, June 1965, pp. 384–399; Dorwin Cartwright and Alvin Zander, eds., *Group Dynamics: Research and Theory,* third edition (New York: Harper and Row, 1968); and the two-volume series published by the A. K. Rice Institute based on work of the Tavistock Institute for Human Relations in London: Arthur D. Colman and W. Harold Bexton, eds., *Group Relations Reader* (Sausalito, CA: GREX, 1975); and Arthur D. Colman and Marvin H. Geller, eds., *Group Relations Reader 2* (Washington, DC: A. K. Rice Institute, 1985).

30. Robert F. Bales, *Interaction Process Analysis* (Reading, MA: Addison-Wesley, 1950).

31. Karl Deutsch also describes authority in regard to attention. "A *source* of messages that receives habitual preferential treatment as regards attention, transmission, and obedience in politics or social life may be said to possess authority . . . Authority consists in the successful claim for the preferential treatment of messages from a particular source, regardless of their content." Karl Deutsch, *Nerves of Government* (New York: Free Press, 1963), p. 179, italics in the original.

32. Harry P. Shelley, "Focused Leadership and Cohesiveness in Small Groups," *Sociometry,* vol. 23, 1960, pp. 209–216; for a group relations view of these

dynamics, see Kenneth Eisold, "Recovering Bion's Contributions to Group Analysis," in Colman and Geller, eds., *Group Relations Reader 2*, p. 43.

33. For a psychoanalytic view of the dynamics by which "central persons" are incorporated into the conscience and ego-ideal of group members, see Sigmund Freud, *Group Psychology and the Analysis of the Ego,* written in 1921, trans. Strachey (New York: Norton, 1959), pp. 25–42; and Fritz Redl, "Group Emotion and Leadership," *Psychiatry,* vol. 5, November 1942, pp. 573–596. Freud emphasizes that widespread bonds of identification throughout the group with the "central person" provide the glue that holds the group together, whereas Redl amends this view by suggesting that in the presence of some styles of "central persons," bonds among members develop as well and generate their own source of cohesion.

34. B. Aubrey Fisher, *Small Group Decision Making,* second edition (New York: McGraw-Hill, 1980), chap. 7.

35. Edwin P. Hollander, *Leadership Dynamics: A Practical Guide to Effective Relationships* (New York: Free Press, 1978).

36. For a sociological analysis of power and authority, see Jeffrey Pfeffer, *Power in Organizations* (Boston: Pitman, 1981); and Jeffrey Pfeffer, *Managing with Power* (Boston: Harvard Business School Press, 1992).

37. The debate among economists within agency theory about "principal-agent slack" parallels the long-standing debate among political scientists between situational/institutional determinists and "great-man" theorists and biographers, as noted earlier (note 15, Chapter 1). Are people captured by their institutions (and constituents) or do they act, to varying degrees, independently of them, occasionally challenging them? In attempting to bridge this debate, the social psychologist, Edwin Hollander, in *Leadership Dynamics,* used the term "idiosyncrasy credits" to refer to the political capital (informal authority) accrued by an authority figure by meeting many of the expectations of constituents. The capital can be spent on creative activity deviant from expectations. Thus, as we see everyday in politics, an authority figure will meet some expectations and frustrate others without losing office. Sometimes she satisfies and frustrates the same constituents, and sometimes she trades off different constituencies, satisfying one and frustrating another. This provides for slack within authorizing relationships that carry a complex bundle of expectations. For an introduction to this debate within agency theory, see Morris P. Fiorina and Kenneth A. Shepsle, "Formal Theories of Leadership: Agents, Agenda Setters, and Entrepreneurs," in Bryan D. Jones, ed., *Leadership and Politics: New Perspectives in Political Science* (Lawrence, KS: University Press of Kansas, 1989), pp. 17–40; Kevin B. Grier, ed., "Empirical Studies of Ideology and Representation in American Politics," *Public Choice,* vol. 76, June 1993 (entire issue); Joseph P. Kalt and Mark A. Zupan, "The Apparent Ideological Behavior of Legislators: Testing for Principal-Agent Slack

in Political Institutions," *Journal of Law and Economics,* vol. 33, April 1990, pp. 103–131; and Joseph P. Kalt and Mark A. Zupan, "Capture and Ideology in the Economic Theory of Politics," *The American Economic Review,* vol. 74, June 1984, pp. 279–300.

38. Some scholars disagree. David Easton applies the term authority broadly to cover all "command-obedience" relationships; thus, a thief with a gun has authority over his victim, although the victim would challenge the legitimacy of that authority. His distinction turns on legitimacy. David A. Easton, *A Systems Analysis of Political Life* (New York: Wiley, 1965), p. 208.

39. The classic studies on habitual deference were performed by Milgram. They are reported in Stanley Milgram, "Some Conditions of Obedience and Disobedience to Authority," *Human Relations,* vol. 18, 1965, pp. 57–76. For an expansion and application of Milgram's themes, see Herbert C. Kelman and V. Lee Hamilton, *Crimes of Obedience: Toward a Social Psychology of Authority and Responsibility* (New Haven: Yale University Press, 1989).

40. Numerous efforts have been made to assess levels of "maturity" among members of organizations, including characteristics like motivation to achieve, ability and willingness to take responsibility, and inclinations toward dependency. See Loren I. Moore, "The FMI: Dimensions of Follower Maturity," *Group and Organizational Studies,* vol. 1, 1976, pp. 203–222; Paul Hersey and Kenneth Blanchard, *Management of Organizational Behavior: Utilizing Human Resources* (Englewood Cliffs, NJ: Prentice-Hall, 1977); and Robert Kegan and Lisa Laskow Lahey, "Adult Leadership and Adult Development: A Constructionist View," in Barbara Kellerman, ed., *Leadership: Multidisciplinary Perspectives* (Englewood Cliffs, NJ: Prentice-Hall, 1984), pp. 199–230.

41. Margaret J. Rioch, "'All We Like Sheep—' [Isaiah 53:6]: Followers and Leaders," in Colman and Bexton, eds., *Group Relations Reader,* p. 175.

42. For an economic analysis of the role of the state in protecting public goods as well as market institutions like property rights, see "A Neoclassical Theory of the State," in Douglass C. North, *Structure and Change in Economic History* (New York: Norton, 1981), chap. 3.

43. Mikhail Gorbachev, *Perestroika: New Thinking for Our Country and the World,* updated edition (New York: Perennial/Harper and Row, 1988), p. 52.

44. See "Leadership in the Gang," in Frederick M. Thrasher, *The Gang: A Study of 1,313 Gangs in Chicago,* second revised edition (Chicago: University of Chicago Press, 1936), chap. 43, for a vivid description of the kinds of power-for-service exchange that takes place between members and heads of gangs.

45. See Janine Ludlam, "Reform and the Redefinition of the Social Contract

under Gorbachev," *World Politics,* vol. 43, January 1991, pp. 284–312; and Erich Fromm, *Escape from Freedom* (New York: Rinehart, 1941).

46. One can say that the trade-off was between various forms of freedom, for example, political and economic freedom versus freedom from insecurity and deprivation. This argument is analogous to Amartya Sen's analysis of various forms of equality. See "Equality of What?" in Amartya Sen, *Inequality Reexamined* (Cambridge: Harvard University Press, 1992), chap. 1.

47. See Lessnoff's *Social Contract* for a history of social contract theory. Among other things in his treatment, he provides a history of the bargains reached between rulers and ruled, from ancient times through feudal arrangements to the current age. Also see Vincente Medina, *Social Contract Theories: Political Obligation or Anarchy?* (Savage, MD: Rowman and Littlefield, 1990); and Ron Replogle, *Recovering the Social Contract* (Savage, MD: Rowman and Littlefield, 1989).

48. "Typically, in political systems, at least in those in which the political authorities are not being fundamentally challenged, the capacity of the authorities to rule is closely connected to the presence of an ingrained belief, usually transmitted across the generations in the socialization processes, that the occupants of the political authority roles have a right to command and the other members of the system a duty to obey. The major source of power for these roles resides in the prevalence of the conviction of their legitimacy." Easton, *A Systems Analysis of Political Life,* p. 208.

49. Jean-Jacques Rousseau, *The Social Contract and Discourses,* written in 1762 (London: Dent, 1973). In fact, Rousseau and many others believed they were providing an accurate account of the genesis of authority structures, and not simply a dramatic vehicle for presenting an aspiration. For a critique, see Fred H. Willhoite Jr., "Primates and Political Authority: A Biobehavioral Perspective," *American Political Science Review,* vol. 70, December 1976, pp. 1110–1126, who uses an analysis of primate social systems to counter the supposition of Hobbes, Rousseau, and Locke that people in some "original" state were at one time free of authority structures.

50. As Freud put it, "A great change takes place [in our ability to construct civilizations] only when the authority is internalized through the establishment of the super-ego." *Civilization and Its Discontents,* p. 80. Also see Jerome H. Barkow, "Attention Structure and the Evolution of Human Psychological Characteristics," in Chance and Larsen, eds., *The Social Structure of Attention,* pp. 206–209, for a discussion of how the capacity to internalize representations of authority enables an economy of attention.

51. The idea that individuals "contain" groups of internalized representations of those people and aspects of people that have been significant in their lives has its roots in Freudian psychology, which then gave rise to object

relations theory and ego psychology. In 1921, Freud wrote, "The contrast between individual psychology and social or group psychology, which at a first glance may seem to be full of significance, loses a great deal of its sharpness when it is examined more closely. It is true that individual psychology is concerned with the individual man and explores the paths by which he seeks to find satisfaction for his instinctual impulses; but only rarely and under certain exceptional conditions is individual psychology in a position to disregard the relations of this individual to others. In the individual's mental life someone else is invariably involved, as a model, as an object, as a helper, as an opponent; and so from the very first individual psychology, in this extended but entirely justifiable sense of the words, is at the same time social psychology as well." Freud, *Group Psychology and the Analysis of the Ego,* p. 1. For an introduction to object relations theory, see Melanie Klein, "Our Adult World and Its Roots in Infancy," *Human Relations,* vol. 12, 1959, pp. 291–303; reprinted in Colman and Geller, eds., *Group Relations Reader 2,* pp. 1–19; and Otto F. Kernberg, *Object Relations Theory and Clinical Psychoanalysis* (New York: Jason Aronson, 1976). For an introduction to ego psychology, see Heinz Hartmann, *Ego Psychology and the Problem of Adaptation* (New York: International Universities Press, 1958); and Erik Erikson, *Childhood and Society* (New York: Norton, 1950).

52. Ants can also achieve very large societies of up to 20 million members. In contrast to human organization, however, ant organization is based not upon a flexible set of learned and evolving norms and rules but upon a rigid set of genetically programmed behaviors. See Burt Hölldobler and Edward O. Wilson, *The Ants* (Cambridge: Belknap/Harvard University Press, 1990).

53. The concept of norms replacing authority is applied to the international system by Robert Keohane. He suggests that in the absence of a hegemon (a dominant world power), key hegemonic coordinating functions could be performed by a set of multilateral institutions and international regimes. That is, institutions and regimes may be able to function in place of a hegemon to facilitate cooperation if they are able to furnish a sense of certainty and confidence in the system formally provided by hegemonic authority. See Robert Keohane, *After Hegemony: Cooperation and Discord in the World Political Economy* (Princeton: Princeton University Press, 1984); see also note 90, Chapter 7, below.

54. David B. Truman, *The Governmental Process* (New York: Knopf, 1951), p. 194.

55. For a discussion of how intact networks of civic engagement enable societies to meet an ongoing stream of adaptive problems, see Robert Putnam, *Making Democracy Work.* Putnam's study of Italy explains the divergent political and economic experiences of the northern and southern regions

in terms of the degree to which each exhibits civic values—political equality, civic engagement, solidarity, trust, tolerance, cooperation, and honesty. Northern Italy, which exhibits a much higher degree of civic values, also has a more effective and democratic system of governance than does the South (p. 115). Putnam explains the self-reinforcing dynamics of the uncivic communities prevailing in southern Italy in terms of game theory: "The strategy of 'never cooperate' is a stable equilibrium, for reasons that are well explicated in standard accounts of the prisoner's dilemma. Once trapped in this situation, no matter how exploitative and backward, it is irrational for any individual to seek a more collaborative alternative, except perhaps within the immediate family" (p. 177).

56. According to Levi-Strauss, a system of chieftainship or headship seems always to exist in traditional societies. Claude Levi-Strauss, "The Nambikuara of Northwestern Mato Grosso," in Ronald Cohen and John Middleton, eds., *Comparative Political Systems: Studies in the Politics of Pre-Industrial Societies* (Garden City, NY: Natural History Press, 1967), p. 25.

57. See Lorna Marshall, "!Kung Bushman Bands," in Cohen and Middleton, eds., *Comparative Political Systems* (Garden City, NY: The Natural History Press, 1967), pp. 15–43. The !Kung are a hunter-gatherer society, and as such may provide insight into the ways human beings lived during most of our history.

58. Indeed, when the headman of the Gura band died without leaving any kin to succeed him, the band went on without a headman for at least two years (at which time the observers left the country). Marshall, "!Kung Bushman Bands," p. 38.

59. Ibid., p. 39.

60. Max Weber, *On Charisma and Institution Building*, ed. S. N. Eisenstadt (Chicago: University of Chicago Press, 1968), chap. 5.

61. For both a broad and in-depth view of charisma, see Jay A. Conger and Rabindra N. Kanungo, eds., *Charismatic Leadership: The Illusive Factor in Organizational Effectiveness* (San Francisco: Jossey-Bass, 1988).

62. See Harrison M. Trice and Janice M. Beyer, "Charisma and Its Routinization in Two Social Movement Organizations," in Barry M. Staw and L. L. Cummings, eds., *Research in Organizational Behavior,* vol. 8 (Greenwich, CN: JAI Press, 1986), pp. 113–164.

63. Weber called this *Amtcharisma,* the charisma of the office. See Weber, *On Charisma,* p. xxi.

64. The literature on stress and the emergence of leadership shows a strong correlation between the degree of distress experienced by a group and the style of behavior they authorize. In more routine contexts authority can be exercised less directly, more participatively, but in times of crisis a group will often withdraw authorization from a person who maintains a partici-

pative style, and it will then invest authority in someone who is directive, who makes quick, forceful decisions. See "Stress and Leadership," in Bass, *Bass and Stogdill's Handbook of Leadership,* chap. 29.

65. See Edward Shils, "Charisma, Order, and Status," *American Sociological Review,* vol. 30, April 1965.

66. Cited in Arthur M. Schlesinger Jr., *The Coming of the New Deal* (Boston: Houghton Mifflin, 1958), pp. 1–2. For an analysis of the context and sources of Roosevelt's charisma, see Ann Ruth Willner, *The Spellbinders: Charismatic Political Leadership* (New Haven: Yale University Press, 1984), pp. 111–117, 153–171.

67. See Max Weber, *The Theory of Social and Economic Organization,* ed. Talcott Parsons (New York: Free Press, 1964); Max Weber, *On Charisma and Institution Building,* p. 18; and Sidney Hook, *The Hero in History* (New York: John Day, 1943).

68. J. O. Hertzler, "Crises and Dictatorships," *American Sociological Review,* vol. 5, 1940, pp. 157–169.

69. See Mauk Mulder and Ad Stemerding, "Threat, Attraction to Group and Need for Strong Leadership," *Human Relations,* vol. 16, 1963, pp. 317–334. For a comparative analysis of this dynamic, see Richard H. Dekmejian and Margaret J. Wyszomirski, "Charismatic Leadership in Islam: The Mahdi of the Sudan," *Comparative Studies in Society and History,* vol. 14, 1972, pp. 195–214.

70. Adolf Hitler, "In Behalf of Christ" (Munich: Voelkischer Beobachter, April 12, 1922), cited in Gordon Prange, ed., *Hitler's Words* (Washington, DC: American Council on Public Affairs, 1944).

71. The perception of Churchill's charisma at the start of the war changed when the war was over; likewise, Roosevelt seemed far less magical to the nation during his second term than during the acute national emergency of his first. Tucker, "The Theory of Charismatic Leadership," p. 744. Of course, the person who gains charismatic authority has to have the personal skills and capacity to receive these projections. Not just anybody can step into the role. See Willner, *The Spellbinders,* pp. 59–171. For analyses of the contextual determinants of charisma, see H. H. Gerth and C. Wright Mills, eds., *From Max Weber: Essays in Sociology* (New York: Oxford University Press, 1946), pp. 245–252; Tucker, "The Theory of Charismatic Leadership," pp. 731–756; Irvine Schiffer, *Charisma* (Toronto: University of Toronto Press, 1973); Rioch, "'All We Like Sheep,'" in Colman and Bexton, eds., *Group Relations Reader,* pp. 159–177; Jerrold M. Post, "Narcissism and the Charismatic Leader-Follower Relationship," *Political Psychology,* vol. 7, 1986, pp. 675–688; and James G. Hunt, B. Rajaram Baliga, H. Peter Dachler, and Chester A. Schriesheim, eds., *Emerging Leadership Vistas* (Lexington, MA: Lexington Books, 1988), pp. 5–83. On

Hitler, see Robert C. Tucker, *Politics as Leadership* (Columbia, Missouri: University of Missouri Press, 1981), pp. 89–97.

72. In his study of Latin American economic development, Albert Hirschman suggests that one of the attitudinal changes required for development is the *perception* that progress is being made by the society, and that skilled rather than charismatic leadership may be required to change that attitude, particularly if charismatic authority is based on the "leader's ability 'to accentuate the sense of being in a desperate predicament.'" Albert O. Hirschman, "Underdevelopment, Obstacles to the Perception of Change, and Leadership," *Daedalus,* vol. 97, summer 1968, pp. 925–937; and Hirschman quoting Tucker, "The Theory of Charismatic Leadership," p. 751.

73. Elliott Jaques, *Requisite Organization: The CEO's Guide to Creative Structure and Leadership* (Arlington, VA: Cason Hall, 1989), p. 122.

4. Mobilizing Adaptive Work

1. For an example, see Floyd Alwon, "Response to Agencywide Crisis: A Model for Administrative Action," *Child Welfare,* vol. 59, June 1980, pp. 335–346. For an introduction to organizational studies of executive functions, see Chester Barnard's two volumes, *The Functions of the Executive* (Cambridge, MA: Harvard University Press, 1938), and *Organization and Management* (Cambridge, MA: Harvard University Press, 1948); Philip Selznick, *Leadership in Administration* (Berkeley: University of California Press, 1984); Daniel Katz and Robert L. Kahn, *The Social Psychology of Organizations,* second edition (New York: Wiley, 1978); Edwin P. Hollander, *Leadership Dynamics: A Practical Guide to Effective Relationships* (New York: Free Press, 1978); Leonard Sayles, *Leadership: What Effective Managers Really Do . . . And How They Do It* (New York: McGraw-Hill, 1979); and Thomas Gilmore, "Leadership and Boundary Management," *Journal of Applied Behavioral Science,* vol. 18, 1982, pp. 343–356. Many studies of executive functioning tend to equate leadership with the fulfillment of the social functions of authority. They have relevance to the uses of authority to accomplish adaptive change, but they do not focus on this process per se.

2. What I have identified as the social functions of authority (direction, protection, orientation, conflict control, and norm maintenance) are analogous to what political economists term the reduction of transaction costs (for example, costs to monitoring and enforcing agreements) and uncertainties critical to cooperation and collective action. See Douglass C. North, *Institutions, Institutional Change, and Economic Performance* (New York: Cambridge University Press, 1990), pp. 48–51.

3. David A. Easton, *A Systems Analysis of Political Life* (New York: Wiley, 1965), p. 213.

4. The names in this vignette are changed to protect privacy.

5. See "Substitutes for Leadership," in Bernard M. Bass, *Bass and Stogdill's Handbook of Leadership*, third edition (New York: Free Press, 1990), pp. 682–686.

6. For a psychoanalytic view of the dependency dynamic, see Wilfred R. Bion, *Experiences in Groups* (New York: Basic Books, 1961); and Edward R. Shapiro and A. Wesley Carr, *Lost in Familiar Places* (New Haven: Yale University Press, 1991), pp. 67–69, 124, and 157–177.

7. See Peter R. Andreas, Eva C. Bertram, Morris J. Blachman, and Kenneth E. Sharpe, "Dead-End Drug Wars," *Foreign Policy*, vol. 85, winter 1991, pp. 106–128.

8. According to a national poll of 1,000 people, taken for this study in September 1993 by pollster Gerry Chervinsky, consultant to *The Boston Globe*, 86% of Americans know of Manuel Noriega; 65% know if they have a mayor and know his or her name; 58% know of Pablo Escobar; 45% know of Medellín; and 28% "have any information or know anything" about their local drug treatment facility.

9. For a discussion of how the demands upon the authority figure's role increase with the size of a group, see John K. Hemphill, "Relations between the Size of the Group and the Behavior of 'Superior' Leaders," *Journal of Social Psychology*, vol. 32, 1950, pp. 11–22. In regard to attacking or replacing authority figures, see Muzafer Sherif and Carolyn Sherif, *Groups in Harmony and Tension* (New York: Harper and Brothers, 1953), pp. 199–202; Robert Hamblin, "Leadership and Crises," *Sociometry*, vol. 21, December 1958, pp. 322–335; and David Korten, "Situational Determinants of Leadership Structure," in Dorwin Cartwright and Alvin Zander, eds., *Group Dynamics: Research and Theory*, third edition (New York: Harper and Row, 1968), pp. 351–361.

10. This case is disguised to protect privacy.

11. See Plato, *The Republic*, trans. Cornford (Oxford: Oxford University Press, 1941), chaps. 2 and 3; Renford Bambrough, "Plato's Political Analogies," in Peter Laslett, ed., *Philosophy, Politics, and Society*, 1st ser. (Oxford: Blackwell/Oxford University Press, 1956); and Robert C. Tucker, *Politics as Leadership* (Columbia, Missouri: University of Missouri Press, 1981), pp. 1–3.

12. By technical expertise, I am generally referring to substantive expertise. Clearly, process expertise is also technical, in the sense that it consists of techniques. The purpose of this study, in fact, is to improve the technical expertise required to lead people through processes of adaptive change.

13. Robert Tucker suggests that "The validity of definitions of the situation may be a matter of degree. There is a possibility, theoretical if not practical

in any particular case, of a more inclusive diagnosis that would make room for some, if not all, of the purposes and concerns of both sides." Tucker, *Politics as Leadership*, p. 53.

14. See Thomas C. Schelling, "Climatic Change: Implications for Welfare and Policy," in the National Academy of Sciences study, *Changing Climate: Report of the Carbon Dioxide Assessment Committee* (Washington, DC: National Academy Press, 1983), pp. 449–482; and more recently John Broome, *Counting the Cost of Global Warming* (Cambridge, England: White Horse Press, 1992), chaps. 1 and 2, who refutes Schelling based on more recent scientific findings.

15. This illustration is based primarily on Henry Lee and Esther Scott, "Managing Environmental Risk: The Case of Asarco" (Cambridge: John F. Kennedy School of Government Case Program, Harvard University, 1985), Case #C16–88–847. Quotations, unless otherwise noted, are taken from this study.

16. Barnett Kalikow, "Environmental Risk: Power to the People," *Technology Review,* vol. 87, October 1984, p. 57.

17. William Ruckelshaus, "Letter: On Tacoma's Air—How E.P.A. Faces the Arsenic Risk," *The New York Times,* July 23, 1983, p. 22.

18. Personal communication, William Ruckelshaus, March 1992.

19. Personal communication, Colin Conant, June 1993.

20. Personal communication, Doug Sutherland, County Executive, Pierce County, WA; June 1993.

21. Personal communication, Professor Lawrence Susskind, MIT, February 1992.

22. One of the effects of this distinction was to broaden the scope of risk assessment, generating comparative risk assessments of communities and regions across the United States. Personal communication, Clark Goulding, Visiting Senior Lecturer, University of Washington; and former Chief, Air Program Branch, Region 10, EPA; June 1993. For discussions of this change, see Mark K. Landy, Marc J. Roberts, and Stephen R. Thomas, *The Environmental Protection Agency: Asking the Wrong Questions* (New York: Oxford University Press, 1990), pp. 258–259; and the report sponsored by Lee Thomas, the EPA Administrator from 1985–1989: Environmental Protection Agency, Office of Policy Planning and Evaluation, *Unfinished Business: A Comparative Assessment of Environmental Problems,* Overview Report (Washington, DC: Environmental Protection Agency, 1987). The quarterly journal of the EPA has provided periodic analyses of the distinction between risk assessment and risk management in the ongoing development of the Agency's mission. For example, see "Profiles in Risk Assessment: New Science, New Contexts," *EPA Journal,* vol. 19, no. 1, 1993.

23. Robert B. Reich, *Public Management in a Democratic Society* (Englewood-Cliffs, NJ: Prentice-Hall, 1990), p. 171.

24. There is, of course, a rich literature on the dynamics of plant closings in the United States, although it is weighted heavily toward studies on the outcome of workers rather than the outcome of the community as a whole. For an introduction to this literature, see Jeanne P. Gordus, Paul Jarley, and Louis A. Ferman, *Plant Closings and Economic Dislocation* (Kalamazoo, MI: W. E. Upjohn Institute for Employment Research, 1981). For studies that include accounts of community outcomes, see Robert L. Aronson and Robert B. McKersie, *Economic Consequences of Plant Shutdowns: Final Report* (Ithaca, NY: New York State School of Industrial and Labor Relations, Cornell University, 1980); David Bensman and Roberta Lynch, *Rusted Dreams: Hard Times in a Steel Community* (New York: McGraw-Hill, 1987); Gregory Pappas, *The Magic City: Unemployment in a Working Class Community* (Ithaca, NY: Cornell University Press, 1989); Lloyd Rodwin and Hidehiko Sazanami, eds., *Deindustrialization and Regional Economic Transformation: The Experience of the United States* (Boston: Unwin Hyman, 1989); and Peter B. Doeringer, et al., *Turbulence in the American Workplace* (New York: Oxford University Press, 1991).

25. Cited in Robert B. Reich, "Policy Making in a Democracy," in Robert B. Reich, ed., *The Power of Public Ideas* (Cambridge: Harvard University Press, 1990), pp. 149–150.

5. Applying Power

1. This distinction is similar to the distinction drawn between headship and leadership, where headship is equated with the formal powers of office (formal authority), and leadership with informal influence (informal authority). In my terms, although both formal and informal authority might be used as tools in the exercise of leadership, neither constitute leadership per se. The headship/leadership model does not help us focus on the task of adaptive work because it uses influence and formal authority as its units of analysis. For discussions of the distinction between formal powers and informal influence (or headship and leadership), see Richard E. Neustadt, *Presidential Power and the Modern Presidents: The Politics of Leadership from Roosevelt to Reagan,* third edition (New York: Free Press, 1990); Cecil A. Gibb, "Leadership," in Gardner Lindzey and Elliot Aronson, eds., *The Handbook of Social Psychology,* second edition (Reading, MA: Addison-Wesley, 1969), vol. 4, pp. 212–213; and Jean Blondel, *Political Leadership: Towards a General Analysis* (Beverly Hills, CA: Sage, 1987), pp. 13–15.

2. See "Public Prestige," in Neustadt, *Presidential Power,* chap. 5.

3. See Donald Winnicott, *The Maturational Process* (New York: International Universities Press, 1965); Arnold H. Modell, "The 'Holding Environment' and the Therapeutic Action of Psychoanalysis," *Journal of the American Psychological Association,* vol. 24, 1976, pp. 285–307; Edward R. Shapiro, "The Holding Environment and Family Therapy with Acting Out Adolescents," *International Journal of Psychoanalytic Psychotherapy,* vol. 9, 1982, pp. 209–226; Robert Kegan, *The Evolving Self* (Cambridge: Harvard University Press, 1982); and Edward R. Shapiro and A. Wesley Carr, *Lost in Familiar Places* (New Haven: Yale University Press, 1991).

4. For a discussion of the uses and misuses of prisons as holding environments to produce developmental change, see Kegan, *The Evolving Self,* pp. 175–177.

5. See David Good, "Individuals, Interpersonal Relations, and Trust," in Diego Gambetta, ed., *Trust* (Oxford: Blackwell, 1988), p. 32. For an organizational study of trust, see John J. Gabarro, "The Development of Trust, Influence, and Expectations," in Anthony G. Athos and John J. Gabarro, *Interpersonal Behavior: Communication and Understanding in Relationships* (Englewood Cliffs, NJ: Prentice-Hall, 1978), pp. 290–303; and John J. Gabarro, *The Dynamics of Taking Charge* (Boston: Harvard Business School Press, 1987), chap. 5.

6. For example, dogs subjected to small but random electric shocks become listless compared with dogs receiving large but predictable shocks. Martin E. P. Seligman, Steven F. Maier, and Richard L. Solomon, "Unpredictable and Uncontrollable Aversive Events," in F. Robert Brush, ed., *Aversive Conditioning and Learning* (New York: Academic Press, 1971); also see Good, "Individuals, Interpersonal Relations, and Trust."

7. Diego Gambetta, "Mafia: The Price of Distrust," in Gambetta, ed., *Trust,* pp. 162–163. Also see Anthony Pagden, "The Destruction of Trust and Its Economic Consequences in the Case of Eighteenth-Century Naples," in the same volume, pp. 127–141; Robert D. Putnam, *Making Democracy Work: Civic Traditions in Modern Italy* (Princeton: Princeton University Press, 1993), pp. 146–148, 167–180.

8. This discussion begins to introduce the skills and temperament that one would want to strengthen in any leadership development effort. A treatment of this subject awaits another volume.

9. This dynamic can be analyzed further. The doctor, by drawing attention to her own well-being, distracts the family from the work itself. And the distraction generates distrust by the following mechanism. People have ambivalent feelings about adaptive work: they want to make progress on hard problems, but they also want to avoid the associated distress. Consequently, the Buchanans might have welcomed the doctor's distraction as an escape from their problems and, at the same time, they might have been

annoyed with the doctor for her implicit breach of contract: "We are the patients. We are supposed to be cared for here, not you."

10. Speech delivered at the John F. Kennedy School of Government, Harvard University, January 1981.

11. Personal Communication, Ernesta Barnes Ballard, March 1993. For an in-depth discussion of the role of public involvement in environmental risk management, see the National Academy of Sciences study, *Improving Risk Communication* (Washington, DC: National Academy Press, 1989).

12. Personal communication, Alex Smith, former Director of the Hazardous Waste, Air and Water Division, Region 10 (Seattle), EPA; April 1993. As she put it incredulously at the time of Ruckelshaus' directive, "We're going to do public workshops on NISHAPS [this kind of regulation]?"

13. The reasons why Ruckelshaus chose risk management are, of course, complex. He might also have chosen the issue of acid rain, or ozone depletion, both of which were getting a lot of public attention (acid rain more than ozone). But the White House had no interest in pursuing these issues, while it approved the notion of risk management. Although Ruckelshaus' authority gave him some power to frame the public debate, his authorization from above constrained him within clear boundaries. See Landy, Roberts, and Thomas, *The Environmental Protection Agency,* pp. 252–258.

14. Without the benefit of historical perspective, I would pursue the logic of this argument with the following questions about President Clinton's strategy. Did he see the issue of gays in the military as an adaptive problem or a technical problem for which authoritative action might make perfect sense? The latter assessment would have been a fairly obvious mistake. The ban on gays in the military posed an adaptive challenge, both for the institution of the military and for the nation as a whole, requiring fundamental changes in institutional norms and procedures and public attitudes and habits. But if the President knew that this was an adaptive challenge, did he know that this issue was also unripe? And if so, was bold action meant to ripen this issue? Clearly, there are alternatives to ripening issues by bold authoritative action. Were these considered in light of the costs to him in terms of attention to other issues and informal authority?

15. Personal communication, Susan Hall, the consultant in charge of designing the public involvement process in Tacoma for the EPA; April 1993.

16. As mentioned in an earlier note, for a thought-provoking analysis of various decisionmaking modes and when to use them, see Victor Vroom and Arthur Jago, *The New Leadership: Managing Participation in Organizations* (Englewood-Cliffs, NJ: Prentice-Hall, 1988).

17. Personal communication, William Ruckelshaus, March 1992.

18. William Ruckelshaus, "Letter: On Tacoma's Air—How EPA Faces the Arsenic Risk," *The New York Times,* July 23, 1983, italics in the original.

6. On a Razor's Edge

1. See "Leader or Clerk?" in Richard E. Neustadt, *Presidential Power and the Modern Presidents: The Politics of Leadership from Roosevelt to Reagan,* third edition (New York: Free Press, 1990), chap. 1; and Warren Bennis, *Why Leaders Can't Lead: The Unconscious Conspiracy Continues* (San Francisco: Jossey-Bass, 1989).

2. Robert D. Putnam's study, *Making Democracy Work: Civic Traditions in Modern Italy* (Princeton: Princeton University Press, 1993), shows a strong positive correlation between institutions of civic engagement (for example, soccer clubs, choral societies, and literary guilds) and community performance (for example, economic development, legislative innovation, and bureaucratic responsiveness).

3. For example, many scholars attribute the greatness of George Washington to his foresight and ability to strengthen the central government in its first years. Washington placed highest priority on increasing the federal government's credibility and prestige. He did so by staying out of "entangling alliances" (during the French Revolution), displaying overwhelming military power (the Whiskey Rebellion), and maintaining the financial solvency of the government (by supporting Hamilton's proposal to fund the debt). Richard Ellis and Aaron Wildavsky describe this as "substituting the appearance of power for the reality of power," which I think confuses the difference between formal powers and informal authority. The source of the government's informal authority lay in perceptions of credibility. That does not make it unreal; it simply suggests that trust is a major source of informal and ultimately formal authorization. In my terms, Washington aimed to strengthen the holding environment provided by central government, and this boosted critically the government's power to hold the nation together through its stage of infancy. See Richard Ellis and Aaron Wildavsky, "'Greatness' Revisited: Evaluating the Performance of Early American Presidents in Terms of Cultural Dilemmas," *Presidential Studies Quarterly,* vol. 21, winter 1991, pp. 18–22.

   Also see Chapters 4 and 5, above, for the example of Ruckelshaus and his efforts to restore the credibility of the EPA as a mediating institution in the society on environmental issues.

4. For a discussion of the relationship between empowerment and the dispersion of authority, see Herbert C. Kelman and V. Lee Hamilton, *Crimes of Obedience: Toward a Social Psychology of Authority and Responsibility* (New Haven: Yale University Press, 1989), pp. 322–327.

5. I use the term *black American* instead of the contemporary phrase *Afri-*

can-American because this case takes place in the 1960s, a time when the term *black American* was becoming an authentic expression of the demand for equality and respect.

6. Quotations from Doris Kearns, *Lyndon Johnson and the American Dream* (New York: New American Library, 1976), pp. 180–181.

7. Ibid., pp. 184–185.

8. It is, of course, hard to say which of Johnson's successes matters most. As Joseph Califano summarizes, "Johnson changed the country more than most of us realize. By the time he left office, he had pushed through Congress Medicare and Medicaid to provide health care for the aged and most of the poor; funds for preschool, elementary, secondary, and higher education; air, water, and noise pollution laws; measures to preserve land; civil rights legislation; food stamps for the needy; a massive housing bill, and a score of consumer-protection laws. He had articulated the concept of affirmative action, dramatized the blight of poverty amid unprecedented wealth, signed the Freedom of Information Act, and created the National Endowments for the Arts and Humanities, the John F. Kennedy Center for the Performing Arts, the Corporation for Public Broadcasting, several cabinet departments and agencies, and he changed the role of the federal government in American life." Joseph A. Califano Jr., *The Triumph and Tragedy of Lyndon Johnson: The White House Years* (New York: Simon and Schuster, 1991), p. 12.

9. Kearns, *Lyndon Johnson*, p. 239.

10. The exception was Eisenhower's 1957 Civil Rights Act which survived the Senate because Senate Majority Leader Lyndon Johnson, eyeing his 1960 run for the presidency, got it passed. See Robert Dallek, *Lone Star Rising: Lyndon Johnson and His Times: 1908–1960* (New York: Oxford University Press, 1991), pp. 517–528.

11. Quotations from Richard N. Goodwin, *Remembering America* (Boston: Little, Brown, 1988), pp. 313, 314, italics added.

12. Quotations from Kearns, *Lyndon Johnson*, p. 194.

13. Robert A. Caro, *The Years of Lyndon Johnson: Means of Ascent* (New York: Vintage Books, 1990), p. xvi.

14. Cited in Califano, *The Triumph and Tragedy of Lyndon Johnson*, p. 53.

15. "Troopers Rout Selma Marchers," *The Washington Post*, March 8, 1965, p. A1.

16. Caro, *Means of Ascent*, p. xv; and J. L. Chestnut Jr., and Julia Cass, *Black in Selma: The Uncommon Life of J. L. Chestnut, Jr.* (Farrar, Straus and Giroux, 1990), p. 207.

17. Kearns, *Lyndon Johnson*, p. 239. The National Guard consists of troops normally under the command of the various state governors. "Calling out the national guard" consists of federalizing these troops, which then fall under the President's command.

18. "King is Dismayed by U.S. 'Timidity,'" *The Washington Post,* March 8, 1965, p. A2.

19. *Brown v. Board of Education,* 347 U.S. 483 (1954) (Brown I). For a summary, see Laurence H. Tribe, *American Constitutional Law,* second edition (Mineola, NY: The Foundation Press, 1988), pp. 1474–1480.

20. Dallek, *Lone Star Rising,* pp. 521–522.

21. According to Califano, "On February 9, 1965, the President met with Martin Luther King at the White House to hear a report on King's campaign to register blacks to vote in Selma, the capital of Dallas County, Alabama. As a political leader preparing to persuade Congress to pass a voting rights bill, Johnson appreciated King's choice of Selma . . . Johnson told King that he would soon send voting-rights legislation to Congress. He thought that the public pressure of Selma would help and hoped there would be no violence." Califano, *The Triumph and Tragedy of Lyndon Johnson,* p. 55.

22. For example, in 1941 the civil rights movement threatened a massive march on Washington to demand equal opportunity for the jobs, both civilian and military, created as the country geared up for World War II. The threat of the march forced Roosevelt, two weeks before the target date, to issue an Executive Order promoting fair employment practices. The march was then called off. See Thomas R. Brooks, *Walls Come Tumbling Down: A History of the Civil Rights Movement 1940–1970* (Englewood Cliffs, NJ: Prentice-Hall, 1974).

23. "Trooper's Rout Selma Marchers with Tear Gas," *The Washington Post,* March 8, 1965, p. A3.

24. Chestnut and Cass, *Black in Selma,* p. 209.

25. Lyndon B. Johnson, *The Vantage Point: Perspectives of the Presidency 1963–1969* (New York: Holt, Rinehart and Winston, 1971), p. 162.

26. Ralph David Abernathy, *And the Walls Came Tumbling Down* (New York: Harper and Row, 1989), p. 334.

27. I discuss the events and tactics of this moment in greater depth in Chapter 9. I do not think Johnson intended to stop the Selma demonstrations altogether, but once the federal court order had been issued, he was obligated to slow King down. Had King broken the law, Johnson would have been forced to take action against King, and both Johnson's and King's strategies would have backfired. See Abernathy, *And the Walls Came Tumbling Down,* pp. 335–342.

28. "President's Statement," *The Washington Post,* March 10, 1965, p. A3.

29. See James Henderson, Philip B. Heymann, Richard E. Neustadt, Glenn Reichardt, and Mark H. Moore, "Voting Rights Act of 1965 (B): LBJ and the Department of Justice" (Cambridge: John F. Kennedy School of Government Case Program, Harvard University, 1975), Case #694–75–114.

30. "Cleric's Death Saddens Selma Crowd," *The Washington Post,* March 12, 1965, p. A8; Abernathy, *And the Walls Came Tumbling Down,* p. 325.
31. Kearns, *Lyndon Johnson,* p. 239.
32. Goodwin, *Remembering America,* p. 320.
33. Kearns, *Lyndon Johnson,* p. 239.
34. Goodwin, *Remembering America,* p. 323.
35. "Transcript of News Conference at the White House," *The Washington Post,* March 14, 1965, p. A12.
36. "Crowd of 15,000 at Lafayette Park Protests Federal Inaction in Selma," *The Washington Post,* March 15, 1965, p. A6; Caro, *Means of Ascent,* p. xviii; and Goodwin, *Remembering America,* p. 324.
37. Some of the consequences of federal initiatives in civil rights have now been studied a generation later. The consequences are impressive. For an analysis linking structural to attitudinal change, see Thomas F. Pettigrew, "Advancing Racial Justice: Past Lessons for Future Use," in Harry J. Knopke, Robert J. Norrell, and Ronald W. Rogers, eds., *Opening Doors: Perspectives on Race Relations in Contemporary America* (Tuscaloosa, AL: University of Alabama Press, 1991), pp. 165–178. For an in-depth case study of an integrated public middle school as a vehicle for attitudinal change, see Janet Ward Schofield, *Black and White in School: Trust, Tension, or Tolerance?* (New York: Praeger, 1982). As well, there are earlier case studies of institutional change leading to attitudinal change. For example, see Leo Bogart, ed., *Social Research and the Desegregation of the U.S. Army* (Chicago: Markham, 1969), pp. 1–41, for an analysis of the way authoritative action and structural change played a critical role in changing attitudes to desegregate the U.S. Army beginning in 1948.
38. Goodwin, *Remembering America,* p. 316.
39. In the terms of political economy, one could analyze the adaptive capacity and resilience of a community in terms of the concept "social capital," which can be understood as "the features of social organization, such as trust, norms, and networks, that can improve the efficiency of society by facilitating coordinated actions . . ." See Putnam, *Making Democracy Work,* p. 167. The more social capital, the stronger the holding environment of the community and thus the higher the limit of tolerance of stress the community can withstand without resorting to work avoidance.
40. Of course, not all action reduces the general level of stress. Urgent or extreme action in a situation that seems not to call for it will generate alarm. I describe one such example in Chapter 7: President Carter's mass firing of his cabinet in July 1979.
41. Goodwin, *Remembering America,* pp. 319–320.
42. As Senate Minority Leader, Johnson had used a similar strategy in the Senate's efforts to repudiate Joseph McCarthy. As he told Maury Maverick,

"You have got to realize that . . . the hysteria around the country and in the Government . . . can be dispelled only by letting it run its course so that people can see for themselves what is really behind all the noise." Johnson waited faithfully for McCarthy to alienate his conservative Senate colleagues and then the American people, both of which McCarthy eventually did. When McCarthy's own Republican colleagues were set to censure him, Johnson called a meeting of the Democratic Policy Committee and persuaded its members to refrain from taking a stand for fear "that it would play into McCarthy's hands and put him back in the good graces of the Republican Party." Instead, the committee recommended that each senator vote his own conscience. He then arranged for a bipartisan committee to investigate McCarthy, and selected meticulously a group of conservative Democrats and Republicans with indisputable credentials and reputations to condemn McCarthy, which it did. The Senate concurred in a vote of 67-to-22.

Issues have their own rate of ripening. The rate can be sped up, as the Selma events demonstrate, but ultimately the rate is determined by the speed at which people learn. I believe Johnson understood both the possibility of ripening issues, as he demonstrated by calling Roy Wilkins in January 1964, as well as the limits to which one could accelerate the process of ripening. Johnson spoke to these limits when he told Elizabeth Rowe after McCarthy had been censured, "You see, you always wanted me to hurry, to speed it up, but I kept telling you, you can't speed it up. You have got to know when the time has come." Dallek, *Lone Star Rising,* pp. 451–459.

43. Kearns, *Lyndon Johnson,* p. 239.
44. Ibid., p. 239. Wallace did run for President in 1968 on this platform.
45. See Goodwin, *Remembering America,* p. 323.
46. Charles E. Fager, *Selma: The March that Changed the South* (Boston: Beacon Press, 1985), pp. 148–149.
47. For a detailed account of the bargaining between King, Abernathy, and LeRoy Collins, Johnson's emissary, which led to turning the march around after reaching the spot where Sunday's beatings had taken place, see Abernathy, *And the Walls Came Tumbling Down,* pp. 337–341.
48. From "Text of Johnson Address to Joint Session of Congress," *The Washington Post,* March 16, 1965, p. A14.
49. Thomas Schelling describes this as a "commitment strategy." By committing himself publicly, Johnson communicated his resolve to Congress. Schelling used the term somewhat differently given the context in which he developed it: nuclear arms control, where commitment to retaliate made deterrent threat credible, and thereby *reduced* the probability of ever having to act on the commitment. Thomas C. Schelling, *The Strategy of Conflict* (Cambridge: Harvard University Press, 1960), p. 14.

50. Dallek, *Lone Star Rising*, pp. 496, 517–528.
51. Caro, *Means of Ascent*, p. xvii.
52. "President Seizes Rights Movement Leadership," *The Washington Post*, March 17, 1965, p. A14.
53. Johnson, *The Vantage Point*, p. 157.
54. Johnson's great speech to Congress was written by Richard Goodwin, one of Johnson's speechwriters. Johnson deliberately picked Goodwin for the job, and not another of his writers, because he felt Goodwin knew best how to put his values and sentiments into words. According to Goodwin, the speech would have been altogether different had it been written for another man. See Goodwin, *Remembering America*, p. 328.
55. The legislation was more powerful than any previously imagined to address the issue. By a double trigger mechanism, federal registrars would replace local officials in those states where discrimination was widely used, and the Attorney General would have virtual veto power over any state legislation on voter qualifications. See Henderson et al., "Voting Rights Act of 1965 (B): LBJ and the Department of Justice."
56. Chestnut and Cass, *Black in Selma*, pp. 233–235.

7. Falling Off the Edge

1. See Ernest R. May, *"Lessons" of the Past: The Use and Misuse of History in American Foreign Policy* (New York: Oxford University Press, 1973), chap. 4; and Yuen Foong Khong, *Analogies at War: Korea, Munich, Dien Bien Phu, and the Vietnam Decisions of 1965* (Princeton, NJ: Princeton University Press, 1992).
2. Larry Berman, *Planning a Tragedy: The Americanization of the War in Vietnam* (New York: Norton, 1982), p. 131.
3. See George C. Herring, *America's Longest War: The United States and Vietnam 1950–1975* (New York: Wiley, 1979); and Larry Berman, *Planning a Tragedy*.
4. According to former American ambassador to Vietnam, General Maxwell Taylor, "In 1965 we knew very little about the Hanoi leaders other than Ho Chi Minh and General Giap and virtually nothing about their individual or collective intentions. We were inclined to assume, however, that they would behave about like the North Koreans and the Red Chinese a decade before; that is, they would seek an accommodation with us when the cost of pursuing a losing course became excessive. Instead, the North Vietnamese proved to be incredibly tough in accepting losses which, by Western calculation, greatly exceeded the value of the stake involved." Cited in Berman, *Planning a Tragedy*, p. 143.
5. Contrary to the image that Johnson's advisers fell into a pattern of groupthink (Irving Janis, *Groupthink*, second edition [Houghton Mifflin: Boston,

1982], chap. 5), recently published documents show that Johnson received a great many competing points of view, not only from Undersecretary of State George Ball but also from Clark Clifford, Vice-President Humphrey, Jack Valenti, Senator Mansfield, CIA Director William Raborn, and Ambassador Llewelyn Thompson. In Burke and Greenstein's view, a major problem was not the absence of diverse opinions but the lack of a process for following through analytically on these differences. They contrast Johnson's policymaking process with Eisenhower's. Eisenhower, as a military commander, had a better understanding of how easily one can be misled in foreign policy and thus made systematic reality testing a priority in his decisionmaking process. As a result, he established as President a quite formal procedure to appraise and test foreign policy questions, and acted much less the part of the lone warrior. See John P. Burke and Fred I. Greenstein, *How Presidents Test Reality: Decisions on Vietnam, 1954 and 1965* (New York: Russell Sage Foundation, 1989).

6. See Richard E. Neustadt, *Presidential Power and the Modern Presidents: The Politics of Leadership from Roosevelt to Reagan,* third edition (New York: Free Press, 1990), pp. 209–212.

7. Herring, *America's Longest War,* p. 116.

8. Arthur M. Schlesinger Jr., *The Imperial Presidency* (Boston: Houghton Mifflin, 1989), p. 179.

9. Richard N. Goodwin, *Remembering America* (Boston: Little, Brown, 1988), p. 362.

10. Herring, *America's Longest War,* p. 120.

11. Gordon Silverstein, "Constitutional Constraints: How Constitutional Interpretation Shapes the Making of American Foreign Policy" (Ph.D. diss., Harvard University, 1991), pp. 200–201.

12. Doris Kearns, *Lyndon Johnson and the American Dream* (New York: New American Library, 1976), p. 207. Regarding the Senate's perception of this event, see U.S. Senate Committee on Foreign Relations, "Hearing on U.S. Commitments to Foreign Powers," 90th Congress, 1967, p. 139.

13. Goodwin, *Remembering America,* p. 359.

14. Berman, *Planning a Tragedy,* p. 33.

15. Goodwin, *Remembering America,* pp. 357, 361.

16. Burke and Greenstein, *How Presidents Test Reality,* pp. 118–149; quotation on p. 126.

17. From a State Department report on "Congressional Attitudes on SVN [South Vietnam]," cited in Burke and Greenstein, *How Presidents Test Reality,* pp. 148–149. An Associated Press poll of 83 senators on January 6, 1965, found that only eight favored the commitment of American forces in Vietnam and only three favored immediate withdrawal. Ten senators wanted immediate negotiations, and 31 favored a negotiated settlement

after strengthening the U.S. and South Vietnamese bargaining position. Ibid., p. 148.

18. Ibid., pp. 130, 192–194.

19. Cited in Berman, *Planning a Tragedy*, p. 55.

20. Ibid., p. 57; and "Chronology of Presidential Decisions," in "Vietnam Documents" (Cambridge: John F. Kennedy School of Government Case Program, Harvard University), Case #C14–80–271D.

21. Robert McNamara, "Memorandum for the President: Recommendations of Additional Deployments to Vietnam," July 20, 1965, and "Summary Notes of 553rd NSC Meeting," July 27, 1965, in "Vietnam Documents." Also Berman, *Planning a Tragedy*, pp. 112–123.

22. Cited in Burke and Greenstein, *How Presidents Test Reality*, p. 230.

23. Herring, *America's Longest War*, p. 141.

24. Kearns, *Lyndon Johnson*, p. 294.

25. Excerpts from McGeorge Bundy, "Memorandum for the President: The Situation in Vietnam," Saigon, February 7, 1965, in "Vietnam Documents," italics in the original. Bundy's belief that the American people had the will for such a war was merely conjecture, although not stated as such. In fact, the public had never been challenged to think about the hard questions. If anything, Johnson's landslide victory against hawkish Senator Goldwater suggested that the people did not have the will for war. The Gallup Poll of June 9, 1965, reported that 20 percent of the public wanted to "continue our present course of action," 21 percent wanted to "increase military action," 26 percent wanted to "stop military action," and 28 percent expressed no opinion. Hardly a consensus. The issue had not formed clearly in people's minds. Poll reported in Burke and Greenstein, *How Presidents Test Reality*, p. 253.

26. In regard to the reasons for deception, see Herring, *America's Longest War*, pp. 142–143; and Neustadt, *Presidential Power*, p. 211.

27. See Lyndon B. Johnson, *The Vantage Point: Perspectives of the Presidency 1963–1969* (New York: Holt, Rinehart and Winston, 1971), pp. 150–151. Senator Mansfield had been a long-time supporter of American involvement in South Vietnam. Indeed, he was a founding member of the Friends of Vietnam in the 1950s. But a major reversal in his views followed a fact-gathering trip at President Kennedy's request in November 1962. In his report to Kennedy, he gave a poor prognosis on the counterinsurgency program and the Diem regime's survivability. After eight years of major U.S. commitment, "substantially the same difficulties remain if, indeed, they have not been compounded." Douglas J. MacDonald, *Adventures in Chaos: American Intervention for Reform in the Third World* (Cambridge: Harvard University Press, 1992), p. 223. See also Schlesinger, *The Imperial Presidency*, p. 327.

28. See Silverstein, "Constitutional Constraints."
29. Kearns, *Lyndon Johnson*, pp. 289–290; also see Schlesinger, *The Imperial Presidency*, p. 46.
30. Cited in Schlesinger, *The Imperial Presidency*, p. 89. Up until World War II, although presidents claimed greater prerogative, they typically acknowledged the need for Congressional authority in many foreign policy problems, even if after the fact. For example, Jefferson engaged in battle with Barbary Coast pirates and went to Congress for authorization after the fact. Polk got into a war with Mexico and presented Congress with a *fait accompli*. Lincoln asked for Congressional authorization for the Civil War after the war had started. Although each stretched the limits of presidential authority, each also acknowledged that he had done so. Also see Silverstein, "Constitutional Constraints," chap. 2.
31. Silverstein, "The Emergence of an Executive Prerogative Interpretation of the Constitution," in "Constitutional Constraints," chap. 3.
32. Schlesinger, *The Imperial Presidency*, p. 141. Not all members of Congress thought it so. After the Korean War began to go badly, Congressman Coudert submitted a resolution to "prevent the commitment of armed forces abroad in advance of aggression solely by executive decision." Senator Taft argued, "I think that the value of such aid and comfort [to the enemy] is grossly exaggerated. The only thing that can give real aid and comfort to the enemy is the adoption of a policy which plays into their hands." Ibid., p. 137.
33. Ibid., p. 128.
34. For the role of covert operations in American foreign policy, see Gregory F. Treverton, *Covert Action: The Limits of Intervention in the Post-War World* (New York: Basic, 1987). Schlesinger suggests that by Eisenhower's day, withholding information from Congress had become routine. The Courts, as well, reinforced this trend. Two Supreme Court rulings in the 1930s, *Curtiss-Wright* and *Belmont*, spoke to the President's control over foreign affairs. In *Curtiss-Wright*, Justice Sutherland wrote that Congress "must often accord to the President a degree of discretion and freedom from statutory restriction which would not be admissible were domestic affairs alone involved." For "in this vast external realm, with its important, complicated, delicate and manifold problems, the President alone has the power to speak and listen as a representative of the nation." Cited in Schlesinger, *The Imperial Presidency*, p. 102.
35. For example, Senator Barry Goldwater claimed in 1971: "We have only been in five declared wars out of over 150 that we have fought." Cited in Schlesinger, *The Imperial Presidency*, p. 53. For a more extensive discussion of these so-called wars, see *The Imperial Presidency*, chap. 3.
36. Ibid., p. 99.

37. Silverstein, "Constitutional Constraints," p. 182.
38. Cited in Schlesinger, *The Imperial Presidency,* p. 160.
39. Kearns, *Lyndon Johnson,* p. 264.
40. Lyndon B. Johnson Oral History, August 12, 1969, Johnson Library; cited in Burke and Greenstein, *How Presidents Test Reality,* p. 191.
41. Schlesinger, *The Imperial Presidency,* p. 14.
42. James Madison, *Debates in the Federal Convention of 1787,* vol. 2 (Buffalo: Prometheus, 1987), pp. 457–458. Jefferson cited by Schlesinger, *The Imperial Presidency,* p. 14.
43. Kearns, *Lyndon Johnson,* p. 297.
44. Senator Frank Church in the *Congressional Record,* Senate, June 20, 1969, p. 16748; cited by Silverstein, "Constitutional Constraints," p. 218.
45. Benjamin Cohen cited by Schlesinger, *The Imperial Presidency,* p. 109.
46. Ibid., p. 110.
47. During his 1940 presidential campaign Roosevelt promised, "I have said this before, but I shall say it again and again and again: Your boys are not going to be sent into any foreign wars." Cited in Califano, *The Triumph and Tragedy of Lyndon Johnson,* p. 172.
48. Kearns, *Lyndon Johnson,* p. 327.
49. By 1966 Johnson was quite deliberately letting this happen. In an effort to protect his Secretary of Defense, he instructed his staff, "They'll destroy that man. This isn't his war. If it belongs to anybody, it's my war. Let's stop him from talking about it so much, and I'll defend it. Make it the President's War, not McNamara's War." Califano, *The Triumph and Tragedy of Lyndon Johnson,* p. 47.
50. Kearns, *Lyndon Johnson,* pp. 277, 296.
51. Neustadt, *Presidential Power,* p. 200.
52. For example, one of the key lessons Ronald Reagan and his staff apparently drew from Jimmy Carter's presidency was the need to focus on one major issue at a time rather than overload the carrying capacity of Congress. Personal communication, Stuart Eizenstat, Domestic Policy Adviser in the Carter Administration, May 1983.
53. Letter to Chester Bowles, cited in Robert Dallek, *Lone Star Rising: Lyndon Johnson and His Times: 1908–1960* (New York: Oxford University Press, 1991), p. 528.
54. Califano, *The Triumph and Tragedy of Lyndon Johnson,* p. 124. In my terms, Johnson knew how to pick ripe issues, and how to ripen green ones. For an account of his skill in ripening an issue, see "Lyndon Johnson and the War on Poverty," in Barbara Kellerman, *The Political Presidency* (New York: Oxford University Press, 1984), chap. 7.
55. Kearns, *Lyndon Johnson,* pp. 268–269.

56. Richard E. Neustadt and Ernest R. May, *Thinking in Time: The Uses of History for Decision-Makers* (New York: Free Press, 1986), p. 88.

57. This is an application of Neustadt and May's analytic term "placement," with somewhat different connotations. By placement, they meant placing the person or organization that one is analyzing in the context of the major public events taking place that serve as background in the formation of the individual or organizational character. Neustadt and May, *Thinking In Time*, pp. 238–240.

58. Kearns, *Lyndon Johnson*, p. 206.

59. According to Burke and Greenstein, up until the Pleiku attack in February 1965, Johnson had quite a bit of room to broker work on the issue, both in Congress and with the public. Pleiku added greatly to the momentum toward involvement. Burke and Greenstein, *How Presidents Test Reality*, pp. 270–271.

60. Johnson lost his first race for the Senate by a thousand votes, and won in 1948 by 87. See Robert A. Caro, *The Years of Lyndon Johnson: Means of Ascent* (New York: Vintage Books, 1990), which describes these two campaigns in vivid detail; Robert Dallek, *Lone Star Rising*, pp. 223, 346; and Kearns, *Lyndon Johnson*, p. 215.

61. Burke and Greenstein, *How Presidents Test Reality*, pp. 205–206.

62. Caro, *Means of Ascent*, p. 15.

63. Idaho Senator Frank Church reported in a Congressional Research Service interview in the summer of 1965 his impressions after taking a trip with Johnson to San Francisco in June for the twentieth anniversary celebration of the United Nations. Johnson had told him of his sleepless nights waiting to hear how many American planes would be lost after a raid. Johnson "had personalized the war by this time and that disturbed me greatly, because I thought it meant that he was losing his capacity to render an objective judgement by losing his detachment." Cited in Burke and Greenstein, *How Presidents Test Reality*, p. 240.

64. "The extreme measures he took to defend his Vietnam policy against enemies real and imagined led directly to the Watergate scandals which would eventually force his resignation." Herring, *America's Longest War*, p. 251; also see Jonathan Schell, "The Nixon Years: Parts I–VI," *The New Yorker:* June 2, 1975, pp. 42–83; June 9, 1975, pp. 70–111; June 16, 1975, pp. 55–96; June 23, 1975, pp. 60–91; June 30, 1975, pp. 39–77; and July 7, 1975, pp. 38–62.

65. Schell, "The Nixon Years," Part I, p. 54.

66. Herring, *America's Longest War*, pp. 221–225.

67. Quoted in Schell, "The Nixon Years," Part I, p. 46.

68. Speech on October 30, 1969, quoted in Schell, "The Nixon Years," Part I, p. 75.

69. William Safire, *Before the Fall: An Inside View of the Pre-Watergate White*

House (New York: Doubleday, 1975), pp. 178–179; and Schell, "The Nixon Years," Part I, p. 77.

70. Nixon began wire-tapping senior administration officials and prominent newsmen in May 1969 when news of the Cambodian bombings leaked to the press. Schell, "The Nixon Years," Part I, p. 57.

71. Safire, *Before the Fall,* p. 190.

72. Ibid., p. 308.

73. Ibid., p. 366.

74. Cited in Schlesinger, *The Imperial Presidency,* p. 217.

75. Charles W. Colson, *Born Again* (Old Tappan, NJ: Chosen Books, 1976), p. 41.

76. Neustadt, *Presidential Power,* p. 188.

77. Schlesinger, *The Imperial Presidency,* p. 267.

78. For various renditions of the Watergate story, see Elizabeth Drew, *Washington Journal: The Events of 1973–1974* (New York: Random House, 1974); Sam Ervin, *The Whole Truth: The Watergate Conspiracy* (New York: Random House, 1980); and John Wesley Dean, *Blind Ambition: The White House Years* (New York: Simon and Schuster, 1976).

79. Neustadt, *Presidential Power,* p. 189.

80. Schlesinger, *The Imperial Presidency,* p. 189.

81. See Henry Kissinger's memoirs: *White House Years* (Boston: Little, Brown, 1979), and *Years of Upheaval* (Boston: Little, Brown, 1982).

82. See Bruce Mazlish, *In Search of Nixon* (New York: Basic Books, 1972).

83. According to Schlesinger, more than any other President, Nixon went way beyond his Constitutional authority in domestic affairs, from his use of the pocket veto and the impoundment of funds—a substitute for the item veto—to unilaterally abolishing statutory programs. Schlesinger, *The Imperial Presidency,* pp. 235–277.

84. Herring, *America's Longest War,* p. 232.

85. See Herring, *America's Longest War,* pp. 252–254, for an account of how shallow and fragile were the Paris Peace Accords.

86. The effects of Watergate in terms of work neglected were manifold. Not only did the presidency as an institution take the heat from Congress for Congress's failure to take decisive action during the Vietnam War, but substantive issues as well suffered, including détente and arms control with the Soviets and economic policy following the inflationary 1973 oil shocks. Neustadt, *Presidential Power,* p. 213.

87. For a study of the aftermath of war from the perspective of the individual soldier in World War II, see J. Glenn Gray, *The Warriors; Reflections on Men in Battle,* second edition (New York: Harper Torchbook, 1970); for the sequelae of U.S. soldiers in Vietnam, see Tim O'Brien, *The Things They Carried: A Work of Fiction* (Boston: Houghton Mifflin, 1990); Frederick Downs, *Aftermath: A Soldier's Return from Vietnam* (New York: Norton,

1984); and Laura Palmer, "The Nurses of Vietnam, Still Wounded," *The New York Times Magazine*, November 7, 1993, pp. 36–73.

88. Joseph C. Harsh, "Do You Recall Vietnam—And What About Dominoes?" *Louisville Courier-Journal*, October 2, 1975; cited in Herring, *America's Longest War*, p. 265.

89. Herring, *America's Longest War*, p. 265.

90. The pressures toward an autocratic presidency in foreign affairs surely did not arise from domestic expectations alone. The world community added greatly to these expectations. Political scientists and economists have described those expectations in hegemonic stability theory, which "claims that the presence of a single, strongly dominant actor in international politics leads to collectively desirable outcomes for *all* states in the international system. Conversely, the absence of a hegemon is associated with disorder in the world system and undesirable outcomes for individual states." Duncan Snidal, "The Limits of Hegemonic Stability Theory," *International Organization*, vol. 39, autumn 1985, p. 579, italics in the original. Charles Kindleberger describes the expected functions of the hegemon in the context of the Great Depression: "In these circumstances, the international economic and monetary system needs leadership, a country that is prepared, consciously or unconsciously, under some system of rules that it has internalized, to set standards of conduct for other countries and to seek to get others to follow them, to take on an undue share of the burdens of the system, and in particular, to take on its support in adversity by accepting its redundant commodities, maintaining a flow of investment capital, and discounting its paper." Charles P. Kindleberger, *The World in Depression, 1929–39* (Berkeley: University of California Press, 1986), p. 11. Whether or not any dominant actor, be it Britain in the century before 1913, or the U.S. after World War II, has in fact fulfilled the expected functions is a matter of debate. See Joseph S. Nye Jr., *Bound to Lead: The Changing Nature of American Power* (New York: Basic, 1990), pp. 50–52. Less debatable, however, is the observation that hegemons have at least been *expected* to perform a special coordinating role in the international system, a set of expectations that would be felt most acutely in the case of the United States by the President. To some degree, these expectations run parallel to those described in this study: the unrealistic longing for a technical solution to a set of adaptive challenges serves to allow the primary stakeholders to avoid responsibility. The locus of problem-solving shifts to the dominant authority. See Barry Eichengreen, *Golden Fetters: The Gold Standard and the Great Depression, 1919–1939* (New York: Oxford, 1992), pp. 390–399, for an analysis of how the U.S. refusal to support the gold standard has often been considered a key abdication of hegemonic responsibility, when, as he argues, the interwar

years consisted of a complex array of problems not amenable to technical fixes—like the gold standard—from above.

91. See Schlesinger, *The Imperial Presidency,* chap. 9.
92. See Neustadt and May, *Thinking in Time,* pp. 65–74.
93. "Transcript of President's Address to Country on Energy Problems," *The New York Times,* July 16, 1979, p. A10.
94. According to a *New York Times*/CBS News poll, Carter's approval rating went up from 26 percent to 37 percent the day after the speech. "Speech Lifts Carter Rating to 37%; Public Agrees on Confidence Crisis," *The New York Times,* July 18, 1979, p. A1. But one month later, the Gallup Poll showed a decline from the previous January from 38 percent to 27 percent in the percentage of voters believing that Carter had "strong leadership qualities," from 43 percent to 33 percent believing that he was "decisive and sure of himself," and from 29 percent to 19 percent believing that he had a "well-defined program for moving the country ahead." "Many in Poll Place Trust in Carter Despite Doubt over Performance," *The New York Times,* August 12, 1979, p. 25.
95. For two key exceptions, see Neustadt, *Presidential Power;* and Arthur M. Schlesinger Jr.'s three-part series on Franklin Roosevelt: *The Crisis of the Old Order* (Boston: Houghton Mifflin, 1956); *The Coming of the New Deal* (Boston: Houghton Mifflin, 1958); and *The Politics of Upheaval* (Boston: Houghton Mifflin, 1960).
96. Silverstein, "Constitutional Constraints," p. 218.

8. Creative Deviance on the Frontline

1. The NIMBY syndrome has been well studied in an array of public policy areas, from finding hazardous waste disposal sites to siting low income housing projects, airports, and prisons. See Lawrence Bacow, Michael O'Hare, and Debra Sanderson, *Facility Siting and Public Opposition* (New York: Van Nostrand Reinhold, 1983); and The Advisory Commission on Regulatory Barriers to Affordable Housing, *Not In My Backyard: Removing Barriers to Affordable Housing,* Report to President Bush and Secretary Kemp (Washington, DC: U.S. Department of Housing and Urban Development, 1991).
2. Robert C. Tucker distinguishes "constituted" (legitimate) from "nonconstituted" (informal) leaders, which I describe in this volume as leadership with and without authority. See his *Politics as Leadership* (Columbia: University of Missouri Press, 1981), pp. 77–113. Tucker's distinction points primarily to the differences between leading with and without *formal* authority, hence the term "constituted." This points in the right direction. I believe we also need to acknowledge the power of informal

authority alone and the exercise of leadership with it, as well as leadership without either formal or informal authority.

3. Washington, Jefferson, Madison, and Monroe were but a few of the Southern founders of the nation, and all except Washington were towering figures throughout Lincoln's early life. The dates alone are revealing when we try to imagine how fresh and alive were the ideas represented by Union during Lincoln's growth and professional development. Abraham Lincoln was born in 1809. Thomas Jefferson was President from 1801–1809 and lived until 1826, when Lincoln was seventeen years old. James Madison was President from 1809–1817 and lived until 1836, when Lincoln was twenty-seven. James Monroe was President from 1817–1825 and lived until 1831, when Lincoln was twenty-two.

4. By and large, I have stayed away from the term *leader* in this study, preferring to use the active phrase "exercising leadership," except when using the word colloquially within the context of someone else's usage in these case studies. I tend to avoid the term *leader* because it generally connotes an authority figure (the leader of the band) or a specific set of personal traits (*He's* a real leader). Instead, I wish to keep our primary focus on the activity of leading and not on the role of authority or the intrinsic qualities of any person. Occasionally, however, I will use *leader* as a simple shorthand to refer to a person who is exercising leadership or who intends to. I use the term *leader* primarily in discussing leadership without authority because in this context there is no noun with which to refer to an individual actor in the way I use the phrase *authority figure*.

The reader may have noticed that I have also cast aside even more fully the word *follower.* It seems to me that *follower* hopelessly entangles us in an inappropriate social contract and logic. Although our common use of language makes us think that there is an inherent truth to the couplet *leader–follower,* just as we do with pairs like *up–down* and *good–bad,* I think there is no truth here, merely custom. Indeed, the word *follower,* which connotes somewhat mindless, lemming-like behavior, fails to suggest how it feels and what it means to be mobilized to do adaptive work. As a member of a community, the feelings are less a "going along with" than what Bernard Bass describes as stimulation in *Leadership and Performance beyond Expectations* (New York: Free Press, 1985). For example, when Martin Luther King Jr. stimulated white conservative citizens to imagine a different balance of values and power, he led them, and they changed in the process; but they did not follow. They were stimulated to think and feel new thoughts, but they were not in the least his followers. King's black constituents as well were stimulated and empowered to rethink their values, self-images, and habits. However, to call them followers captures not at all their role in shaping the process of change in America or the way they experienced that role.

5. Even revolutionaries like Mao Zedong build their movements and philosophies upon the fundamental values and traditions of their societies. Mao may have rejected the Confucian virtue of manners, but he espoused primary Chinese values when he attacked imperialism, and he spoke to fundamental high Confucian standards of conduct for authority figures when he attacked corruption, warlords, local bullies, and evil gentry. See James MacGregor Burns, *Leadership* (New York: Harper Colophon, 1978), pp. 228–240.

6. See Taylor Branch, *Parting the Waters: America in the King Years: 1954–1963* (New York: Simon and Schuster, 1988), chaps. 18–20.

7. Ibid., pp. 837, 838, and 850.

8. Gandhi's strategies and philosophical roots are described both in his own writings and in a variety of biographical efforts. See Mohandas K. Gandhi, *An Autobiography: The Story of My Experiments with Truth* (Boston: Beacon Press, 1957); Gopinath Dhawan, *The Political Philosophy of Mahatma Gandhi* (Ahmedabad, India: Navajivan Publishing House, 1946); and Louis Fischer, *The Life of Mahatma Gandhi* (New York: Harper and Row, 1950). For a psychological interpretation of Gandhi's political behavior, see Erik Erikson, *Gandhi's Truth: On the Origins of Militant Nonviolence* (New York: Norton, 1969).

9. For an account of Gandhi's visit to the Lancashire cotton mills in 1931, ten years after Gandhi had started the Indian boycott of British cotton fabric with cloth-burning, see William L. Shirer, *Gandhi: A Memoir* (New York: Washington Square Press, 1979), pp. 182–186.

10. See Fischer, *The Life of Mahatma Gandhi,* pp. 123–137, for Gandhi's understanding of India's adaptive challenge on his return to India and his first major speech to those with authority and power in which he pointedly describes the discrepancy between espoused values and concrete reality.

11. See Fischer, *The Life of Mahatma Gandhi,* pp. 184–198.

12. There are many such examples, including Gandhi's 1932 fast from prison to protest the caste system and Untouchability. Upon announcement that an election would be held in which Untouchables would vote separately from the rest of the population, Gandhi vowed to fast to the death. His target audience was not the British but Indians. He achieved astonishing results. Within five days he had performed what many considered a "miracle" by provoking Hindus throughout India to open Temples to Untouchables and to begin the breakdown of an ancient taboo. See Willner, *The Spellbinders,* pp. 189–191.

13. Fischer, *The Life of Mahatma Gandhi,* pp. 123–133.

14. "The very purpose of a hierarchy is to prevent information from reaching higher layers. It operates as an information filter, and there are little wastebaskets all along the way." Kenneth Boulding, from a speech reported in *Business Week,* February 18, 1967, p. 202; cited in H. Edward Wrapp,

"Good Managers Don't Make Policy Decisions," in *Harvard Business Review: On Human Relations* (New York: Harper and Row, 1980), p. 75. For an analysis of this and other strategic problems, see Jeffrey Pfeffer, "Political Strategy and Tactics," in *Power in Organizations* (Boston: Pitman, 1981), chap. 5; also see James Bruce, *The Intuitive Pragmatist: Conversations with Chief Executive Officers* (Greensboro, NC: Center for Creative Leadership, 1986).

15. Richard E. Neustadt, *Presidential Power and the Modern Presidents: The Politics of Leadership from Roosevelt to Reagan,* third edition (New York: Free Press, 1990), p. 129.

16. Fischer, *The Life of Mahatma Gandhi,* p. 131.

17. The following account of Sanger's life is taken from Ellen Chesler, *Woman of Valor: Margaret Sanger and the Birth Control Movement in America* (New York: Simon and Schuster, 1992).

18. Ibid., p. 63.

19. Ibid., p. 127.

20. Ibid., pp. 131–132.

21. Ibid., p. 374.

22. "Because [Sanger] viewed elected officials as conformists who 'expressed public sentiment,' she focused on changing public opinion first and the law later. When she did lobby for changing the law, she expected not to win, but to gain more publicity and generate more public debate." Ibid., pp. 144–145.

23. The names of the protagonists in these two Vietnam cases have been changed to protect privacy.

24. During World War II, Samuel Stouffer studied extensively the competing sources of formal and informal authority (expectations) on military officers, including those with noncommissioned and midlevel rank, and the stress generated by conflicting role expectations. See "Attitudes toward Leadership and Social Control," in Samuel A. Stouffer, Edward A. Suchman, Leland C. DeVinney, Shirley A. Star, and Robin M. Williams Jr., *The American Soldier: Adjustment during Army Life* (Princeton, Princeton University Press, 1949), vol. 1, chap. 8, esp. pp. 401–410.

9. Modulating the Provocation

1. Although the case of Selma used later in this chapter illustrates the senior formal authority figures as barometers of systemic stress, this idea can also be applied to senior informal authority figures within the bounds of their informal constituency. Their informal constituents will often expect them to provide direction, protection, and order in much the same way as a formal constituency.

2. Parts of the following account are based on J. L. Chestnut Jr. and Julia Cass, *Black in Selma: The Uncommon Life of J. L. Chestnut, Jr.* (New York: Farrar, Straus and Giroux, 1990). In addition, parts are taken verbatim from excerpts of the teaching case prepared by James Henderson, Philip B. Heymann, Richard E. Neustadt, William Mates, and Mark H. Moore, "The Voting Rights Act of 1965 (A): The Selma Campaign" (Cambridge: John F. Kennedy School of Government Case Program, Harvard University, 1977), Case #C14–75–113. Quotations are from this teaching case, except where otherwise noted.

3. Chestnut and Cass, *Black in Selma,* pp. 135–136.

4. Ibid., pp. 153–154.

5. Ibid., pp. 160.

6. Lafayette quoted in ibid., p. 166.

7. According to Chestnut, Judge Hare was the decisionmaker in the white community, and the initiative to suppress the demonstrations came from him and not primarily from Sheriff Clark. "Judge in a Nutshell," in Chestnut and Cass, *Black in Selma,* chap. 10.

8. Ibid., p. 188. (The excerpts from "The Voting Rights Act of 1965 [A]: The Selma Campaign" end here.)

9. Chestnut and Cass, *Black in Selma,* p. 212.

10. Martin Luther King Jr., *Why We Can't Wait* (New York: Mentor, 1963), pp. 81–82.

11. Ralph David Abernathy, *And the Walls Came Tumbling Down* (New York: Harper and Row, 1989), pp. 297, 300, 393.

12. Chestnut and Cass, *Black in Selma,* pp. 260, 194.

13. Charles E. Fager, *Selma: The March that Changed the South* (Boston: Beacon Press, 1985), pp. 3–11.

14. Ibid., p. 7.

15. Chestnut and Cass, *Black in Selma,* p. 194.

16. Chestnut and Cass, *Black in Selma,* p. 191.

17. "Chronology of Events at Selma, Ala.," *The Washington Post,* March 22, 1965, p. A9; and Abernathy, *And the Walls Came Tumbling Down,* p. 325.

18. Chestnut and Cass, *Black in Selma,* p. 204.

19. According to Abernathy, Governor Wallace had engineered the breaking up of the march so that it would occur just inside the city line, and thus could be attributed to Clark and not to him. On Monday Wallace then met with Clark and "chewed him out angrily for allowing Sunday's violence." Abernathy, *And the Walls Came Tumbling Down,* p. 326; also see Fager, *Selma,* p. 101.

20. Chestnut and Cass, *Black in Selma,* p. 198.

21. For an analysis of the parallel problem of hasty economic reform, see

Shang-Jin Wei, "Gradualism Versus Big Bang: Speed and Sustainability of Reforms," Working Paper Series #R93-2 (Cambridge: John F. Kennedy School of Government, Harvard University, March 1993).

22. Fager, *Selma*, p. 57.
23. Abernathy, *And the Walls Came Tumbling Down*, pp. 322–323; Henderson et al., "The Voting Rights Act of 1965 (A): The Selma Campaign," p. 5.
24. "Dr. King Sees Johnson, Asks U.S. Registrars," *The Washington Post*, March 6, 1965, p. A2.
25. "Demands Rise across U.S. for Selma Action," *The Washington Post*, March 13, 1965, p. A8.
26. Abernathy, *And the Walls Came Tumbling Down*, p. 325.
27. As time would prove, a restraining order along with both planning and national guard protection could not guarantee safety when the three-day march to Montgomery began two weeks later, on March 21. Mrs. Viola Liuzzo, a white Detroit housewife, was shot and killed in her car while shuttling demonstrators back to Selma at the end of the march. "Mother of 5 Slain after March," *The Washington Post*, March 26, 1965, p. A1. See also Henderson et al., "The Voting Rights Act of 1965 (A): The Selma Campaign," p. 14; Abernathy, *And the Walls Came Tumbling Down*, pp. 335–342.
28. Fager, *Selma*, p. 101.
29. For accounts of some of King's personal and strategic mistakes, see Abernathy, *And the Walls Came Tumbling Down;* and Branch, *Parting the Waters.*
30. William L. Shirer, *Gandhi: A Memoir* (New York: Washington Square Press, 1979), p. 167.
31. Chesler, *Woman of Valor*, pp. 219–220.
32. I mentioned one such example in Chapter 7, when Undersecretary of State George Ball rewrote numerous critical memos on Vietnam policy to President Johnson, less alarming and more palatable, to no avail.
33. Abernathy, *And the Walls Came Tumbling Down*, p. 342.
34. See Taylor Branch, *Parting the Waters*, p. 824.
35. King, *Why We Can't Wait*, p. 79.
36. Chestnut and Cass, *Black in Selma*, p. 235.

10. Assassination

1. For an economic model of this problem, see Raquel Fernandez and Dani Rodrik, "Resistance to Reform: Status Quo Bias in the Presence of Individual-Specific Uncertainty," *American Economic Review*, vol. 81, December 1991, pp. 1146–1155.

2. In his analysis of political leadership after World War II, Jasper Shannon suggests that people have been inclined throughout history to endow their political authorities with magical gifts, in societies from traditional to modern. Even in democratic societies, "The principle trend is . . . the perhaps naïve belief, deliberately propagandized by politicians themselves to get votes, that leaders are accountable for the evils or the goods of society." Jasper B. Shannon, "The Study of Political Leadership," in Jasper B. Shannon, ed., *The Study of Comparative Government* (New York: Greenwood, 1949), p. 322. Aaron Wildavsky attributes this dynamic to the stability of political cultures that routinely interpret their problems in a characteristic way: "for or against existing authority." See Aaron Wildavsky, "A Cultural Theory of Leadership," in Bryan D. Jones, ed., *Leadership and Politics: New Perspectives in Political Science* (Lawrence, KS: University Press of Kansas, 1989), pp. 98–100.

3. Quoted in Stanley Karnow, "Cory Aquino's Downhill Slide," *The New York Times Magazine,* August 19, 1990, p. 25.

4. Edwin O. James, "Expiation and Atonement," in *Sacrifice and Sacrament* (New York: Barnes and Noble, 1962), chap. 5, p. 106.

5. Amando Doronila, chairman of the editorial board of the *Manila Chronicle,* described the "people power" revolution as "extremely limited and flawed" in which "the return to political warlordism or tribal politics dominated by the family dynasties foreshadows the reassertion of the oligarchic tendencies in Philippine politics." Doronila argued that the alliance to overthrow Marcos "had no ideological motivation to change the social and power structure; it merely sought to change rulers without restructuring society." David Joel Steinberg, *The Philippines: A Singular and a Plural Place,* second edition (Boulder, Colorado: Westview Press, 1990), pp. 147–148. Conversations with Professor John Thomas at the Harvard Institute for International Development provided insight into the government transition in the Philippines. In the United States, Nixon's downfall apparently did not solve the fundamental problem of the shift of power from Congress to the President. See Gordon Silverstein, "Constitutional Constraints: How Constitutional Interpretation Shapes the Making of American Foreign Policy" (Ph.D. diss., Harvard University, 1991).

6. As Steinberg suggests, "There are unique moments in history when it is possible to reorganize the social hierarchy and to redistribute power. William Howard Taft had such a chance at the turn of the century [when the Philippines became an American colony]. Douglas MacArthur, as supreme allied commander in Japan, exercised that opportunity to alter in the most profound ways the fabric and structure of Japanese society. During the period when President Aquino had virtually limitless power under the freedom constitution, she had dramatic opportunity to address frontally

the social contradictions and economic tensions of her nation." Steinberg, *The Philippines*, pp. 150–152.

7. For an analysis of the strengths and weaknesses of a coalition-building style of leadership, see Kerry Mullins and Aaron Wildavsky, "The Procedural Presidency of George Bush," *Political Science Quarterly*, vol. 107, spring 1992, pp. 31–62. They suggest that "coalitions are Bush's preferred method of problem resolution. He emphasizes the involvement of all parties, including those who disagree, particularly when encountering difficult issues. His approach to educational reform calls for 'all of the players—administrators, school boards, local business leaders, parents, teachers' unions—around the table working together.' His policies on the environment, drug use, and the transportation system, all problems defying easy resolution, also call for widespread involvement on all levels. Indeed, they were not 'his' policies until they emerged out of this consensus-raising process. Much of this consultation can be attributed to his desire for the widest possible inclusion. But it also serves as a substitute for strong ideological commitment and a vision for how these problems might be solved" (p. 42). I agree with Mullins and Wildavsky that simply pulling a coalition together is insufficient to make progress on hard problems. In my view, one must also (1) hold the parties tightly in facing the issues, and (2) have a substantive idea about how the parties need to be challenged. If this is what Mullins and Wildavsky mean by vision, then vision must often take the form not of answers but of the hard questions that demand resolution. Otherwise, coalitions often end up avoiding the pain of change and producing the least common denominator; decisionmaking takes the form of "splitting the difference," and not much adaptive work gets done.

8. The most the framers thought they could do in addressing slavery without losing the Southern states was to give Congress the power to outlaw the importation of slaves after 1808. Even that date was a compromise. They had initially set the year of 1800, but the Southern representatives wanted the year set back. In any case, the Constitutional clause meant little. By the time of the federal convention, Virginia and Maryland had already stopped importation of slaves because the birth of American born slaves proved sufficient for their economic aims. See James Madison, *Debates in the Federal Convention of 1787*, vol. 2 (Buffalo: Prometheus, 1987), Sessions of August 21, 22, and 25, 1787, pp. 442–447, 467–469.

9. See Milton Friedman, "Using the Market for Social Development," *Cato Journal*, vol. 8, winter 1989, pp. 567–579.

10. China, for example, used a gradual approach, instituting agricultural reforms in 1979, followed by urban/industrial reforms five years later. This approach was successful, in part, because it kept the level of conflict

generated by the change within socially and politically sustainable levels. Although agricultural reform displeased urban workers and bureaucrats because it meant an increase in food prices, reform pleased the majority of the population, which was rural. Then, when urban/industrial reforms were enacted, the farmers, although upset by the rise in cost of inputs (tractors, fertilizers), had already benefitted from reforms. They had developed a favorable attitude toward the entire reform package and thus accepted industrial reform. Had the Chinese government enacted both reforms simultaneously, however, angering both farmers and urban residents, the whole package might have been "shot down by street demonstrations or other forms of unrest." Shang-Jin Wei, "Gradualism Versus Big Bang: Speed and Sustainability of Reforms," Working Paper Series #R93-2 (Cambridge: John F. Kennedy School of Government, Harvard University, March 1993), p. 3.

11. Califano, *The Triumph and Tragedy of Lyndon Johnson*, p. 209.

12. See Plato, *The Last Days of Socrates,* trans. Tredennick (New York: Penguin, 1969), pp. 45–76.

13. For example, see Socrates' trial defense in "The Apology," in Plato, *The Last Days of Socrates,* pp. 45–76.

14. Califano, *The Triumph and Tragedy of Lyndon Johnson.* Johnson quote, p. 142; Califano quote, p. 338.

15. See Sidney Hook, *The Hero in History* (New York: John Day, 1943), chap. 1.

16. Ann Ruth Willner analyzes the indicators of the charismatic political relationship along three dimensions: (1) idealized images of the person, (2) unconditional acceptance, and (3) complete emotional commitment of the person and, "by extension, to his vision or to the order he has created." See Willner, *The Spellbinders,* pp. 18–29. Also see Robert C. Tucker, "The Theory of Charismatic Leadership," *Daedalus,* vol. 97, summer 1968, pp. 742–753. For Freud's analysis of charismatic dependency, see Sigmund Freud, *Totem and Taboo,* written in 1913, trans. Strachey (New York: Norton, 1989); and Sigmund Freud, *Group Psychology and the Analysis of the Ego,* written in 1921, trans. Strachey (New York: Norton, 1959).

17. There are many such examples of persistent charismatic attachment, even when the charismatic is not killed. Although Lenin was not murdered, Lenin-worship took hold after his premature death and his mausoleum became a key national shrine. See Tucker, "The Theory of Charismatic Leadership," p. 754. As Willner describes, "The image of a past and even of a defeated charismatic leader may serve as a standard of measure against which those who succeed him are viewed." Willner, *The Spellbinders,* pp. 199–200.

18. David J. Garrow, *Bearing the Cross: Martin Luther King, Jr., and the*

Southern Christian Leadership Conference (New York: Vintage, 1988), p. 603; see also pp. 577–617.

11. The Personal Challenge

1. Max Weber, "Politics as A Vocation," in H. H. Gerth and C. Wright Mills, eds., *From Max Weber: Essays in Sociology* (New York: Oxford University Press, 1946), p. 127, italics in the original.
2. Argyris also suggests that loneliness at the top is a product of a reciprocal isolating dynamic of aloofness between subordinates and the executive. See Chris Argyris, *Overcoming Organizational Defenses: Facilitating Organizational Learning* (Boston: Allyn and Bacon, 1990), p. 73. For an account of how several CEOs view their "loneliness," see James Bruce, *The Intuitive Pragmatist: Conversations with Chief Executive Officers* (Greensboro, NC: Center for Creative Leadership, 1986). Also see Jeffrey Lynn Speller, *Executives in Crisis: Recognizing and Managing the Alcoholic, Drug Addicted, or Mentally Ill Executive* (San Francisco: Jossey-Bass, 1989).
3. "Stunned Japanese Offer Sympathy as Some Are Struck by Symbolism," *The New York Times,* January 9, 1992, p. A8.
4. These ideas derive in part from research performed by members of the A. K. Rice Institute and its parent organization, the Tavistock Institute for Human Relations, in London, England. The reader interested in pursuing the development of some of these personal skills in experiential workshops may wish to explore the Group Relations Conferences produced by the A. K. Rice Institute; the national office is in Jupiter, Florida. For an in-depth description of these workshops and their pedagogical theory, see A. K. Rice, *Learning for Leadership: Interpersonal and Intergroup Relations* (London: Tavistock, 1965). For conceptualizations of group dynamics within the Tavistock tradition, see Jonathon Gillette and Marion McCollom, eds., *Groups in Context: A New Perspective on Group Dynamics* (Reading, MA: Addison-Wesley, 1990); Kenwyn Smith and David Berg, *Paradoxes of Group Life: Understanding Conflict, Paralysis, and Movement in Group Dynamics* (San Francisco: Jossey-Bass, 1987); Edward R. Shapiro and A. Wesley Carr, *Lost in Familiar Places* (New Haven: Yale University Press, 1991); and the two edited volumes published by the A. K. Rice Institute: Arthur D. Colman and W. Harold Bexton, eds., *Group Relations Reader* (Sausalito, CA: GREX, 1975); and Arthur D. Colman and Marvin H. Geller, eds., *Group Relations Reader 2* (Washington, DC: A. K. Rice Institute, 1985).
5. On the skill of reflection in action, see Donald A. Schön, *The Reflective Practitioner: How Professionals Think in Action* (New York: Basic, 1983); and Weber's "Politics as A Vocation." The Whitman quotation is from "Leaves of Grass," verse 4, in Walt Whitman, *Leaves of Grass,* original

edition (New York: Viking Compass, 1959), ed. Malcolm Cowley, p. 28. Athletic examples courtesy of Professor Michael O'Hare, University of California, Berkeley.

6. Neustadt describes this as the need to identify the sense of responsibility individuals have to the constituents to whom they answer. "The essence of a President's persuasive task, with congressmen and everybody else, is to induce them to believe that what he wants of them is what their own appraisal of their own responsibilities requires them to do in their interest, not his." Richard E. Neustadt, *Presidential Power and the Modern Presidents: The Politics of Leadership from Roosevelt to Reagan,* third edition (New York: Free Press, 1990), p. 40.

7. The corollary, well studied in the social sciences, is that people with particular personalities are drawn to roles with related characteristics. Thus, the behavior of an individual in a particular role says as much about the role and the institutional expectations that shape it as it does about the person. See Glenn D. Paige, *The Scientific Study of Political Leadership* (New York: Free Press, 1977), pp. 109–113.

8. The idea that people routinely embody issues, and its corollary, that people routinely discuss and work issues not as abstractions but using the "players" involved as proxies, has its roots in group relations theory as well as political science. See Wilfred R. Bion, *Experiences in Groups* (New York: Basic Books, 1961); and Aaron Wildavsky, "A Cultural Theory of Leadership," in Bryan D. Jones, ed., *Leadership and Politics: New Perspectives in Political Science* (Lawrence, KS: University Press of Kansas, 1989), pp. 97–100. For an analysis of the mirroring dynamic and how people import views from the task environment, see "Contextual Influences: The Process of Importing and Exporting Frames of Reference," in Smith and Berg, *Paradoxes of Group Life,* chap. 8.

9. See Shapiro and Carr, *Lost in Familiar Places,* pp. 111–122, 137–143.

10. This case has been altered to protect privacy.

11. See Pierre M. Turquet, "Leadership: The Individual and the Group," in Colman and Geller, eds., *Group Relations Reader 2,* pp. 71–87.

12. See Sonja M. Hunt, "The Role of Leadership in the Construction of Reality," in Barbara Kellerman, ed., *Leadership: Multidisciplinary Perspectives* (Englewood Cliffs, NJ: Prentice-Hall, 1984), pp. 157–178; and Bobby J. Calder, "An Attribution Theory of Leadership," in Barry M. Staw and Gerald R. Salancik, eds., *New Directions in Organizational Behavior* (Chicago: St. Clair, 1977), chap. 5. For an overview of attribution theory, see Michael Ross and Garth Fletcher, "Attribution and Social Perception," in Gordon Lindzey and Elliot Aronson, eds., *The Handbook of Social Psychology,* third edition (New York: Random House, 1985), pp. 73–122. For a prescriptive view on testing and evaluating attributions, see Chris Argyris, *Strategy, Change, and Defensive Routines* (Boston: Pitman, 1985).

13. See Chapter 1 for a discussion of scapegoating in the Nazi context.

14. Tape Recording and Transcripts of the Cuban Missile Crisis Meetings, Presidential Recordings, October 16, 1962, John F. Kennedy Library, Meeting #1, p. 27. It is, of course, difficult to attribute a particular emotional state, like outrage, to someone else at a distance. What seems minimally clear from the tape recordings is Kennedy's very strong determination to take action. To my ears, his responses sound like a very disciplined form of outrage. Robert Kennedy describes the dominant feelings as "stunned surprise" and "shocked incredulity." Robert Kennedy, *Thirteen Days: A Memoir of the Cuban Missile Crisis* (New York: Norton, 1968), pp. 2, 5. In their Afterword to *Thirteen Days,* Richard Neustadt and Graham Allison interpret President Kennedy's feelings as startled and personal anger of the form: "He can't do that to *me*" (p. 122).

15. According to the Soviet decisionmakers, the Soviet government put missiles in Cuba both to achieve strategic parity and to deter a potential U.S. invasion of Cuba to overthrow Castro's regime. See James G. Blight and David A. Welch, *On the Brink: Americans and Soviets Reexamine the Cuban Missile Crisis* (New York: Hill and Wang, 1989), pp. 238–239.

16. Kennedy, *Thirteen Days,* pp. 64–88.

17. For a review of the sources of role–self and role–role conflict, see "Conflict and Legitimacy in the Leadership Role," in Bernard M. Bass, *Bass and Stogdill's Handbook of Leadership,* third edition (New York: Free Press, 1990), chap. 15.

18. See John P. Burke and Fred I. Greenstein, *How Presidents Test Reality: Decisions on Vietnam, 1954 and 1965* (New York: Russell Sage Foundation, 1989).

19. Geraldine A. Ferraro with Linda Bird Francke, *Ferraro: My Story* (New York: Bantam, 1985), pp. 155–180.

20. Speech at Valley College, Van Nuys, California, November 1984, in Geraldine Ferraro, *Ferraro: My Story* (New York: Bantam, 1985), p. 292, italics in the original.

21. For an analysis of partnerships and their importance in a military context, see Major General Baron Hugo von Freytag-Loringhoven, "The Power of Personality in War," in *Roots of Strategy: 3 Military Classics,* Book 3 (Harrisburg, PA: Stackpole, 1991), pp. 326–341.

22. Regarding his note, see Kennedy, *Thirteen Days,* p. 9. Robert Kennedy does not explain exactly what he meant to communicate by his note. I am inferring these meanings, as have other scholars, including Robert C. Tucker, in *Politics as Leadership* (Columbia: University of Missouri Press, 1981), p. 48.

23. See Allan R. Cohen and David L. Bradford, *Influence without Authority* (New York: Wiley, 1989).

24. Margaret J. Rioch, "'All We Like Sheep—' [Isaiah 53:6]: Followers and Leaders," in Colman and Bexton, eds., *Group Relations Reader,* p. 170.
25. See Wilfred R. Bion, "Selections from: *Experiences in Groups,*" in Colman and Bexton, eds., *Group Relations Reader,* pp. 11–20; Shapiro and Carr, *Lost in Familiar Places,* pp. 78–94; and Larry Hirschhorn, *The Workplace Within: Psychodynamics of Organizational Life* (Cambridge: MIT Press, 1988), pp. 110–113.

Acknowledgments

There are no public words adequate to the feelings I have for the people who have seen me through this work.

Sousan Abadian, my wife, provided extraordinary assistance with the manuscript. She made contributions of the most fundamental kind to the clarity of the analysis: to the broad conceptual framework, the structure of chapters, and the details of paragraphs and sentences. Moreover, she provided the right mix of loving patience and limit-setting to help me keep my priorities straight at home. I cannot imagine this book without her personal, moral, and intellectual help.

Riley Sinder and I have generated ideas together for twenty-three years. Some of these ideas are published jointly in other places. Many serve as the intuitions and underpinnings of this book, which he painstakingly edited. Crossing disciplines has not been an easy enterprise for me, intellectually or personally, and Sinder helped fashion the path.

My colleagues at Harvard University's John F. Kennedy School of Government invested ten years in this synthesis. Deans Graham Allison and Albert Carnesale took the risk that the subject of leadership could be given conceptual clarity and that critical elements of its practice could be taught. Several current and former colleagues, Alan Altshuler, Philip Heymann, Robert Klitgaard, "Dutch" Leonard, Martin Linsky, Ernest May, Mark Moore, Richard Neustadt, Joseph Nye, Michael O'Hare, Robert Reich, Thomas Schelling, Edith Stokey, and Peter Zimmerman, brought me along from the start, giving me courage and steadfast personal and intellectual assistance. Each of these friends in a quite unique way contributed greatly to the rigor of these ideas and to the process of writing them down. Each went far beyond the call of duty. Some even read the manuscript twice. Several served the essential and quite personal role of confidant. From the fall of 1989 through June 1991, our Faculty Seminar on Leadership, chaired by Altshuler, provided a spirited forum that catalyzed and enriched these efforts. Chris Argyris, who joined our seminar from the Harvard Business School, offered consistent partnership. Theresa Monroe provided extraordinary and enduring colleagueship.

I am also very grateful to my colleagues—both from within the Kennedy School/Harvard community and from other educational institutions—who generously read an entire draft of the manuscript and gave me the benefit of their substantial insights. I thank James David Barber, Eugene Bardach, Derek Bok, James MacGregor Burns, John Gardner, Jerome Kagan, Joseph Kalt, Barbara Kellerman, Steven Kelman, Sharon Daloz Parks, Jerrold Post, Howard Prince, Joseph Rost, Dennis Thompson, Walter Ulmer, William Ury, and the late Aaron Wildavsky. I hope they can see the signs of their handiwork (Aaron from on high).

Several friends outside the academy also did yeoman's service in reading and commenting on the whole manuscript. I am truly grateful to Bahman Abadian, Merribel Ayers, Donald Laurie, Hillel Levine, David Margulies, Lawrence Navon, Scott Peck, and Robert Ronnow. They contributed with great care.

Edward Shapiro, who helped to train me in psychiatry, has continued over the years to lend his point of view on my teaching and writing. I appreciate his help in applying psychiatric insight and group relations theory to politics, organizations, and teaching.

Other people helped greatly with specific portions of the book. My father and eldest brother, Milton Heifetz and Laurence Heifetz, both doctors, helped with the Buchanan case and analysis. Professors Richard Wrangham and Marc Hauser of the Harvard Department of Anthropology each reviewed a draft of Chapter Three on the roots of authority and corrected large and small errors in my thinking about primate behavior. John Thomas at the Harvard Institute for

International Development gave me years of encouragement as well as specific help on the Aquino material. Ashton Carter, Professor of Science and International Affairs at the Kennedy School, reviewed my analysis of Reagan's Strategic Defense Initiative. Henry Lee, Executive Director of our Energy and Environmental Programs, gave me assistance in researching the Tacoma case. Dr. Jo Ann Van Tilburg of the Institute for Archeology at UCLA assisted generously with the Easter Island case. William Kovach, David Lax, James Sebenius, and a group of Nieman fellows and friends graciously and with good humor helped me find a title for the book.

I am deeply indebted to my former students. Not only have they provided me with the invaluable opportunity to learn from their stories and insights, but many of them have continued to give encouragement of the most essential kind to my teaching and writing efforts. Some of them have become major collaborators in the area of leadership education—at the Kennedy School and in other settings more distant—both professional and academic. I mention only a few who contributed specifically to encouraging and improving this book: Thomas Bennett, Stephen Boyd, Jenny Gelber, Thomas Landy, Daniel Mulhern, Majd Nurishafiq, Hugh O'Doherty, Galia Saouma, and Pamela Steiner.

John Hilliard served heroically as my research assistant during the first two years of the project. Wendy Kaminer came on board in the last year to help transform a rough set of chapters into a viable manuscript. Mary Jane Rose worked steadily during the frenetic last phase, recovering hundreds of books and articles from the libraries at Harvard as I checked the notes. Their wit, spirit, and remarkable efforts are much appreciated.

My editors at Harvard University Press, Susan Wallace Boehmer and Aïda Donald, went way beyond their standard procedures—already prodigious—in shepherding the manuscript through its last phases and supervising its production. Marc Jaffe and Joy Harris gave me much needed professional advice on the publishing industry, as well as useful feedback on drafts. Linda Healey shaped the concept of the book at the outset. Susan Grant scanned the manuscript for prejudicial language.

Finally, three institutions gave sustained and generous funding to support this research. The money, however, provided even more than the time and resources that I bought with it. In a moral sense, the money represented a trust that gave me the heart to begin and press on despite recurrent doubts. Marianna Bridge, Richard Broholm, Craig Dykstra, Fred Hofheinz, and Susan Wisely at the Lilly Endowment have been partners in the truest sense. Robert Armstrong and Henry Luce III of the Henry Luce Foundation believed in this effort when it was not too much more than a rough set of ideas coupled with enthusiasm; so did Bayley Mason at our development office. Marvin Moss, Fred Saalfeld, Philip Selwyn, and Albert Wood from the Office of Naval Research gave me the courage to find applications that at first I did not see. I am truly grateful for all of their confidence.

Index

343